**THE CENTURY PSYCHOLOGY SERIES**

*Richard M. Elliott, Gardner Lindzey,
and Kenneth MacCorquodale*
EDITORS

# Child Development

# contributors

ANNE ANASTASI
Fordham University

NATHAN H. AZRIN
Anna State Hospital

DONALD M. BAER
University of Kansas

SIDNEY W. BIJOU
University of Illinois

JAY S. BIRNBRAUER
University of North Carolina

JOHN A. COOLEY
National Institute of Mental Health

MARIAN K. DEMYER
Indiana University Medical Center

C. B. FERSTER
Institute of Behavioral Research

GILBERT FREITAG
Yale University

JACOB L. GERWIRTZ
National Institute of Mental Health

VIVIAN J. GOLD
University of California (Los Angeles)

ISRAEL GOLDIAMOND
Institute of Behavioral Research

FLORENCE R. HARRIS
University of Washington

WENDELL E. JEFFREY
University of California (Los Angeles)

IRENE C. KASSORLA
University of California (Los Angeles)

HERBERT KAYE
Brown University

FRED S. KELLER
Arizona State University

NANCY KERR
Arizona State University

JOHN D. KIDDER
University of Washington

OGDEN R. LINDSLEY
University of Kansas

LEWIS P. LIPSITT
Brown University

O. IVAR LOVAAS
University of California (Los Angeles)

HAYDEN L. MEES
University of Oregon

LEE MEYERSON
Arizona State University

JACK L. MICHAEL
Arizona State University

ROBERT MOORE
Arizona State University

DELMONT C. MORRISON
Reis-Davis Clinic

ROBERT ORLANDO
Peabody College

ROBERT F. PETERSON
University of Illinois

HARRIET L. RHEINGOLD
University of North Carolina

TODD R. RISLEY
University of Kansas

HELEN W. ROSS
National Institute of Mental Health

JAMES A. SHERMAN
University of Kansas

EINAR R. SIQUELAND
Brown University

B. F. SKINNER
Harvard University

WALTER C. STANLEY
National Institute of Mental Health

CECILIA TAGUE
Rainier School, Washington

GLENN TERRELL
University of Illinois

ROBERT G. WAHLER
University of Tennessee

CARL D. WILLIAMS
University of Miami

GARY H. WINKEL
University of Washington

MONTROSE M. WOLF
University of Kansas

# Child Development:
## readings in experimental analysis

edited by
**SIDNEY W. BIJOU**
University of Illinois

**DONALD M. BAER**
University of Kansas

New York

APPLETON-CENTURY-CROFTS

Educational Division

MEREDITH CORPORATION

# preface

This collection of readings is intended to supplement the authors' preceding two volumes as well as future volumes in their series on child behavior and development. It is also intended to stand by itself as a compilation of research relevant to several of the problems of modern society and especially education. Although some of the studies are devoted to abstract principles of behavior, an effort has been made to show the direct contribution of such studies to immediate and significant social problems. The principles cited, even the most abstract ones, are *action* principles: they are mechanisms of behavioral change and maintenance. A large part of this volume is devoted to studies that have treated these principles as prescriptions and have attempted to remediate problem behavior. We have chosen examples which are mainly experimental applications. This means that when the application succeeds, it is deliberately changed in some specific respect to see if that respect was essential to the change observed. As a result, the investigator learns what aspect of this procedure to extend and intensify and what aspect to revise.

In the same spirit, we have, for the most part, chosen studies in which the behavior of a single child is analyzed, modified, or developed. Thus what is displayed in these pages are not attempts to describe statistically the characteristics of some group or population in the manner of the census. Rather, they are attempts to demonstrate that certain principles are powerful enough to operate clearly in the interaction of an individual child and environmental events. Many conditions and factors which obviously play a role in determining child development are not noted in this collection, primarily because studies dealing with them still fail to meet this above stated specification. Thus, we have a selective assembly of theoretical comments and research, biased in the direction of a natural science approach to child behavior and development.

We wish to thank the students in our undergraduate courses in child behavior and development and our colleagues for their assistance in developing these readings and comments during the past four years. We also wish to express our indebtedness to the authors and publishers for granting permission to reprint the papers and to Miss Anona Bangs and Mrs. Blanca

Law for typing the manuscript, preparing the figures, and assisting in the correspondence entailed in such an undertaking. Finally, we wish to thank the National Institute of Mental Health, United States Public Health Service, for supporting our research on normal and deviant development (MH-02208 and MH-02232 before 1965, and MH-12067 after 1965). Our research has enriched our teaching and in the process has generated materials such as this compilation.

S. W. B.

D. M. B.

# contents

# PART I

# Basic Principles
# and Concepts

# Introduction

This collection of papers is a sample from a substantial body of current work, most of which has been written since 1956. Prior to that time, with the exception of a series of studies on respondent (classical) conditioning in the young infant and one or perhaps two investigations on operant behavior in young children,[1] this literature was virtually non-existent. The possibility of such work, however, was anticipated by Fred S. Keller in a 1950 paper entitled "Animals and Children." For this reason it seems appropriate to introduce these readings with Keller's paper.

Keller was asked by the Society for Research in Child Development to participate in a symposium on "Permissiveness Versus Rigidity in Relation to Child Rearing, Personality and Culture." The title promised a set of papers dealing with conditions and processes specific to child behavior. Keller was considered an expert in animal behavior, especially in animal learning. For many in his audience, animal learning and child learning were distinct topics, each with its own principles, techniques, and subjects; the conclusions of one area were not necessarily, perhaps not even probably applicable to the other. In particular, many must have thought that Keller's experimental studies of pigeons and rats could hardly

---

[1] E.g., A. B. Warren and R. H. Brown, "Conditioned Operant Response Phenomenon in Children," *J. genet. Psychol.*, 1943, *28*, 181–207.

prove more than an analogy to parental practices such as permissiveness and rigidity, and would have little relevance to personality and culture.

However, as the following pages show, Keller believed that a set of principles which could describe behavior in general is not only possible, but is the prime target of behavioral scientists. He outlined what was known of those principles in 1950 with the clarity and conciseness for which he has long been known. (Indeed, for the reader with little or no knowledge of the principles which the studies in this collection exemplify, Keller's brief outline may go far in helping him to understand the rest of this volume.)

Keller proposed that generalized descriptions of behavior in the laboratory animal should be taken as theoretical descriptions of the behavior of human children and adults, and that systematic research be pursued to evaluate the usefulness of doing so. His insistence upon research rather than extrapolation to "behavioral analogues and parallels in the everyday life of human beings" is a point that needs to be made many times over.

At the time of the writing, Keller could only hope that research of this sort would be pursued. Now, seventeen years later, it seems clear from a review of the literature of child development that such research has indeed been pursued, and at a constantly increasing rate. The majority of the investigations in this recent surge of research has an obvious relationship to experimental techniques developed with laboratory animals. The details of these techniques have been modified to make them suitable for children; but the concepts and principles are much the same.

The rest of this book presents a sample of the research proposed by Keller. The reader may judge if this research will result in the unification of child and animal behavior under a general set of theoretical principles and an expansion in theory. He will agree that Keller made an accurate prediction.

# 1

# Animals and Children

### Fred S. Keller

Before anything relevant to the topic of this symposium can be said, a more general question must be raised. What can the student of child development expect from the student of animal behavior? This question is answerable, although the answer may not be quieting or readily accepted. One thing that may certainly be expected from animal behavior study is theory.

Theory, of course, is what the animal worker has, for some time back, been offering. Since the time of John Watson, systematists in psychology have leaned heavily, sometimes exclusively, upon research with animal subjects; and there are no signs, among the experimentalists, that this dependency is decreasing. The opposite, if anything, appears to be the case. Today, in reinforcement theory (sometimes called behavior theory), a fresh offer is in the making, an offer that is likely to be pressed more vigorously and more insistently than any of those in the past.

Reinforcement theory is an integration of experimental facts commonly associated with the names of Hull and Skinner, but it has already grown beyond a point where any important purpose is served by talking about Hullians or Skinnerites. Reinforcement theorists are now to be found in many of our universities; and the age of discipleship in psychology seems, happily, to be passing. Indeed, historians of the present epoch may well decide that Pavlov, Thorndike, and (despite his non-experimentalism) Freud were the fathers of this movement, giving to Hull and Skinner the status of founders.

A comprehensive treatment of this theory would include an account of elicited and emitted (voluntary) behavior, of conditioning, extinction, discrimination, and several other basic principles. It would consider the interrelation of these principles, now a matter of major concern; and it would deal with their extension within classical areas of experimental psychology to give an interlocking account of many previously insulated topics. Such a treatment, of course, cannot be presented here; but some-

Fred S. Keller, "Animals and Children," *Child Development*, 1950, *21*, 7–12. Reprinted by permission of The Society for Research in Child Development, Inc., and the author.

thing may be said about those aspects of the system which bear, more or less directly, upon the present discussion.

In the remarks to follow, it will be impossible to avoid using one or two terms that may seem unduly technical for the present occasion. I should like to dispense with them here, but they do provide a degree of specification that is lacking in "plain English" and in their psychological predecessors. It is only to be hoped that a regard for scientific clarity will outweigh the objection to a little novelty.

The reinforcement theorist is obviously concerned with reinforcement, of which two kinds may be identified. There is positive reinforcement and negative reinforcement. Reinforcement refers to a function of stimuli, and we may speak of positively reinforcing stimuli or positive "reinforcers" as those stimuli which, when presented to an organism, strengthen the response that they follow. Negative reinforcers weaken the response that they follow; but this weakening is not the equivalent of an eradication or extinction of the response. Rather, it is more a suppression. The effect is that of punishment; and there is evidence to show that the punished response will, under certain circumstances, exhibit all its pristine strength.

Positive reinforcers may be primary, like food, water, and sex mates for suitably motivated organisms; or they may be secondary, like tones, lights, or other initially neutral stimuli which have often served as cues for primarily reinforced responses. These are the derived, or conditioned, reinforcers that have sometimes been called token rewards. Approval, in the form of a word, a nod, or a smile, often qualifies as a secondary reinforcer. Money, for most of us, is another. For the child of our culture, the mother, in any or all of her stimulus aspects, early becomes a powerful agent of this sort.

Primary negative reinforcers include such things as slaps, blows, shocks, burns, and other forms of intense stimulation. Secondary negative reinforcers comprise those initially neutral stimuli which, through association with primary reinforcers, come to exercise a similar depressive effect upon the behavior with which they are correlated. If secondary positive reinforcement is thought of as a promise of reward, secondary negative reinforcement may be thought of as a threat of punishment. Again, in our society, the mother may have a negatively reinforcing status as well as a positively reinforcing one. She may take on the character of the wicked witch no less than that of the fairy godmother. The two functions, unfortunately for the child, may sometimes be exercised with reference to the same form of activity.

Negative reinforcers may also be treated as stimuli the removal of which is strengthening. For example: an electric shock may exert a weakening effect upon whatever behavior is in progress at the time of its application; but, if this shock is continued and its intensity is not so great as to disorganize behavior completely, any response that is permitted to remove it will be strengthened. This is especially clear in the case of primary negative reinforcers, as in the classical picture of escape behavior; but it holds also for secondary negative reinforcers. An organism's reinforcement may consist only in the removal of a light, a tone, or even a "general situation," provided that some primary reinforcer, like shock, has previously been associated with such stimulation. Some writers have gone further, to say that in presenting such secondary reinforcers we arouse a state of anxiety, which is only reduced by their removal.

These generalizations arise from observations of animal behavior in various experimental situations, and they are paralleled by age-old statements about human conduct. It is unlikely that many would disagree with the suggestion that primary reinforcement, positive or negative, is related to such a problem as that of permissiveness and rigidity in child training; isn't this "reward" and "punishment" all over again? Probably, too, not many would take issue with the assertion that the reinforcers of child behavior are often of the secondary sort; we have all heard of "approval" and "disapproval." There might even be some agreement with the animal worker's definition of avoidance and anxiety.

Very few, however, would feel that they had learned anything new, helpful, or inspiring from this way of treating behavior. Still fewer would be willing to replace the old familiar terms with "reinforcement jargon." And many would reject forcefully the implication that human behavior, in all its complexity, is amenable to analysis with the tools provided by the white rat, the dog, or the anthropoid ape.

These reactions are understandable, but they miss some important points. The first one is that, for the reinforcement theorists, the degree of control and prediction achieved through his initial formulation marks the beginning, rather than the end, of research. He may be pleased to find behavioral analogues and parallels in the everyday life of human beings and at other levels of descriptive rigor—he would be unnatural if he didn't. But a good theory, as often noted, is autocatalytic; and he soon finds himself confronted with a host of new experimental problems. The solutions of these problems may, or they may not, have obvious counterparts elsewhere, but they cannot fail to further his understanding. There is but one path open to him, and he is duty-bound to take it.

Such a development is now underway and we have scores of observations which indicate its fruitfulness. In the field of secondary reinforcement alone, considerable progress has been made. We have learned, among other things, that (1) many neutral stimuli thus far tested, including the proprioceptive or response-produced, may acquire reinforcing power through its connection with some type of primary reinforcement. A tone, a light, or the making of some movement, which has regularly been followed by food or water, may itself be used to strengthen, say, a running, a lever-pressing, or a chain-pulling response. (2) The response that is strengthened by such a secondary reinforcer may be entirely different from the one with which primary reinforcement has been correlated. Thus, an auditory stimulus, formerly associated with running to food, may be used to strengthen a lever-pressing response. (3) A secondary reinforcer, established under one dominant motive (e.g., thirst) may serve to strengthen a response under some other dominant motive, say hunger. (4) Recently we have found that a stimulus must be discriminative if it is to take on reinforcing value. It has been shown that the reinforcing effect of a light upon a white rat's running is a function of the degree to which this light had become a discriminative stimulus for this response. Mere temporal contiguity of a neutral stimulus and a primary reinforcer is apparently not enough to set up the neutral stimulus as a secondary reinforcer.

Similar findings have been obtained in connection with secondary negative reinforcement, although the work in this area is not well advanced. I have been especially impressed, during the past year, with an apparent demonstration, with white rats, that a postural response (holding a door open) may be maintained for long periods of time because it removes proprioceptive stimuli that have been associated with the negatively reinforced act of letting the door close. The primary reinforcer, in this instance, was a fairly intense light, from which escape had been possible by opening the door. The animal came ultimately to escape from some of his own responding, merely because it had previously been accompanied by the noxious light.

Such findings go beyond elementary statements concerning reward and punishment, approval and disapproval, and so on. They tell us about a few of the circumstances under which stimuli may operate to strengthen or weaken behavior and, more significantly, they aid in the systematic integration of fact and principle which is theory in the best sense of the word. They do not, of course, transcend the influences of heredity and maturation—influences which set limits to behavioral change, but they are independent of physiological or psychic assumptions. They enhance appreciably our powers of control and prediction, and the number of research problems they suggest is embarrassingly great.

A second point concerns the general relevance of animal studies to an account of human behavior. Professor Beach has recently given us a picture of the Pied Piper, in the form of a white rat, leading psychologists to destruction. Beach was speaking in jest, and in behalf of other animal species, but the vivid figure will undoubtedly be put to use by those who feel that principles derived from rat behavior can never encompass the complexity of human response—even, perhaps, at the pre-verbal or pre-social stage.

Extrapolation from rats or dogs or apes to man is always dangerous, but not because man is complex and the animal simple, or because man is a social creature and the animal is not, or because man alone exhibits verbal behavior. The simplicity of the rat has been exaggerated, and the problems of social and verbal behavior are still problems of behavior, to be dealt with as any other by appeal to controlling variables in the environment, past or present. Whatever uniqueness attaches to such behavior appears to arise from the fact that its reinforcement is mediated by the behavior of other organisms.

The danger in extrapolation lies, rather, in the fact that it may be superficial or premature, reflecting a failure to recognize complexity at the animal, no less than at the human, level. And, in this respect, the animal worker who naively treats man as a kind of king-sized rat is no more at fault than the student of, say, child behavior who utilizes animal research uncritically whenever it seems to serve his purpose.

There is a final point. Extrapolation is not the life line of the reinforcement theorist who wishes to reach human conduct at any stage of its development. There is an obvious, and better, solution: he may, in many cases, deal with human subjects in his research. Some experimental problems, it is true, are best approached with animals. Others, such as those of verbal behavior, are not; and a systematic program which fails to attack these problems frontally will always be under fire.

The recent progress of reinforcement theory has depended largely upon the choice of behavior samples that could be measured in terms of their frequency of occurrence in time—as in the case of the lever-pressing response. This choice has made it possible to discover a good deal of orderliness in the behavior of individual animals without a laborious restriction of experimental conditions. Many of the most interesting and satisfying results have been obtained under circumstances no more artificial than that represented by an infant in his play-pen or crib, and with fewer subjects than are commonly available in a nursery group. Some advance has even been made with animal subjects having a known history of research participation. In view of these facts, it is hard to believe that animals are more suitable than infants and young children in many studies aimed at the further development of behavior theory. The fundamental requirements of technique and design should be met easily.

It is, however, improbable that any great number of animal workers will forsake their rat colonies and their plans of research to enter this promising area. In addition to their understandable inclination to stay on familiar ground, and their personal frustrations in rearing their own offspring, they may have unconsciously accepted the "hands-off" admonitions of their critics. Nor is it to be expected that students of child behavior will suddenly reorient their research in line with theoretical proposals from "below." One surmises that there are difficulties in the way of this which stem from the nature of their subject matter. To the animal worker, from whom nothing very useful is expected, it sometimes appears that research in child behavior is hampered by its own best friends. So much is demanded, and so soon. The very theme of this symposium seems to reflect practical considerations somewhat remote from the atmosphere of inquiry in which basic research prospers.

Nevertheless, an understanding of behavior, animal or child, cannot be expected in the absence of theory. If it is not one theory, it will have to be another. There is no escaping an ultimate organization of the facts. Reinforcement theory is a step in this direction. It has met with some initial success at the animal level and within the field of experimental psychology in general; and it has made suggestive points of contact with ideas of clinical or psychoanalytic origin. Its future will depend upon the ease with which it handles questions of social and verbal interaction. The experimental investigation of infant and child behavior presents itself as an alluring approach to this goal. It will be a pity if outmoded objections and extrascientific considerations stand in the way of its attainment.

# Basic Mechanisms:
# Operant and Respondent

The next three studies were chosen to represent two basic types of behavioral development and modification in infancy: operant and respondent conditioning. The first is a study of a primitive form of operant exploration in the human infant. The second represents a successful study of the conditionability of respondent sucking responses in 3- and 4-day-old babies. The third involves both operant and respondent mechanisms, but most notably the discrimination of an operant response to stimuli which signal a reinforcement contingency.

# 2

# Method for Studying
# Exploratory Behavior in Infants

### Harriet L. Rheingold, Walter C. Stanley, and John A. Cooley

## ABSTRACT

An experimental crib has been designed for use in studying the effect of visual feedback upon the exploratory behavior of the human infant. It can be easily adapted to older children, to some animals, and to problems other than the development of exploratory behavior.

Exploratory behavior is clearly apparent in human infants by the time they are 3 months old (Gesell & Thompson, 1934; Piaget, 1952; Rheingold, 1961). An apparatus designed for use in studying the beginnings of this behavior, especially in relation to feedback from the external environment, is also adaptable to the study of other kinds of early behavior, both human and animal. The apparatus holds the infant in a suitable position, permits measurement of certain behavior, and provides for sensory feedback from that behavior.

A specially designed crib is approximately 5 feet long, 3 feet wide, and 4 feet high. It stands on legs 2 feet 5 inches long. Interior surfaces are made of Acoustitex nonperforated sound-insulation boards, painted ivory. Six 6-watt bulbs are mounted at the top of the wall behind the infant. The sides of the crib are double sliding panels. Behind the infant is a double observation window, 28 inches long by 18 inches wide, glass on the outside and plastic on the inside. At the other end is a double glass window, 16 by 17 inches, set at an angle of 60°, through which images can be projected on a screen. The screen is frosted Plexiglass, 34 by 31 inches, also set at an angle of 60°. The crib is ventilated by a blower of capacity 60 ft³ /min.

The infant faces the screen at a distance of 30 inches, supported in a commercially available canvas seat (Welsh Company, St. Louis, Mo.), on a modified frame adjustable at angles between 45° and 90°. A cloth strap holds the infant across the chest and abdomen, leaving its hands and feet free. The seat can be rocked by the observer's pressing a pedal.

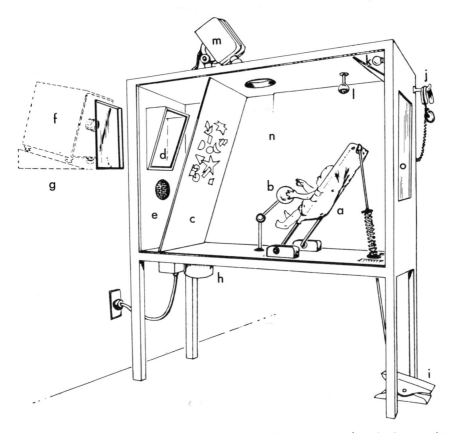

Figure 1.   Experimental crib: *a*, seat; *b*, manipulandum; *c*, screen; *d*, projection opening; *e*, sound source; *f*, projector; *g*, control room; *h*, ventilator; *i*, rocker; *j*, intercom; *k*, crib lights; *l*, microphone; *m*, television camera; *n*, doors of crib; *o*, window

A hollow nonshiny stainless-steel sphere, 4 inches in diameter, mounted on an adjustable rod, is positioned so that only its near and visible surface can be touched by the infant. Touching the sphere activates a capacitance relay, the sensitivity of which is adjusted by a variable frequency oscillator. Control equipment in an adjacent room operates a cumulative recorder, counters, and stimulus-producing elements, namely, a continuous-movie projector (Cinesalesman, modified) and a closed-loop tape system (Mohawk Business Machines). Images are projected on the crib screen; auditory stimuli come from a speaker located directly behind the screen. Stimuli presented either way can be controlled by the infant's responses to the sphere, by a clock, or manually by the operator. The duration of the movie, the sound, and the experimental conditions are controlled by timers (Time delay timers, series TDAF, Industrial Timer Corp.). A variable resistance-capacitance relay is included to make the inter-response interval adjustable from 50 msec. to 5 sec. As we have used the apparatus, responses which are spaced in accordance with a predetermined interval (typically, 0.2 second) appear on a cumulative recorder, while counters accumulate all responses spaced more than 17 msec. apart.

The infant's behavior is monitored in the control room by closed-circuit television (Kin Tel) and earphones. The television camera is mounted on the ceiling of the crib, while a microphone over the infant's head transmits his vocalizations both to the operator and to a tape recorder. An intercom system connects observer and operator. The infant's behavior can be photographed from the television screen.

Most 4- to 6-month-old infants will perform in the apparatus for at

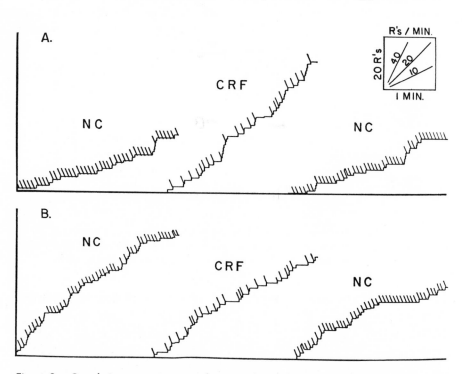

Figure 2.  Cumulative response curves for two infants, showing (A) performance sensitive to changes in experimental conditions and (B) performance not sensitive. Under the noncontingent (NC) condition the movie appeared for alternate 1½-second periods regardless of the infant's behavior, under the continuous reinforcement (CRF) condition the movie followed each of the infant's responses.

least 8 minutes without fussing, a period of time comparable to that used by other investigators studying conditioning in human infants (Papousek, 1960; Simmons & Lipsitt, 1961). Some preliminary work with older children, 2 to 5 years of age, suggests that the experimental period for this group may be extended to 20 minutes or longer. If the infant fusses, the observer rocks him, but if the infant cries, he is removed at once.

Mothers assist in placing their infants in the crib and then go to the control room to observe their infants on the television screen.

The reinforcing effects of visual stimuli on exploratory behavior are currently under investigation. Sample performances are shown in the cumulative records of Figure 2. In both cases, touching the sphere produced a motion picture of brightly colored geometric paper figures moving over a black velvet drum for 1.5 seconds.

A great variety of visual and auditory stimuli can be used, programmed as either reinforcing or discriminative. The projected images may be of things or people, known or strange, and such stimulus properties as complexity and novelty can be varied systematically. The effect of auditory reinforcement, alone or coupled with visual reinforcement, can be analyzed, while other manipulanda can be introduced to study response differentiation.

## REFERENCES

Gesell, A., & Thompson, H. *Infant behavior.* New York: McGraw-Hill, 1934.

Papousek, H. Conditioned motor alimentary reflexes in infants. II. A new experimental method of investigation. *Cesk. Pediatr.,* 1960, *15,* 981.

Piaget, J. *The origins of intelligence in children.* Trans. by Margaret Cook. New York: International Universities Press, 1952.

Rheingold, H. L. The effect of environmental stimulation upon social and exploratory behavior in the human infant. In B. Foss (Ed.), *Determinants of infant behavior.* London: Methuen, 1961. Pp. 143–171.

Simmons, M. W., & Lipsitt, L. P. An operant-discrimination apparatus for infants. *J. exp. Anal. Beh.,* 1961, *4,* 233.

### EDITORS' COMMENTS

The preceding study is primarily a report on a method of infant study. However, there are three points about it that need emphasis. The first concerns its place in this section on Basic Mechanisms; the second concerns the nature of the stimuli used as reinforcers in the sample performances; and the third concerns the relationship between these stimuli and exploratory behavior.

The study is first in this section because it describes a method of illustrating the importance of a reinforcement contingency in forming and maintaining simple behavior. The simplicity of the contingency, the clarity of its effect on behavior, and the age of the infant make this brief study a highly relevant document in an experimental analysis of child development. With respect to the clarity of its effect on behavior, we are generalizing beyond the sample data given in this article. Our basis for doing so is the data provided by a subsequent study by Rheingold, Stanley, and Doyle.[1] Using the same method and the same stimulus and response measures, they show similar orderly data on 25 children from 2 to 5 years of age.

In these studies by Rheingold and her co-workers the nature of the reinforcing stimuli deserves special attention. Apparently, a changing pattern of light and sound can be enough of a stimulus consequence of a young infant's response to affect the future strength of that response. This stimulus complex is not one of the biologically powerful reinforcers typically used in studies of learning mechanisms. Yet it functions to reinforce behavior much as do food or water. The study alerts us to the need for a more thorough analysis of reinforcement contingencies in the infant's world than those involving food, water, shelter, pain, etc. A wealth of other reinforcing stimuli in the infant's environment may teach him a corresponding wealth of skills. Thus, some of the inevitable patterns of behavioral development in children may not have to be conceived of as "emergent." Experimental studies of the contingencies between these behaviors and a variety of stimuli may produce a precise analysis of their origins and development. In *Child Development,* Vol. 2: *Universal Stage of Infancy*[2] such reinforcers are called "ecological," and the uniformity of development to which they contribute is said to be the "Universal" stage of development, following J. R. Kantor's terminology.

Finally, there is the wise use of the term "exploration" by Rheingold *et al.,* to characterize the infant's behavior in this study. Some readers may find the analysis of a sphere-touching response, involving only hand and arm, too limited or too repetitive to be called exploration. However, if exploration has any essential characteristic, it is that it is controlled by the stimulus aspects of the environment to which it is directed. In other words, when we are exploring something, we are finding out what it is like. This study shows us that one characteristic of the infant's environment was sufficient to keep him behaving in it, with it, and toward it: the environment responded to the infant's behavior, his touch, by changing the visual and auditory feedback to the infant. Because of this, the infant's skill in

[1] "Visual and Auditory Reinforcement of a Manipulatory Response in a Young Child," *J. exp. child Psychol.,* 1964, *1,* 316–326.
[2] Sidney W. Bijou and Donald M. Baer, New York: Appleton-Century-Crofts, 1965.

manipulating one part of the environment, the sphere, increased. From an observer's point of view, the infant learned "what the sphere was like." Many environments will offer enough feedback of an ecologically reinforcing kind to keep a child attending, differentiating, and discriminating—in a word, exploring.

# 3

# Conditioned Sucking in the Human Newborn

## Lewis P. Lipsitt and Herbert Kaye

### EDITORS' COMMENTS

The next article is the only study in this collection emphasizing respondent (classical, or Pavlovian) conditioning. This is not necessarily testimony to the unimportance of respondent mechanisms in child development. Rather, studies of respondent conditioning using children as subjects are few. The child is not often the most convenient subject for studies of the basic mechanisms of learning. Children must be handled with great care; the stimuli to which they can be exposed must be mild; and the duration of an experimental study must be short, at least in any one session. However, it is true that investigators of child development more often have been interested in the social, intellectual, and verbal repertoires of children than in their respondents; thus operant procedures have predominated.

Nevertheless, this study is noteworthy on several grounds. (1) It is a meaningful study of respondent processes in the child, despite the considerations mentioned in the preceding paragraph. (2) It concerns early mechanisms of development demonstrable in 3- to 4-day-old infants. (3) The study was successful: respondent conditioning is not easy to demonstrate in the newborn, despite the widespread opinion that it occurs. Thus this study should be attended to not only as a demonstration of a particular mechanism of behavioral development in the newborn human, but also as a sophisticated application of technology to a difficult problem.

Future investigations of respondent conditioning in the infant may well make use of the techniques developed by Lipsitt and Kaye for this study. Such studies might demonstrate a much greater role

Lewis P. Lipsitt and Herbert Kaye, "Conditioned Sucking in the Human Newborn," *Psychonomic Science*, 1964, *1*, 29–30.

The writers thank Mrs. Dorothy Westlake for her assistance. This study was carried out as part of a project entitled Sensory Discrimination and Learning in Human Infants under a USPHS grant (NB-04268) to Lewis P. Lipsitt. The writers are indebted to the staff of the Providence Lying-In Hospital for their cooperation.

of respondent processes, even in the social, intellectual, and verbal repertoires of children, than is currently recognized. This study alone accomplishes an interesting analysis of the conditionability of the sucking response of newborns, a behavior of obvious importance and prominence in babies, and a very common activity occurring at the end of many other operant chains of behavior out of which grow motor, social, intellectual, verbal, and many other behavior repertoires. Indeed, we may guess that the babies of the study cited just before this one might well have sucked on the sphere which they touched if they could have gotten it to their mouths.

The report was written for a technical journal in which space is allotted in small amounts. Consequently, it exemplifies the severe standards of brief scientific reporting. The reader will discover that, even so, the essential terms and abbreviations are defined, most of them in the second paragraph of the study. One exception may be remedied here: the abbreviation "O" stands for the observer who watched the conditioning procedures and recorded the sucking responses. There were two such observers working together.

## ABSTRACT

Classical conditioning of the sucking response was demonstrated. Sucking in response to a tone was greater in infants who received paired presentations of the tone and a sucking device than in infants who received unpaired presentations of the same stimuli.

## PROBLEM

To determine whether classical conditioning is possible within the first days of human life, a tone was used as a conditioning stimulus (CS), and insertion of a nipple in the baby's mouth to elicit sucking movements constituted the unconditioned stimulus (UCS). If conditioning takes place, more sucking to the tone should occur following paired presentations of CS and UCS (experimental group, E) than following unpaired presentations (control group, C).

## METHOD

Two groups of 10 hospital Ss in their third or fourth day were studied between 8 and 9:15 A.M., at least 3 hrs. after the previous feeding. For both groups, the CS was a low-frequency, loud (about 93 db) square-wave tone with a fundamental component of 23 cps and lasting 15 sec. For Group E, the nipple[1] was inserted in the infant's mouth 1 sec. after onset of the CS and remained to the end of the 15-sec. CS. For Group C, the CS and UCS were not paired; the nipple was inserted for 14 sec. approximately 30 sec. following offset of the CS.

All Ss first received 5 basal trials of CS alone. Presence and number of sucking movements to each 15-sec. tone were recorded independently by 2 Os. These trials were administered approximately 1 min. apart. Both groups then received 25 training trials, every 5th trial being a test in which sucking responses to the CS alone were recorded. For Group E, CS and UCS were paired for 14 sec. on the 20 conditioning trials. On these trials, Group C received the CS and UCS stimulations with a variable interval of 25–45 sec. (average, 30 sec.) between offset of CS and introduction of UCS. For Group E, intertrial interval was 1 min.; for Group C about 30 sec. Thus the conditioning session for Group E took approximately 31 min.; for Group C, about 38 min.

Following the conditioning period, all Ss received no less than 10 nor more than 30 extinction trials like the basal trials, these being discontinued when no responses occurred for 3 successive trials, the extinction criterion.

## RESULTS

O agreement was high for both measures, the results being essentially identical when each O's results were considered independently. Averages for both Os are plotted in Figure 1 for the three phases of the study: 5 basal trials, 5 CS trials during conditioning, and 2 blocks of 5 extinction or test trials. The per cent measure, indicating proportions of trials in which sucking occurred during CS-alone presentations, showed an increase for Group E from beginning to end of the session, while this measure leveled off for Group C. A similar trend was present for the number-of-sucks measure. Analyses of variance for both measures yielded highly significant interactions between groups and phases [$F$ (3, 54) $= 19.4$ and 12.3, $p < .001$, respectively], indicating increasing differences between groups over time. Individual Ss in Group E showed a significantly greater amount of change from basal to extinction periods in both per cent of response and number of sucks [$t$ (18) $= 2.14$ and $t$ (18) $= 2.41$, $p < .05$,

---

[1] The non-nutritive nipple used was an automatic device for the recording of sucking responses developed by Grunzke (1961) for work with monkeys. For work with humans, Levin and Kaye (1964) adapted this stainless-steel mouthpiece, shaped like a nipple and containing a small lever attached to a microswitch, by covering it with a sterile rubber nipple. As the infant sucks, the lever is depressed and released, producing digital blips on a polygraph record.

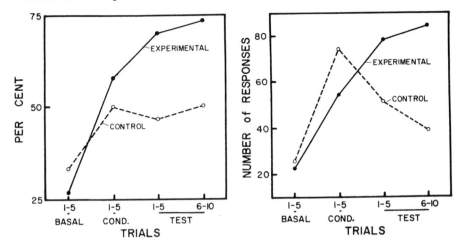

Figure 1. Percentage and number of sucking responses to the CS (tone) in the Experimental and Control Groups

respectively]. Finally, the trials-to-criterion measure in extinction showed that Group E gave responses on the average of 24.1 of 30 trials compared with 11.1 for Group C [t (18) = 2.42, p < .05].

## DISCUSSION

The study design attempted to control for sensitization or pseudo-conditioning (Wickens & Wickens, 1940) by giving both groups identical stimulation but in different CS-UCS temporal relationships. There are two indications that this procedure did not completely eliminate such an effect: (1) Group C gave slightly (not significantly) more responses to CS than Group E during the conditioning period, and (2) Group C responded more during the extinction phase than during the basal phase. When the individual averages from the basal trials of Group C are compared with averages from the first 10 extinction trials, the t is 2.45 for the per cent measure (df = 9, p < .05) and for the number-of-sucks measure, the t is 2.59 (p < .05). Thus the Group C treatment was itself effective in increasing response, possibly due to (1) sensitization, (2) the unlikely possibility of trace conditioning having occurred in Group C, or (3) increase in hunger or other arousing conditions, 35–40 min. having elapsed between the basal and extinction periods. Regardless, it has been established that the paired stimulation administered to Group E increased response more than did the control condition.

While 20 paired presentations of CS and UCS constitute a relatively small number of trials, the frequency of sucking during presentation of the

UCS is such as to produce many "pairings" within each trial. Groups E and C responded with means of 13.1 and 13.0 sucks, respectively, per nipple presentation, and they did not differ over trials in numbers of sucks made to successive UCS presentations. If each sucking response is considered independently, then an average of 260 "pairings" of CS and UCS occurred in the conditioning session for the experimental Ss. Thus sucking is an efficient response for administering many paired CS-UCS presentations in a brief period.

These data agree with a much earlier experiment by Marquis (1931) and, more recently, with Papousek (1961) that conditioning of responses involving mouth-stimulation can occur in newborns, and contrast with reservations expressed by Kessen (1963) and Scott (1963). While age-determined changes in conditioning rate apparently occur (Kantrow, 1937; Morgan & Morgan, 1944; Papousek, 1961), failures to establish conditioning in neonates may be due as much to the use of ineffective experimental techniques as to chronological or neurophysiological deficiencies.

## REFERENCES

Grunske, M. E. A liquid dispenser for primates. *J. exp. Anal. Beh.*, 1961, *4*, 326.

Kantrow, R. W. An investigation of conditioned feeding responses and concomitant adaptive behavior in young infants. *Univ. Ia. Stud. Child Welf.*, 1937, *13*(3).

Kessen, W. Research in the psychological development of children. *Merrill-Palmer Quart.*, 1963, *9*, 83–94.

Levin, G. R., & Kaye, H. Non-nutritive sucking by human neonates. *Child Developm.*, 1964, *35*, 749–758.

Marquis, D. P. Can conditioned responses be established in the newborn infant? *J. genet. Psychol.*, 1931, *39*, 479–492.

Morgan, J. J. B., & Morgan, S. S. Infant learning as a developmental index. *J. genet Psychol.*, 1944, *65*, 281–289.

Papousek, H. Conditioned head rotation reflexes in infants in the first months of life. *Acta Pediatr.*, 1961, *50*, 565–576.

Scott, J. P. The process of primary socialization in canine and human infants. *Monogr. Soc. Res. Child Developm.*, 1963, *28*(1).

Wickens, D. D., & Wickens, C. A study of conditioning in the neonate. *J. exp. Psychol.*, 1940, *26*, 94–102.

# 4

# Conditioned Head-Turning
# in Human Newborns

## Einar R. Siqueland and Lewis P. Lipsitt

### EDITORS' COMMENTS

The following study is notable in that only a few clear-cut demonstrations of discrimination in newborns had existed previously. Despite this, it has been apparent to many students of human development that all of the environmental conditions necessary for discrimination are present in the neonate's situation, and therefore discrimination could begin in the earliest days of postnatal life. A possibility, of course, is not as good as a demonstration; therefore, this study is particularly significant.

We suggest to the reader that he ask, as he reads the article, what type of behavior is being studied. Head-turning, he will learn, is often considered one of the "unconditioned responses" of the human neonate, i.e., it is seen in newborns early in postnatal life with no *obvious* history of conditioning preceding it. It is closely tied to apparently eliciting stimuli; specifically, the infant turns his head in the direction of a touch on his cheek (an "ipsilateral" head-turning response). Knowing nothing more about the response, one might be tempted to classify it as respondent. Such a responsiveness to touch may serve the infant well: it may often cause him to turn his head in the direction in which a nipple may be found. (If the infant is being held against his mother's breast, the tactile touch of a nipple against his cheek is quite likely; turning towards that touch will make it much more probable that his mouth will make contact with the nipple.) However, this fact does not clarify the nature of the response.

Einar R. Siqueland and Lewis P. Lipsitt, "Conditioned Head-Turning in Human Newborns," *Journal of Experimental Child Psychology,* 1966, *3,* 356–376. Reprinted by permission of Academic Press Inc.

This research was supported by Grant No. NB 04268 (National Institute of Health) to Lewis P. Lipsitt for the study of sensory discrimination and learning in infants. These studies were conducted while the first author was a Postdoctoral Fellow of the United States Public Health Service. We wish to thank the staff of the Providence Lying-In Hospital for their continued encouragement and cooperation.

Many respondents have considerable adaptive value for the organism (e.g., the sneeze). On the other hand, it is clear that if the response makes food more probable than it would be otherwise, a *possible* reinforcement contingency may operate for this response.

In this study the authors have simply changed the probability that head-turning in the direction of the touched cheek will make food available. They have created for the infant a small and temporary world in which turning *toward* a touch on the cheek produces food, while turning *away* from that touch consistently produces no food. A respondent would not be affected by such differential consequences; an operant would. The reader will note the outcome of these procedures, and of their reversal, and agree that a basic study has been performed.

The authors draw a careful conclusion, with commendable scientific caution. In addition, they refer to the first volume of Bijou and Baer's *Child Development*[1] noting that the distinction between operant and respondent processes in the young organism may not always be clear-cut, since operants and respondents often interact with one another. We suggest another possibility as well: some behaviors of the infant may first appear as respondents, in that they are attached to stimuli which elicit them independently of any *previous* history of reinforcement. However, these stimulus-response relationships may be adaptive (e.g., aid in finding food). Suppose that these behaviors, unlike most respondents, *are* sensitive to reinforcing stimulus consequences. If so, they could be attached to new stimuli, and even detached from the original eliciting stimulus, by new reinforcement contingencies. The paper by Siqueland and Lipsitt might well be viewed in this context.

## ABSTRACT

Three experiments demonstrated learning in human newborns, utilizing techniques involving the strengthening of a head-turning response through reinforcement contingencies. The first study demonstrated that administration of a dextrose-water solution contingent upon an ipsilateral response to tactile stimulation of the cheek increases the frequency of such responding. A second study presented the tactile stimulus on the opposite cheeks on alternate trials, right- and left-sided stimulation being paired with differential auditory stimuli. Reinforcement was given differentially for ipsilateral responding to the two "eliciting" stimuli, and learning was revealed through increased occurrence of the reinforced response, in con-

[1] *Child Development,* Vol. 1: *A Systematic and Empirical Theory,* New York: Appleton-Century-Crofts, 1961.

trast to habituation of the non-reinforced response. In the final experiment, involving tactile stimulation on only one side, the two auditory stimuli served as positive and negative cues. Ipsilateral turns to right-sided stimulation in the presence of one cue were reinforced, while such turns in the presence of the other cue were not. Infants acquired the discrimination and demonstrated reversal behavior when the cue-reinforcement contingencies were reversed. All subjects in these studies were under four days of age, and all experimental treatments were given in one session lasting no longer than one hour. No major effect of age was obtained, nor did amount of time since previous feeding within the range studied exert any effect. Since the demonstrated acquisition of discriminative behavior resulted from experimental procedures in which arousal level and sensitization were controlled, the effect of reinforcing circumstances on the head-turning behavior must be ascribed to learning.

## INTRODUCTION

Recent studies (Papousek, 1961; Lipsitt & Kaye, 1964) have shown that certain behavior patterns of human newborns can be viewed as learning phenomena, and traditional learning concepts such as reinforcement, conditioning, and extinction are useful in the analysis of infant behavior. These investigations suggest that, with increasing refinement of experimental techniques, analyses of learning processes are now possible in young organisms whose immature neuromuscular status has been a barrier previously to extensive behavioral study.

It was the purpose of this investigation to explore the use of instrumental conditioning procedures with newborns. As yet there has been little experimental data clearly demonstrating that some environmental circumstances act as reinforcing stimuli to shape or selectively strengthen behavior in infants in the first days of life (Lipsitt, 1963).

Papousek (1961) has shown that head movements in infants is a response suitable for conditioning studies, and Siqueland (1964) recently reported successful operant conditioning of head-turning in four-month infants. These results recommended the head-turning response for further investigation with the newborn. The most complete description of newborn head-turning, which is a well-developed response at birth and is elicited by various stimuli, has been provided by Prechtl (1958). In the present investigation head rotation in response to touch on the infant's cheek was selected for investigation. This response appears to serve an important function in the early feeding history of the infant and a number of investigations, other than those of Prechtl, have focused on parameters of head movement in newborn infants as an unconditioned response (Pratt, Nelson & Sun, 1930; Gentry & Aldrich, 1948; Blauvelt & McKenna, 1961; Turkewitz, Gordon & Birch, 1965). These investigations suggest the influence of such parameters as duration and intensity of stimulus, deprivational state, arousal level, age of infant, and medication of mother during delivery.

The focus of the present investigation was to evaluate the cumulative effect of reinforcement operations on head-turning in newborns, i.e., whether certain environmental consequences of the response can function to maintain or strengthen the response. Clinical observations of the initial feeding interaction between mother and newborn (Gunther, 1961) have resulted in speculation concerning the role of reinforcement on subsequent behavior in the feeding situation. Gewirtz (1961) has suggested that instrumental learning concepts may be useful in understanding behavior of young organisms in which specific components of unconditioned responses are shaped or selectively strengthened by immediate environmental consequences functioning as reinforcing stimuli.

The studies investigated the responses of lateral head movements as a component of the newborn's "unconditioned response" to tactile stimulation of the cheek. The first experiment studied the effect of experimentally presenting reinforcement upon the occurrence of ipsilateral head movements to the tactile stimulus. The effect of reinforcement contingencies upon probability of response occurrence over successive presentations of the tactile stimulus was assessed; thus the data were evaluated for evidence of instrumental conditioning in the first days of human life.

## EXPERIMENT 1

### Subjects and Design

The Ss were 36 full term newborns tested between 40 and 93 hrs. after birth at the Providence Lying-In Hospital. The Ss, selected from a population of awake infants, were all bottle-fed, and were studied in the morning between 8:00–9:15 and between 10:30–12:00. The Ss were assigned to two deprivation groups on the basis of time from previous feeding when brought to the laboratory. All infants in this hospital are routinely fed at intervals of four hours. Thus, time from previous feeding reflects an approximation of the naturally occurring food deprivation of this population. Group L (low hunger) was brought to the laboratory 30 to 90 min. (Mdn. 60) following previous feeding, and Group H (high hunger) was tested 120 to 180 min. (Mdn. 150) following feeding. Both deprivation groups were subdivided further by random assignment of infants to experimental and control groups (L-E, L-C, H-E, and H-C).

### Apparatus

All testing procedures were accomplished in a stablimeter crib described previously by Lipsitt and DeLucia (1960). Breathing was monitored by a Phipps and Bird infant pneumograph strapped around the abdomen. Respiration and general body activity were recorded continuously during experimental sessions on a Grass S5 polygraph. A manually operated event marker was used to record presentation of auditory and tactile stimulation and to designate observation periods on the polygraph record. Auditory stimuli were presented from an Eico audio-oscillator and a 10-watt amplifier, connected to an 8 in. Quam 6A speaker placed approximately 10 in. above S's head.

## Experimental Procedures

Infants were brought individually from the nursery to the laboratory by a nurse who assisted in experimental procedures. Swaddling with arms positioned on the chest prevented the infant's arms and hands from touching the face during testing. The Ss were placed supine in the experimental crib and testing began approximately 4 min. later.

During training all four groups received 30 presentations of tactile stimulation during a 5 sec. presentation of "buzzer" (a low frequency square wave tone, approximately 80 db. with a fundamental component of 23 cps). A 3 sec. tactile stimulus was presented to S's left cheek 2 sec. following buzzer onset and coincided with the last 3 sec. of buzzer. The tactile stimulus consisted of three light strokes of E's finger moving vertically on infant's left cheek a distance of 2.5 cm. beginning approximately 1.5 cm. from the corner of the lips. The response measure was the occurrence of an ipsilateral head rotation on each trial. A trial was defined as the 6-sec. time interval beginning with onset of buzzer. Two observers (E and an experimentally naive nurse) independently scored Ss for occurrence or absence of an ipsilateral head movement on each trial.

All Ss received 30 training trials, one every 30 sec. Following training, all infants received at least 12, but not more than 30, extinction trials. Extinction was terminated when Ss met an extinction criterion of four successive trials without occurrence of a response. Training for the experimental groups consisted of a 2-sec. presentation of a 5% dextrose solution via nipple contingent upon response occurrence within the 6-sec. interval. Control Ss were matched trial for trial with experimental Ss on reinforcements over training trials, but dextrose presentation always occurred 8–10 sec. following termination of the tactile stimulus.

## Results and Discussion

Agreement between observers in scoring head-turn responses was high (no. agreements minus no. disagreements, divided by total no. of observations), ranging from .89 to 1.0 over individual Ss, with a mean agreement ratio of .97 (Mdn .97) for the 36 infants. On the few trials in which the two observers disagreed, no response was inferred.

The measure of performance in this experiment was the percent occurrence of left-turn responses over training and extinction trials. The mean percent response for each of the four subgroups is presented in Table 1 in blocks of three trials for the ten blocks of training and four

Table 1

Mean Percent Response for Each of the Four Experimental Groups Over the Ten Blocks of Training Trials and Four Blocks of Extinction Trials
(Three Trial Blocks)

| Conditions | | Training Trials | | | | | | | | | | Extinct. Trials | | | |
|---|---|---|---|---|---|---|---|---|---|---|---|---|---|---|---|
| | | 1 | 2 | 3 | 4 | 5 | 6 | 7 | 8 | 9 | 10 | 11 | 12 | 13 | 14 |
| High Depriv. | Exp. | 30 | 44 | 58 | 63 | 67 | 55 | 63 | 89 | 85 | 89 | 85 | 70 | 52 | 67 |
| | Con | 30 | 26 | 41 | 22 | 18 | 41 | 30 | 15 | 33 | 22 | 26 | 22 | 07 | 15 |
| Low Depriv. | Exp. | 30 | 44 | 41 | 55 | 63 | 59 | 52 | 70 | 72 | 78 | 70 | 55 | 70 | 44 |
| | Con | 37 | 15 | 30 | 26 | 41 | 22 | 15 | 15 | 30 | 18 | 15 | 18 | 30 | 07 |

blocks of extinction trials. Figure 1 summarizes these results by comparing the experimental group (N-18) and the control group (N-18), deprivation disregarded, over training and extinction trials. The training and extinction data, presented in Table 1, were treated separately by Type III analyses of variance (Lindquist, 1953). Three significant effects were obtained from the analysis of the training data: Treatments ($F = 45.25$; df $= 1/32$; $p < 0.001$), Trials ($F = 2.70$; df $= 9/288$; $p < 0.01$), and Treatments X Trials ($F = 5.86$; df $= 9/288$; $p < 0.001$). Although an examination of the group means presented in Table 1 suggests a separation of the two experimental groups over the last four blocks of training trials, with more responding in the high deprivation group than for the low deprivation group, this effect was not reliable. Neither the main effect of deprivation nor its interaction with other variables was significant.

The analysis performed on the extinction data revealed two significant effects: Treatments ($F = 45.26$; df $= 1/32$; $p < 0.001$), and Treatment X Deprivation ($F = 4.36$; df $= 3/96$; $p < 0.010$). The extinction analysis suggested a trials effect ($F = 2.69$; df $= 3/96$; $p < 0.10$), but apparently not enough trials were available for this analysis to produce a striking effect.

These results indicate that the procedure of pairing reinforcement with the response of turning to tactile stimulation resulted in more responding by experimental Ss than control Ss during training and extinction. The fact that the control group who received the same number of dextrose presentations during training, failed to show similar response increments indicates that this increased probability of response for the experimental group was not attributable to simple arousal effects of dextrose presentation. In contrast to the relatively stable base rate of response for the control Ss, experimental Ss demonstrated a reliable acquisition effect over the ten blocks of training trials, shifting in probability of response occurrence from .30 to .83. Of 17 infants in the experimental group who shifted between the 1st and 10th blocks, all showed an increase (p < 0.01, Wilcoxon matched-pairs test[1]), whereas 6 of 7 Ss that shifted in the control group showed a decrease. A similar analysis of the shifts by these two groups between the 1st block of training trials and the 1st extinction block showed that 15 of 16 experimental Ss who shifted, increased in response probability (p < 0.01, Wilcoxon matched-pairs test), whereas 7 of the 9 control Ss who changed, decreased in response.

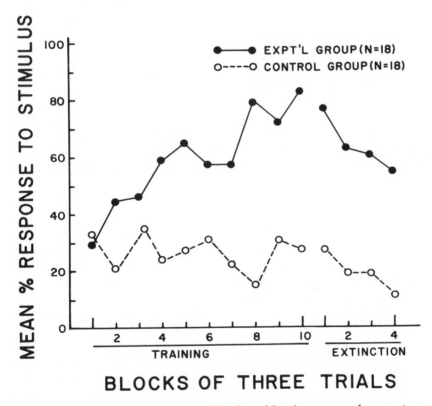

Figure 1.   Mean percentage occurrence of ipsilateral head movements for experimental Ss and control Ss, deprivation disregarded, over 10 blocks of 3 training trials and 4 blocks of 3 extinction trials (Experiment 1)

The analysis of the extinction data indicates that the pairing of reinforcement with left-turn responses for the experimental groups resulted in more responding for these groups as compared with the control group fol-

[1] Wherever Wilcoxon matched-pairs tests (two tailed) were used, t-tests for correlated pairs showed essentially similar results.

lowing termination of reinforcement. Although the limitations on number of trials available for analysis in extinction precluded the demonstration of a treatments by trials interaction, the experimental groups were observed to further decrease in responding over subsequent extinction trials with 15 of 18 infants meeting the extinction criterion within 30 trials. The mean numbers of responses to the extinction criterion (four successive trials without responding) were 11.55 for Group H-E, 8.77 for Group L-E, 2.50 for Group H-C, and 2.22 for Group L-C. The difference between Group H-E and Group L-E was not reliable ($t = 1.13$, $df = 16$).

The deprivation by trials interaction obtained in the analysis of the extinction data reflects largely an elevation in response by four infants in the low deprivation group on the third block of extinction trials (see Block 13, Table 1). This reversal in a trend of decreased responding on one of four blocks of extinction trials was not observed over the subsequent extinction trials.

Although an apparent treatments by deprivation effect could be observed in the response curves of the four groups during both training and extinction, these effects were not reliable. Prechtl (1958) has suggested that in newborns high ratings on "wakefulness" 30 min. following feeding coincide with low amounts of milk ingested at previous feeding. Thus, our procedure of selecting an experimental sample from a population of "awake" infants may have biased the present "low deprivation" $S$s in the direction of higher deprivation.

A more general problem for experimental investigations with newborns is the rapid fluctuation in sleep-awake cycles during the first days of life. Behavioral effects of experimental procedures, even of brief duration, may be confounded by rapid shifts in arousal of the subject. In the present experiments, the use of an auditory stimulus preceding and overlapping the tactile stimulus reflects an attempt to maintain a more stable baseline of arousal for the duration of the experimental procedure.

In the present experiment, there were no reliable differences between experimental and control $S$s in the occurrence of responses to buzzer alone (i.e., left-turn responses during the 2-sec. interval between onset of auditory stimulus and presentation of the tactile stimulus). The primary experimental effect was an increase in ipsilateral responding to tactile stimulation as a result of pairing reinforcement with the occurrence of the turning response. These results suggest that the effect of the reinforcement procedure was to produce stable responding in the presence of a stimulus which normally functioned as a "relatively weak eliciting stimulus." Results similar to these were obtained by Lipsitt, Kaye and Bosak (1965) who demonstrated conditioning of the sucking response under a procedure where the CS was a rubber tube which functioned as a weak eliciting stimulus for the sucking response. On the basis of a demonstrated increase in sucking to the tube following reinforcement trials, compared with an habituation of sucking effect in the non-reinforced control Ss, it was concluded that "a non-optimizing sucking stimulus can be transformed into a more effective elicitor of sucking through pairing with it of a suitable reinforcing agent . . ." (Lipsitt, 1965).

## EXPERIMENT 2

This experiment was designed to assess the experimental effect of pairing reinforcement differentially with two responses for individual Ss. It was assumed that experimental evidence for differential changes in probability of response occurrence for reinforced and non-reinforced head-turning responses would represent learned differentiation in human newborns.

### Subjects and Design

The Ss were 40 full-term infants, tested 120 to 180 min. following feeding. They were selected from newborns ranging from 24 to 112 hr. of age. The experiment involved a 2 × 2 factorial design. Infants were assigned to two groups on the basis of their age at time of testing, Group Y (younger, tested 24 to 48 hr. from birth; Mdn. 36 hr.), and Group O (older, tested 64 to 112 hr. from birth; Mdn. 80.5 hr.). Both age groups were subdivided further by random assignment of Ss to experimental and control groups (Groups Y-E, Y-C, O-E, and O-C).

### Experimental Procedures

The apparatus and pre-experimental preparations with Ss were identical to those used in the first experiment. Testing procedures were initiated approximately 4 min. after swaddled infants had been placed in the experimental crib.

The procedure of presenting tactile stimulation to infants overlapping the last 3 sec. of a 5 sec. auditory stimulus was continued in the present experiment with the following modifications. On alternate trials the tactile stimulus was presented to the right or left cheek of the infant. For individual Ss right- and left-sided stimulation were consistently paired with distinctive auditory stimuli (labeled "buzzer" and "tone" in this experiment). The buzzer was identical to that in the first experiment. The tone was a square wave, 230 cps (90db.). This single alternation procedure of presenting right- and left-sided tactile stimulation to infants paired with buzzer and tone was maintained over experimental trials. The order of stimulus presentation and pairing of the two auditory stimuli with loci of tactile stimulation were counterbalanced across Ss within each of the four subgroups.

The response measure was the occurrence or absence of an ipsilateral head rotation on each trial (i.e., left rotation to left-sided stimulation and right turn to right-sided stimulation). A trial was defined as the 4-sec. interval beginning with the onset of the 3-sec. tactile stimulus. The $S$s were scored as not responding on each trial in which the initial response to the tactile stimulus was a contralateral turn. The reinforcing stimulus (i.e., 2-sec. presentation of dextrose solution) was identical to that used in the previous experiment.

All four groups received six baseline, 48 training, and 36 extinction trials, one trial every 30 sec. During training trials, experimental $S$s received reinforcement following each ipsilateral turn to the positive stimulus ($R^{s+}$), but no reinforcement following turns to the negative stimulus ($R^{s-}$). Control $S$s were matched with individual experimental $S$s on total number of reinforcements over training trials, but presentation of the dextrose solution, 8 to 10 sec. following tactile stimulation, was not contingent upon head rotation responses. Because preliminary data, obtained from an independent sample of newborns, had suggested rather stable response biases for individual $S$s (i.e., individual infants demonstrated differential probabilities of ipsilateral turning to right- and left-sided tactile stimulation), individual response biases in the present experiment were assessed over the six baseline trials. Baseline data from each infant determined which of the two responses would be paired with reinforcement during training. The response with the lower incidence of occurrence was designated $R^{s+}$ for both experimental and control $S$s, but for the former, it was paired with dextrose presentation (i.e., the response with the lower probability of elicitation was always reinforced). The response with the higher probability of elicitation for each $S$ over baseline trials was designated $R^{s-}$ and was the nonreinforced response for experimental $S$s. $R^{s+}$ and $R^{s-}$ were assigned randomly to infants who responded equally to left- and right-sided tactile stimulation over baseline trials.

## Results and Discussion

The response measure was the percent occurrence of ipsilateral head turns to the positive and negative stimulus over blocks of six trials during baseline, training and extinction procedures. The measure of learning is reflected in the relative shift in percent occurrence of $R^{s+}$ and $R^{s-}$ over trials as a function of differential reinforcement of the two responses during training. Figure 2 summarizes the results by comparing experimental $S$s ($N = 20$), with age disregarded, on percent occurrence of $R^{s+}$ and $R^{s-}$ over baseline, training and extinction trials. The graph presents individual curves showing the mean percent occurrence of $R^{s+}$ and $R^{s-}$ separately in blocks of three trials each for each group. Table 2 presents the same data for each of the four subgroups over the nine blocks of baseline and

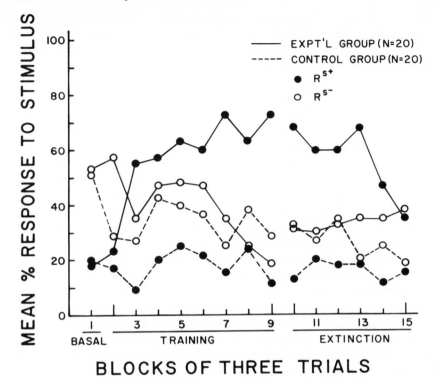

Figure 2. Mean percentage occurrence of $R^{s+}$ and $R^{s-}$ for the experimental and control Ss, age disregarded, over blocks of baseline, training and extinction trials (Experiment 2)

Table 2

Mean Percent Occurrence of $R^{s+}$ and $R^{s-}$ for Each of the Four Subgroups Over Baseline, Training and Extinction Trials

(Blocks of Three Trials)

|  | Basal | Training Trials | | | | | | | | Extinction Trials | | | | | |
|---|---|---|---|---|---|---|---|---|---|---|---|---|---|---|---|
| GRP. | 1 | 2 | 3 | 4 | 5 | 6 | 7 | 8 | 9 | 10 | 11 | 12 | 13 | 14 | 15 |
| O-E | 10 | 50 | 70 | 67 | 67 | 63 | 83 | 60 | 73 | 73 | 63 | 70 | 67 | 63 | 43 |
| O-C | 13 | 13 | 10 | 20 | 27 | 27 | 33 | 23 | 13 | 17 | 23 | 23 | 23 | 17 | 27 |
| Y-E | 27 | 30 | 40 | 47 | 60 | 57 | 63 | 67 | 73 | 70 | 57 | 53 | 70 | 30 | 27 |
| Y-C | 27 | 20 | 20 | 20 | 23 | 30 | 10 | 27 | 10 | 10 | 17 | 13 | 13 | 07 | 03 |
| O-E | 60 | 67 | 40 | 47 | 47 | 47 | 40 | 33 | 17 | 33 | 37 | 40 | 40 | 47 | 53 |
|  | 52 | 20 | 23 | 53 | 50 | 40 | 33 | 43 | 37 | 43 | 40 | 50 | 33 | 40 | 30 |
|  | 47 | 47 | 30 | 47 | 50 | 47 | 30 | 17 | 20 | 30 | 23 | 27 | 30 | 23 | 23 |
|  | 50 | 37 | 30 | 33 | 30 | 33 | 17 | 33 | 20 | 23 | 13 | 20 | 07 | 10 | 07 |

training trials and six blocks of extinction trials. The training and extinction data presented in Table 2 were treated separately by Type III analyses of variance. Analyses were conducted separately for the $R^{s+}$ and the $R^{s-}$ data.

### Training Data

Three significant effects were obtained from the analysis of $R^{s+}$ occurrence over training trials (including the baseline block): Treatments ($F = 56.67$; df $= 1/36$; $p < 0.001$), Trials ($F = 5.58$; df $= 8/288$; $p < 0.01$), and Treatments X Trials ($F = 6.50$; df $= 8/288$; $p < 0.01$). The analysis performed on incidence of $R^{s-}$ over comparable trials resulted in two significant effects: Trials ($F = 4.97$; df $= 8/288$; $p < 0.001$), Treatments X Trials ($F = 2.21$; df $= 8/288$; $p < 0.05$). None of the age effects was significant in either of these analyses.

It is clear from these results that experimental $S$s as compared with control $S$s demonstrated a higher total incidence of $R^{s+}$ over training. The increasing separation between the two groups in occurrence of $R^{s+}$ over training trials, moreover, is reflected in the curves of Figure 2 which show that the experimental group shifted from a baseline probability of .18 to .73 by the end of training, while the control group showed a decrease from .20 to .12. Analysis of these shifts by the two groups between baseline and the end of training indicates a reliable increase by the experimental group ($p < 0.01$, Wilcoxon matched-pairs signed-ranks test) and a reliable decrease ($p < 0.01$) by the control group. Of 18 $S$s in the experimental group who shifted in incidence of $R^{s+}$ over training, all showed an increase, whereas 10 of 10 $S$s in the control group that changed, demonstrated a decrease.

Examination of Figure 2 shows also that both experimental and control groups decreased in $R^{s-}$ occurrence over training, this decrease being reflected in the reliable trials effect. In both groups 15 of 17 $S$s who shifted between baseline and the end of training showed a decrease in incidence of $R^{s-}$. This decrease was a reliable shift ($p < 0.01$, Wilcoxon matched-pairs test) for both groups. The reliable treatments by trials interaction obtained in the analysis of $R^{s-}$ occurrence over training trials may reflect an initial generalization of the reinforcement effect in the experimental group. As seen in Figure 2, $R^{s-}$ occurrence for the experimental group was elevated above that of the control group over the first part of training, but there was an inversion of these two groups on the last two blocks of training trials.

### Extinction Data

The analysis of $R^{s+}$ occurrence over extinction trials resulted in four significant effects: Treatments ($F = 58.71$; df $= 1/36$; $p < 0.001$), Age

(F = 4.73; df = 1/36; p < 0.05), Trials (F = 3.79; df = 5/180; p < 0.005), and Treatment X Trials (F = 2.63; df = 5/180; p < 0.005). Only one significant effect was obtained from the analysis of $R^{s-}$ occurrence over extinction trials, that of Age (F = 13.32; df = 1/36; p < 0.001).

The reliable age effects obtained in both analyses indicate that the older infants were responding more than the younger infants during extinction. The mean number of $R^{s+}$ occurrence were 5.55 for Group Y and 7.65 for Group O. The $R^{s-}$ means for these two age groups were 3.55 and 7.30 respectively.

It is clear that the experimental group had a higher probability of $R^{s+}$ occurrence than the control group during extinction. Moreover, a reliable extinction effect was reflected in the treatments by trials inter-action, and the decrement in occurrence of $R^{s+}$ between the first and last blocks of extinction trials for the experimental group was reliable (p < 0.01, Wilcoxon matched-pairs test). Fourteen of 17 infants who shifted showed a decrease. The control group showed no reliable change in $R^{s+}$ over extinction trials.

The results of this experiment demonstrate learned discrimination as a function of differential reinforcement of the two responses. In contrast to the general habituation demonstrated by the $R^{s+}$ and $R^{s-}$ decrement over trials by the control Ss, experimental Ss showed a similar response decrement for the non-reinforced response ($R^{s-}$), but demonstrated a reliable acquisition effect for the reinforced response ($R^{s+}$). Thus, for the experimental Ss relative response to two "eliciting stimuli" was influenced by the differential reinforcement contingencies employed. Ipsilateral head movement to right- and left-sided stimulation (the two loci of tactile stimulation paired with distinctive auditory stimuli) clearly reflected the effects of differential reinforcement.

Turkewitz, Gordon and Birch (1965) have reported evidence of right turn bias in newborns (i.e., higher probability of ipsilateral turns to right-sided stimulation than ipsilateral turns to left-sided stimulation). Although the experimental parameters of stimulation were quite different in the present experiment, a similar effect was observed in the baseline response measures of the 40 infants tested. These infants made significantly more right turns to right-sided stimulation than left turns to left-sided stimulation (Wilcoxon matched-pairs test, p < 0.01). The mean percentages of ipsilateral turns to right-sided and left-sided stimulation were 40 and 32, respectively. In addition, it was found that although the two age groups did not differ in total number of ipsilateral responses to stimulation during baseline, they did differ significantly with respect to a right-sided bias (Mann-Whitney U test, p < 0.05). Of 20 infants in Group O, 14 (70%) showed a right turn bias, 5 (25%) responded more to left-sided stimulation, and 1 (5%) responded equally to right- and left-sided stimulation. In contrast, only 3 of 20 infants in Group Y (15%) gave more right turns to right-sided stimulation than left turns to left-sided stimulation, 6 (30%) showed a left turn bias, and 11 (55%) responded equally to right- and left-sided stimulation. An examination of the performance of control Ss over training trials gave evidence of relative stability of these response biases in newborns. This apparent age effect may reflect differences in deprivational conditions or number of feedings, progressive evidence of TNR over the first days of life, or diminishing effects of drugs administered maternally at birth.

## EXPERIMENT 3

In this experiment the two auditory stimuli served experimentally as the positive and negative cues for reinforcement. Initially, ipsilateral turns to right-sided stimulation in the presence of one auditory stimulus were reinforced while ipsilateral turns to right-sided stimulation in the presence of the other were not. In a subsequent stage, the relation of reinforcement to the auditory stimuli was reversed so that turning to the previously reinforced cue was now non-reinforced and vice versa.

### Apparatus

Modification of a head-turning apparatus previously described in a study with 4-month infants (Siqueland, 1964) provided instrumentation and automatic recording of head movements with newborns. The present apparatus consisted of a light-weight plastic headpiece connecting with a potentiometer circuit by means of a flexible shaft. A photograph of the head apparatus is shown in Figure 3. The photograph shows the flexible plastic headpiece resting on the infant's temples, held in position by an adjustable, elastic headband. Measures of lateral head movements were obtained with the potentiometer circuit which polygraphically recorded changes in potential occurring with rotations about the horizontal axis. The flexible shaft, connecting the headpiece with the potentiometer circuit, allowed infants complete freedom of head movements, but only lateral movements about the horizontal axis were recorded polygraphically. The apparatus was calibrated to give directional deflections of 1 mm. from baseline with each 5 degrees of rotation. A polygraph-record sample obtained in this experiment is shown in Figure 4. The sample shows two continuous minutes of recording obtained from one S over the last block of training trials, the 28th min. at the top and the 29th min. below. Four trials are presented in this record, two buzzer presentations and two tone presentations, one each 30 sec. The event markers on the first line show the onset of the 5-sec. auditory stimuli and the overlapping 3-sec. tactile stimulus. The second and third lines show analog records of lateral head movements and respiration, respectively.

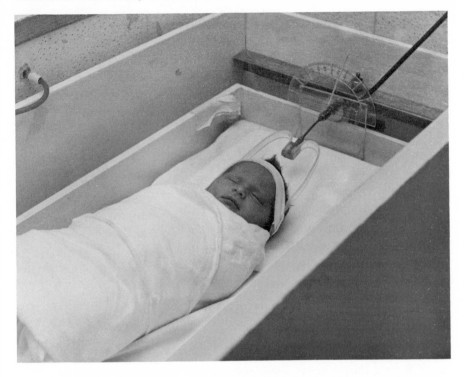

Figure 3. Photographic representation of the head-turning apparatus

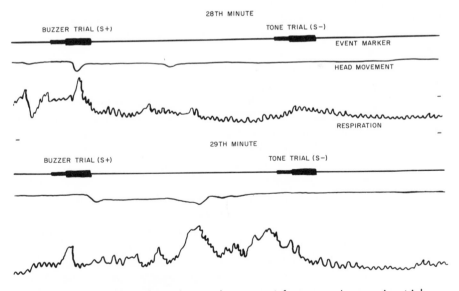

Figure 4. Sample polygraph record on one infant over 4 successive trials

## Subjects and Design

The $S$s were two groups of eight infants, 6 males and 10 females, 48 to 116 hr. of age. They were tested approximately two to three hours following previous feeding. In this experiment tactile stimulation to the right side was presented in the presence of buzzer or tone on alternate trials and right turns to the tactile stimuli. The infants were randomly assigned to two groups. For half, (Group 1), tone was the positive stimulus ($S^+$, turning right to right-sided stimulation in presence of tone being paired with reinforcement), while buzzer was the negative stimulus ($S^-$, turning right to right-sided stimulation in the presence of buzzer not followed by reinforcement). For the other half, (Group 2) the buzzer functioned as $S^+$ and the tone as $S^-$. Subsequent to original training, reversal training was presented to both groups.

## Experimental Procedures

Pre-experimental preparations were identical to those of the previous experiments, and testing began approximately 4 min. after swaddled infants had been placed in the experimental crib with the head apparatus and pneumograph adjusted. The two auditory stimuli ("buzzer" and "tone") were the same as those used in the previous experiment. Both groups received 60 training trials (30 with each of the two auditory stimuli), followed by 60 reversal trials, one trial every 30 sec. A 3-min. interval separated the last training trial and the first reversal trial. Stimulus presentations on each trial consisted of right-sided tactile stimulation overlapping the last 3 seconds of the 5-sec. presentation of buzzer or tone.

The response measure was the occurrence of a 10° rotation of the head to the right of baseline position on each trial. As in the previous experiment, a trial was defined as the 4-sec. interval beginning with the onset of the tactile stimulus. The $S$s were scored as giving no response on each trial that the initial response to the tactile stimulus was a 10° rotation to the left of baseline. Reinforcement presentation was contingent upon polygraphically recorded deflections of 2 mm. or greater in the appropriate direction. As seen in the sample record (Figure 4), downward deflections of the polygraph pen from a baseline position indicate right turn movements of the infant's head, and opposite deflections indicate left turns. A research assistant continually observed the polygraph record throughout the procedure and provided $E$ with a digital output of the analog record, signalling $E$ on each trial that a deflection from baseline of 2 mm. was observed. The reinforcing stimulus was the presentation of 0.2 cc. of a 5% dextrose via nipple, the nipple being presented for 4-sec. period.

## Results and Discussion

The results are summarized in Figure 5 which presents the mean percent occurrence of ipsilateral turns to right-sided stimulation in the presence of S+ and S− over the 10 blocks of original training and 10 of reversal. Separate analyses of variance were performed on S+ and S− responding over trial blocks. These analyses indicated that the primary

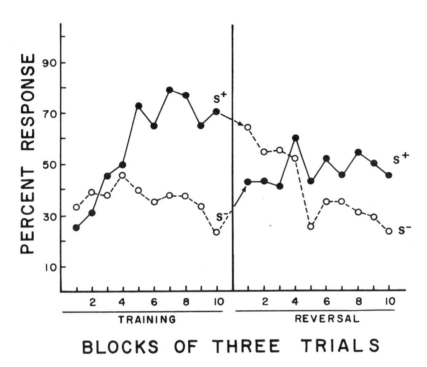

Figure 5. Mean for 16 experimental Ss on percentage occurrence of right turns to right-sided tactile stimulation in the presence of the positive (S+) and the negative (S−) stimuli

experimental effect during original training was to increase the probability of response occurrence to the positive stimulus over training trials (F = 7.46; df = 9/126; p < 0.001), while responding in the presence of the negative stimulus showed negligible change (F = 0.87; df = 9/126). The 16 Ss demonstrated a reliable increase in S+ responding between the 1st and 10th block of training trials (p < 0.01, Wilcoxon matched-pairs test) with 12 of 14 who shifted showing an increase in response occurrence. A similar analysis of shifts in response occurrence on S− trials showed no reliable change.

By contrast, the primary experimental effect during reversal was a decrease in response occurrence in the presence of S⁻ (the positive stimulus during original training) over trials (F = 3.57; df = 9/126; p < 0.001), while S⁺ responding (S⁻ during original training) showed no significant change over reversal trials (F = 0.69; df = 9/126). A reliable decrease in S⁻ responding was found between the 1st and 10th blocks of reversal (Wilcoxon matched-pairs test, p < 0.01) with 13 of 15 infants who shifted demonstrating a decrease. Although extinction of the acquired response to S⁺ is now reflected in the response decrement during reversal to S⁻, there is also the possibility that this decrement is due in part to a satiation effect. The total number of ipsilateral responses to right-sided stimulation in the presence of both positive and negative cues decreased between the 1st and 10th reversal blocks (p < 0.05, Wilcoxon matched-pairs test). Thus the decrease in response to S⁻ may reflect both extinction and satiation effects, while the failure to find a reliable increase in S⁺ responding during reversal may reflect combined effects of acquisition training and satiation. As seen in Figure 5, the effects of the reinforcement contingencies during reversal are reflected by the Ss' relative response to the positive and negative stimuli. At the end of reversal training the 16 infants were responding more to the positive than to the negative stimulus (p < 0.01, Wilcoxon matched-pairs test).

Separate analyses of variance were used to compare (1) the two experimental groups on response occurrence to *tone* over training trials (S⁺ for Group 1, and S⁻ for Group 2), and (2) on response occurrence to *buzzer* (S⁻ for Group 1, and S⁺ for Group 2). The comparison of the two groups to tone over the 10 blocks of training trials indicated significantly higher responding for Group 1 than for Group 2 (F = 8.44; df = 1/14; p < 0.025), and also an increasing separation between the two groups over trials (F = 2.86; df = 9/126; p < 0.01). The difference between the two groups in total number of responses to buzzer over training was in the predicted direction, although not statistically reliable (F = 4.22; df = 1/14; p < 0.10). However, a reliable treatments by trials effect (F = 3.29; df = 9/126; p < 0.005) indicated an increasing separation between these two groups as a result of differential reinforcement. Although Group 2 showed increased responding to the buzzer (S⁺) over training, Group 1 showed no change to buzzer (S⁻).

The evidence of auditory discrimination in this experiment reflects primarily an increased probability of ipsilateral head movements to the positive stimulus, while probability of ipsilateral head movements to the negative stimulus showed negligible change. However, it was observed during training procedures that although Ss were responding less to the negative stimulus than to the positive one, contralateral movements to the negative stimulus appeared to increase in frequency. To further assess this apparent effect, response differentiation ratios were computed for the positive and negative stimuli which relates the frequency of ipsilateral responses to contralateral responses (i.e., number of ipsilateral turns divided by the number of ipsilateral and contralateral responses). Ratios above .50 indicate more turns toward than away from the tactual stimulus, and below .50 indicate more contralateral responses. Figure 6 summarizes

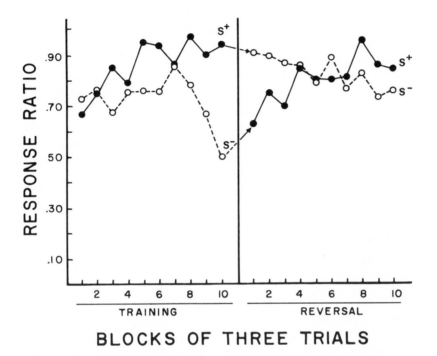

BLOCKS OF THREE TRIALS

Figure 6. Response differentiation ratios (no. of ipsilateral responses divided by no. of ipsilateral and contralateral responses) computed on the total response occurrence for 16 Ss to the positive and negative stimuli over 10 blocks of training and 10 blocks of reversal trials

these results by showing the response ratios for the 16 infants to the positive and negative stimuli over training and reversal. The initial ratios of approximately .70 for both the positive and negative stimuli indicate that most of the turns were in the direction of the tactile stimulus. However, over training Ss show an increased ratio of ipsilateral responses to the positive stimulus, while the response ratio to the negative stimulus dropped sharply over the last 4 blocks of training. This decreased ratio in the presence of the negative stimulus largely reflects an increase in contralateral responses. The increased ratio to the positive stimulus reflects both a sharp increase in ipsilateral and an apparent decrease in contralateral responses. Subsequent shifts in the ratios over reversal trials also reflect the change in experimental reinforcement contingencies. The shift in response ratio to the newly positive stimulus during reversal (negative stimulus originally) reflects a decrease in contralateral responses. On the other hand, the decreased S⁻ ratio during reversal (formerly the positive stimulus) reflects a decrease in ipsilateral responses (extinction of the reinforced response class) over trials.

Prechtl (1958) has reported the occurrence of contralateral responding in habituation studies with newborns. He reports that following habituation of ipsilateral responses to the presentation of lateralized tactile stimulation, continued presentation of the tactile stimulus results in increased contralateral responding. The phenomenon, following habituation of ipsilateral turning, may reflect a type of conditioned inhibition or escape responding. On the other hand, the decrease in contralateral responding to the positive stimulus may reflect a type of learned response differentiation. Although this phenomenon reflects an apparent learning effect, the design of the present experiment does not provide the necessary controls for further interpretation of this particular effect.

The present data provide evidence of an acquired auditory discrimination in the first days of human life. The newborn infants' responding to the positive and negative stimuli clearly reflect the effects of the discrimination training procedures employed in this experiment.

## General Discussion

These experiments show that, under certain experimental conditions, environmental events can function as reinforcing stimuli to shape or selectively strengthen components of "unconditioned responses." The results indicate that presentation of dextrose via nipple can function as a positive reinforcing stimulus for head movement responses in human newborns. Bilateral head movements, of the amplitude observed and quantified in these studies, were brought under the control of instrumental reinforcement contingencies. It is suggested that the rapid acquisition effects demonstrated in these experiments may reflect the immediate temporal relationship between response occurrence and the reinforcing event. Head rotations of a specified response class were followed immediately by presentation of a stimulus event which provided infants with both oral-tactile and taste stimulation.

In the first experiment the effect of reinforcement was to produce stable responding to a stimulus (tactual stimulation of cheek) which functioned initially as a "low level elicitor" of the to-be-reinforced response class. For control Ss, the presentation of the response-reinforcement contingency resulted in a reliable acquisition effect, and termination of the experimental contingency resulted in extinction. One interpretation of this acquisition effect suggests that the "low level eliciting stimulus" acquired discriminative cue value for the reinforcement of turning responses. This suggestion implies that some stimuli may have complex functions, reflecting interactions and summations of eliciting and discriminative properties.

It should be noted that the initially low probability of response elicitation obtained in the present series of experiments may reflect the specific and somewhat arbitrary selection of experimental stimulation parameters. Turkewitz, Gordon and Birch (1965) have reported higher probability of response elicitation with newborns using experimental procedures quite different from those employed in the present study. Other investigators (Prechtl, 1958; Blauvelt & McKenna, 1961) have reported inter- and intra-subject variability in response elicitation and have indicated that the response may be controlled by such factors as food deprivation, age, arousal level, and medication during delivery. Comparison between baseline response measures among studies is difficult because of differences in experimental procedures such as response criterion, preparation and positioning of Ss during testing, arousal effects of testing procedures, inter-trial interval, and parameters of the tactile stimulus. Papousek (1965), with procedures similar to those used here, reports comparable baseline responding in his newborn population. He also reports a shaping procedure with milk reinforcement prior to obtaining stable turning to tactile stimulation in the newborn population.

Our second experiment suggests a type of learned discrimination in newborns in that responding to two different eliciting stimuli, in the context of differential reinforcement, was brought under control of these reinforcement contingencies. Individual infants demonstrated not only a decrement in the non-reinforced response (habituation), but also showed increased occurrence of the reinforced response (acquisition). Reliable extinction effects were demonstrated following termination of reinforcement.

Evidence of an acquired stimulus discrimination was seen in the last experiment. When response to an eliciting stimulus was differentially reinforced in the presence of two auditory stimuli, newborns showed increased responding to the eliciting stimulus in the presence of the positive auditory cue, but response to the same eliciting stimulus in the presence of the negative auditory cue did not change.

Possibly the type of learning experiences provided for newborns in the normal feeding situation may not be too different from the experimental prototypes investigated in these experiments. Stimuli that function as low level elicitors in the initial feeding situation may acquire discriminative function because they provide cues for reinforcing environmental consequences. The breast-fed infant may demonstrate a higher probability of ipsilateral turning to tactile stimulation when held in feeding position at the mother's breast than when lying supine on the mother's lap. This suggests that infants may readily learn to turn differentially to the tactile stimulus when it is presented in the context of complex visual and postural cues signaling that reinforcement or non-reinforcement will follow occurrence of the turning response.

It is difficult to specify clearly the type of learning processes involved in these experiments. The distinction between respondents and operants as labels for response classes in the newborn become somewhat blurred and may be interactions between these response classes (Bijou & Baer, 1961, pp. 71–73). It was observed in the course of these experiments that marked increases in spontaneous turning responses occurred during the inter-trial intervals following a few trials of reinforced responding. A similar observation has been reported by Papousek (1965). The only quantitative data on this observed increase in inter-trial turning was provided by the third experiment. Examination of the analog records indicated that infants showed a marked increase in spontaneous turning over the last blocks of training trials, reaching asymptote by the 4th and 5th blocks of trials. They subsequently showed a gradual decrease in spontaneous turning over the last five blocks of training trials. It is not possible to determine from these results whether the observed increase in spontaneous head movements reflected a general arousal effect or whether it specifically reflects the reinforcement of the response class.

It is clear from these results that head turning to tactile stimulation in newborn infants may be influenced by environmental events which function as reinforcers. It is suggested also that some environmental stimuli may under certain conditions have complex functions for the human newborn's behavior and very early in the history of the organism begin to reflect interactions between eliciting and learned cue functions.

## REFERENCES

Bijou, S. W., & Baer, D. M. *Child development.* Vol. 1. *A systematic and empirical theory.* New York: Appleton-Century-Crofts, 1961.

Blauvelt, Helen, & McKenna, J. Mother-neonate interaction: capacity of the human newborn for orientation. In B. M. Foss (Ed.), *Determinants of infant behavior.* New York: Wiley, 1961. Pp. 3–29.

Gentry, E. F., & Aldrich, C. A. Rooting reflex in newborn infants: incidence and effect on it of sleep. *Amer. J. Dis. Children,* 1948, *75,* 528–539.

Gewirtz, J. L. A learning analysis of the effect of normal stimulation privation and deprivation on the acquisition of social motivation and attachment. In B. M. Foss (Ed.), *Determinants of infant behavior.* New York: Wiley, 1961. Pp. 213–290.

Gunther, Mavis. Infant behavior at the breast. In B. M. Foss (Ed.), *Determinants of infant behavior.* New York: Wiley, 1961. Pp. 37–40.

Lindquist, E. F. *Design and analysis of experiments in psychology and education.* Boston: Houghton-Mifflin, 1953.

Lipsitt, L. P. Learning in the first year of life. In L. P. Lipsitt & C. C. Spiker (Eds.), *Advances in child development and behavior*. Vol. 1. New York: Academic Press, 1963. Pp. 147–195.

Lipsitt, L. P. Learning processes of human newborns. *Merrill-Palmer Quart.* Paper delivered to Merrill-Palmer Conference on Infant Development, February, 1965. In press.

Lipsitt, L. P., & DeLucia, C. A. An apparatus for the measurement of specific response and general activity in the human neonate. *Amer. J. Psychol.*, 1960, *73*, 630–632.

Lipsitt, L. P., & Kaye, H. Conditioned sucking in the human newborn. *Psychon. Sci.*, 1964, *1*, 29–30.

Lipsitt, L. P., Kaye, H., & Bosack, T. The facilitation of sucking behavior in the human newborn through reinforcement. In preparation, 1965.

Papousek, H. Conditioned head rotation reflexes in infants in the first months of life. *Acta Pediatr.*, 1961, *50*, 565–576.

Papousek, H. Experimental appetitional behavior in human newborns and infants. Reported at Social Science Research Council Conference on Learned and Non-Learned Behavior in Immature Organisms, Stillwater, Minn., June, 1965.

Pratt, K. C., Nelson, A. K., & Sun, K. H. The behavior of the newborn infant. *Ohio State Univ. Stud. Contr. Psychol.*, 1930, No. 10.

Prechtl, H. F. R. The directed head turning response and allied movements in the human baby. *Behavior*, 1958, *13*, 212–242.

Siqueland, E. R. Operant conditioning of head-turning in four-month infants. *Psychonom. Sci.*, 1964, *1*, 223–224.

Turkewitz, G., Gordon, E. W., & Birch, H. G. Head-turning in the human neonate: effect of prandial condition and lateral preference. *J. comp. physiol. Psychol.*, 1965, *59*, 189–192.

# Extensions to Social Dimensions

The principles exemplified in the next three readings are essentially laboratory demonstrations. However, when such principles are expected to describe the development of the child in natural surroundings, laboratory research takes on a curiously mixed character. The researcher attempts to retain the highly controlled atmosphere of the laboratory. Since that is not where children live, some aspects of the child's natural world must be transplanted into the laboratory. Some of the most interesting of these hybridizations of real world and laboratory have involved the introduction of social stimuli into an otherwise highly controlled, laboratory-like setting. (An alternative technique would be to take the procedures of the laboratory into the real life setting of the child. A number of studies using this approach are included in the second part of this collection, Applications.)

# 5

# Social Conditioning
# of Vocalizations
# in the Infant

### Harriet L. Rheingold, Jacob L. Gewirtz,
### and Helen W. Ross

### EDITORS' COMMENTS

Vocal behavior is obviously an important response class in young children. It is the repertoire out of which will be differentiated the verbal behavior that will make up the child's (and the adult's) basic communication repertoire. Similarly, social reinforcement is an important process in the development of infants. It is the kind of stimulation which follows a great deal of the young child's behavior in the presence of adults. Thus, any analysis of the development of vocal behavior is valuable, and any establishment of the reinforcing function of particular classes of social stimuli is significant, from a systematic point of view.

In the following study, Rheingold, Gewirtz, and Ross contribute clearly to both goals. They apply to the vocal behavior of young infants a complex of social stimuli similar to the sort in everyday use by parents. A clear demonstration of operant conditioning results. Extinction is then programmed, with the usual outcome of weakening the vocalization rate. Reinstatement of the reinforcement contingency readily restores a strong rate of vocalization.

Despite the clarity of these findings, note the authors' concern in the discussion section of this paper that perhaps they have not completely separated the reinforcing function of the social stimuli from their possible eliciting or "releasing" function. That is, perhaps the effect of the social stimuli is not to reinforce the last vocalization, but to elicit the next one. The authors suggest ways of checking this possibility. Several years later, Paul Weisberg followed

Harriet L. Rheingold, Jacob L. Gewirtz, and Helen W. Ross, "Social Conditioning of Vocalizations in the Infant," *Journal of Comparative and Physiological Psychology*, 1959, *52*, 68–73.

their suggestions and found that only a reinforcing function of the stimuli was involved,[1] as Rheingold, Gewirtz, and Ross had supposed. Thus the present study portrays classic scientific caution, careful analysis of possible weaknesses in itself, and subsequent vindication—a standard scientific drama.

By three months of age the infant gives a well-defined social response to the appearance of adults. He looks at them intently, smiles, becomes active, and vocalizes. This behavior is repeated again and again in sequence. Adults often respond to these acts of the infant; they may only look at the child, but they may also smile to him, touch or caress him, or vocalize in return. Frequently one observes "answering" social and, in particular, vocal play between mother and child. The adults' responses may therefore play an important part in maintaining and developing social responsiveness in the child (Rheingold, 1956). The principles of operant conditioning (Skinner, 1953) suggest that some of these adult responses, functioning as reinforcers, may affect the development of the child's social behavior (Gewirtz, 1956). Thus, smiling in the infant has been shown to respond to conditioning (Brackbill, 1958).

The present study was an attempt to condition vocalizations in infants. Vocalizations were selected for study because they seem to provide an index of the whole social response (Rheingold, 1956). The reinforcing stimulus was a complex of social acts which resembled those an attentive adult might naturally make when a child vocalizes. If temporal contiguity between the infant's vocalization and the reinforcing stimulus, which follows it, brings about an increase in the vocalizations, conditioning may be said to have occurred. The possibility that the reinforcing stimulus may also have functioned as an arouser of vocalizations will be considered. In any case, the results of the study should provide further understanding about the development of social responsiveness, as well as of speech.

## METHOD

Two parallel experiments were carried out in sequence. In the first, 11 babies (Ss) were studied, with one experimenter (E) and one observer-recorder (O), both women. In the second, 10 other Ss and one S from Experiment I were studied with the E and O of the first experiment exchanging roles. An experiment was composed of three successive units in each of which three or four Ss were studied at one time.

[1] "Social and Nonsocial Conditioning of Infant Vocalization," *Child Develpm.*, 1963, *34*, 377–388.

**Subjects**

The Ss were 21 infants, all residents almost from birth in the same institution. (We are grateful to Sister Thecla and the staff of St. Ann's Infant Asylum, Washington, D.C., for their generous cooperation.) Their median age was 3.0 months; three-quarters of them were no more than three days older or younger than the median. In each experiment six Ss were male, five were female. Age was the main criterion for selection. Four possible Ss were rejected: one seemed immature, two had a very high rate of vocalizing during the first baseline measure, and one was markedly fussy.

The institution offers excellent care and, as is characteristic of institutions, there are multiple caretakers. In general, the Ss were well developed, healthy, alert, and socially responsive. The Es asked for no modifications in the usual caretaking routines. The caretakers knew that the Es were observing the development of social behavior, but they did not know the details of the experiment. The caretakers' usual behavior toward the Ss appeared not to be modified by the conditions of the experiment.

**Experimental Conditions**

Baseline

On experimental Days 1 and 2 (first and second Baseline days) E leaned over the crib with her face about 15 in. above S's and looked at him with an expressionless face, while O tallied vocalizations, out of S's sight. The E moved her head as necessary to remain in S's line of vision, a condition which was obtained throughout the experiments.

Conditioning

During experimental Days 3 and 4 (first and second Conditioning days), E again leaned over the crib with an expressionless face except that when S vocalized, E made an immediate response and then resumed the expressionless face until the next vocalization. The response, or reinforcing stimulus, consisted of three acts executed by E simultaneously, quickly, and smoothly. They were a broad smile, three "tsk" sounds and a light touch applied to the infant's abdomen with thumb and fingers of the hand opposed. No more than a second of time was required to administer the reinforcer.

At the beginning of the conditioning periods each vocalization was reinforced. Sometimes, as the rate of vocalizing increased, only every second, and later, every third, vocalization was reinforced. In Experiment

I, 72% of the reinforcers occurred after each vocalization; in Experiment II, 94%. Less frequent reinforcing seemed to depress the rate, at least initially, and because of the rather severe time restrictions, was abandoned altogether by the end of the study.

### Extinction

Experimental Days 5 and 6 (first and second Extinction days) were the same as Days 1 and 2; E leaned over the crib with an expressionless face and made no response to S's vocalizations.

## The Vocal Response

Every discrete, voiced sound produced by S was counted as a *vocalization*. A number of other sounds characteristically made by very young infants, e.g., straining sounds and coughs, and the whistles, squeaks, and snorts of noisy breathing, were not counted as vocalizations. Sounds falling under the categories of protests, fusses, and cries (see Emotional Behavior below) were recorded separately. No attempt was made to record the phonetic characteristics of any of the sounds or their duration.

### Observer Agreement

Agreement between two Os on the number of vocalizations produced by Ss in 3-min. periods was high. Counts for 27 periods, using 13 different Ss, yielded a median percentage agreement of 96 (range, 67 to 100). About half of these reliability measures were obtained at the Ss' cribs, and the rest from tape recordings made during the experiment. These two techniques yielded similar percentages of observer agreement.

### The Unit of Measurement

The unit for statistical analysis was the number of vocalizations an S gave in a 3-min. period. The counts were recorded by half-minutes and these were summed to give the score for the 3-min. period. After a rest period of 2 min., in which both E and O walked away from the baby's crib, another 3-min. count was made. After a second rest period a third count was made.

In each day nine such 3-min. counts were planned, and distributed thus: one block of three in the first part of the morning, the second block of three in the late morning, and the third block of three after the midday meal. The minimum amount of time between blocks was 10 min., although usually an hour or more elapsed.

Actually, nine periods of observations were obtained during only 80% of the 132 subject-days (22 Ss × 6 experimental days). Since three or four Ss were studied at a time, it was not always possible to find nine periods in a day when each was awake, alert, and content. Further, because the experiments were carried out in the nursery which the Ss shared with 12 other infants, the presence and activities of these other babies, and of the caretakers in carrying out their routines, sometimes made it impossible to obtain the desired number of periods.

## Emotional Behavior

A number of responses which seemed to be "emotional" were recorded during the observation periods. These were: "protests," discrete sounds of a whining nature; "fusses," a series of sounds separated by a catch in the voice, whimpering; "cries," continuous loud, wailing sounds; "persistent looking away from E," rolling of the head from side to side or staring to one side or the other of E; and "marked hand activity," hand play, finger sucking, or face or head rubbing. The last two activities seemed to be attempts to avoid E. Measures of observer-agreement in the recording of these responses were not made.

Each of these responses was given a credit of one for each half-minute in which it occurred. From the sum for each S a mean score was obtained for each experimental day.

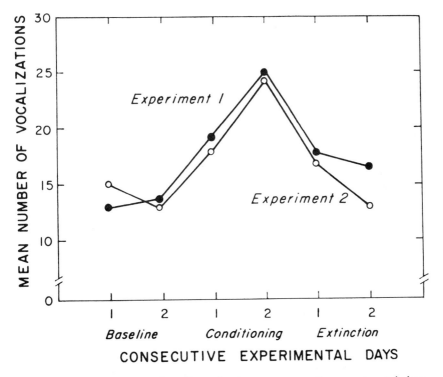

Figure 1.  Mean number of vocalizations on consecutive experimental days

# RESULTS

## Similarity Between Experiments

Figure 1 presents the means of both experiments for the six experimental days. Each point represents the mean of 11 individual means. It was expected that the effect of the experimental conditions would be similar from experiment to experiment, but the extent to which the slopes of the curves would be congruent was not predicted.

The amount of similarity between the two experiments was estimated by an analysis of variance (Table 1), using Lindquist's Type VI design (1953). The analysis reveals no evidence of a difference between Experiments. Further, no source of variation involving Experiments is significant. (The difference between the two experiments in second Extinction day means is not significant; it suggests, however, that the less frequent reinforcement in Experiment I may have made the behavior more resistant to extinction.)

### Table 1
#### Analysis of Variance of Effect of Consecutive Experimental Days

| Source of Variation | df | MS | F |
|---|---|---|---|
| Between Subjects | 21 | | |
|   Experiments (1 vs. 2) | 1 | 1218 | 0.03 |
|   Error | 20 | 45322 | |
| Within Subjects | 110 | | |
|   Conditions (Baseline vs. Conditioning vs. Extinction) | 2 | 71243 (1)[a] | 10.63* |
|   Days within Conditions (1 vs. 2) | 1 | 4205 (2)[a] | 1.88 |
|   Conditions X Days | 2 | 22917 (2)[a] | 9.24* |
|   Days X Experiments | 1 | 1738 (2)[a] | 0.78 |
|   Conditions X Experiments | 2 | 2031 (1)[a] | 0.30 |
|   Conditions X Days X Experiments | 2 | 866 (3)[a] | 0.35 |
|   Error 1 | 40 | 6703 | |
|   Error 2 | 20 | 2233 | |
|   Error 3 | 40 | 2481 | |

[a]Number in parentheses refers to the error term used. The terms were not pooled because of statistically significant differences among them.
*Significant at .001 level.

Three conclusions may be drawn from such close agreement in the results of two parallel experiments, each using different Ss and different Es: first, we are dealing with some relatively stable characteristics of three-month-old infants; second, the results may be accepted with confidence; and third, the results of the separate experiments may be pooled for all remaining analyses.

## Effect of Experimental Conditions

Table 1 shows that there was a difference in the effect of the three two-day experimental conditions (p < .001), and, also, in the effect of successive days within conditions (p < .001). These effects were assessed by $t$ tests (for paired data) on the amount of change from one day to another in the mean number of vocalizations given by individual Ss. The error term was derived only from the scores for the two days being compared. The tests on the pooled sample (21 df) show that:

1. There was no statistically significant difference in the mean number of vocalizations given in a 3-min. period from the first to the second Baseline day ($t = 0.87$, p > .30).

2. The mean number of vocalizations increased from the second Baseline day to the first Conditioning day ($t = 2.69$, p < .01).

3. A further increase occurred from the first to the second Conditioning day ($t = 3.61$, p < .001).

4. On the first Extinction day, vocalizations decreased ($t = 3.19$, p < .0025).

5. The mean number of vocalizations on the second Extinction day was smaller than on the first Extinction day, but the difference was not reliable ($t = 1.35$, p < .10).

6. There was no statistically significant difference between the mean number of vocalizations given on the second Extinction day and on the second Baseline day ($t = 1.20$, p > .20).

The tests between Baseline days and between Baseline and Extinction days were two-sided tests; the others were one-sided.

If final days within conditions are compared, the differences are more marked: the mean for the second Conditioning day is higher than that of the second Baseline day at p < .0005 ($t = 4.80$), and the second Extinction day mean is lower than the second Conditioning day mean at p < .005 ($t = 4.08$). Similar differences occur between the means of experimental conditions, obtained by averaging the first- and second-day results for each condition.

## Amount of Change in Number of Vocalizations

The treatment effects have been found reliable. It seems in order, therefore, to present the means of vocalizations for each day and to calculate the amount of change produced by the experimental conditions. Under baseline conditions the three-month-old infants gave about 13 to

14 vocalizations in a 3-min. period. Individual differences were wide and ranged from 3 to 37 vocalizations. Using the social reinforcer for one day raised the rate to 18 vocalizations, an increase of 39%. A second day of conditioning elevated the rate to 25, a further increase of 34%. In all, conditioning brought about an increase of 86%. Removing the reinforcer depressed the rate to 17 during the first and to 15 during the second day, the latter approaching very closely the level of baseline performance.

## Emotional Behavior

Emotional behavior, while striking when it occurred, was observed infrequently. The largest mean for any day in both experiments was 3.0, the smallest was 1.9. The order of the means by experimental days was identical in the two experiments. It was: first Extinction day, second Extinction day, second Baseline day, second Conditioning day, first Conditioning day, and first Baseline day. The greater number of emotional responses during Extinction agrees with the findings of others (e.g., Brackbill, 1958; Skinner, 1953; Verplanck, 1955). Because the responses labeled emotional occurred so infrequently and because observer-agreement measures were not made, no further statistical analysis seemed warranted.

## Additional Findings

### Performance of Successive Groups

It will be recalled that in any one experimental week the Ss were studied in groups of three or four. Inspection of the results suggests that in each successive group of each experiment an increasing number of Ss conformed to expectation, showing an increase in vocalizations during Conditioning and a decrease during Extinction. The Es apparently became more adept in executing the reinforcer as each experiment progressed.

### Performance of Individual Subjects

Although differences between experimental conditions have been demonstrated for the Ss as a group, the performance of individual Ss is of interest. Of the 22 Ss, 19 showed an increase in vocalizations under Conditioning. For 14 of these 19 the increase was significant at the .05 level, according to the Mann-Whitney Test (1947). Under Extinction, 16 of the 22 Ss showed some decrease, and for 10 of these 16 the decrease was significant at the .05 level.

Three Ss departed widely from the group pattern. For two, not only did Conditioning depress the rate of vocalizing, but Extinction restored it to its Baseline rate. The first chewed her thumb more during Conditioning than before or after. The second strained (in an apparent effort to defecate) during Conditioning whenever anyone, E or the nurse, leaned over his crib. Both activities precluded vocalizing. Both babies were very active, and it is possible, therefore, that in the very first Conditioning period E may have inadvertently reinforced these activities. For the third S, in Experiment I the experimental conditions appeared not to affect the frequency of vocalizations. Developmental immaturity seemed the most likely reasons, for two weeks later he was studied again in Experiment II (the only S to be used in both experiments) with satisfactory results.

### Effect of Baseline Performance Upon Conditioning

The Ss tended to maintain their relative positions under Baseline and Conditioning. The rank-order coefficient of correlation (R) was .66, $p < .0005$. Further, the amount of gain under Conditioning was not correlated with original position ($R = .24$, $p > .05$).

### Sex Differences

The 12 male Ss gave slightly more vocalizations during Baseline and gained more under Conditioning than the 10 female Ss, but the differences were not reliable.

## DISCUSSION

The results of these experiments suggest that:

1. Infants' vocal behavior in a social situation can be brought under experimental control; that is, it appears to be conditionable.

2. A social event composed of an everyday complex of acts, performed by an adult who is not a caretaker, can function as a reinforcing stimulus.

3. The incidence of such behavior can be very quickly modified in as young an organism as the three-month-old infant.

### Alternative Explanation

The question raised in the introduction may now be considered. Did the reinforcing stimulus function as an arouser of vocalizations? Would infants have vocalized more often because of the stimulation it provided, even if it had *not* been made contingent upon the infant's behavior? Or, did some part of the reinforcing stimulus (say, the smile) act as a social "releaser"? The findings appear to be compatible with the conclusion that conditioning occurred: The rate of vocalizing continued to rise on the second day of Conditioning; the rate did not fall to the Baseline level on the first day of Extinction; it continued to fall on the second day of Extinction; and Ss with low Baseline rates of vocalizing gained under Conditioning, although for them there was often a relatively long time interval (30 sec. or more) between the reinforcing stimulus and the occurrence of the next vocalization. Still, the decisive answer to the question must await an experiment in which the reinforcing stimulus is administered with equal frequency, but never directly after the infant vocalizes.

## Nature of the Reinforcer

The results seem to show that some everyday behavior of adults can function as a reinforcing stimulus for an infant. One would like to know from what sources its reinforcing properties arise. In the simplest case, the smiles, sounds, and caresses of adults may be reinforcing only because they provide a change in stimulation. Further information on this matter could be obtained by working with the separate parts of the reinforcing stimulus, one by one; by substituting for them lights or sounds dispensed by a machine; or by using a reinforcer of a less "affectionate" nature than the one used here appears to be. On the other hand, even for the three-month-old infant the smiles, sounds, and caresses of the adults may function as conditioned reinforcers because of their past association with caretaking acts.

It is possible that the Ss of this study, living in an institution, may have had a less rich experience with adults. Institutional babies were used as Ss only because they were more readily available, because more of them could be studied at one time, and because the complicating variable of differences in maternal care could be bypassed. They did not appear however to be "starved" for attention or affection. Indeed, the attendants were often observed responding to babies when they vocalized. While it is possible that mothers would respond more often, in the absence of a comparative study we believe that infants in general would respond as these infants did.

## Relation of Results to Theories of Speech

Since this study was limited to the vocalizing of infants in a social situation, attempts to reconcile the results with theories which account for all classes of prelinguistic utterances (babbling is the class frequently mentioned) cannot be complete. Thus, nothing in the findings of this study is incompatible with, for example, Holt's theory (1931) that the sound which the child hears himself make has reinforcing properties; with Lewis' theory (1951) that the adult's speech calls forth the infant's speech (a kind of imitation); or with Piaget's theory (1952) that vocalizing is perpetuated for its own sake by the processes of assimilation and accommodation. These may be labeled circular theories, for they do not postulate the necessity for any class of events prior to the moment when the infant responds to his own or another's vocalization. The theories of Miller and Dollard (1941) and of Mowrer (1950), on the other hand, are based upon the infant's associating the gratification of his needs and the accompanying vocalizations of the caretaker. Again, the results do not contradict this possibility.

The present study, however, does demonstrate the operation of still another principle: that the speech of the infant, if only in a social situation, can be modified by a response from the environment which is contingent upon his vocalizing. Hence, what happens *after* the infant vocalizes has been shown to be important.

### Significance of Results

On the basis of the results of these experiments it is seen that responses of adults which do not involve caretaking can affect the vocalizing of the young in a social setting. If the results can be extended to life situations, then mothers might be able to increase or decrease the vocal output of their children by the responses they make when the children vocalize. Other kinds of social behavior in addition to vocalizing behavior should respond similarly to conditioning. Brackbill (1958) has shown smiling in the four-month-old infant may be increased when followed by a social response from an adult. It is likely that still other kinds of social behavior in babies, such as showing an interest in people, reaching out to them or turning away, perhaps even fear of the stranger, may also be affected by the responses adults make to them.

# SUMMARY

Infants often vocalize as part of the response they give to the appearance of an adult. The central question of this study is: Can the frequency of vocalizing be increased if the adult makes a social response contingent upon it?

The Ss were 21 normal infants, three months of age, living in an institution. Eleven of them were studied in Experiment I with one E; 10 different Ss and one S from Experiment I were studied in Experiment II with a different E.

During the first and second Baseline days E leaned over S with an expressionless face, and the number of vocalizations was tallied. During the next two days, the first and second Conditioning days, E reinforced vocalizations by simultaneously smiling, clucking, and touching S's abdomen. During the last two days, the first and second Extinction days, E returned to Baseline conditions.

The results indicated that: (a) there was no difference between Experiments, (b) Conditioning raised the rate of vocalizing above the Base-line level, (c) while Extinction lowered it until it approached the Baseline level.

The results suggest that the social vocalizing of infants and, more generally, their social responsiveness may be modified by their responses adults make to them.

## REFERENCES

Brackbill, Y. Extinction of the smiling responses in infants as a function of reinforcement schedule. *Child Develpm.*, 1958, *29*, 115–124.

Gewirtz, J. L. A program of research on the dimensions and antecedents of emotional dependence. *Child Develpm.*, 1956, *27*, 205–221.

Holt, E. B. *Animal drive.* London: Williams & Norgate, 1931.

Lewis, M. M. *Infant speech: a study of the beginnings of language.* (2nd ed.) New York: Humanities Press, 1951.

Lindquist, E. F. *Design and analysis of experiments in psychology and educa-tion.* Boston: Houghton Mifflin, 1953.

Mann, H. B., & Whitney, D. R. On a test of whether one of two random vari-ables is stochastically larger than the other. *Ann. Math. Statist.*, 1947, *18*, 50–60.

Miller, N. E., & Dollard, J. *Social learning and imitation.* New Haven: Yale, 1941.

Mowrer, O. H. *Learning theory and personality dynamics.* New York: Ronald, 1950.

Piaget, J. *The origins of intelligence in children.* New York: International Uni-versities Press, 1952.

Rheingold, H. L. The modification of social responsiveness in institutional babies. *Monogr. Soc. Res. Child Develpm.*, 1956, *21*, No. 63 (No. 2).

Skinner, B. F. *Science and human behavior.* New York: Macmillan, 1953.

Verplanck, W. S. The control of the content of conversation: reinforcement of statements of opinion. *J. abnorm. soc. Psychol.*, 1955, *51*, 668–676.

# 6

# The Reinforcement of Cooperation
# Between Children

## Nathan H. Azrin and Ogden R. Lindsley

Most methods for the development and experimental analysis of cooperation between humans require specific instructions concerning the cooperative relationship between the individual responses. Peters and Murphree (1954) have developed one of the most recent of these methods. Skinner (1953) has suggested, and shown with lower organisms (1952), that cooperation between individuals can be developed, maintained, and eliminated solely by manipulating the contingency between reinforcing stimuli and the cooperative response.

The advantages of eliminating instructions concerning cooperation are that (a) the initial acquisition of cooperation can be studied, (b) subjects (Ss) that learn by demonstration and instruction with difficulty (i.e., infants, certain classes of psychotics, and lower organisms) can be studied, and (c) no problems involving the effects of instructions upon the behavior of the Ss are involved.

Some more general advantages of operant conditioning techniques are (a) a more continuous record of the cooperative process is obtained, (b) extraneous environmental variables are minimized, and (c) relatively long periods of experimental observation are possible.

## PROBLEM

Can cooperation between children be developed, maintained, and eliminated solely by the presentation or nonpresentation of a single reinforcing stimulus, available to each member of the cooperative team, following each cooperative response?

Nathan H. Azrin and Ogden R. Lindsley, "The Reinforcement of Co-operation Between Children," *Journal of Abnormal and Social Psychology*, 1956, 2, 100–102.

This paper was read at a meeting of the Eastern Psychological Association on April 10, 1954, New York City.

## Cooperative Teams

Twenty children, seven to twelve years of age, were formed into ten cooperative teams of two children. The children in each team were matched as to age and sex. Seven teams were boys and three were girls.[1] Selection was made via the request, "Who wants to play a game?" The first two volunteers of the same age and sex were chosen for each team. The age given by the children was verified against available community center records. No information concerning the game was given during the selection. No teams were rejected.

## Cooperative Response

Cooperation was assured by designing an apparatus that (a) could not be operated by one individual alone (assuring group behavior), and (b) demanded that one individual respond to the behavior of the other individual in order to produce reinforcement (assuring cooperation).

## Procedure

The two children of each cooperative team were placed at opposite sides of a table with three holes and a stylus in front of each child (see

Figure 1. Apparatus used for the reinforcement of cooperation between children

[1] We wish to thank the Harriet Tubman House and the South Bay Union of Boston, Mass., for providing the subjects and the use of their facilities.

Figure 1). A wire screen down the center of the table prevented each child from manipulating the other child's stylus, which was on the other side of the table.

The following instructions were given: "This is a game. You can play the game any way you want to or do anything else that you want to do. This is how the game works: Put both sticks (styli) into all three of the holes." (This sentence was repeated until both styli had been placed in the three available holes.) "While you are in this room some of these" (the experimenter, E, held out several jelly beans) "will drop into this cup. You can eat them here if you want to or you can take them home with you." The instructions were then repeated without reply to any questions, after which E said: "I am leaving the room now; you can play any game that you want to while I am gone." Then E left the room until the end of the experimental session.

If the styli were placed in opposite holes within 0.04 seconds of each other (a cooperative response), a red light flashed on the table (conditioned reinforcing stimulus) and a single jelly bean (reinforcing stimulus) fell into the cup that was accessible to both children.[2] Cooperative responses were recorded on counters and a cumulative response recorder in an adjoining room.

## Experimental Design

Each team was studied for one continuous experimental session divided into the following three consecutive periods without experimental interruption:

1. *First reinforcement period.* Every cooperative response was reinforced for over 15 minutes. If the rate of response was not steady at this time, the reinforcement was continued until five minutes passed with no noticeable change in the rate of cooperation.

2. *Extinction period.* The cooperative responses were not reinforced for a period of at least 15 minutes and until a steady rate of response for at least five minutes was observed.

3. *Second reinforcement period.* The cooperative responses were again reinforced until at least three minutes of a stable rate occurred. This was done to determine whether a reduction in rate during the extinction period was due to extinction, satiation, or fatigue.

## RESULTS

All teams learned to cooperate without specific instructions in the first 10 minutes of experimentation. Observation through a one-way vision

[2] Skinner (1952) presented two reinforcing stimuli (one to each pigeon) following each cooperative response.

screen disclosed that leader-follower relationships were developed and maintained in most cases. Almost immediately eight teams divided the candy in some manner. With two teams, one member at first took all the candy until the other member refused to cooperate. When verbal agreement was reached in these two teams, the members then cooperated and divided the candy. Most vocalization occurred during the initial acquisition period and throughout the extinction period. This vocalization was correlated with a higher variability in rate during these periods. (See below.)

Figure 2 contains cumulative records of the cooperative responses

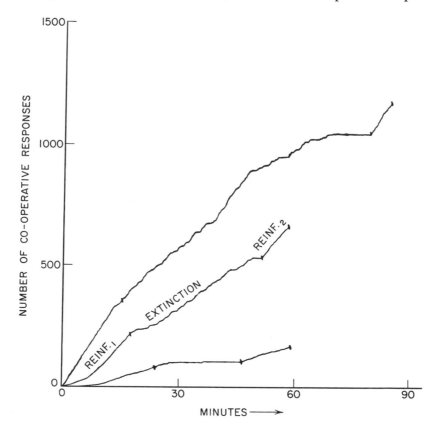

Figure 2. Cumulative response records for the teams with the highest, median, and lowest rates of cooperation

of the three teams with the highest, the median, and the lowest number of cooperative responses for the experimental session. These curves show a large difference in the rate of acquisition of cooperation. One team took almost 10 minutes to acquire a high cooperative response rate. Stable rates of cooperation can be observed during the latter parts of the first reinforcement period. The gradual, rather than immediate, decline in cooperation during extinction suggests an orderly extinction of cooperative behavior as is found with individual extinction curves. In all cases the variability of rate was greater during extinction than during reinforcement. Skinner has found this increased variability in rate during extinction with lower organism and has described it as emotional behavior (Skinner, 1953, p. 69). The high rate of response following the first reinforcement of the second reinforcement period shows that reacquisition is almost immediate.

Table 1 contains a quantification of the records for statistical analysis. The median and range of the number of cooperative responses per minute for all 10 teams during the critical periods of the experiment are given. The number of cooperative responses per minute for the first three minutes of the first reinforcement period was significantly lower than the rate during the last three minutes of the first reinforcement period (p < .02).[3] This shows that the rate of cooperation was significantly lower during initial acquisition than during maintenance of cooperation. The number of cooperative responses per minute during the last three minutes of extinction was significantly lower than the rate during the last three minutes of the first reinforcement period (p < .001). This shows that the removal of reinforcement during extinction significantly lowered the rate of cooperation between these children.

Table 1

The Median and Range of the Number of Cooperative
Responses per Minute for the Critical Experimental Periods

| | Number of Cooperative Responses per Minute | | | |
|---|---|---|---|---|
| N 10 | First three mins. of first reinf. period | Last three mins. of first reinf. period | Last three mins. of extinction period | Last three mins. of second reinf. period |
| Median | 5.5 | 17.5 | 1.5 | 17.5 |
| Range | 1–26 | 6–26 | 0–7 | 6–27 |

The number of cooperative responses per minute during the last three minutes of the second reinforcement period was significantly above the rate during the last three minutes of the extinction period (p < .001). This shows that the rate of cooperation was significantly increased during the second reinforcement period and that the drop in rate during extinction was due to the absence of the reinforcing stimulus rather than satiation or fatigue. The rates of cooperation during the second reinforcement period were not significantly different and show that the rate was almost immediately restored to its pre-extinction value upon the presentation of reinforcement for the second time. The rate of cooperative responding during the first three minutes of the second reinforcement period

[3] Wilcoxon's (1949) nonparametric T for paired associates was used in all statistical treatments.

was significantly higher than during the first three minutes of the first reinforcement period (p < .02). This again shows that the reacquisition of cooperation was not gradual, as was initial acquisition, but occurred almost immediately.

## CONCLUSIONS

Operant conditioning techniques can be used to develop, maintain, and eliminate cooperation between children without the use of specific instructions concerning cooperation. The rate of a cooperative response changes in much the same way as a function of single reinforcement as does an individual response. In the reinforcement of cooperative responses, a reinforcing stimulus need not be delivered to each member of the cooperative team following each cooperative response. The presentation of a single reinforcing stimulus, available to each member of the cooperative team, is sufficient to increase the rate of cooperation. The cooperative response gradually increases in frequency when reinforced and gradually decreases in frequency when no longer reinforced (extinction). Cooperative responses are maintained at a stable rate during reinforcement but occur in sporadic bursts during extinction. Reinforcement following extinction results in an almost immediate restoration of the rate of cooperation to its pre-extinction value.

## REFERENCES

Peters, H. N., & Murphee, O. D. A cooperative multiple-choice apparatus. *Science,* 1954, *119,* 189–191.

Skinner, B. F. *Science and human behavior.* New York: Macmillan, 1953.

Skinner, B. F. Classroom demonstration. Personal communication, 1952.

Wilcoxon, F. *Some rapid approximate statistical procedures.* New York: American Cyanamid Co., 1949.

### *EDITORS' COMMENTS*

The preceding study by Azrin and Lindsley sets up a simple relationship between two children, such that their combined behavior may be called "cooperative." The study has been cited many times in textbooks and articles, and has been reprinted in several other collections of readings. That such a brief study, embodying so simple a social task, should attract so much attention may seem puzzling at first. In retrospect, however, one may note several of its characteristics as possible explanations for its stature.

In the first place, this study succeeds in introducing a social

variable into a laboratory setting without sacrificing the thorough-
ness of environmental control essential to laboratory precision—an
accomplishment which is not commonplace in the research literature
of psychology. Second, the situation embodies a simple analysis of a
cooperative relationship between two children: for each child to cooperate he need only discriminate his own response to the corresponding response of the other child and reduce his response time (latency)
in doing so to a sufficiently brief duration. Since the only condition
operating to produce this discrimination and response adjustment is
the reinforcement produced, the development of the cooperative behavior is related to that contingency. Proof is afforded by the fact
that discontinuing the reinforcement contingency (extinction) results
in a lowering of the rate of cooperative responses, whereupon a resumption of the reinforcement contingency restores the rate to its
previous high level. Cooperative behavior is seen clearly in each
pair of children studied and as an ongoing series of interactions,
every repetition of which is objectively and clearly recorded.

Thus, simple cooperation has been produced, manipulated, and
observed as a class of behavior developing over time, and shown to
be shaped by a reinforcement contingency operating on the discrimination by one child of another's behavior. To simplify interpreta-
tions, instructions to cooperate were carefully avoided.

This study led Donald Cohen to embark on an investigation
with more elaborate procedures involving both cooperation and competition. Among other things, he was interested in determining which
subject leads and which one follows in cooperation between pairs of
children (and adults) with a variety of known or suspected relationships prior to the study. Cohen's study is discussed in more detail in
Part III of this collection.

# 7

# Reinforcement Control of Generalized Imitation in Young Children

## Donald M. Baer and James A. Sherman

Three imitative responses (head-nodding, mouthing, and strange verbalizations) were established in young children by social reinforcement from a puppet. A fourth imitative response (bar-pressing), which was never reinforced, was found to increase in strength when reinforcement followed the other three imitative responses. This increase in imitative bar-pressing was taken to indicate that a generalized similarity of responding between puppet and child could be a reinforcing stimulus dimension in the child's behavior. Two additional procedures were applied to demonstrate further the dependence of imitative bar-pressing upon the reinforcement following the other imitative responses. These additional procedures were extinction of the other imitative responding, and time-out from the other imitative responding. In extinction, reinforcement was no longer presented following imitative head-nodding, mouthing, and strange verbalizations, but was instead presented in a noncontingent manner during the normal conversation between puppet and child. As a consequence, imitative bar-pressing decreased in strength. When reinforcement was reinstated for the other imitative responses, imitative bar-pressing again rose in strength. During time-out periods, the puppet ceased to provide the child with head-nodding, mouthing, and strange verbalization performances for the child to imitate. Again, social reinforcement was continued at the same rate but was delivered during the normal puppet-child conversation. The effect of the time-out was to decrease the strength of imitative bar-pressing. Reinstatement of the cues and reinforcement for imitative head-nodding,

Donald M. Baer and James A. Sherman, "Reinforcement Control of Generalization Imitation in Young Children," *Journal of Experimental Child Psychology*, 1964, *1*, 37–49. Reprinted by permission of Academic Press Inc.

This research was supported in part by grant M-2208 from the National Institutes of Health, United States Public Health Service.

The authors are grateful to Miss Judith Higgins and Miss Sharon Feeney for their reliable and intelligent assistance. Appreciation is also due to Mrs. Mildred Reed, Director, and Mrs. Mildred Hall, Seattle Day Nursery Association, for their cooperation and assistance.

mouthing, and strange verbalizations produced increased imitative bar-pressing.

The term "imitation" has seen much use in the literature of child psychology. However, experimental work in this area has often failed to invoke its most powerful meaning. In experimental situations, behavior frequently has been called imitative because it resembled that of a model previously observed by the subject. But there rarely has been any guarantee that the *similarity* of the two behaviors was functional in producing the behavior in the observer. Instead, it has been common to require the observer to learn a reinforced response after having watched a model perform the same response and receive reinforcement for it. The observer often does profit from this observation of a correct performance. However, it is quite possible that he does so because certain stimuli of the situation have been paired with the sight of the reinforcement secured by the model. Since the sight of reinforcement should be a powerful secondary reinforcer, observational learning, not of a similar response, but of the cues which will facilitate that response may very well take place. When the observer is placed in the situation, his learning (of what typically is the only reinforced response in the situation) is speeded by his previously acquired sensitivity to the cues in the situation.

For example, a child may watch a model turn a crank on a green box and receive nothing, then turn a crank on a red box and receive reinforcement consistently and repeatedly. As a result of this observation, the observer subsequently may learn the same discrimination more quickly than a control subject. This may be due simply to the establishment of red as a discriminative cue for reinforcement. The observer is better reinforced for approaching red than green as a consequence of his observation, and thereby is more likely to turn the crank on the red box and be reinforced for it. There is no need in this example to assume that the *similarity* of his crank-turning response and the model's is involved. The similarity may lie in the eye of the experimenter rather than in the eye of the observer, and, in this situation, only a similar response will be reinforced. Hence the similarity is both forced and (perhaps) irrelevant.

However, there can be a more powerful use of imitation in the experimental analysis of children's learning if it can be shown that similarity per se functions as an important stimulus dimension in the child's behavior. The purpose of the present study is to add another demonstration of this role of similarity to the small body of literature already produced (e.g., Bandura & Huston, 1961) and to show the function of certain social reinforcement operations in promoting responding along the dimension of similarity in behavior. Specifically, a response is considered which is imitative of a model but never directly reinforced. Instead, other responses also imitative of a model, are controlled by reinforcement operations. The strength of the unreinforced imitative response is then observed as a function of these reinforcement operations. An animated talking puppet, used previously in studies of social interaction with children (Baer, 1962), serves both as a model to imitate and as a source of social reinforcement.

## METHOD

### Apparatus

The apparatus was an animated talking puppet dressed as a cowboy and seated in a chair inside a puppet stage. The puppet was capable of making four kinds of responses: (1) raising and lowering his head, or *nodding;* (2) opening and closing his mouth, or *mouthing;* (3) *bar-pressing* on a puppet-scaled bar-pressing apparatus located beside his chair, almost identical in appearance to a regular-sized bar-pressing apparatus located beside the child; and (4) *talking,* accomplished by playing $E$'s voice through a loudspeaker mounted behind the puppet's chair, while the puppet's jaw was worked in coordination with the words being spoken. (For a more complete description and a photograph, cf. Baer, 1962.)

### First Sequence of Procedures

#### Introduction

The experiment was conducted in a two-room mobile trailer-laboratory (Bijou, 1958) parked in the lot of a day-care nursery. $E$ observed the child and puppet through a one way mirror from the other room. The child sat in a chair immediately in front of the puppet stage. An adult assistant, $A$, brought the child to the laboratory, introduced him to the puppet, seated him in his chair, and then sat in a screened corner of the room, out of the child's sight. The introduction for the first session was, "This is Jimmy the puppet. He wants to talk to you. And this (pointing) is your bar. See, it's just like Jimmy's bar, only bigger (pointing). Do you know how it works?" The usual answer was "No," in which case $A$ demonstrated a bar-press, saying "Now you try it." (Some children pressed the bar without demonstration.) $A$ then said, "You can talk to Jimmy now." On all later sessions, $A$ said simply, "Hello Jimmy, here's (child's name) to talk to you again," and, to the child, "Now you can talk to Jimmy again."

After $A$'s introduction, the puppet raised his head and began speaking to the child. He followed a fairly standard line of conversation, starting with greetings, and progressing through expressions of pleasure over the chance to talk with the child to alternating questions about what the child had been doing and colorful stories about what the puppet had been doing. This type of conversation was maintained throughout all the sessions; the social reinforcement procedures used as the independent variable in this study were interjected within the conversation according to the experimental design.

### Operant Level

The first session was to acquaint child and puppet and to collect an operant level of the child's bar-pressing, imitative or otherwise. Shortly after the puppet began talking to the child, he began to press his bar, alternating between a slow rate of 1 response per 15 seconds and a fast rate of about 3 responses per second. The puppet's bar-pressing was recorded on a cumulative recorder.

The operant level period was interrupted after 5–10 minutes of the puppet's bar-pressing for a special procedure. The special procedure was designed to establish whether the child could generalize from the puppet's bar to his own. After the puppet had stopped bar-pressing, he would nod twice and say, "This is my head. Show me your head." Invariably, the child would move his head or point to it. The puppet then said, "Good," and began mouthing, saying, "This is my mouth. Show me your mouth." The child would move his mouth or point to it. Then the puppet said, "Good," and bar-pressing twice, said, "This is my bar. Show me your bar." Some children imitated the response; some pointed to their bar. A few did neither; of these, some appeared puzzled, and others tentatively reached for the puppet's bar. These were the children the procedure was designed to detect. In their cases, the puppet explained that they had a bar of their own and helped them find it, which usually sufficed to produce either a bar-press or a pointing toward the bar. The puppet gave no reinforcement for the bar-pressing response, and instead resumed the conversation about his adventures or the child's. With some subjects there then followed another 5–10 minutes of bar-pressing by the puppet to determine whether this procedure in itself had promoted imitative bar-pressing by the child. No imitative bar-pressing ever did develop as a result of this procedure alone in the children subjected to it. For the rest of the subjects, this extra portion of the operant level period was dropped.

Still another 5–10 minutes of bar-pressing by the puppet was sometimes displayed. On these occasions, the puppet took up a very approving line of conversation, dispensing a great deal of "Good," "Very good," and "You're really smart" to the child. This was to determine the effect of noncontingent social reinforcement on the child's imitative bar-pressing. However, no child subjected to this procedure ever developed imitative bar-pressing as a result. The other subjects had a similar kind of noncontingent approval incorporated into the earlier portions of their operant level periods.

The typical rate of imitative bar-pressing during operant level periods was zero. In fact, of 11 children seen in this study, only one showed a slight tendency to imitate the puppet's bar-pressing, but this disappeared early in her operant level period. Two others showed a non-imitative bar-pressing rate during the initial session.

### Reinforcement of Some Imitative Responses

After collecting the child's operant level of bar-pressing, the puppet stopped bar-pressing and began to present a series of other responses, one after another at first, and then at scattered points in his conversation. Each time he would first ask the child, "Can you do this?" These responses consisted of nodding, mouthing, and a variety of nonsense statements (such as "Glub-flub-bug," "One-two-three-four," or "Red robins run rapidly"). In each case if the child imitated the responses, the puppet reinforced the child's response with approval consisting mainly of the words "Good," "Very good," and "Fine." Almost without exception, the children did imitate virtually every response the puppet presented in this way, and after a few reinforcements, the puppet stopped asking "Can you do this?" in preface to the response.

After the child was consistently imitating each of these other responses without the prefatory "Can you do this?", the puppet resumed bar-pressing, alternating fast and slow rates. He continued to display nodding, mouthing, and verbal nonsense statements at scattered points in his conversation, and maintained a continuous schedule of reinforcement for every imitation of these by the child. The child's bar-pressing from this point on was the basic dependent variable of the study. An increase over operant level in this never-reinforced[1] bar-pressing by the child, especially insofar as it matched the puppet's bar-pressing, would be significant: It would be attributable to the direct reinforcement of the other responses (nodding, mouthing, and verbal). These responses have very slight topographical resemblance to bar-pressing; they are like it essentially in that they all are imitative of a model's behavior. Thus an increase in imitative bar-pressing by the child would indicate that similarity of responding per se was a functional dimension of the child's behavior, that is, similarity of responding could be strengthened as could responding itself.

This program of reinforcement for all imitative responding (other than bar-pressing) was usually begun during the first session. With some children, it was started early in their second session. Children were seen as many as 7 sessions in the course of the study. These sessions were separated by 3–7 days.

## RESULTS

In the design of this study, both individual and group performances are relevant to the central question. If any child showed a significant in-

---

[1] On one occasion with one child, a bar-press was accidentally reinforced. This will be noted in the results.

crease in imitative bar-pressing over his operant level, as a result of direct reinforcement of other imitative responses, this would demonstrate the functional role of similarity in behavior for that child. Hence each child represented an experiment in himself. As a group, the sample allows some estimation of the probability of the effect occurring in children from this population.

Of 11 children studied, 4 failed to show any development of an imitative bar-pressing response during the course of reinforcement of nodding, mouthing, and verbal imitations. Two of these were the only two children showing a high level of non-imitative bar-pressing during their operant level periods. The remaining 7 children showed varying degrees of increase in bar-pressing, as illustrated in Figure 1. This figure shows 4 records,

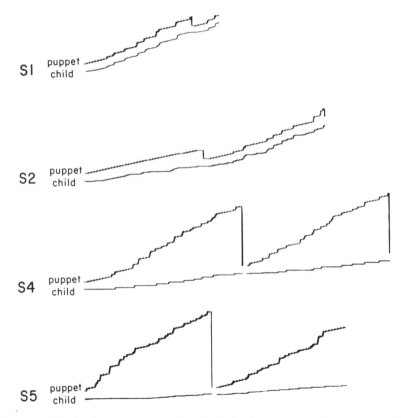

Figure 1.    The development of generalized imitative bar-pressing in four representative Ss

selected to indicate the range of increase in bar-pressing obtained. A fact not always apparent in these records (necessarily compressed for publication) is that virtually every bar-pressing response by the child occurs closely following a response (or response burst) by the puppet, and hence is clearly imitative.

## FURTHER PROCEDURE AND RESULTS

The increased imitative bar-pressing by some of the children was brought about by reinforcement of other imitative responding by the child (nodding, mouthing, and verbal performances). Further procedures were developed to show the dependence of the generalized imitative bar-pressing on this reinforcement. These procedures were of two kinds: extinction of the other imitative responding, and time-out from the other imitative responding.

### Extinction of Imitation

Extinction was instituted with two children, one of whom had developed a near-perfect rate of imitative bar-pressing, the other showing a low rate. After a stable rate of imitative bar-pressing had been established by each child, the puppet stopped giving any reinforcement for imitation of his nodding, mouthing, or verbal nonsense performances (imitation of which in the immediate past he had reinforced continuously). However, he continued performing these actions at the same rate. He also continued to reinforce the child at the same rate, but at appropriate points in the child's conversation rather than for imitation. This continued for several sessions, until the child had shown a stable or marked decrease in imitative bar-pressing. Then reinforcement was shifted back to imitations of nodding, mouthing, or verbal nonsense performances and maintained as before, until the child showed a stable or marked increase in imitative bar-pressing. As usual, bar-pressing was never reinforced.

The subjects chosen for this procedure were S1 and S4 of Figure 1; both were girls. Their records (Figure 2) include the early sessions that show operant level and the development of generalized imitation, already seen in Figure 1, as a baseline against which the effect of extinction of other imitative responding is seen. (Sessions 4 and 5 are omitted from a record of S4 because they are virtually identical in procedure and performance to Session 3 and would needlessly enlarge Figure 2 if included.) It is clear that S1 was very responsive to the extinction and reinforcement operations: Her near-perfect rate of imitative bar-pressing weakened considerably after nearly one complete session of extinction for other imitative responding, but promptly recovered its near-perfect aspect when reinforcement was resumed.[2] The record of S4 shows the same pattern, but

[2] In the case of S1, it can be seen that the effects of extinction are markedly stronger with the beginning of Session 4, and that the effects of resumed reinforcement, clear in the last half of Session 5, are even more pronounced with the beginning of Session 6. This interaction between session changes and experimental conditions remains an unexplained complication of the data; however, it need not greatly alter the conclusions drawn.

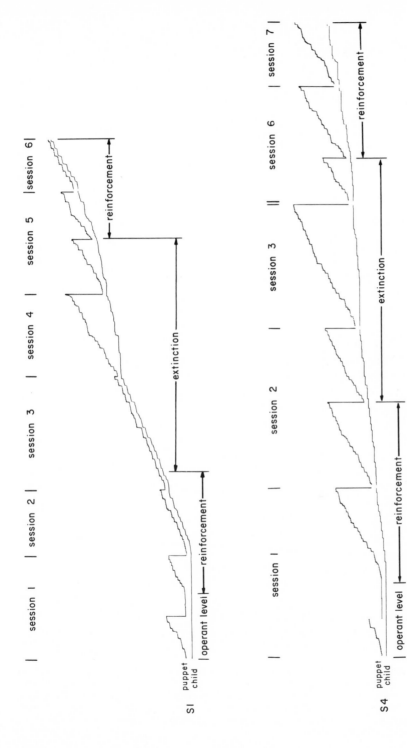

Figure 2. The effects of extinction of previously reinforced imitation on generalized imitative bar-pressing in two Ss

73

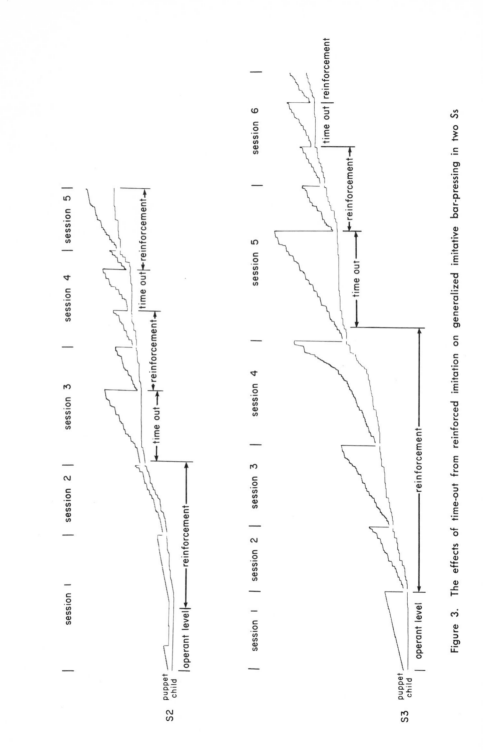

Figure 3. The effects of time-out from reinforced imitation on generalized imitative bar-pressing in two Ss

the differences are not so apparent. This may be due to the low rate of imitative bar-pressing induced in S4 under the previous reinforcement conditions. Sighting along the curve, however, will make clear the same pattern of rate changes apparent in the record of S1.

### Time-Out from Imitation

Time-out procedures were instituted with two other children, one of whom had a high rate of imitative bar-pressing, and the other only a modest rate. After a stable rate of imitative bar-pressing had been established by each child, the puppet ceased providing any nodding, mouthing, or verbal nonsense performances for the child to imitate, hence eliminating any reinforcement of imitation by eliminating the previously established cues for the occurrence of imitation. Social reinforcement was continued at the same rate, but was delivered for appropriate comments in the child's conversation rather than for imitation.

This time-out was continued until the child showed a stable or marked decrease in imitative bar-pressing. Then the puppet resumed performances of nodding, mouthing, and verbal nonsense statements, and shifted his reinforcement back to the child's imitations of these performances until the child showed a stable or marked increase in imitative bar-pressing. Then the whole cycle of time-out and reinforcement was repeated in exactly the same way. Bar-pressing, of course, was never reinforced.

The subjects chosen for this procedure were S2 of Figure 1 and S3, both girls. Their records are shown in Figure 3. (The early portion of the record of S2 has already been seen in Figure 1.) It is apparent that the time-out condition produced a quick and drastic weakening of imitative bar-pressing in these children, and that a resumption of reinforcement of other imitative responses, when these were again displayed by the puppet for the child to imitate, quickly generalized to the nonreinforced imitative bar-pressing. (By accident, S3 received one reinforcement for bar-pressing during Session 1. It is assumed that the effect of this single reinforcement was negligible.)

## DISCUSSION

In this study, social reinforcement has been used to strengthen a set of behaviors directly. The responses of nodding, mouthing, and saying nonsense syllable chains have been established through instructions ("Can you do this?") and reinforcement, and maintained with reinforcement. These responses have in common the fact that they are all imitative of a model's behavior and that the child does them only when the model does. It is in this context that the strengthening of imitative bar-pressing becomes significant. Bar-pressing was never reinforced directly; nor was the child ever instructed to bar-press imitatively. (The simple instructions dealing with the child's bar—"Show me your bar"—never promoted imitative bar-pressing in the children observed specifically for this possibility.) Bar-pressing has little physical or topographical resemblance to nodding, mouthing, and verbal nonsense chains. What it does have in common with these responses is the fact that it too is imitative of one of the model's performances. Hence its strengthening, following the direct strengthening of nodding, mouthing, and verbal responses, may be attributed to generalization along a dimension of similarity between the child's response and the model's response. In other words, the child is responsive to the stimulus of similarity between responses per se, apparently independently of the particular physical stimuli involved in specific responses.

It can be important to demonstrate that similarity between behaviors of model and child can be a functional stimulus dimension. Such a demonstration would be essential in at least some reinforcement analyses of imitation, especially in any analysis trying to show that imitation should be a strong response in a child, even when it does not produce extrinsic reinforcement. One such analysis might proceed as follows:

In ordinary course of his early life, a child will form many hundreds of discriminations that involve the sight or sound of a model's behavior as a cue for a response by the child which achieves the same (or a similar) reinforcing outcome. In effect, in all such situations, the child is in a position to learn what response on his part reproduces the effect produced by the model's behavior. Many times, the world will be such that only a response similar in physical make-up or topography will reproduce the same effect. For example, many times a child will need to get through a latched door. He will often observe an older or more skillful model turn the knob and pass through. The child will eventually differentiate his own behavior to the point where it succeeds in opening the door. But doors are such that very few responses will succeed, and consequently the child's behavior will be very similar to the model's. In this situation, and in many others like it, the stimulus of similarity between the child's behavior and the model's is consistently programmed and sets the occasion for reinforcement of the child. Given enough of these situations, of adequate consistency and variety, the stimulus of similarity between behaviors in general may become discriminative for reinforcement. Since a stimulus which is discriminative for reinforcement becomes (secondarily) reinforcing in its own right, then responses which produce similarity between behaviors will thereby be strengthened. Responses of the child which "produce similarity" are those responses which have a topography that the child can compare to the topography of the model's responses, e.g., he can see both his response and the model's or can hear both. Hence the child will become generally "imitative," and, if similarity has great strength as a discriminative and therefore reinforcing stimulus, imitative behavior will be correspondingly more prevalent and apparently autonomous.

Certain details of procedure in this study may be worthy of note. One involves the fact that noncontingent social reinforcement given by the puppet to the child was not sufficient to induce imitation of the puppet. Furthermore, once a generalized imitation had been set up, noncontingent reinforcement was not sufficient to maintain it. Only when other imitative responses were being reinforced would imitative bar-pressing (never directly reinforced) remain at any strength. The puppet would, as the design required, shift his reinforcement from imitative responses to other appropriate moments in the interactions, but the general amount and spacing of this reinforcement remained the same. Hence the effects on imitative bar-pressing noted here cannot be attributed to the simple presence or absence of reinforcement, but rather are related to its contingent or noncontingent use. This is at some variance with the results of other studies (cf. Bandura & Huston, 1961), in which a prior condition of noncontingent social reinforcement from a model evoked more imitation of the model from the child than otherwise. This may be due to the particular response used in this study to observe generalized imitation, which was bar-pressing. Bar-pressing may be an unusual response for a young child and may have relatively little resemblance to the strong responses already in his repertoire. For this reason, it may be a relatively inefficient response with which to demonstrate a generalized imitation of the puppet. On the other hand, it may be that while similarity between behaviors is reinforcing for children, this reinforcing value is closely dependent on similarity remaining discriminative for at least some reinforcement in the situation. Possibly, when similarity clearly is no longer discriminative for reinforcement, it loses its own reinforcing function rather quickly. It will take an extensive program of research to provide useful data on this question, but the question may well be worth it, since such arguments about imitation can figure heavily in a conceptual account of socialization or "identification."

Another point, possibly important, is that all of the subjects showing imitation were girls. Since the group sampled was composed largely of girls, this may not be unusual. However, the puppet was clearly a male cowboy, and since cross-sex interactions are prevalent where social reinforcement is involved (especially with young children), it may be that later data will demonstrate that the sex of the subject and the model is an important variable. No conclusion is possible from the present data.

Finally, the increased imitative bar-pressing demonstrated here is not simply part of a generalized increase in activity; its clearly imitative nature denies that. Furthermore, it was apparent to the observers that there was no general increase of other observable activities as imitative bar-pressing developed in the child.

# REFERENCES

Baer, D. M. A technique of social reinforcement for the study of child be-
    havior avoiding reinforcement withdrawal. *Child Develpm.*, 1962, *33*,
    847–858.
Bandura, A., & Huston, Aletha C. Identification as a process of incidental
    learning. *J. abnorm. soc. Psychol.*, 1961, *63*, 311–318.
Bijou, S. W. A child study laboratory on wheels. *Child Develpm.*, 1958, *29*,
    425–427.

*EDITORS' COMMENTS*

Many readers, upon their initial acquaintance with the technology
of behavior development described in these readings, show some
puzzlement over the possibility that these principles can be a comprehensive account of the complex behavioral repertoire and potential of the human. Common expressions of this bewilderment may
be the questions: Do you have to reinforce every response that is to
develop in the child? Doesn't he contribute anything on his own
initiative? How could any parent, teacher, or school system hope to
reinforce *all* the behaviors they want changed in a child? People
concerned with the moral development of children may say that they
want the child to learn not specific acts of virtue (which they see
could readily be reinforced to any degree of strength) but rather the
values which underlie those specific acts and which tie them together
into a class of moral behavior. The preceding study is relevant to
these issues. It is a preliminary exercise in the analysis not only of
social responses, but of social response classes. A response class is a
group of responses which develop together. All grow strong or weak,
even though the environment may be acting directly *on only some of
them*.

The class chosen was imitation, an eminently social set of behaviors. Four imitative responses were studied in each child. Three
of these were reinforced directly, but the fourth was not. When the
first three were strengthened by reinforcement contingencies, the
fourth increased in rate; when the first three were weakened or made
impossible, the fourth decreased as well. The four responses have
little in common physically (i.e., topographically); basically, they resemble one another only in that they all are imitations. Thus, the
study shows that a class of behaviors can develop which contains
more members than those directly reinforced. Indeed, the study shows
a response growing stronger even though it is apparently undergoing
an extinction contingency! Perhaps this could be called "contributing

something on his own initiative." However, it is clear why the response develops: it is imitative of the child's source of social reinforcement, and other imitations of that source are being reinforced.

This study represents only a model in miniature of the process of developing response classes; four responses do not constitute an exhaustive survey of the problem. However, it is the kind of research which might provide more comprehensive answers to the possibility of establishing complex repertoires of behavior through simple reinforcement contingencies.

An unusual feature of technique in this study is the use of an animated, talking puppet as both a model for the child to imitate and as a source of social reinforcement. The puppet has a number of advantages for this type of research, but the most important ones are the ease of controlling the exact nature of the demonstrations to be imitated and the nature and timing of the social approval given.[1]

A detail of the history of this research may interest the reader; it affords one more example of the role of serendipity in directing experimental analyses of behavior. The original goal of the experimenters was to establish an imitative response in a child which could serve as a baseline to reflect changes in the social relationship between the child and the puppet-model. For example, it might be asked: If the child is imitating the puppet, what change would occur in his rate of imitation if the puppet became angry? Or rejecting? Or distant? However, such questions could not be answered satisfactorily in the early attempts, because the imitative response, set up by instructions ("Whenever I do this, you do it too," said the puppet), proved so powerful that nothing else the puppet could do seemed to affect it once it was established stably enough to serve as a baseline. Consequently, the experimenters cast about for a "gentler" technique of setting up an imitative response, such that the imitation might prove both stable and sensitive to changing conditions. It was thought that perhaps the child might be prompted to develop a particular imitation (bar-pressing) without instructions, if other imitations (like nodding, mouthing, and verbal statements) were first established directly. As the study shows, this idea proved practical. In doing so, the original questions seemed less interesting than the new behavioral phenomenon: Why does an unreinforced behavior grow in strength? What conditions allow this, what conditions undo it? And so the preceding study was pursued.

---

[1] A fuller discussion of these advantages and of the difficulties inherent in the procedure may be found in L. P. Lipsitt & C. C. Spiker, eds., *Advances in Child Behavior and Development,* New York: Academic Press, 1963.

# Discrimination Mechanisms
# in Development

Two of the basic mechanisms of behavioral elaboration in child development are discrimination and differentiation (Bijou & Baer, *Child Development,* Vol. 2). Discrimination is the development of different strengths of the same response to different stimuli; differentiation is the shaping of chosen forms or topographies of response, topographies which may not exist in the previous repertoire of the child. The two are rarely separated in reality, but frequently one is emphasized over the other in laboratory analyses. In this section, discrimination is taken as a topic in development; differentiation is involved in these studies but little emphasized. In the second part of this collection, Applications, differentiation is more clearly the focus of experimental effort. However, discrimination is not more of a "basic principle and concept" than differentiation. Both are equally basic; both are brought about by selective use of reinforcement contingencies (cf. Bijou & Baer, *Child Development,* Vol. 1). It is simply that in the literature of child development, discrimination has received attention by researchers primarily interested in basic processes, and differentiation has received attention from investigators concerned primarily with problems of application. The organization of this collection of readings reflects that fact of history.

# 8

# Rapid Acquisition
# of Multiple-Schedule Discrimination Performance
# in a Single Response Free-Operant Situation
# with Retardates

## Robert Orlando and Sidney W. Bijou

### EDITORS' COMMENTS

Early in the development of psychoanalysis, there appeared an experimental demonstration of anxiety, a practically useful technique, and a parlor game—all in one procedure. The procedure involves the use of word association: a subject is presented with a series of words, one at a time, and is asked to respond as quickly as possible to each word, with the first word that occurs to him. Two aspects of this response can be noted: the content of each response (i.e., the meaning of the word he says relative to the meaning of the word presented to him) and the time he requires before he makes the response (i.e., latency). At first, only innocuous or everyday words are presented to the subject, and his responses usually are equally ordinary, and prompt. But if a special word is presented to him, one which is uniquely aversive, both the content and the promptness of his response are likely to be different from his preceding responses.

"Rapid Acquisition of Multiple-Schedule Discrimination Performance in a Single Response Free-Operant Situation with Retardates" is a revision of a paper published in the *Journal of the Experimental Analysis of Behavior*, 1961, *4*, 7–16, entitled "Rapid Development of Multiple-Schedule Performances with Retarded Children." The revision incorporates procedural refinements developed since 1961 with over 50 retarded children. Orlando further extends this line of investigation in a paper entitled "Shaping Multiple Schedule Performances in Retardates: Establishment of Baselines by Systematic and Special Procedures" published in the *Journal of Experimental Child Psychology*, 1965, *2*, 135–153.

This investigation was supported by a research grant (M-2232) from the National Institute of Mental Health, Public Health Service.

The authors are grateful to Russell M. Tyler and David A. Marshall, Research Assistants, for their assistance in conducting the study and to Charles H. Martin, Superintendent of the Rainier School, for his cooperation in making available research space and subjects.

For example, suppose we are playing this game with a child who has been stealing candy which he has been forbidden to eat. The game begins by presenting a series of words, one at a time, such as "cat," "mouse," "black," etc. The boy probably would respond within a few seconds of each word with such ordinary associations as "dog," "home," "white," and so on. But if, without any particular warning, the word "candy" were presented, then his response might suddenly take 10 or 15 seconds instead of the usual one or two, and its content might be unusual as well, such as "not me." Thus, by the unusual character of the child's response, relative to his typical response to such stimuli, we detect a class of stimuli with unusual function *for that child*. Another child might respond to the same stimuli very promptly, perhaps saying "cane" after "candy."

A modern example of a similar technique is the polygraph "lie detector." In this case, a variety of responses are observed constantly: breathing rate, heart rate, electrical conductivity of the skin, etc. The subject is asked questions. In answering them, he shows changes in these other responses, but typically small changes when the questions are routine. However, if a question with an aversive or arousing function is asked, these changes are likely to become suddenly large; or if the subject is aroused by the act of lying in response to a question, then again the changes may be major. Thus the observer detects an area of sensitivity by noting the character of the subject's responses to that area relative to his usual response.

Note that in both these examples it is not the behavior which is of major interest, but rather a *change* in that behavior. Therefore, these techniques are often called "baseline," or "single-subject" methods; often it is said that the subject "serves as his own control." There are several advantages to this approach.

One advantage is that these methods allow the observer to see a mechanism or law of behavior at work within an individual. Psychologists usually state the laws of behavior as if they described the behavior of an individual in response to a certain stimulational field. Thus, for example, the principle of discrimination states that the effects of reinforcement contingencies applied to a subject's behavior will become specific to the stimulus conditions with which they are associated. If he is reinforced in the presence of a red light and extinguished in the presence of a green light, then the response to which these contingencies are applied will be strong in the presence of red lights and weak in the presence of green ones. This statement does not imply merely that the average response of a group of subjects so treated will be high in red light and low in green light conditions. It states a principle of learning which should be observable in the behavior of every organism to whose behavior discrimination contingencies are applied. If any individual fails to show a discrimination of red and green lights under these conditions, the question then becomes: What is unusual about this organism? rather than one of diluting the statement of discrimination into a sometime process. The organism may be color blind, he may not respond to the reinforcer in question as positive, he may be physically ill or emotionally upset, he may have a past history making extinction a condition in which he has often been reinforced for persevering long enough (and thus will require a long time before discrimination appears, etc.). Analysis of the single subject may thus contribute not only to an understanding of him as a behaving organism, but also to the general meaning of discrimination as a behavioral process, by clarifying the conditions under which it may be modified, augmented, combined with other processes, or, indeed, combined with itself. The last example given above illustrates this. Suppose a subject has had a history in which extinction was made a condition in which, if he did continue to respond, eventually he was again reinforced. In other words, initial nonreinforcement of a response served to signal the subject that in fact he was now on a variable-ratio schedule of reinforcement rather than on an extinction schedule. If the subject now is presented with a condition in which red lights mark periods of reinforcement and green lights mark periods of extinction, he may well respond according to his previous training and continue to respond throughout many green light periods at a high rate. At first glance, he may appear to be violating the principle of discrimination. But it is simply that he has been taught that nonreinforcement is discriminative for continued responding. When we present him with nonreinforcement during the green light periods, he responds, as taught, with a continuing high rate. In other words, a current discrimination contingency is failing to show its effects only because a prior discrimination contingency established different functions for some of the stimuli involved. But the *principle* of discrimination is the same in both the prior and the current situations; only the details (the choice of stimuli to which discriminative function is to be attached) are different, and these details are not essential to the principle. The prior discrimination has worked according to the principle; the current discrimination contingency is not now working *because of the same principle,* but, given time or special helping conditions, it will work *according to the same principle.*

The following paper illustrates all of these points. It exemplifies baseline methods of child study, in which any behavioral process can be seen in the behavior of a single child at a time, with all of the unique details, special to that child, of responding according to principle. Again the behavior itself is of little interest: bar-pressing is not one of the everyday intellectual, social, or esthetic activities of the child. It is the *stability* of the behavior, its steady strength in the presence of one stimulus and its reliably low rate in the presence of the other, which makes the behavior a valuable candidate as a baseline for studying the effects of other variables. Furthermore, there is to be seen in this paper the application of a technique which facilitates the forming of a discrimination usable as a baseline. The technique itself is a discrimination process, one which teaches the subject that when his responding has ceased, a stimulus discriminative for reinforcement will be presented. Thus, the stimuli associated with nonresponse (visual, auditory, tactual, and kinesthetic) are given discriminative function as cues for reinforcement. Finally, this paper demonstrates the procedure of "fading," of gradually introducing and establishing new stimuli or conditions and thereby creating a behavioral change which might have been difficult had the new problem been presented full blown at first presentation. This technique, in various settings, appears frequently in these readings; it is an application of discrimination procedures itself, one that has proven to be useful in many practical applications.

Note that the term "multiple schedule" is only a technical name for the process of discrimination; it refers to a schedule in which one stimulus is associated with a different reinforcement schedule, typically an extinction schedule. Thus the programming of discrimination in this way is a combination of two schedules in a recurrent cycle, i.e., a "multiple" schedule.

When a child enters an experimental situation, receives instructions, and begins responding on an experimental task, the behavior displayed is, of course, dependent upon his behavioral repertoire, functional features of the current situation, and effects of previous learning. The influences of antecedents may be conceptualized as effects of independent variables such as rate of change in operant conditioning (Skinner, 1953). Effects of this sort may be quantified psychometrically, by such devices as inventories of traits and scales of abilities, or they may be quantified by experimental procedures. The latter approach, which involves observation of the successive changes in behavior that are required to perform an experimental task to criterion, may be carried out in two ways. One way is to present the task and record the time (and "errors"). Such a procedure is often abortive. If the task is complex, even slightly so, learning may take an unreasonable length of time, or may not be achieved at all. The other way is to present the child with a series of graded conditions and reinforcing responses that approximate more and more the final performance required. The child sets the pace; that is, each response class is strengthened to a criterion before the next condition is introduced.

This alternative of tailoring the procedure to the child's performance has several advantages. Most important, it yields not only measures in terms of time, but also an account of the strengthening and weakening operations necessary to arrive at final performance. Furthermore, studying initial behavior is especially pertinent from the point of view of technique, particularly for investigations on human subjects using individual baselines. At the current stage of our knowledge of operant procedures with humans, many experimenters spend considerable time and effort establishing baseline performance on a schedule or on multiple schedules.

The objective of this paper is to describe and illustrate a method that has proven useful for the rapid establishment of multiple-schedule performance in a single-response, free operant, experimental situation with retarded subjects. A multiple schedule has been defined as one "in which reinforcement is programmed by two or more schedules alternating, usually at random. Each schedule is accompanied by a different stimulus, which is present as long as the schedule is in force" (Ferster & Skinner, 1957, p. 7). The multiple schedules discussed here have two components (one involving extinction), presented in regular alternation.

Initial attempts to establish discriminated operant baselines in children (Bijou, 1961) started with principles outlined for infrahuman subjects (Keller & Schoenfeld, 1950) and "hand-shaping" techniques popular as classroom demonstrations and developed most fully in animal training (Breland & Breland, 1951). Satisfactory two-component baseline performances were obtained, but only after an investment of seven or more weekly sessions. The technique reported here is the result of subsequent studies using progressively refined procedures.

## THE LABORATORY SITUATION

The experimental setting is a well-illuminated room, 10 x 8 feet, with a standard table and two chairs. A wooden box approximately 12 x 12 x 16 inches is on the table. A wooden chute with tray attached for presenting reinforcers is at the left of the box. The upper end of the chute extends through an opening in the wall that separates the experimental and control rooms. On the front panel of the box are a red jewel light in the upper left-hand side, a blue jewel light in the upper right-hand side, and a sturdy metal lever (a handle grip for the squeezer of an O'Cedar sponge mop) protruding from a rectangular opening in the center. Pressing the lever down is always accompanied by a relay click and occasionally by a reinforcer dispensed by a Gerbrands Universal Feeder in the control room. Reinforcers are: M & M's, Hersheyettes, candy corn, Payroll mint coins, and Sixlets. These candies were selected because they are readily consumed, easily dispensed, and not sticky (Bijou & Sturges, 1959).

Control and recording equipment similar to devices used with infrahuman Ss (Ferster & Skinner, 1957; Skinner, 1957; Verhave, 1959) is located in the adjoining room. Impulse counters and a Gerbrands cumulative recorder are used to record responses on the lever. The cumulative recorder also indicates reinforcements and the type and duration of discriminative stimuli. "Blips" on the cumulative curve indicate reinforcements, and the event-pen baseline under each curve records which of the two discriminative stimuli is present.

## INSTRUCTIONS

Instructions are treated as setting events (Bijou & Baer, 1961), which are considered to be verbal and nonverbal procedures that may affect the subject's rates and patterns of responding. The instructions described here, deliberately simple and brief, were designed to initiate lever-pressing behavior at a moderate rate. Uncomplicated instructions such as these may be applied without modification to a wide range of subjects (e.g., those with physical immaturities, sensory defects, or emotional disturbances, as well as normal children), and are not likely to contain discriminative and conditioned stimuli which may successfully compete with shaping the experimental operant (Azrin & Lindsley, 1956; Bijou & Sturges, 1959).

The discriminative stimulus (to be referred to as $S^D$) is on when the subject enters the room (e.g., red light is illuminated). The investigator instructs the subject to sit in the chair facing the apparatus. The investigator then says, *"Watch me, I'll show you how we get candy here."* The investigator makes five lever responses separated by intervals of about two seconds. Candy comes down the chute after the fifth response. *"See, here's some candy. Take it, it's for you. Now you do it. You get some candy."* If the subject makes five responses, the fifth is reinforced, and the investigator leaves the room, saying, *"You go ahead and get candy. I'll be back when it is time to leave."* If the subject is hesitant, or fails to make the five responses, the investigator demonstrates again, starting with *"Watch me."* If the subject fails again, the investigator takes the subject's hand and works the lever five times, gets reinforced for the fifth, and repeats instructions from *"Now you do it."* Subjects who still do not make five independent responses can be eliminated or trained further, depending on the nature of the study.

## TECHNIQUE

The five steps in training to a two-component multiple schedule are described in detail, not because it is expected that they will be followed as given, but because it is a convenient way of giving an account of the technique. Investigators will find it necessary to modify the steps in accordance with the nature of their subjects, the type of multiple schedules desired, and variations in experimental situations.

## Rate Evaluation

The purpose of this phase is to estimate the subject's initial rate of responding (or operant level). If the rate is sufficient to withstand the next phase, no training is given. If, however, the rate is low, special training designed to strengthen response rate is applied.

*Duration:* one minute ($S^D$ on)
*Reinforcement Schedule: FI 15″* (reinforcers are delivered at fixed intervals of 15 seconds)
*Criterion:* more than 20 responses in one minute.

If the criterion is not met but the rate appears to be increasing, an additional minute is given. The criterion for sufficient rate is then *more than 40 responses in two minutes*. The criterion can, of course, be adjusted according to the kind of subjects to be used.

## Rate Strengthening

This phase is included only for those subjects who do not meet the rate-evaluation criterion. Any one of a number of differential-reinforcement-of-high-rate (drh) procedures could be applied to build up a higher workable rate. For developmentally retarded children, an indirect method consisting of an "increasing ratio" has proven effective. With the $S^D$ on, this schedule requires a gradually increasing number of unreinforced responses between successive reinforced responses. The schedule is continued until rate has increased to a criterion of 20 responses per minute or better. For example, counting responses from the first in this phase, the following responses are reinforced: 1, 2, 4, 6, 9, 12, 16, 20, 25, 30, etc. The gradualness of the ratio increase can be adjusted to suit each subject's initial rate. For those whose rate is very low in the evaluation phase, a "richer" schedule can be used (e.g., reinforcements could be programmed for responses 1, 2, 3, 5, 7, 9, 12, 15, 18, 22, 26, etc.). It is important that rate be built up only to a moderate level, since very high rates are likely to prolong the next phase of training.

## Pause Building

For the two-component multiple schedule in which one of the discriminative stimuli is associated with nonreinforcement, training is specifically designed to establish "withholding" of responding in the presence of that cue (e.g., blue light) referred to as S delta ($S^\Delta$). That is, reinforcement is made contingent on successful refraining from responding during $S^\Delta$ periods. Later this discriminative behavior will be combined with the previously established responding in the presence of the $S^D$, to make up the complete multiple-schedule performance.

The procedure consists essentially of differentially reinforcing low rates (drl) with a sequence which requires more and more withholding behavior. After rate evaluation (and strengthening if necessary), $S^D$ is removed and $S^\Delta$ presented. The subject then is required to pause (not respond on the lever) for a specified interval. When this requirement is met, $S^\Delta$ is removed and $S^D$ presented. The first response is reinforced, and the cues changed again. This procedure is repeated several times for each step in a series in which the interval is gradually increased. The criterion consists of withholding of responses in the presence of $S^\Delta$ and a relatively short latency of response to the onset of $S^D$, for one complete series of a given pause interval.

As an illustration, the pause-building phase that has been found effective with developmentally retarded children is presented below:

*Step 1*—Five 5-sec. pauses required (ten if five are not made in 5 min.)
*Step 2*—Five 10-sec. pauses required (ten if five are not made in 5 min.)
*Step 3*—Five 15-sec. pauses required (ten if five are not made in 5 min.)
*Step 4*—Five 30-sec. pauses required (ten if five are not made in 10 min.)

The sequence can be terminated at the end of step 2 or 3 if all criteria have been met without necessity for repeating a pause series. The pause-building procedure does not *insure* that discriminative performance will develop (a low rate of responding could simply be established), but short latencies to the $S^D$, onset almost always indicate discrimination.

### Rate-Recovery Evaluation

The recovery-evaluation phase is included to estimate the degree to which a reasonably high rate will re-occur in the presence of the $S^D$, since a low rate of responding is necessarily established during pause building. The phase is identical to the original rate evaluation (i.e., one minute for 20 or more responses). If the criterion is not met, $S^D$ remains on, and the rate-strengthening procedure is applied.

### Multiple Schedule

This is the final phase of training. Its content depends on the particular values of the multiple schedule desired. If the schedule of reinforcement is not larger than a ratio of 50 or an interval of one minute, and if the period between alternations of discriminative stimuli does not exceed two minutes, these conditions may be instituted immediately after the rate-recovery evaluation (and if necessary, restrengthening phase). For multiple schedules involving larger values, a gradual approach is recommended. For example, if a final schedule of mult *VR 100* ext (variable ratio of 100 responses, and extinction) with 3-minute alternation of cues is desired, the approach may be made with a 10-minute period of *VR 25* ext (variable ratio of 25 responses, and extinction) with 2-minute alternation of cues. The reason for using a gradual approach is that there is a possibility of extinction during the initial long $S^\Delta$ periods, especially after a large number of reinforcements have been earned during earlier phases.

With the majority of institutionalized developmentally retarded children, this procedure can be completed in a single session of one hour or less. If the series must be interrupted because of excessively slow development, it is recommended that succeeding sessions begin with a rate-evaluation phase, followed by the *beginning* of the interrupted phase.

## SAMPLE DATA

The performances of four subjects in two experimental sessions each are presented as illustrations. These subjects show some of the range of differences in pattern of baseline development that are obtained with this procedure. The clinical diagnosis is included in the brief description of each subject. To facilitate identification of the figures, each record is identified by the subject's initials (e.g., EMN) and session number (e.g., S-1, S-2).

The top two records in Figure 1 show the first and second sessions of EMN, a 16-year-old girl with an MA of 5 years 3 months and an IQ of 42. She has been living at the Rainer School for 4 years and was diagnosed as "undifferentiated." In these records, as well as in the others, the horizontal line under the cumulative-response curve indicates the discriminative stimulus in force. When the line is elevated, the blue light was on; when depressed, the red light was on. Which of the colored lights served as $S^D$ can be inferred from the reinforcement marks in the cumulative curve.

Since in Session 1 (S-1) EMN's initial rate was high, rate strengthening was omitted. Pause building proceeded slowly and steadily. When shifted to mult *VR 25* ext (variable ratio of 25 responses and extinction) with fixed 1-minute alternation of lights, she performed at a steady rate under *VR 25* and showed some anticipatory responses during $S^\Delta$. The Session 2 (S-2) performance on mult *VR 25* ext with fixed 2-minute alternation is orderly, although some tendency to respond during $S^\Delta$ is present.

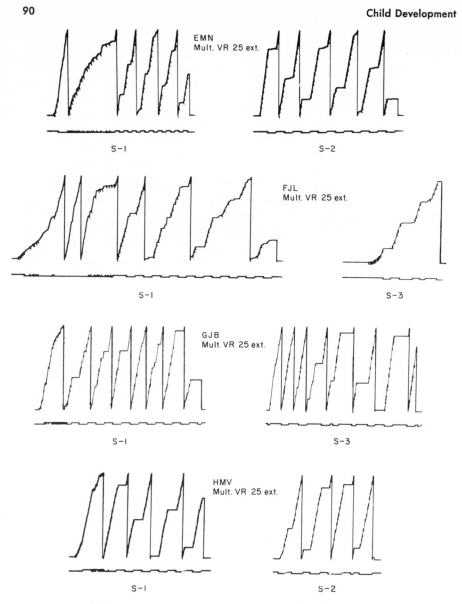

Figure 1.   Records of two sessions each for four subjects showing the development of
multiple with a variable ratio 25 and extinction components

The second subject (FJL) is a 14-year-old mongoloid girl with an
MA of 3 years 1 month and IQ of 32. She had lived at the Rainier
School for 4 years. The initial reaction to pause building in Session 1
consisted of a rate increase. After pause building, a rate-recovery interval

showed that rate strengthening was not necessary, and she was shifted immediately to mult $VR$ 25 ext with fixed 2-minute alternation of $S^D$ and $S^\Delta$. Evidence of a discrimination is shown during the middle part of the session. Performance is fair, but rate drops toward the end. This extinction trend was continued during the second session (S-2, not shown), in which only two responses were made. In the third session (S-3), the increasing-ratio schedule recovered the rate, and discriminative performance on mult $VR\ 25$ ext with variable 2-minute alternation followed.

The third subject (GJB) is a 21-year-old mongoloid girl with an MA of 3 years 5 months and an IQ of 30. She has lived at the institution for 11 years. She began Session 1 with a high rate; and although pause-building progressed well, she responded to the onset of $S^D$ with "runs" of responses. Rate recovery was good; when shifted to mult $VR\ 25$ ext with fixed 2-minute alternation, discrimination was only fair, because of the large numbers of responses during $S^\Delta$ shown in the middle of the session.

Session 2 for GJB is not shown. The performance in Session 2 consisted of almost continuous responding, very much as in the initial part of Session 3. In Session 3 excellent performance developed on mult $VR\ 25$ ext, with variable 2-minute alternation of the stimulus conditions.

The final subject (HMV) is a 21-year-old mongoloid boy with an MA of 4 years 9 months and an IQ of 32. He has been institutionalized for only 3 years. His initial high rate and virtually continuous responding during pause building quite suddenly gave way to rapid learning to pause. The pause series was terminated at the end of five 10-second pauses, and rate recovery showed no necessity for strengthening. Performance on mult $VR\ 25$ ext with fixed 2-minute alternation was nearly perfect, and this high level of discrimination was continued in Session 2 on mult $VR\ 25$ ext with variable 2-minute alternation.

## SUMMARY

This paper describes a technique for modifying simple operant behavior of institutionalized retarded children observed at the beginning of studies concerned with the establishment of multiple-schedule control. Such procedures have promise for an experimental analysis of individual differences, and for the development of multiple-schedule baseline performances. Concern here is with the latter aspect. This "shaping" procedure is designed to establish a two-component multiple schedule performance. The final multiple schedule desired may be a variation of the one described here with the restriction that one component be extinction. The particular reinforcement schedule employed during $S^D$ and the sequence and duration of cue-periods is flexible. Sample data are presented on four subjects illustrating some of the phases and some of the terminal performances.

## REFERENCES

Azrin, N. H., & Lindsley, O. R. The reinforcement of cooperation between children. *J. abnorm. soc. Psychol.*, 1956, *52*, 100–102.

Bijou, S. W. Discrimination performance as a baseline for individual analysis of young children. *Child Develpm.*, 1961, *32*, 163–170.

Bijou, S. W., & Baer, D. M. *Child development*. Vol. 1. *A systematic and empirical theory*. New York: Appleton-Century-Crofts, 1961.

Bijou, S. W., & Sturges, Persis T. Positive reinforcers for experimental studies with children—consumables and manipulatables. *Child Develpm.*, 1959, *30*, 151–170.

Breland, K., & Breland, Marion. A field of applied animal psychology. *Amer. Psychol.*, 1951, *6*, 202–204.

Ferster, C. B., & Skinner, B. F. *Schedules of reinforcement*. New York: Appleton-Century-Crofts, 1957.

Keller, F. S., & Schoenfeld, W. N. *Principles of psychology*. New York: Appleton-Century-Crofts, 1950.

Skinner, B. F. *Science and human behavior*. New York: Macmillan, 1953.

Skinner, B. F. The experimental analysis of behavior. *Amer. Scientist*, 1957, *45*, 343–371.

Verhave, T. Recent developments in the experimental analysis of behavior. *Proceed. Eleventh Res. Conf., Amer. Meat Inst. Found. of the Univer. of Chicago*, 1959.

# 9

# Variables in Early Discrimination Learning:
# 1. Motor Responses in the Training
# of a Left-Right Discrimination

**Wendell E. Jeffrey**

## EDITORS' COMMENTS

The following study by Jeffrey is an example of experimental research which is truly developmental. There are a number of well-used definitions of developmental research. Probably the oldest definition is simply to state the behavioral characteristics of children. A more elaborate ambition is to describe changes in behavior with increasing age. But an analytically oriented investigation would ask: What is it that happens with age to change the behavior of children? Age refers to the passage of time, and time allows experience. Thus, an analysis of the kind, sequence, and extent of experience necessary to any progressive change in behavior is thereby a developmental study; it may tell us what has been happening to children at certain times such that they will be more capable later.

Jeffrey takes a simple behavior to illustrate this type of analysis: a discrimination between left and right. This discrimination, he finds, typically is not present in young children. But a few years later those children will almost certainly display the discrimination in many aspects of their behavior: in putting the right shoes on the right feet, writing their letters from left to right, distinguishing "b" from "d," etc. Furthermore, Jeffrey notes that under straightforward and direct methods of teaching, four-year-old children fail to learn a left-right discrimination despite extensive trials, although children a few years older would learn the same discrimination with ease.

Wendell E. Jeffrey, "Variables in Early Discrimination Learning: 1. Motor Responses in the Training of a Left-Right Discrimination," *Child Development,* 1958, *29,* 269–275. Reprinted by permission of The Society for Research in Child Development, Inc., and the author.

This research was supported by a grant from the research committee of the University of California and by research grant M-1498 from the National Institute of Mental Health, U.S. Public Health Service. I wish to express my appreciation to the staffs of the Small Fry and Peter Pan Nursery Schools for their cooperation in this research.

Such findings, taken alone, constitute what is usually called an "age difference" in the traditional child psychology literature. The difference might well have been interred in the literature as such and added one more detail to the description of the difference between four-year-olds and other children.

Happily, Jeffrey was not content with the demonstration of one more age difference. Instead, he analyzed the experiences that could be prerequisite to forming a left-right discrimination in young children who lack one at the moment. His analysis consisted of finding a simpler experience which provided a helping step to the more complex problem. Given the step, even the young children were able to form the complex left-right discrimination, and without benefit of several years passage of time. The study which follows details the procedures which allow this experimentally accelerated development.

We have no guarantee that somewhere in the course of their early years, children undergo experiences similar to the ones Jeffrey studied and thereby become able to learn the left-right discriminations which their everyday world presents to them almost constantly. The observation and analysis of the natural sequence of learning through which the individual child progresses towards his adult capabilities is another problem. Jeffrey's study shows us *one* of the processes we may look for if we attempt that analysis. Almost certainly, there are many other ways in which the initial problem could have been made simpler. Jeffrey refers to one possibility in the second paragraph of his discussion. He suggests that he might have simplified the stimulus differences which the children were asked to discriminate, possibly by accentuating the left-right differences which are critical to the discrimination. If a sufficiently blatant stimulus difference could be made which the young children could successfully discriminate, then once they were performing the discrimination successfully, these accentuated differences could be gradually diminished, until only the original stimuli of the left-right discrimination were left. This technique is called "fading." It has been alluded to in the remarks preceding the Orlando and Bijou paper and will be referred to again in the studies by Moore and Goldiamond, and Bijou, Birnbrauer, Kidder, and Tague.

Jeffrey's study is ordinarily labelled as an investigation of the "acquired distinctiveness" of stimuli; however, it may also be viewed as a simple example of "programming."[1] Programming refers to

---

[1] The student interested in this area should read the review by Joan H. Cantor, "Transfer of Stimulus Pretraining in Motor Paired-Associate and Discrimination Learning Tasks," in L. P. Lipsitt & C. C. Spiker, eds., *Advances in Child Development and Behavior*, Vol. 2, New York: Academic Press, 1965.

the sequences in which stimuli are presented. If the sequences are properly designed, they can bring about the rapid development of a new behavior, a desirable skill, or the loss of an undesirable or hindering behavior. To understand development, it is essential to understand what the programming of experiences can accomplish, as well as what change each individual experience can accomplish. We have defined development elsewhere as progressive changes in the interactions between stimuli and responses.[2] The progression of such changes is an important factor in determining what the successive interactions themselves will accomplish in the future behavior of the child.

Recently there have been various discussions of perceptual development (Gibson & Gibson, 1955; Postman, 1955), response factors in learning (Mandler, 1954), or early discrimination learning (Hebb, 1949) which are in general concerned with an organism's early experience with stimuli and the effects of this experience on subsequent performance. Experiments with both rats (Forgus, 1955) and chimpanzees (Riesen, 1947) have also demonstrated that early environment is important for later discrimination learning. For practical as well as theoretical purposes it would be valuable to know the type and amount of experience that is necessary, and the time at which it should occur, if the time factor is critical at all. Young children may be particularly good $S$s for such research inasmuch as discriminations can be found which they do not normally make and seem to learn only with great difficulty before certain ages. The ability to learn these discriminations may then be taken as a critical indication of the effect of various types of experience in a pretraining situation.

A number of studies have been done (Cantor, 1955; Jeffrey, 1953; Spiker & Terrell, 1955) following such a plan but, in most cases, the problem presented to the child was simply one of learning which response to attach to each stimulus, inasmuch as the basic distinction among stimuli had probably already been learned.

For the present study a situation was sought where the presentation of differential stimuli apparently aroused no differential responses beyond those involved in receptor activation. This would provide a situation that would coincide more closely with Hebb's notion of early learning and would also fit closely with what others have referred to as perceptual development. A study by Swanson and Benton (1955) suggested that left-right distinctions provide a difficult learning task for young children. After some preliminary research indicated that most four-year-olds were not capable of placing differential labels on stimuli that differed only in

[2] Bijou & Baer, *Child Development*, Vol. 1, 1961.

terms of left-right orientation, this task was chosen as a criterion discrimination.

It seemed possible that the ability to learn to respond discriminatively to stimuli differing in spatial orientation, i.e., left-right, might vary with the nature of the response to be learned. It was presumed that a response like pointing in the same direction in which stick figures were pointing would be easy to learn, and that the acquisition of this response would facilitate the acquisition of other responses. After preliminary research indicated that such a response was indeed easier than the labeling task, this experiment was set up to evaluate specifically the transfer effect from learning a discriminative motor response to the more difficult labeling task. It should be noted that, inasmuch as the direction of the motor response was not varied, no conclusion can be drawn regarding the importance of the symmetrical relationship of that response to the discriminative stimuli.

## METHOD

### Apparatus

The stimuli were two stick figures, with either a left or a right arm raised, each drawn in India ink on a 3 by 5 white card. A duplicate set of cards was available and was substituted during training to make certain that the children were not learning to discriminate dirt smudges or other nonexperimental but consistent stimuli.

Two push buttons mounted 12 inches apart on top of a box provided the motor response. Tape recorded children's music through earphones served as incentive and reinforcement. The music was controlled by a foot button and Hunter timer, so that for a correct motor or verbal response $E$ pushed the foot button permitting $S$ to listen to 10 seconds of the recorded material.

### Procedure

The experiment followed what was essentially an X-Y-X transfer design in which the X task involved training to label the stick figures differentially, and the Y task trained $S$ to make button pressing responses in the general direction toward which the figures could be said to be pointing. The control group received only the X, or labeling, training.

Each $S$ was asked to come into an adjoining room to play a game. At this time, he was introduced to the earphones and seated in a chair in front of the box. Typically there was some small talk about earphones and airplane pilots. Then, to help accustom the child to the situation, the music was turned on and allowed to play for a minute or two.

To start the initial training on the criterion, or X, task, the music was stopped and the stimuli were placed side by side on the box in front of S. He was then asked if he could tell how the two figures differed. None of the Ss gave any evidence of seeing the difference or of knowing what was meant by the word, "difference." The differences were then pointed out, and S was told that the figure with the arm pointing "in this way" would be call "Jack," and the figure with the arm pointing "this way" would be called "Jill," and that the music would come on only if he gave the right name for each picture whenever the picture was presented. The stimuli were presented successively following a randomized order.

For the control group, training proceeded as described above until S met a criterion of 10 successive correct responses, or until he quit and refused to return, or until such time as E decided to discontinue training. The latter was done only when there was no evidence of learning after at least 80 trials. At intervals from 10 to 20 trials, instructions were given again, pointing out the relationship between the names and directions in which the arms were pointing.

The experimental group first received 20 trials of the same training as the control group with instructions repeated after the 10th trial. After this initial training on the control task, the experimental Ss were instructed to push the button toward which the stick figure was pointing, and the appropriate button for each stick figure was indicated by E. The experimental Ss were trained on this task to a criterion of 10 successive correct responses and then returned to the labeling task. Two of the nine children who were given the experimental treatment went back to the original task in the same session. Seven Ss came back on a second day one week later, and were given 10 more button pressing trials before returning to the labeling task.

### Subjects

Twenty-eight children were divided into two groups, matched for mean CA of four years and four months and range from three years, eleven months, to four years, nine months. The training procedure was assigned to each S by the toss of a coin. There were seven girls and seven boys in each group.

## RESULTS

A contingency table showing the number of Ss in the experimental and control groups who were able to meet the criterion of 10 successive correct discriminations in the labeling task is presented in Table 1. The Fisher exact probability test, which tests the hypothesis as to whether two groups differ significantly in the proportion of passes and fails attributed to them, indicates that the null hypothesis can be rejected at better than the .005 level of confidence.

However, it should be noted that three Ss in the control group were able to perform the labeling task without the experimental treatment. The control Ss can be categorized roughly into three groups: first, three who performed at a high level from the beginning and completed the criterion within 30 to 40 trials; second, four who refused to continue after rather limited number of trials and five who refused to return after low success in the initial session; third, two who continued to come back with no evidence of ever responding above chance.

Table 1

Contingency Table Showing Numbers in Control and Experimental
Groups Passing and Failing the Labeling Task

|              | Pass | Fail |
|--------------|------|------|
| Experimental | 13   | 1    |
| Control      | 3    | 11   |

Inasmuch as the labeling task proved to be less difficult than was indicated by other studies (Davidson, 1935; Swanson & Benton, 1955), it seemed important to try to identify any members of the experimental group who might learn the labeling task without the experimental treatment, in order to eliminate them from consideration in the final results. Thus, two Ss in the experimental group were given an extra 20 trials on the initial test task because of high performance on the first 20 trials. One of these met the criterion while the other did not, even though the instructions had been repeated before the 21st and 31st trials. Four other children in the experimental group also showed evidence of learning or met the criterion task during the initial 20 training trials.

Table 2 gives a picture of the results if one removes from Table 1 the three Ss of the control group and the five Ss of the experimental group who learned the criterion task so readily that it seems reasonable to assume they were not examples of early or original learners. This table gives a more striking picture of what has taken place. Again, the null hypothesis can be rejected at the .005 level of confidence. As can be seen, those Ss in the control group who did not show promise of learning from very early in the training did not learn subsequently. In the experimental group, when those who apparently were capable of learning the criterion task with some ease were excluded from the group, thus making this group comparable to the non-learning controls, we still found that all but one of these Ss learned the criterion task quickly after the experimental treatment. The one $S$ who did not learn was performing consistently above chance (eight out of 10, and nine out of 10 in the last 20 trials) but was apparently too distractable to meet the criterion of 10 successive correct responses. It should be noted that in the experimental treatment four $S$s performed perfectly after instructions alone, four $S$s

## Table 2
### Contingency Table of Numbers Passing and Failing the Labeling Task When Children Who Apparently Learned with Ease Were Rejected from Both Groups

|              | Pass | Fail |
|--------------|------|------|
| Experimental | 8    | 1    |
| Control      | 0    | 11   |

completed the criterion in 20 trials, and one took 30 trials. Subsequent to this training, seven $S$s completed the criterion on the test task within 20 trials, one completed the criterion within 30 trials, and, as mentioned above, one failed to meet the criterion within 50 trials and training was discontinued.

## DISCUSSION

The exploratory nature of this research makes it hazardous to discuss it on a theoretical level. The left-right discrimination is really somewhat easier than had been expected. Thus, it is probably gratuitous to suggest that we are getting at early learning in the sense that we had hoped. We are now working with pitch discrimination which appears to be almost universally difficult and better meets our criterion for early learning. From this experiment, however, it seems reasonable to conclude that some discriminations that may be difficult for children to make can be simplified so that the child can learn the simpler task, and that, as the result of learning the simpler discrimination, performance may be facilitated in more complex situations.

Simplification can be specified in both the stimulus and response dimensions. In this experiment the response was simplified. What will happen if the stimulus dimension is manipulated remains to be demonstrated. It may be that exaggerating the differences between stimuli in order to simplify them may have the net effect of eliciting a response more easily. Thus, in the present experiment lengthening the arms of the stick figures might have increased the number of successful performances with the naming task by producing in the observing response the sort of distinct stimulation now produced by the button pressing response. It should be reiterated that the button pressing response apparently did more than simply call attention to the appropriate part of the stimuli inasmuch as the importance of the direction that the arms were pointing was demonstrated to S several times during the test trials.

Whether the button pressing served a mediating function was not clear. Preliminary research most definitely indicated that it was not necessary to set up a series of trials attaching names to the buttons. A number of the children, however, obviously used the button pressing response or fractional parts of it in learning to apply the names. In one case, a child who had to be told twice to discontinue the button pressing started lifting the appropriate shoulder for each stimulus before applying labels. Other children would look at the appropriate button before supplying the name of the figure. The majority, however, displayed no obvious remnant of the motor response when learning the names. Further research manipulating both stimulus and response variables is obviously a necessity before one speculates further about the basic processes involved or about other levels of mediation.

At a practical level, these data can be interpreted as having fairly direct implications with regard to specific instruction, such as teaching of reading. Research by Davidson (1935) has indicated that children are not normally capable of discriminating "b" from "d" until seven and one-half years of age. The present data indicate that a child incapable of performing this discrimination at a given time can be taught it very quickly, even as early as four years of age, if conditions are properly arranged.

The recommendation to delay training after the failure of children to meet certain readiness criteria probably arises from observations of the frustration produced when children attempt to learn discriminations that are too difficult for them, rather than from knowledge of the processes involved in discrimination learning. The refusal of a number of the children in this experiment to remain in the situation under conditions providing 50 per cent reinforcement was striking when compared with the extended periods of time others spent if success was relatively high. Four-year-old children have already learned to label such performance as failure and react by withdrawing from the situation. However, it should be noted that the situation in general was sufficiently reinforcing, if success was relatively high, to keep children in the experimental situation for extended periods of time and also to keep them coming back on subsequent days. Furthermore, these children were from schools which attempted to minimize the importance of high performance and competition. Thus, it undoubtedly is wise not to push the child when he has difficulty. However, the present study suggests that one can continue training at a different level and thus achieve the desired results without concomitant frustration.

## SUMMARY

An experiment was devised to test the facilitative effect of attaching simple motor responses to stimuli differing in spatial (left-right) orientation on the subsequent labeling of these stimuli. Four-year-old children were used as Ss and it was found that, except for a few children who learned the labeling task with ease, the majority of four-year-olds found the task essentially impossible.

The experimental treatment of learning to press buttons oriented in the directions the stick figures used as stimuli were pointing was readily learned by all Ss in the experimental group and this training was found to have a significant effect on subsequently learning to apply labels.

## REFERENCES

Cantor, G. N. Effects of three types of pretraining on discrimination learning in preschool children. *J. exp. Psychol.*, 1955, *49*, 339–342.

Davidson, H. P. A study of the confusing letters, d, b, p, and q. *J. genet. Psychol.*, 1935, *47*, 458–468.

Forgus, R. H. Early visual and motor experience as determiners of complex maze-learning ability under rich and reduced stimulation. *J. comp. physiol. Psychol.*, 1955, *48*, 215–220.

Gibson, J. J., & Gibson, E. J. Perceptual learning—differentiation or enrichment? *Psychol. Rev.*, 1955, *62*, 32–41.

Hebb, D. O. *Organization of behavior.* New York: Wiley, 1949.

Jeffrey, W. E. The effects of verbal and nonverbal responses in mediating an instrumental act. *J. exp. Psychol.*, 1953, *45*, 327–333.

Mandler, G. M., Response factors in human learning. *Psychol. Rev.*, 1954, *61*, 235–244.

Postman, L. Association theory and perceptual learning. *Psychol. Rev.*, 1955, *62*, 438–446.

Riesen, A. H. The development of visual perception in man and chimpanzee. *Science*, 1947, *106*, 107–108.

Spiker, C. C., & Terrell, G. Factors associated with transposition behavior of preschool children. *J. genet. Psychol.*, 1955, *86*, 143–158.

Swanson, R., & Benton, A. L. Some aspects of the genetic development of right-left discrimination. *Child Develpm.*, 1955, *29*, 123–133.

# 10

# Errorless Establishment of Visual
# Discrimination Using Fading Procedures

### Robert Moore and Israel Goldiamond

EDITORS' COMMENTS

Many accounts of discrimination treat it as a unitary phenomenon. That is, it is a basic behavior of the child—he discriminates or does not discriminate, just as he takes a step or does not. Under this assumption the study of child development became in part a study of the discriminations a child has at various ages and in various environments. Thus, for example, children of the lower classes were said to discriminate between activities mainly in terms of their immediate consequences, but middle- and upper-class children could distinguish both the immediate and later consequences of activities, and choose their responses more meaningfully.

With the application of techniques derived from animal and laboratory investigations (as Keller prophesied in the first reading of this collection), the discriminations of organisms (including children) were analyzed into more basic processes of behavior. Discrimination then was seen as a result of two different procedures applied to the same behavior, but in different stimulus settings. In one setting, the behavior might be strengthened by an appropriate reinforcement contingency; in another setting, the behavior would be relatively weakened by either a punishment or extinction contingency. The need to weaken the learned behavior in the "incorrect" stimulus settings was attributed to generalization of the learning accomplished in the "correct" stimulus setting. Generalization was seen as an inevitable accompaniment of any learned alteration

Robert Moore and Israel Goldiamond, "Errorless Establishment of Visual Discrimination Using Fading Procedures," *Journal of the Experimental Analysis of Behavior*, 1964, 7, 269–272.

Performed under contract with the Operational Applications Laboratory, Electronic Systems Defense, Air Force Cambridge Research Center. L. G. Hanscom Field, Bedford, Massachusetts.

Based on a master's thesis in the Department of Psychology, Arizona State University, Tempe, by the senior author, under supervision of the junior author.

of behavior. Thus, when it occurred in inappropriate stimulus conditions, it had to be "corrected" by extinction or punishment. This analysis of discrimination greatly increased the detail of corresponding analyses of child development, at least potentially. It leads inevitably to questions about the contingencies under which any discrimination in a child was formed. It would not be enough any longer to say that lower-class children do not discriminate between activities in terms of their long-term consequences whereas middle-class children do. Instead, it would be asked: Are middle-class children likely to be differentially reinforced for considering long-term outcomes of their acts, and are lower-class children not differentially reinforced for this? The answers to such questions would greatly improve our understanding of class differences in development, and would also relate such differences to general behavior theory.

However, general behavior theory, like any other theory rooted in objectively defined data, should never be considered complete. An understanding of discrimination as a result of a generalized strengthening of behavior followed by a selective weakening of it in inappropriate settings did add greatly to analyses of children's discriminations—greatly, but incompletely. In 1963 a fundamental addition was made to the understanding of discrimination. Terrace[1] showed that a pigeon could be taught to respond to a disc illuminated with one color and not respond when the disc was differently colored—and without making errors in the process. In other words, the pigeon did *not* have to learn to peck at discs, incorrectly generalize to discs of all colors, and then, through extinguished or punished errors, lose his response to all but the correctly colored disc. Instead, he learned from the start to respond only to the correct color. Incorrect colors were introduced gradually such that he was extremely unlikely to respond to them. For example, they might have been presented only for a few seconds at moments when the pigeon was not pecking. Gradually, they were introduced for longer and longer durations; but since the pigeon was equally gradually, but perfectly consistently, reinforced for waiting through incorrect colors until the correct color appeared (whereupon he could peck and be reinforced), incorrect behaviors virtually never appeared.

Once this "errorless" discrimination was formed, the pigeon could then be taught further discriminations, and these too were established without error (as the following paper will describe). In short, a new technique of instruction had been developed, one not

[1] Terrace, H. S., "Discrimination Learning With and Without 'Errors,'" *J. exp. Anal. Behav.*, 1963, *6*, 1–27.

characterized by inappropriate generalization which would have to be undone by the teacher. The relevance of this possibility to educational technology is obvious and exciting. However, one pigeon does not make a technology of education. The need for further exploration of this technique and its characteristics is also obvious. Especially necessary is the application of errorless discrimination techniques to children.

The following study by Moore and Goldiamond is thus of great value. In itself, it shows that preschool children can learn a simple visual discrimination without making mistakes in the process. The discrimination is simple in terms of its structure: it requires only the discriminating of differing angles of rotation of triangles. Although simple, it is not easy for such children. Nevertheless, under this procedure, they acquired it virtually without error. Learning without inappropriate generalization is apparently possible in young children. Further elaboration of the conditions under which it can be made to occur, and of the consequences of learning lessons in this way, are the obvious next steps in an important and lengthy program of research.

The last paragraph cites the need to study the "consequences of learning lessons in this way." The point is emphasized for several reasons. The prospect of "errorless" education will prove exciting to many educators and psychotherapists. The correction of incorrect or inappropriate behavior often is accompanied by emotional displays that are painful to both teacher and pupil, therapist and patient. However, the development of a technology of errorless, and thus emotionless, frustration-free behavior changes may not necessarily have an entirely benevolent outcome. It may be, for example, that errorless discriminations are not transferred to other settings where they *would* be appropriate as readily as discriminations established by more traditional methods. If so, this would be a drawback. It would perhaps make a less flexible, less creative student. There is no reason for suspecting such an outcome; but there is always reason for checking all the characteristics of a new behavioral technique before over-applying it. This might reduce the errors in our own learning about children's learning.

## ABSTRACT

A visual discrimination task involved presenting a triangle briefly as a sample; when it was withdrawn, this triangle and two others differing slightly in degree of rotation were presented in different positions, with $S$ required to locate the sample that had been presented. Discrimination proved difficult for preschool children. When only the correct triangle was illuminated, discrimination was readily established. The brightness difference between correct and incorrect matches was gradually faded out by increasing the intensity of the incorrect matches, until they were equal in brightness to the correct match. The discrimination established by brightness difference was maintained in its absence, thereby transferring stimulus control from brightness to form, in an almost errorless sequence.

In laboratory discrimination experiments, the establishment of discrimination often requires numerous extinction trials. In programmed instruction (Holland, 1960), on the other hand, the experimental aim is to program the presentations so as to preclude such trials, which are considered to be "errors." In the present investigation, such "errorless" procedures were applied to a laboratory situation to minimize $S^\Delta$ responding, using preschool children as $S$s, in a task involving form discrimination.

The procedure is adapted from an experiment by Terrace (1963), who minimized the considerable $S^\Delta$ responding previously associated with the establishment of responding to vertical rather than horizontal stripes by pigeons. The easier discrimination between red and green was first established. Each stripe was then embedded in a color, and the colors were then gradually faded out. The discrimination was transferred to the stripes alone almost without error.

## METHOD AND PROCEDURES

Six children attending private day nursery schools[1] served as $S$s, with ages (to the nearest year), and sexes as follows: S-1, 3F; S-2, 5M; S-3, 4F; S-4, 5F; S-5, 4M; S-6, 4M. They were children of working mothers, engaged mainly in clerical tasks (with one nurse and one teacher); the fathers included clerical, maintenance, and skilled industrial workers. The experiment was conducted in a special room at the nursery schools set aside for that purpose.

The $S$ faced a masonite panel, about 24 in. square, containing four small windows, each of milk plastic, 2 in. wide by 3 in. high. The sample window was centered toward the top of the panel, with the other three windows symmetrically arranged in an arc below it, so that the center of each was 4 in. from the center of the sample window. Arranged in an arc beneath each of the matching windows were three small buttons, the manipulanda, with a pilot light above each. This light went on when the correct button was pressed.

[1] The authors wish to express their appreciation to the Little Papoose Nursery School and to Collier's Nursery School, Scottsdale, Arizona, for making their resources available.

Two types of series were run, *full* presentations and *fading* series, for the same or different Ss. In the *full* presentations, the sample window at the top went on, projecting a triangle at full 110 v. intensity. The sample window then went off, and simultaneously, the current was switched to the three matching windows below, each of which contained a triangle presented at full 110 v. intensity. One of these was matched in degree of rotation with the sample triangle, and the other two differed. The S was required to select the one that matched the withdrawn sample, a delayed matching to sample task (Ferster & Appel, 1961). In the *fading* series, the sample window was presented and withdrawn, as in the full series, but of the three windows *only the correct match was presented at full 110 v. intensity,* the two incorrect matches being presented at a lower intensity, ranging from O and up. This distinction between correct and incorrect was enhanced by a marked phi-phenomenon effect as the current was switched from the sample to the correct matching window. This series began with three presentations of the incorrect windows at O, then one presentation each at settings .35, .40, .50, .60, .65, .70, .75, .80, .83 (or .82), .86, .88, .90, .92, .94, .96, .98 of full voltage. There were then at least seven presentations at 1.00 (110 v.) in this series. It will be noted that at this final level, the *settings are identical to those of the full series,* and that the gradual increase in voltage whereby this identity is produced represents a gradual *fading of the brightness difference* between incorrect and correct, since the latter is always presented at full intensity. A correct response advanced the presentation to the next in this series; an incorrect response resulted in a repetition of the step (with a new slide). Two errors in a row resulted in a regression to a previous step.[2]

Three triangles differing in angle of rotation were used as stimuli (Reynolds, 1961). They were inverted isosceles skeleton triangles altitude 1.75 in., base 1.25 in. centered in each window. The apex was either straight down (D), rotated 25° to the left (L), or to the right (R). All three appeared in the matching windows, in varied positions; the sample was also varied. The order of sample presentations (with match presentations in parentheses) was: L (LDR), D (RLD), R (LRD), L (RDL), D (DRL), R (DRL), R (RDL), L (DLR), D (LDR), recycle. Nine sheets of acetate formed the slides, which incorporated these presentations, and which were inserted into position before each presentation, with all lights off.

The S faced the panel, with E visible at the side, with controls behind the panel. The sample was illuminated for approximately 4 sec. as S was told: "Look at the picture in the top window. See which way it's pointing." It was then turned off, illuminating the matching windows, and

---

[2] In four Ss, the fading series was extended between two and four presentations by unsystematic errors by E, which seemed to have no effect upon the data. These errors included repeating the voltage of the preceding presentation, and increasing by steps of .05 where .10 was scheduled.

*E* said: "Find another pointing the same way; touch it and push the button underneath it." If a correct response was made, the pilot light above the button illuminated immediately, and *S* was handed a small consumable or trinket, which he had previously been instructed to put into a small plastic bag. If an incorrect response was made, nothing was said by *E*. Recording was manual.

## RESULTS

Results are presented in Figure 1. The ordinate is cumulative correct responses, and the abscissa is number of presentations. Establishment of discrimination by the fading schedule is most clearly demonstrated by

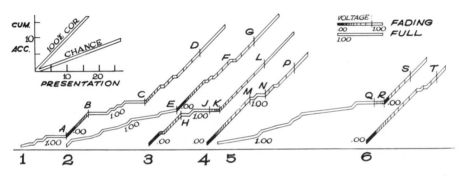

Figure 1. Accuracy rates as functions of differential reinforcement of correct and incorrect matches of triangles when presented at full intensity during training (Full), as compared to initial presentation at differing intensities for correct and incorrect matches, with the difference gradually faded out (Fading) by increasing the intensity of the incorrect matches until they were as full as the correct matches

the curve for *S-1,* who was begun on the full series, with incorrect windows at voltage setting 1.00. Accuracy was no better than chance. At A, fading was introduced, with the incorrect windows set at O. These were then increased in voltage to .60, at B. All responses in this series were accurate. The brightness differences between correct and incorrect were then eliminated, with the full series replacing the fading series, from B to C, during which the settings of the incorrect windows were 1.00. Accuracy immediately deteriorated to chance values. At C, fading procedures were reintroduced, with the voltage setting at .60, where it had been before the total elimination of differences between the windows. Accuracy immediately returned, with only two errors occurring during the ascending voltage (but decreasing brightness difference) series. At D, the voltages of all three matching windows were the same, and it will be noted that accuracy was maintained under conditions where previously (the full series) it had been no better than chance. Stimulus control had been transferred from brightness to rotation.

Contrasting effects upon the establishment of discrimination using full and fading series are also demonstrated by *S-2,* who was begun on the full series, with accuracy no better than chance. At E, fading was introduced, with the incorrect windows set at O. Discrimination immediately became errorless. At F, there were two errors in a row, and the voltage was lowered one step. Accuracy returned, and the progression was reinstated, culminating in 1.00 at G, when the incorrect and correct windows were equal in brightness, the condition prior to E. In contrast to the latter period, which was under the full series, discrimination was now maintained without error.

The fading procedure initiated the sessions of *S-3* and *S-4,* who accordingly began with errorless discrimination trials. For *S-3,* at H, the setting was .75, and the next settings were at 1.00, the full series, instead of .80 of the fading series. There was an immediate deterioration in accuracy. At J, the .75 setting was reintroduced, with no appreciable effect upon accuracy. The settings were then progressively reduced to .70, .65, and .60, at which point accuracy was reinstated (K), and the progression was then reestablished, with accuracy continuing thereafter through L, at the final setting of 1.00. For *S-4,* setting .82 was followed by full voltage at M, with breakdown to chance performance. Reinstatement of the fading procedure at N, when the setting was returned to .82, was followed by recovery of accuracy, which continued with one error into P, at the final setting of 1.00.

For *S-5,* the series was begun at full setting, with the chance performance characteristic of this procedure evident. At Q, the incorrect windows were lowered to .60 rather than 0, with no appreciable effect upon accuracy. At R, accordingly, fading was introduced by setting the incorrect windows at O, with the complete instatement of accuracy which characterized this procedure. For this *S,* however, the fading series comprised three presentations at O, four at .60, and six at 1.00. Errorless behavior was maintained during transitions whose abruptness disrupted discrimination in the other *S*s. Whether such behavior was a function of the individual *S,* or of the long standard discrimination training period prior to Q, which characterized this record, and during which some discrimination may have been established, cannot be answered from these data. The record certainly contrasts, however, with that of *S-6,* who was begun using the fading procedure, and was continued on it without interruption. By T, the progression had reached 1.00 and was maintained without error. Discrimination was established with only two errors, and in the minimal time. His condensed performance contrasts sharply with that of the other *S*s, and the similarities of his record to those of other *S*s during fading series, suggests that it was the fading procedures themselves that were involved in the rapid establishment of discrimination.

## DISCUSSION

These results indicate that fading procedures may be extended to the errorless establishment of discrimination in matching to sample procedures.[3] Errors produce extinction trials which may make it more difficult to maintain the behavior being studied and serve to prolong the series, and the economy of procedures which minimize error was depicted in the last S presented, whose learning was the most "perfect"—with the least practice. Control of errorless behaviors by the procedures themselves was evident throughout the experiments by the reversibility and reinstatement obtained when the fading procedures were systematically dropped or instated. The results also reiterate that a major variable in the establishment of behavior is the *sequence* (or program) of procedures utilized. On the response side, attention to sequence characterizes *shaping,* which can be considered a program of reinforcement of successive response ensembles, the succession being dictated by increasing presence of behavior along a criterion dimension. Thereby, novel response patterns are established, either for their own sake, or for use in other research. Analogously, in *fading, E* reinforces responses to stimulus differences successively approaching a criterion stimulus dimension, and it is suggested that such procedures may be useful in the establishment of novel discriminations and others required in psychophysical or other perceptual (cf. Goldiamond, 1962) or conceptual research (Goldiamond, 1964).

## REFERENCES

Ferster, C. B., & Appel, J. B. Punishment of $S^\Delta$ responding in matching to sample by time out from positive reinforcement. *J. exp. Anal. Behav.,* 1961, *4,* 45–56.

Goldiamond, I. Perception. In A. J. Bachrach (Ed.), *The experimental foundations of clinical psychology.* New York: Basic Books, 1962. Pp. 280–340.

Goldiamond, I. A research and demonstration procedure in stimulus control, abstraction, and environmental programming. *J. exp. Anal. Behav.,* 1964, *7,* 216.

Holland, J. G. Teaching machines: an application of principles from the laboratory. *J. exp. Anal. Behav.,* 1960, *3,* 275–287.

Reynolds, G. S. Contrast, generalization, and the process of discrimination. *J. exp. Anal. Behav.,* 1961, *4,* 289–294.

Terrace, H. S. Discrimination learning with and without "errors." *J. exp. Anal. Behav.,* 1963, *6,* 1–27.

[3] Discrimination of selected letters of the alphabet, using parallel fading procedures, was also established without error with other children from the same nursery schools.

# Hereditary Mechanisms, Psychological Behavior, and Development

It is standard, almost to the point of being a platitude, to refer all behavioral development to *three* sources: the current environment, the total history of past environmental stimulation, and the heredity of the child. Any aspect of the current environment which changes behavior is relevant to the first two sources, for it becomes a part of the child's history simply with the passage of time. The third source, heredity, has indeed had no emphasis in these pages so far, and, except for the article which follows, will have no role in future pages.

The reason is simple: relatively little has been found on the contributions of inheritance per se to child development. It is clear that a great variety of the behavioral and structural characteristics of animals other than man can be determined by properly selecting their ancestors in controlled breeding experiments extending over many generations. As a result of such studies, there have grown up both a science of genetics and a technology of breeding organisms, plant and animal. Man, however, is not subject to controlled breeding experiments; thus, relatively little is known to date about how heredity contributes to his development.

As Anne Anastasi will show, another difficulty with this area of study has been the insistent asking of the wrong questions about heredity and man's traits. It is a mistake to ask *which* traits are hereditary and which are learned. Similarly it is a mistake even to ask *how much* heredity and environment contribute respectively to any specified pattern of development. The correct question, as always, is *how* development takes place, in detail, step by step through the causal chains found operating in a specific individual under study. Anastasi is prescribing a causal analysis of development, rather than sorting development into predetermined logical categories.

Three points might well be stressed further. One is that a sensitivity of any pattern of development to the child's heredity does not thereby make it insensitive to current environmental action. Quite to the contrary, it should be assumed that any behavior, genetically influenced or not, is nevertheless modifiable by experience. The assumption may not be sound, of course, but that will be discovered only by trying to change the behavior by environmental variables. If such an attempt succeeds, it shows that the previous understanding of the behavior and its development was incomplete. And if such an attempt fails, it reminds us that other environmental actions may exist and should be tried as soon as possible. The essence of this argument is that neither the suspicion nor the affirmation of genetic influence in any pattern of development must ever produce an aura of hopelessness, especially when the development is an undersirable one. Nor must it produce the idea that the analysis of this pattern of development is thus complete. Both conclusions are incorrect and potentially tragic.

The second point is the difficulty of affirming that any behavior has a clear debt to heredity. Anastasi is rightly critical of the possibility of settling such questions through "twin studies." For any organism other than the human child, effective techniques involving the experimental breeding of strains of the organism would give powerful answers to such questions. These techniques are impossible in the case of the human child, however, and other techniques seem relatively weak and unsatisfactory to us.

To discover that a behavior has been significantly influenced in its development by the child's ancestry is informative (if it *can* be discovered), but leaves us helpless when confronted by the question: What can we do about it? We cannot unbreed the child and reconstitute his genes in a happier combination. We are left only with the possibility of modifying his behavior through current environmental action.

As a causal analysis finds that human development involves the genetic constitution of the organism in specific ways, textbooks will result which, we predict, will not classify environmental and hereditary mechanisms into different chapters, as is the practice now, but instead will treat both throughout all of their pages. Attention to the following presentation, which contains further support for a functional analysis of child development, we hope will hasten the day when such textbooks will make their appearance.

# 11

# Heredity, Environment, and the Question "How?"

**Anne Anastasi**

Two or three decades ago, the so-called heredity-environment question was the center of lively controversy. Today, on the other hand, many psychologists look upon it as a dead issue. It is now generally conceded that both hereditary and environmental factors enter into all behavior. The reacting organism is a product of its genes and its past environment, while present environment provides the immediate stimulus for current behavior. To be sure, it can be argued that, although a given trait may result from the combined influence of hereditary and environmental factors, a specific difference in this trait between individuals or between groups may be traceable to either hereditary or environmental factors alone. The design of most traditional investigations undertaken to identify such factors, however, has been such as to yield inconclusive answers. The same set of data has frequently led to opposite conclusions in the hands of psychologists with different orientations.

Nor have efforts to determine the proportional contribution of hereditary and environmental factors to observed individual differences in given traits met with any greater success. Apart from difficulties in controlling conditions, such investigations have usually been based upon the implicit assumption that hereditary and environmental factors combine in an additive fashion. Both geneticists and psychologists have repeatedly demonstrated, however, that a more tenable hypothesis is that of interaction (Haldane, 1938; Loevinger, 1943; Schwesinger, 1933; Woodworth, 1941). In other words, the nature and extent of the influence of each type of factor depend upon the contribution of the other. Thus the proportional contribution of heredity to the variance of a given trait, rather than being a constant, will vary under different environmental conditions. Similarly, under different hereditary conditions, the relative

Anne Anastasi, "Heredity, Environment, and the Question 'How?'" *Psychological Review*, 1958, *65*, 197–208.

Address of the President, Division of General Psychology, American Psychological Association, September 4, 1957.

contribution of environment will differ. Studies designed to estimate the proportional contribution of heredity and environment, however, have rarely included measures of such interaction. The only possible conclusion from such research would thus seem to be that both heredity and environment contribute to all behavior traits and that the extent of their respective contributions cannot be specified for any trait. Small wonder that some psychologists regard the heredity-environment question as unworthy of further consideration!

But is this really all we can find out about the operation of heredity and environment in the etiology of behavior? Perhaps we have simply been asking the wrong questions. The traditional questions about heredity and environment may be intrinsically unanswerable. Psychologists began by asking *which* type of factor, hereditary or environmental, is responsible for individual differences in a given trait. Later, they tried to discover *how much* of the variance was attributable to heredity and how much to environment. It is the primary contention of this paper that a more fruitful approach is to be found in the question *"How?"* There is still much to be learned about the specific *modus operandi* of hereditary and environmental factors in the development of behavioral differences. And there are several current lines of research which offer promising techniques for answering the question "How?"

## VARIETY OF INTERACTION MECHANISMS

### Hereditary Factors

If we examine some of the specific ways in which hereditary factors may influence behavior, we cannot fail but be impressed by their wide diversity. At one extreme, we find such conditions as phenylpyruvic amentia and amaurotic idiocy. In these cases, certain essential physical prerequisites for normal intellectual development are lacking as a result of hereditary metabolic disorders.

A somewhat different situation is illustrated by hereditary deafness, which may lead to intellectual retardation through interference with normal social interaction, language development, and schooling. In such a case, however, the hereditary handicap can be offset by appropriate adaptations of training procedures. It has been said, in fact, that the degree of intellectual backwardness of the deaf is an index of the state of development of special instructional facilities. As the latter improve, the intellectual retardation associated with deafness is correspondingly reduced.

A third example is provided by inherited susceptibility to certain physical diseases, with consequent protracted ill health. If environmental conditions are such that illness does in fact develop, a number of different behavioral effects may follow. Intellectually, the individual may be handicapped by his inability to attend school regularly. On the other hand, depending upon age of onset, home conditions, parental status, and similar factors, poor health may have the effect of concentrating the individual's energies upon intellectual pursuits. The curtailment of participation in athletics and social functions may serve to strengthen interest in reading and other sedentary activities. Concomitant circumstances would also determine the influence of such illness upon personality development. And it is well known that the latter effects could run the gamut from a deepening of human sympathy to psychiatric breakdown.

Finally, heredity may influence behavior through the mechanism of social stereotypes. A wide variety of inherited physical characteristics have served as the visible cues for identifying such stereotypes. These cues thus lead to behavioral restrictions or opportunities and—at a more subtle level—to social attitudes and expectancies. The individual's own self concept tends gradually to reflect such expectancies. All of these influences eventually leave their mark upon his abilities and inabilities, his emotional reactions, goals, ambitions, and outlook on life.

The geneticist Dobzhansky illustrates this type of mechanism by means of a dramatic hypothetical situation. He points out that, if there were a culture in which the carriers of blood group AB were considered aristocrats and those of blood group O laborers, then the blood group genes would become important hereditary determiners of behavior (Dobzhansky, 1950a, p. 147). Obviously the association between blood group and behavior would be specific to that culture. But such specificity is an essential property of the causal mechanism under consideration.

More realistic examples are not hard to find. The most familiar instances occur in connection with constitutional types, sex, and race. Sex and skin pigmentation obviously depend upon heredity. General body build is strongly influenced by hereditary components, although also susceptible to environmental modification. That all these physical characteristics may exert a pronounced effect upon behavior within a given culture is well known. It is equally apparent, of course, that in different cultures the behavioral correlates of such hereditary physical traits may be quite unlike. A specific physical cue may be completely unrelated to individual differences in psychological traits in one culture, while closely correlated with them in another. Or it may be associated with totally dissimilar behavior characteristics in two different cultures.

It might be objected that some of the illustrations which have been cited do not properly exemplify the operation of hereditary mechanisms in behavior development, since hereditary factors enter only indirectly into the behavior in question. Closer examination, however, shows this distinction to be untenable. First it may be noted that the influence of heredity upon behavior is always indirect. No psychological trait is ever inherited as such. All we can ever say directly from behavioral observations is that a given trait shows evidence of being influenced by certain "inheritable unknowns." This merely defines a problem for genetic research; it does not provide a causal explanation. Unlike the blood groups, which are close to the level of primary gene products, psychological traits are related to genes by highly indirect and devious routes. Even the mental deficiency associated with phenylketonuria is several steps removed from the chemically defective genes that represent its hereditary basis. Moreover, hereditary influences cannot be dichotomized into the more direct and the less direct. Rather do they represent a whole "continuum of indirectness," along which are found all degrees of remoteness of causal links. The examples already cited illustrate a few of the points on this continuum.

It should be noted that as we proceed along the continuum of indirectness, the range of variation of possible outcomes of hereditary factors expands rapidly. At each step in the causal chain, there is fresh opportunity for interaction with other hereditary factors as well as with environmental factors. And since each interaction in turn determines the direction of subsequent interactions, there is an ever-widening network of possible outcomes. If we visualize a simple sequential grid with only two alternatives at each point, it is obvious that there are two possible outcomes in the one-stage situation, four outcomes at the second stage, eight at the third, and so on in geometric progression. The actual situation is undoubtedly much more complex, since there will usually be more than two alternatives at any one point.

In the case of the blood groups, the relation to specific genes is so close that no other concomitant hereditary or environmental conditions can alter the outcome. If the organism survives at all, it will have the blood group determined by its genes. Among psychological traits, on the other hand, some variation in outcome is always possible as a result of concurrent circumstances. Even in cases of phenylketonuria, intellectual development will exhibit some relationship with the type of care and training available to the individual. That behavioral outcomes show progressive diversification as we proceed along the continuum of indirectness is brought out by the other examples which were cited. Chronic illness *can* lead to scholarly renown or to intellectual immaturity; a mesomorphic physique *can* be a contributing factor in juvenile delinquency or in the attainment of a college presidency! Published data on Sheldon somatotypes provide some support for both of the latter outcomes.

Parenthetically, it may be noted that geneticists have sometimes used the term "norm of reaction" to designate the range of variation of possible outcomes of gene properties (cf. Dobzhansky, 1950b, p. 161). Thus heredity sets the "norm" or limits within which environmental differences determine the eventual outcome. In the case of some traits, such as blood groups or eye color, this norm is much narrower than in the case of other traits. Owing to the rather different psychological connotations of both the words "norm" and "reaction," however, it seems less confusing to speak of the "range of variation" in this context.

A large portion of the continuum of hereditary influences which we have described coincides with the domain of somatopsychological relations, as defined by Barker et al., (1953). Under this heading, Barker includes "variations in physique that affect the psychological situation of a person by influencing the effectiveness of his body as a tool for actions or by serving as a stimulus to himself or others" (p. 1). Relatively direct neurological influences on behavior, which have been the traditional concern of physiological psychology, are excluded from this definition, Barker being primarily concerned with what he calls the "social psychology of physique." Of the examples cited in the present paper, deafness, severe illness, and the physical characteristics associated with social stereotypes would meet the specifications of somatopsychological factors.

The somatic factors to which Barker refers, however, are not limited to those of hereditary origin. Bodily conditions attributable to environmental causes operate in the same sorts of somatopsychological relations as those traceable to heredity. In fact, heredity-environment distinctions play a minor part in Barker's approach.

## Environmental Factors: Organic

Turning now to an analysis of the role of environmental factors in behavior, we find the same etiological mechanisms which were observed in the case of hereditary factors. First, however, we must differentiate between two classes of environmental influences: (a) those producing organic effects which may in turn influence behavior and (b) those serving as direct stimuli for psychological reactions. The former may be illustrated by food intake or by exposure to bacterial infection; the latter, by tribal initiation ceremonies or by a course in algebra. There are no completely satisfactory names by which to designate these two classes of influences. In an earlier paper by Anastasi and Foley (1948), the terms "structural" and "functional" were employed. However, "organic" and "behavioral" have the advantage of greater familiarity in this context and may be less open to misinterpretation. Accordingly, these terms will be used in the present paper.

Like hereditary factors, environmental influences of an organic nature can also be ordered along a continuum of indirectness with regard to their relation to behavior. This continuum closely parallels that of hereditary factors. One end is typified by such conditions as mental deficiency resulting from cerebral birth injury or from prenatal nutritional inadequacies. A more indirect etiological mechanism is illustrated by severe motor disorder—as in certain cases of cerebral palsy—*without* accompanying injury to higher neurological centers. In such instances, intellectual retardation may occur as an indirect result of the motor handicap, through the curtailment of educational and social activities. Obviously this causal mechanism corresponds closely to that of hereditary deafness cited earlier in the paper.

Finally, we may consider an environmental parallel to the previously discussed social stereotypes which were mediated by hereditary physical cues. Let us suppose that a young woman with mousy brown hair becomes transformed into a dazzling golden blonde through environmental techniques currently available in our culture. It is highly probable that this metamorphosis will alter, not only the reactions of her associates toward her, but also her own self concept and subsequent behavior. The effects could range all the way from a rise in social poise to a drop in clerical accuracy!

Among the examples of environmentally determined organic influences which have been described, all but the first two fit Barker's definition of somatopsychological factors. With the exception of birth injuries and nutritional deficiencies, all fall within the social psychology of physique. Nevertheless, the individual factors exhibit wide diversity in their specific *modus operandi*—a diversity which has important practical as well as theoretical implications.

### Environmental Factors: Behavioral

The second major class of environmental factors—the behavioral as contrasted to the organic—are by definition direct influences. The immediate effect of such environmental factors is always a behavioral change. To be sure, some of the initial behavioral effects may themselves indirectly affect the individual's later behavior. But this relationship can perhaps be best conceptualized in terms of breadth and permanence of effects. Thus it could be said that we are now dealing, not with a continuum of indirectness, as in the case of hereditary and organic-environmental factors, but rather with a continuum of breadth.

Social class membership may serve as an illustration of a relatively broad, pervasive, and enduring environmental factor. Its influence upon behavior development may operate through many channels. Thus social level may determine the range and nature of intellectual stimulation provided by home and community through books, music, art, play activities, and the like. Even more far-reaching may be the effects upon interests and motivation, as illustrated by the desire to perform abstract intellectual tasks, to surpass others in competitive situations, to succeed in school, or to gain social approval. Emotional and social traits may likewise be influenced by the nature of interpersonal relations characterizing homes at different socioeconomic levels. Somewhat more restricted in scope than social class, although still exerting a relatively broad influence, is amount of formal schooling which the individual is able to obtain.

A factor which may be wide or narrow in its effects, depending upon concomitant circumstances, is language handicap. Thus the bilingualism of an adult who moves to a foreign country with inadequate mastery of the new language represents a relatively limited handicap which can be readily overcome in most cases. At most, the difficulty is one of communication. On the other hand, some kinds of bilingualism in childhood may exert a retarding influence upon intellectual development and may under certain conditions affect personality development adversely (Anastasi, 1958; Arsenian, 1945; Darcy, 1953). A common pattern in the homes of immigrants is that the child speaks one language at home and another in school, so that his knowledge of each language is limited to certain types of situations. Inadequate facility with the language of the school interferes with the acquisition of basic concepts, intellectual skills, and information. The frustration engendered by scholastic difficulties may in turn lead to discouragement and general dislike of school. Such reactions can be found, for example, among a number of Puerto Rican children in New York City schools (Anastasi & Cordova, 1953). In the case of certain groups, moreover, the child's foreign language background may be perceived by himself and his associates as a symbol of minority group status and may thereby augment any emotional maladjustment arising from such status (Spoerl, 1943).

A highly restricted environmental influence is to be found in the opportunity to acquire specific items of information occurring in a particular intelligence test. The fact that such opportunities may vary with culture, social class, or individual experimental background is at the basis of the test user's concern with the problem of coaching and with "culture-free" or "culture-fair" tests (cf. Anastasi, 1954; 1958). If the advantage or disadvantage which such experiential differences confer upon certain individuals is strictly confined to performance on the given test, it will obviously reduce the validity of the test and should be eliminated.

In this connection, however, it is essential to know the breadth of the environmental influence in question. A fallacy inherent in many attempts to develop culture-fair tests is that the breadth of cultural differentials is not taken into account. Failure to consider breadth of effect likewise characterizes certain discussions of coaching. If, in coaching a student for a college admission test, we can improve his knowledge of verbal concepts and his reading comprehension, he will be better equipped to succeed in college courses. His performance level will thus be raised, not only on the test, but also on the criterion which the test is intended to predict. To try to devise a test which is not susceptible to such coaching would merely reduce the effectiveness of the test. Similarly, efforts to rule out cultural differentials from test items so as to make them equally "fair" to subjects in different social classes or in different cultures may merely limit the usefulness of the test, since the same cultural differentials may operate within the broader area of behavior which the test is designed to sample.

## METHODOLOGICAL APPROACHES

The examples considered so far should suffice to highlight the wide variety of ways in which hereditary and environmental factors may interact in the course of behavior development. There is clearly a need for identifying explicitly the etiological mechanism whereby any given hereditary or environmental condition ultimately leads to a behavioral characteristic—in other words, the "how" of heredity and environment. Accordingly, we may now take a quick look at some promising methodological approaches to the question "How?"

Within the past decade, an increasing number of studies have been designed to trace the connection between specific factors in the hereditary backgrounds or in the reactional biographies of individuals and their observed behavioral characteristics. There has been a definite shift away from the predominantly descriptive and correlational approach of the earlier decades toward more deliberate attempts to verify explanatory hypotheses. Similarly, the cataloguing of group differences in psychological traits has been giving way gradually to research on *changes* in group characteristics following altered conditions.

Among recent methodological developments, we have chosen seven as being particularly relevant to the analysis of etiological mechanisms. The first represents an extension of selective breeding investigations to permit the identification of specific hereditary conditions underlying the observed behavioral differences. When early selective breeding investigations such as those of Tryon (1940) on rats indicated that "maze learning ability" was inherited, we were still a long way from knowing what was actually being transmitted by the genes. It was obviously not "maze learning ability" as such. Twenty—or even ten—years ago, some psychologists would have suggested that it was probably general intelligence. And a few might even have drawn a parallel with the inheritance of human intelligence.

But today investigators have been asking: Just what makes one group of rats learn mazes more quickly than the other? Is it differences in motivation, emotionality, speed of running, general activity level? If so, are these behavioral characteristics in turn dependent upon group differences in glandular development, body weight, brain size, biochemical factors, or some other organic conditions? A number of recent and ongoing investigations indicate that attempts are being made to trace, at least part of the way, the steps whereby certain chemical properties of the genes may ultimately lead to specified behavior characteristics.

An example of such a study is provided by Searle's (1949) follow-up on Tryon's research. Working with the strains of maze-bright and maze-dull rats developed by Tryon, Searle demonstrated that the two strains differed in a number of emotional and motivational factors, rather than in ability. Thus the strain differences were traced one step further, although many links still remain to be found between maze learning and genes. A promising methodological development within the same general area is to be found in the recent research of Hirsch and Tryon (1956). Utilizing a specially devised technique for measuring individual differences in behavior among lower organisms, these investigators launched a series of studies on selective breeding for behavioral characteristics in the fruit fly, *Drosophila*. Such research can capitalize on the mass of available genetic knowledge regarding the morphology of *Drosophila,* as well as on other advantages of using such an organism in genetic studies.

Further evidence of current interest in the specific hereditary factors which influence behavior is to be found in an extensive research program in progress at the Jackson Memorial Laboratory, under the direction of Scott and Fuller (1951). In general, the project is concerned with the behavioral characteristics of various breeds and cross-breeds of dogs. Analyses of some of the data gathered to date again suggest that "differences in performance are produced by differences in emotional, motivational, and peripheral processes, and that genetically caused differences in central processes may be either slight or non-existent" (Scott & Charles, 1953, p. 225). In other parts of the same project, breed differences in physiological characteristics, which may in turn be related to behavioral differences, have been established.

A second line of attack is the exploration of possible relationships between behavioral characteristics and physiological variables which may in turn be traceable to hereditary factors. Research on EEG, autonomic balance, metabolic processes, and biochemical factors illustrates this approach. A lucid demonstration of the process of tracing a psychological condition to genetic factors is provided by the identification and subsequent investigation of phenylpyruvic amentia. In this case, the causal chain from defective gene, through metabolic disorder and consequent cerebral malfunctioning, to feeblemindedness and other overt symptoms can be described step by step (cf. Snyder, 1949; Snyder & David, 1957, pp. 389–391). Also relevant are the recent researches on neurological and biochemical correlates of schizophrenia (Brackbill, 1956). Owing to inadequate methodological controls, however, most of the findings of the latter studies must be regarded as tentative (Horwitt, 1956).

Prenatal environmental factors provide a third avenue of fruitful investigation. Especially noteworthy is the recent work of Pasamanick and his associates (1956), which demonstrated a tie-up between socioeconomic level, complications of pregnancy and parturition, and psychological disorders of the offspring. In a series of studies on large samples of whites and Negroes in Baltimore, these investigators showed that various prenatal and paranatal disorders are significantly related to the occurrence of mental defect and psychiatric disorders in the child. An important source of such irregularities in the process of childbearing and birth is to be found in deficiencies of maternal diet and in other conditions associated with low socioeconomic status. An analysis of the data did in fact reveal a much higher frequency of all such medical complication in lower than in higher socioeconomic levels, and a higher frequency among Negroes than among whites.

Direct evidence of the influence of prenatal nutritional factors upon subsequent intellectual development is to be found in a recent, well controlled experiment by Harrell *et al.,* (1955). The subjects were pregnant women in low-income groups, whose normal diets were generally quite deficient. A dietary supplement was administered to some of these women during pregnancy and lactation, while an equated control group received placebos. When tested at the ages of three and four years, the offspring of the experimental group obtained a significantly higher mean IQ than did the offspring of the controls.

Mention should also be made of animal experiments on the effects of such factors as prenatal radiation and neonatal asphyxia upon cerebral anomalies as well as upon subsequent behavior development. These experimental studies merge imperceptibly into the fourth approach to be considered, namely, the investigation of the influence of early experience upon the eventual behavioral characteristics of animals. Research in this area has been accumulating at a rapid rate. In 1954, Beach and Jaynes surveyed this literature for the *Psychological Bulletin,* listing over 130 references. Several new studies have appeared since that date (e.g., Forgus, 1954; King & Gurney, 1954; Luchins & Forgus, 1955; Melzack, 1954; Thompson & Melzack, 1956). The variety of factors covered ranges from the type and quantity of available food to the extent of contact with human culture. A large number of experiments have been concerned with various forms of sensory deprivation and with diminished opportunities for motor exercise. Effects have been observed in many kinds of animals and in almost all aspects of behavior, including perceptual responses, motor activity, learning, emotionality, and social reactions.

In their review, Beach and Jaynes pointed out that research in this area has been stimulated by at least four distinct theoretical interests. Some studies were motivated by the traditional concern with the relative contribution of maturation of learning to behavior development. Others were designed in an effort to test certain psychoanalytic theories regarding infantile experiences, as illustrated by studies which limited the feeding responses of young animals. A third relevant influence is to be found in the work of the European biologist Lorenz (1935) on early social stimulation of birds, and in particular on the special type of learning for which the term "imprinting" has been coined. A relatively large number of recent studies have centered around Hebb's (1949) theory regarding the importance of early perceptual experiences upon subsquent perform-ance in learning situations. All this research represents a rapidly growing and promising attack on the *modus operandi* of specific environmental factors.

The human counterpart of these animal studies may be found in the comparative investigation of child-rearing practices in different cul-tures and subcultures. This represents the fifth approach in our list. An outstanding example of such a study is that by Whiting and Child pub-lished in 1963. Utilizing data on 75 primitive societies from the Cross-Cultural Files of the Yale Institute of Human Relations, these investi-gators set out to test a number of hypotheses regarding the relationships between child-rearing practices and personality development. This analy-sis was followed up by field observations in five cultures, the results of which have not yet been reported (cf. Whiting *et al.*, 1954).

Within our own culture, similar surveys have been concerned with the diverse psychological environments provided by different social classes (Davis & Havighurst, 1946). Of particular interest are the study of Williams and Scott (1953) on the association between socioeconomic level, permissiveness, and motor development among Negro children, and the exploratory research by Milner (1951) on the relationship between reading readiness in first-grade children and patterns of parent-child interaction. Milner found that upon school entrance the lower-class child seems to lack chiefly two advantages enjoyed by the middle-class child. The first is described as "a warm positive family atmosphere or adult-relationship pattern which is more and more being recognized as a motivational prerequisite of any kind of adult-controlled learning." The lower-class children in Milner's study perceived adults as predominantly hostile. The second advantage is an extensive opportunity to interact verbally with adults in the family. The latter point is illustrated by parental atti-tudes toward mealtime conversation, lower-class parents tending to in-hibit and discourage such conversation, while middle-class parents en-courage it.

Most traditional studies on child-rearing practices have been de-signed in terms of a psychoanalytic orientation. There is need for more data pertaining to other types of hypotheses. Findings such as those of Milner on opportunities for verbalization and the resulting effects upon reading readiness represent a step in this direction. Another possible source of future data is the application of the intensive observational techniques of psychological ecology developed by Barker and Wright (1955) to widely diverse socioeconomic groups.

A sixth major approach involves research on the previously cited somatopsychological relationships (Barker, Wright, Myerson, & Gonick, 1953). To date, little direct information is available on the precise operation of this class of factors in psychological development. The multiplicity of ways in which physical traits—whether hereditary or environmental in origin—may influence behavior thus offers a relatively unexplored field for future study.

The seventh and final approach to be considered represents an adaptation of traditional twin studies. From the standpoint of the question "How?" there is need for closer coordination between the usual data on twin resemblance and observations of the family interactions of twins. Available data already suggest, for example, that closeness of contact and extent of environmental similarity are greater in the case of monozygotic than in the case of dizygotic twins (cf. Anastasi, 1958). Information on the social reactions of twins toward each other and the specialization of roles is likewise of interest (Anastasi, 1958). Especially useful would be longitudinal studies of twins, beginning in early infancy and following the subjects through school age. The operation of differential environmental pressures, the development of specialized roles, and other environmental influences could thus be more clearly identified and correlated with intellectual and personality changes in the growing twins.

Parenthetically, I should like to add a remark about the traditional applications of the twin method, in which persons in different degrees of hereditary and environmental relationships to each other are simply compared for behavioral similarity. In these studies, attention has been focused principally upon the amount of resemblance of monozygotic as contrasted to dizygotic twins. Yet such a comparison is particularly difficult to interpret because of the many subtle differences in the environmental situations of the two types of twins. A more fruitful comparison would seem to be that between dizygotic twins and siblings, for whom the hereditary similarity is known to be the same. In Kallmann's (1953) monumental research on psychiatric disorders among twins for example, one of the most convincing bits of evidence for the operation of hereditary factors in schizophrenia is the fact that the degrees of concordance for dizygotic twins and for siblings were practically identical. In contrast, it will be recalled that in intelligence test scores dizygotic twins resemble each other much more closely than do siblings—a finding which reveals the influence of environmental factors in intellectual development.

## SUMMARY

The heredity-environment problem is still very much alive. Its viability is assured by the gradual replacement of the questions, "Which one?" and "How much?" by the more basic and appropriate question,

"How?" Hereditary influences—as well as environmental factors of an organic nature—vary along a "continuum of indirectness." The more indirect their connection with behavior, the wider will be the range of variation of possible outcomes. One extreme of the continuum of indirectness may be illustrated by brain damage leading to mental deficiency; the other extreme, by physical characteristics associated with social stereotypes. Examples of factors falling at intermediate points include deafness, physical diseases, and motor disorders. Those environmental factors which act directly upon behavior can be ordered along a continuum of breadth or permanence of effect, as exemplified by social class membership, amount of formal schooling, language handicap, and familiarity with specific test items.

Several current lines of research offer promising techniques for exploring the *modus operandi* of hereditary and environmental factors. Outstanding among them are investigations of: (a) hereditary conditions which underlie behavioral differences between selectively bred groups of animals; (b) relations between physiological variables and individual differences in behavior, especially in the case of pathological deviations; (c) role of prenatal physiological factors in behavior development; (d) influence of early experience upon eventual behavioral characteristics; (e) cultural differences in child-rearing practices in relation to intellectual and emotional development; (f) mechanisms of somatopsychological relationships; and (g) psychological development of twins from infancy to maturity, together with observations of their social environment. Such approaches are extremely varied with regard to subjects employed, nature of psychological functions studied, and specific experimental procedures followed. But it is just such heterogeneity of methodology that is demanded by the wide diversity of ways in which hereditary and environmental factors interact in behavior development.

## REFERENCES

Anastasi, Anne. *Psychological testing.* New York: Macmillan, 1954.

Anastasi, Anne. *Differential psychology.* (3rd ed.) New York: Macmillan, 1958.

Anastasi, Anne, & Cordova, F. A. Some effects of bilingualism upon the intelligence test performance of Puerto Rican children in New York City. *J. educ. Psychol.,* 1953, *44,* 1–19.

Anastasi, Anne, & Foley, J. P., Jr. A proposed reorientation in the heredity-environment controversy. *Psychol. Rev.,* 1948, *55,* 239–249.

Arsenian, S. Bilingualism in the postwar world. *Psychol. Bul.,* 1945, *42,* 65–86.

Barker, R. G., Wright, Beatrice A., Myerson, L., & Gonick, Mollie R. Adjustment to physical handicap and illness: a survey of the social psychology of physique and disability. *Soc. Sci. Res. Coun. Bull.,* 1953, No. 55 (Rev.).

Barker, R. G., & Wright, H. F. *Midwest and its children: the psychological ecology of an American town.* New York: Harper & Row, 1955.

Beach, F. A., & Jaynes, J. Effects of early experience upon the behavior of animals. *Psychol. Bull.,* 1954, *51,* 239–263.

Brackbill, G. A. Studies of brain dysfunction in schizophrenia. *Psychol. Bull.,* 1956, *53,* 210–226.

Darcy, Natalie T. A review of the literature of the effects of bilingualism upon the measurement of intelligence. *J. genet. Psychol.,* 1953, *82,* 21–57.

Davis, A., & Havighurst, R. J. Social class and color differences in child rearing. *Amer. sociol. Rev.,* 1946, *11,* 698–710.

Dobzhansky, T. The genetic nature of differences among men. In S. Persons (Ed.), *Evolutionary thought in America.* New Haven: Yale, 1950a. Pp. 86–155.

Dobzhansky, T. Heredity, environment, and evolution. *Science,* 1950b, *111,* 161–166.

Forgus, R. H. The effect of early perceptual learning on the behavioral organization of adult rats. *J. comp. physiol. Psychol.,* 1954, *47,* 331–336.

Haldane, J. B. S. *Heredity and politics.* New York: Norton, 1938.

Harrell, Ruth F., Woodyard, Ella, & Gates, A. I. *The effect of mothers' diets on the intelligence of the offspring.* New York: Teachers College, 1955.

Hebb, D. O. *The organization of behavior.* New York: Wiley, 1949.

Hirsch. J., & Tryon, R. C. Mass screening and reliable individual measurement in the experimental behavior genetics of lower organisms. *Psychol. Bull.,* 1956, *53,* 402–410.

Horwitt, M. K. Fact and artifact in the biology of schizophrenia. *Science,* 1956, *124,* 429–430.

Kallmann, F. J. *Heredity in health and mental disorder: principles of psychiatric genetics in the light of comparative twin studies.* New York: Norton, 1953.

King, J. A., & Gurney, Nancy L. Effect of early social experience on adult aggressive behavior in C57BL10 mice. *J. comp. physiol. Psychol.,* 1954, *47,* 326–330.

Loevinger, Jane. On the proportional contributions of differences in nature and in nurture to differences in intelligence. *Psychol. Bull.,* 1943, *40,* 725–756.

Lorenz, K. Der Kumpan in der Umwelt des Vogels. Der Artgenosse als auslösendes Moment sozialer Verhaltungsweisen. *J. Orn, Lpz.,* 1935, *83,* 137–213; 289–413.

Luchins, A. S., & Forgus, R. H. The effect of differential postweaning environment on the rigidity of an animal's behavior. *J. genet. Psychol.,* 1955, *86,* 51–58.

Melzack, R. The genesis of emotional behavior: An experimental study of the dog. *J. comp. physiol. Psychol.,* 1954, *47,* 166–168.

Milner, Esther A. A study of the relationships between reading readiness in grade one school children and patterns of parent-child interaction. *Child Develpm.,* 1951, *22,* 95–112.

Pasamanick, B., Knobloch, Hilda, & Lilienfeld, A. M. Socioeconomic status and some precursors of neuropsychiatric disorder. *Amer. J. Orthopsychiat.,* 1956, *26,* 594–601.

Schwesinger, Gladys C. *Heredity and environment*. New York: Macmillan, 1933.

Scott, J. P., & Charles, Margaret S. Some problems of heredity and social behavior. *J. gen. Psychol.*, 1953, *48*, 209–230.

Scott, J. P., & Fuller, J. L. Research on genetics and social behavior at the Roscoe B. Jackson Memorial Laboratory, 1946–1951—A progress report. *J. Hered.*, 1951, *42*, 191–197.

Searle, L. V. The organization of hereditary maze-brightness and maze-dullness. *Genet. Psychol. Monogr.*, 1949, *39*, 279–325.

Snyder, L. H. The genetic approach to human individuality. *Sci. Mon.*, N.Y., 1949, *68*, 165–171.

Snyder, L. H., & David, P. R. *The principles of heredity*. (5th ed.) Boston: Heath, 1957.

Spoerl, Dorothy T. Bilinguality and emotional adjustment. *J. abnorm. soc. Psychol.*, 1943, *38*, 37–57.

Thompson, W. R., & Melzack, R. Early environment. *Sci. Amer.*, 1956, *194*, (1), 38–42.

Tryon, R. C. Genetic differences in maze-learning ability in rats. *Yearb. nat. Soc. Stud. Educ.*, 1940, *39*, Part I, 111–119.

Whiting, J. W. M., *et al. Field guide for a study of socialization in five societies*. Cambridge, Mass.: Harvard, 1954 (mimeo.).

Whiting, J. W. M., & Child, I. L. *Child training and personality: a crosscultural study*. New Haven: Yale, 1953.

Williams, Judith R., & Scott, R. B. Growth and development of Negro infants: IV. Motor development and its relationship to child rearing practices in two groups of Negro infants. *Child Develpm.*, 1953, *24*, 103–121.

Woodworth, R. S. Heredity and environment: a critical survey of recently published material on twins and foster children. *Soc. Sci. Res. Coun. Bull.*, 1941, No. 47.

# Retrospect and Prospect

The next article is meant to offer a summary characterization of one of the essential features of the research that has been surveyed so far. Thus, it is retrospective, looking back in an analytical way over what has gone before. At the same time, it will serve as a preface to the second part of this volume (dealing with applications of basic mechanisms) and will thereby provide a prospectus for what is to come. In both functions, it points to the same distinguishing characteristic of the research reported: its simplicity.

Although Terrell's theoretical and methodological orientation differs from Keller's, he and Keller came to the same conclusion about the research needed in child development. It will be recalled that Keller argued for the application to child behavior of the concepts, principles, and methods developed during the past 50 years on infrahuman subjects. In so doing he called for research based on clear-cut and objectively defined stimulus and response. Terrell also argues for simplicity in child research. It is his impression that much of the research in child behavior and development to date is not producing the substance needed for advancing a scientific analysis of human psychological development. He suggests that nebulous concepts such as dependency, rejection, and hostility, and vaguely described explanatory principles such as a child's "drive to realize his full potential" are not paying their way in a discipline that must be part autocatalytic (Keller's term). Furthermore, he points out that correlational analyses, especially those of low order and those dealing with relationships over long time spans fail to provide nourishment for the growth of an empirical theory of child behavior and development.

It might be instructive to point out that research in child behavior and development has been moving along the lines advocated by Terrell and Keller, as indicated by the establishment of the *Journal of Experimental Child Psychology*. This journal, founded in 1964, is devoted to the publication of studies "in which the behavior and development of children is clearly related to its determining variables."

For the reader who appreciates the value of simplicity in studies of development, we recommend the argument simply as a cogent confirmation and suggest that the date of the original publication be noted as an indication of the author's relatively early discernment. For the reader who is still open to instruction in what is simple about such research, we introduce him now to Terrell's excellent advice.

# 12

# The Need for Simplicity
# in Research in Child Psychology

*Glenn Terrell*

Perhaps the best way to begin this paper is to explain what the writer means by simple research in child psychology. A few examples should suffice: (a) the effects of interference on crank-turning behavior (Screven, 1954); (b) an experiment involving the learning of concepts of size (Hicks & Stewart, 1930); (c) an investigation of reinforcement variables affecting the resistance to extinction of a simple response of placing a ball in a hole (Bijou, 1957). In each of these problems the behavior studied is relatively simple, particularly in relation to far more complex responses involved in studies of social development, or in investigations of the effects of child rearing methods on personality growth. It is felt that the best way to begin the argument for the current need for simple research in child psychology is to make an analysis of a characteristic area of research involving exceedingly complex variables. For this purpose, the writer has selected the general area involving the effects of child rearing variables on personality development. Out of this analysis and subsequent argument should come the impression that the writer's main reason for favoring "basic" research is a methodological one. Following this discussion, the writer will present some of the important uses of the study of simple processes in child psychology, and follow this with a treatment of the advantages that such a research orientation has.

The research literature in child development is replete with investigations concerned with the relationships between early guidance or child rearing procedures and personality development of children. The independent and dependent variables of these studies are typically complex,

Glenn Terrell, "The Need for Simplicity in Research in Child Psychology," *Child Development*, 1958, *29,* 303–310. Reprinted by permission of The Society for Research in Child Development, Inc., and the author.

This paper is a longer version of a contribution to a symposium, "Trends in Developmental Psychology," presented at the Rocky Mountain Psychological Association meetings in 1957.

hard-to-measure processes. Many of them involve attempts to measure the effects of such variables as punishment, affection, rejection, breast feeding, and home atmosphere on the adjustment of the child. Measures of these child rearing variables are usually obtained through interviews, rating scales, projective tests, or observational procedures. The adjustment or response measures are typically scores on paper and pencil personality tests, clinical judgments, teacher ratings, or responses in projective doll play situations.

Correlations between these child rearing and adjustment measures are calculated, and if they differ significantly from zero, the investigator typically concludes that he has discovered a useful relationship in the science of child rearing.

Much has been written about the unreliabilities of the interview, the rating scale, personality tests, and clinical judgments. It is not within the scope of this paper to go into a detailed review of the difficulties associated with the use of these methods. Suffice it to say that there are problems of recall of the desired information by the parent, of intentional or unintentional falsification of responses, of definition, and of projections or misinterpretations by clinicians, parents, and teachers.

To illustrate what the writer considers the prematurity of research at this complex level in child psychology, perhaps the analysis of an hypothetical example will prove helpful. Let us suppose that an investigator wishes to study, among other things, the relationship between the duration of breast feeding in infancy and the frequency of dependency behavior of elementary school children. Measures of duration of breast feeding are obtained by the interview, while measures of dependency are taken in a standardized projective doll play situation. For the sake of the argument, let us assume that the investiation is conducted with the greatest possible care. Much preparation has gone into the interview and the doll play procedures in order that the researcher reduce to a minimum the invalidities and unreliabilities of the study due to these factors. Further, let it be assumed that the investigator finds a significant inverse correlation between duration of breast feeding and the frequency of dependency behavior.

To what extent is he justified in claiming the discovery of a relationship between these variables? Obviously the experimenter is not manipulating the independent variable. Though a relevant variable can be isolated and studied without the experimenter's manipulating it, the difficulty with this procedure, as McCandless and Spiker (1956) recently pointed out in an appeal for more experimental research in child psychology, is greatly increased as the number of relevant variables affecting the dependent system is increased. And as McCandless and Spiker in the same paper further point out, "That a very large number of variables affects the behavior of the living organism is a fact that has long been recognized" (p. 76). Here is the crux of the difficulty: the number of relevant variables affecting the dependent system in complex research, as in the hypothetical example, is undoubtedly far greater than those affecting relatively simple responses. Furthermore, they are infinitely more difficult to isolate and control. In fact, the control of variables associated with the study of the effects of child rearing techniques on adjustment is in most cases impossible at the present stage. Indeed, it is highly probable that the great majority of these variables is as yet unidentified. Some of the possible variables more obviously relevant to dependency, other than the duration of breast feeding, are the character structure of the parents, friendship patterns, socioeconomic class, genetic and constitutional factors, and the nature of sibling relationships. Variables such as these are more often than not unconsidered in studies at this level, and even if efforts to study them were made, the outlook would indeed be bleak, since it would be difficult if not impossible to say which has affected the dependent variable, and to what degree. The end result of this state of affairs is, of course, that the experimenter thinks he has discovered a relationship in child rearing variables, when in reality there is a good chance that one or more of the unconsidered variables mentioned above has brought about the change in the dependent variables. Any well trained scientist must admit that because of the above reasoning, there is, at the very best, only a slight, highly equivocal suggestion in the results of the above described hypothetical study that there is a meaningful relationship between the variables studied, certainly not enough to warrant the confident statements about child rearing problems one frequently sees emanating from such research. It is not at all unlikely that many child psychologists have been misled into conducting further research along these lines, to say nothing of the possibly more serious consequences of parents being misled by reports of these studies.

At this point it seems appropriate to point out some important uses of more basic research at the present stage of maturity of developmental psychology. If one has followed recent issues of *Child Development, The Journal of Experimental Psychology,* and other psychological journals, it is unmistakably clear that one of the newer trends in developmental psychology is a preoccupation with basic research problems that relate to some of the significant problems in general psychology, particularly within a stimulus-response framework. Two of these problems will be described briefly, along with some of the research that has been performed with children bearing on these issues.

First, there is the principle of stimulus generalization, which has been used in general behavior theory to explain, among others, such phenomena as the occurrence of sudden or insightful solutions of problems and the persistence of behavior that is not rewarded, or is even punished. One of the important variables assumed to affect the generali-

zation of a response is the number of reinforcements given on the training stimulus. Razran (1949) reports that the evidence from classical
conditioning with infrahuman and adult human subjects demonstrates
fairly conclusively that an increase in the number of reinforcements on
the training (conditioned) stimulus results in an increased amount of
generalization to the test stimuli. Spiker (1956a) has developed a simple
technique to extend these findings to the young child. The Ss, preschoolers,
were trained to pull a lever repeatedly to a stimulus of a given hue in
order to receive marbles. They were then tested on stimuli of different
hues to determine the number of responses that would be made to the
test stimuli without receiving reinforcement. A group given 24 reinforcements to the conditioned stimulus prior to the generalization tests averaged nearly twice as many responses to the test stimuli as did a group
given only 12 preliminary reinforcements. Thus, the same relationship
found to exist at the infrahuman and human adult levels was found to
apply to the preschool child. Spiker (1956b) in a later experiment found
that the steepness of the generalization gradient was also a positive
function of the number of reinforced training trials as well as the intensity
of the stimuli used in the training. In this experiment 60 Ss were given
differential reinforcement to a white (positive) and a blue (negative)
light. For one half the Ss, the positive stimulus was the brightest of four
stimuli differing from each other in brightness; for the other half, it was
the dimmest. One half of each of these groups was given 12 presentations and the other half was given 24 presentations of each of the positive
and negative stimuli. The response was again the repeated pulling of a
lever for marbles during a 3-second presentation of the conditioned stimulus, and the response measure was the number of such responses that
occurred during the 3-second periods. Immediately following training,
the Ss were tested, without reinforcement, on each of the four stimuli
differing in brightness. As was mentioned above, the findings were: (a)
a steeper gradient for the Ss who received the greater number of reinforced training trials, and (b) a steeper gradient for the bright-trained
than for the dim-trained Ss. These results are in agreement with the experiments by Grice and Saltz (1950) and by Brown (1942) at the infrahuman level, and with the prediction made by Hull (1952) on the
basis of the principle of stimulus dynamism.

The second principle from general psychology which has received
recent attention in child psychology is the principle of secondary or
mediated generalization, sometimes referred to as acquired equivalence
of cues. In brief, this principle states that if S had been trained to make
the same response to two or more dissimilar stimuli, there will be an
increased tendency to generalize to the other stimulus other responses
subsequently learned to one of the stimuli. In other words, if S is taught
to make response 1 to stimuli 1 and 2, then taught to make response 2 to

stimulus 1, he will make response 2 to stimulus 2. Jeffrey (1953) has demonstrated the role of mediating responses in generalization. He trained his Ss to move a lever, again a simple dependent variable, in one direction to a white stimulus, and in the opposite direction to a black stimulus. He then taught some Ss to call a gray stimulus "white" and others to call it "black," and next retrained the Ss on the lever moving task to the white and black stimuli. Following this, he presented the gray stimulus interspersed with black and white stimuli to determine how the Ss would respond to the gray stimulus. He found that, if the Ss had been taught to call the gray stimulus "white," they responded to it as they did it to the white stimulus; if they had been taught to call the gray stimulus "black," they responded to it as they did to the black stimulus. He found a similar tendency for another group of Ss who instead of using the names "black" and "white" had been taught to turn the handle to the right or the left for the white, black and gray stimuli. Thus, Jeffrey demonstrates that either verbal or motor responses may serve as mediating responses. Shepard (1954) and Eisman (1955), among others, have also recently demonstrated mediated generalization in young children.

The study of simple responses like the ones described in the experiments above may be made in more applied, pragmatic research with children. For example, in the important area of incentives in children's learning, the writer and Kennedy (1957) have recently shown that a candy reward results in quicker learning and more consistent transfer of a "larger-than" concept than either praise, reproof, a light flash, or a delayed reward. The only exception to this latter statement was the nonsignificant difference that existed in the consistency of transfer between the candy reward group and the group that was given a delayed reward. In this experiment the behavior studied was a simple button-pushing response to the larger of two three-dimensional geometric objects. The nonsignificant difference in the candy (immediate) and delayed reward group of the aforementioned study led the writer (1958) to perform an experiment comparing two types of delayed rewards with each other and with an immediate reward in the learning and transferring of a "larger-than" discrimination. It was hypothesized that Ss assigned to a delayed reward condition which permitted them to observe progress toward the to-be-received reward would learn more quickly and transfer more consistently than would Ss assigned to a delayed reward condition that did not allow them to observe their progress in the learning situation. This hypothesis was convincingly supported by the results of the experiment.

Now what advantages do the studies of simple behaviors in the experiments cited above have, other than their contributions to general psychology? As was stated previously, they are mainly methodological. First of all, when we study basic responses, the variables, both independent and dependent, are easier to manipulate. Compare, for example, the difficulties associated with isolating, controlling, and measuring complex child rearing and adjustment variables with the relative ease and rigor of control in (a) Jeffrey's study of the effects of simple verbal instructions, "say white" or "say black," on crank-turning responses, or (b) Spiker's experiment with the generalization of lever-pulling responses to lights of varying hues, intensities, and frequencies. Because of the more rigorous control exercised in the latter experiments, the experimenter minimizes the danger of masking the basic processes. That we can be less equivocal about interpreting the results of these experiments is obvious.

In most experiments the researcher has a choice in the matter of selecting responses to be studied. For example, Spiker may well have studied the principle of stimulus generalization within a more complex, clinical framework, by obtaining measures of generalization of responses of children from maladjusted teachers to peers or love interests, instead of studying the generalization of lever-pulling responses to lights of differing intensities and hues. Or again, the writer may have studied the effects of various incentives on the solution of higher mathematics problems, or on some of the more intricate aspects of social development in childhood. That we are all interested in the latter problems is a foregone conclusion. In fact, the critics of the writer's position will ask the question, "Of what practical value is it to investigate these simple, trivial behaviors? What we need to know, indeed what society is demanding of us now, is the solution of important practical problems in developmental psychology, such as the complex factors involved in learning and personality development." The writer's answer to this argument is that he believes that ultimately we will be able to supply answers to the complex, immediately relevant social problems associated with child psychology more quickly if we first systematize our knowledge of relationships existing at an elementary behavior level. By doing this we do not get ahead of our limited methodological resources, which has always been one of the greatest tendencies of researchers in child psychology. And what is even more important, we do not run the serious risk of misleading society.

Critics of this position will insist that the writer be more specific about *how* the study of relatively uncomplicated problems eventually will facilitate a rigorous, more fruitful investigation of such phenomena as are involved in complex learning or personality development. It is felt that not only will the current concern for basic research with children mean that we keep our investigations within the limits of our methodological resources, but it is also believed that, because of the above, basic research is likely to result in the discovery of variables relevant to complex human behavior. For example, the writer (1958) has found a strong indication that the speed with which a child learns a simple "larger-than" discrimination without a material reward depends upon a host of child rearing variables associated with social class membership, such as the importance to the middle class child of not appearing unintelligent. Had the relevance of this social class variable been suggested by an experiment involving more complex learning with less rigor of control, it appears reasonable to argue that one would place less confidence in its importance, even in complex learning situations. It is true that a variable related to the learning of a size discrimination may not be important in the learning of principles involved in the solution of quadratic equations, or the variables relevant to the generalization of responses from lights of one intensity to lights of other intensities may not be related to the generalization of responses from maladjusted parents to heterosexual relationships. There is some evidence, however, for contending that the likelihood of variables which are known to apply at a simple behavioral level to be relevant also at a more complex level is greater than the probability that variables suggested as relevant in complicated, poorly controlled studies are in fact relevant at that level. The evidence in support of this statement falls into two categories: (a) the applicability of principles discovered in animal research to more complex human behavior, and (b) the highly inconsistent findings of research in human behavior concerned with such complex phenomena as child rearing variables and their effects on personality development.

Rosenblum (1956) has found that the acquisition and extinction of "copying" responses by fourth and fifth graders are regulated by the same principles of partial reinforcement as found in animal experiments (Skinner, 1938). Kuenne (1946) reports that Spence's (1937) theory of transposition, formulated to account for animal behavior in a discrimination learning situation, also applies to the preverbal child. Consider also the highly controversial research involving the effects of socialization training on personality. Some studies show the techniques of feeding, weaning, and toileting to be related in a substantial way to security, the quality of adjustment, and other important personality traits (Goldman-Eisler, 1953; Holway, 1949; Maslow & Szilagyi-Kessler, 1946); whereas others show no relationship between these variables (Peterson & Spano, 1941; Sewell & Mussen, 1952; Thurston & Mussen, 1951). It is felt that the inconsistencies in these investigations are due, among other things, to false leads concerning relevant variables in socialization and personality that researchers get in focusing attention on problems of this degree of complexity.

The writer does not want to take the position that *all* research in complex human behavior is useless at the present stage of maturity of psychology. It must be acknowledged that some of this research is yielding reasonably consistent results, despite the difficulties discussed above. It is felt, however, that child psychology generally would benefit more by an increased concern on the part of many of us with understanding behavior in its more basic forms. Indeed, it is felt that the great preponderance of the research which is now being done at a more complicated level will have to be redone in the light of the results of the more basic research in child psychology.

## REFERENCES

Bijou, S. W. Patterns of reinforcement and resistance to extinction in young children. *Child Develpm.*, 1957, *28*, 47–54.

Brown, J. S. The generalization of approach responses as a function of stimulus intensity and strength of motivation. *J. comp. Psychol.*, 1942, *33*, 209–226.

Eisman, B. S. Attitude formation: the development of a color preference response through mediated generalization. *J. abnorm. soc. Psychol.*, 1955, *50*, 321–326.

Goldman-Eisler, F. Breast feeding and character formation. In C. Kluckhohn & H. A. Murray (Eds.), *Personality in nature, society and culture.* New York: Knopf, 1953. Pp. 146–184.

Grice, R. G., & Saltz, E. The generalization of an instrumental response to stimuli varying in the size dimension. *J. exp. Psychol.*, 1950, *40*, 702–708.

Hicks, J. A., & Stewart, F. D. The learning of abstract concepts of size. *Child Develpm.*, 1930, *1*, 195–203.

Holway, A. R. Early self-regulation of infants and later behavior in play interviews. *Amer. J. Orthopsychiat.*, 1949, *19*, 612–622.

Hull, C. L. *A behavior system.* New Haven: Yale, 1952.

Jeffrey, W. E. The effects of verbal and non-verbal responses in mediating an instrumental act. *J. exp. Psychol.*, 1953, *45*, 327–333.

Kuenne, M. R. Experimental investigation of transposition behavior in young children. *J. exp. Psychol.*, 1946, *36*, 471–490.

McCandless, B. R., & Spiker, C. C. Experimental research in child psychology. *Child Develpm.*, 1956, *27*, 75–80.

Maslow, A. H., & Szilagyi-Kessler, I. Security and breast feeding. *J. abnorm. soc. Psychol.*, 1946, *41*, 83–85.

Peterson, C. H., & Spano, F. Breast feeding, maternal rejection, and child personality. *J. Pers.*, 1941, *10*, 62–66.

Razran, G. Stimulus generalization of conditional responses. *Psychol. Bull.*, 1949, *46*, 337–365.

Rosenblum, S. The effects of differential reinforcement and motivation on prediction responses in children. *Child Develpm.*, 1956, *27*, 99–108.

Screven, C. G. The effects of interference on response strength. *J. comp. physiol. Psychol.*, 1954, *47*, 140–144.

Sewell, W. H., & Mussen, P. H. The effects of feeding, weaning, and scheduling procedures on childhood adjustment and the formation of oral symptoms. *Child Develpm.*, 1952, *23*, 185–191.

Shepard, W. O. The effects of verbal pretraining on discrimination learning in preschool children. Unpublished doctoral dissertation, State Univer. of Iowa, 1954.

Skinner, B. F. *The behavior of organisms.* New York: Appleton-Century-Crofts, 1938.

Spence, K. W. The differential response in animals to stimuli varying within a single dimension. *Psychol. Rev.,* 1937, *44,* 430–444.

Spiker, C. C. The effects of number of reinforcements on the strength of a generalized instrumental response. *Child Develpm.,* 1956, *27,* 37–44. (a)

Spiker, C. C. The stimulus generalization gradient as a function of the intensity of stimulus lights. *Child Develpm.,* 1956, *27,* 85–98. (b)

Terrell, G. The role of incentive in discrimination learning in children. *Child Develpm.,* 1958, *29,* 231–236.

Terrell, G., & Kennedy, W. A. Discrimination learning transposition in children as a function of the nature of the reward. *J. exp. Psychol.,* 1957, *53,* 257–260.

Thurston, J. R., & Mussen, P. H. Infant feeding gratification and adult personality. *J. Pers.,* 1951, *19,* 449–458.

# Applications

The difference between basic and applied research is a real one, but a minor one for this collection. The distinction is worth perhaps a difference in headings (Part 1 is Basic Principles and Concepts, Part II is Applications), but little else. Basic research usually means that some general question is being asked about behavior, and the experimenter will choose the most *convenient* research setting available to him to find an answer. He may place the subject in an artificial laboratory environment simply to insure that unwanted variations in the environment are avoided. He may choose a similarly artificial response, such as bar-pressing, simply because it is unequivocally operant, easy to perform and record, and simple to integrate with other experimental apparatus. And he may also choose subjects just because they are available (and presumably as good as any other subjects for the study). Applied research is likely to differ on these same dimensions of convenience. It may not be possible to take the subject to the highly controlled laboratory setting because the experimenter is asking a question about the behavior of children, say, in their classrooms, and he wants the answer to apply directly, not speculatively, to classroom behavior. Or the experimenter may not be able to use the easily integrated bar-pressing response because his question concerns, say, thumb-sucking, and he does not wish to assume that thumb-sucking and bar-pressing are essentially the same. Or the experimenter may not be able to use the readily available children, say, in the university's nursery school because his question concerns retardation, and he must have the answer from children who are retarded.

In short, one essential difference between basic and applied research is that applied research is more demanding, leaving the researcher fewer choices of research tactics. For that reason alone, when applied research is well done, it merits more admiration than basic research, because it was probably more difficult to perform. In addition, when applied studies show the same results as "basic" studies of the same process, not only has a scientific principle been shown to be more generally valid, but it may assist our society to move toward a solution of its many behavior problems. Thus, we suggest that the studies reported in this part of the book are no less "science" than those in Part I and are, at the same time, potentially useful social tools. Studies of this sort force us to consider their implications not only for the science of psychology but also for what we might do with them—or what someone else might do with them, perhaps to us.

# To Social Behavior

Man is one of the most thoroughly socialized organisms in all of the animal kingdom. Much of his development can be traced to interactions with the physical and organismic stimuli which comprise his environment; yet his society can and does intrude its controlling stimuli into even these interactions. We learn to walk largely under the control of the law of gravity and the painful consequences of falling on the hard surface of our world; but then we are taught by social means that some walks are more appropriate than others in certain settings. We learn, for example, to walk quietly when others are sleeping, to march in step for the Scouts, and to keep our feet off other people's toes. Similarly, we blink our eyelids for primarily organismic reasons, keeping the eyeball lubricated and clean. But we also learn to blink (wink) at others to signal amusement, a secret, or a discreet invitation.

Thus, in recognition of the importance of social control, our first area of application is to interactions created by and modifiable by the stimuli which other people provide to children.

# 13

# The Elimination of Tantrum Behavior by Extinction Procedures

*Carl D. Williams*

## EDITORS' COMMENTS

One situation promoting "spoiled" or "regressed" behavior in a young child is a period of illness requiring bed care. It is easy to understand how illness can lead to behavior problems. In carrying out the doctor's orders and in doing everything else possible to restore health, the parents typically give their child special care and attention. In most instances this means that a parent, usually the mother, has to be near the child almost constantly and is likely to respond promptly to practically every request. It also means that she has to engage in parent-child practices that will help the youngster make a rapid and complete recovery, e.g., give him or promise him things and activities that will keep him in bed, keep him covered, and have him follow prescribed medical procedures. Thus the typical sickbed regime contains a high saturation of social reinforcement in the form of adult proximity, attention, approval, and affection.

When the child is restored to health, it is natural that the mother will return to her normal household routines. With this shift back to normal living, many of the behaviors she reinforced in her child during illness are no longer reinforced. Such a change constitutes an extinguishing or chain-breaking procedure which leads to gradual weakening of the preceding behavior, and in many instances to the generation of "frustration" or "anger" behaviors. (See the introductory note preceding the Moore and Goldiamond paper.) If the specific component acts of "frustration" behavior (e.g., yelling, screaming, kicking) are given reinforcement by adult attention, such behaviors could be strengthened and become part of the child's operant repertoire. These "spoiled" forms of behavior are distasteful to the parent; even so, they are frequently reinforced, because "giv-

Carl D. Williams, "The Elimination of Tantrum Behavior by Extinction Procedures," *Journal of Abnormal and Social Psychology*, 1959, *59*, 269.

ing-in" stops the distasteful behavior—temporarily. Parental response to the child's "spoiled" behavior thus not only strengthens that behavior in the child but also strengthens the act of catering-to-the-child in the parent: the aversive stimulation produced by the child (e.g., yelling, screaming, and kicking) is terminated by the parent, thereby strengthening whatever behavior the parent employed to accomplish this feat.

This brief report by Williams is an account of a procedure used by parents to eliminate tantrum behavior evidently generated as an aftermath of a period of illness.

It is interesting to note the comment by Williams to the effect that when the tantrum behavior was weakened, no other undesirable behavior came to the fore. It is likely that he was reacting to the hypothesis that the removal of a "psychological symptom" by direct procedures leads to a substitute psychological "symptom." Apparently, he could not confirm that hypothesis in this case.

This paper reports the successful treatment of tyrant-like tantrum behavior in a male child by the removal of reinforcement. The subject (S) was approximately 21 months old. He had been seriously ill much of the first 18 months of his life. His health then improved considerably, and he gained weight and vigor.

S now demanded the special care and attention that had been given him over the many critical months. He enforced some of his wishes, especially at bedtime, by unleashing tantrum behavior to control the actions of his parents.

The parents and aunt took turns in putting him to bed both at night and for S's afternoon nap. If the parent left the bedroom after putting S in his bed, S would scream and fuss until the parent returned to the room. As a result, the parent was unable to leave the bedroom until after S went to sleep. If the parent began to read while in the bedroom, S would cry until the reading material was put down. The parents felt that S enjoyed his control over them and that he fought off going to sleep as long as he could. In any event, a parent was spending from one-half to two hours each bedtime just waiting in the bedroom until S went to sleep.

Following medical reassurance regarding S's physical condition, it was decided to remove the reinforcement of this tyrant-like tantrum behavior. Consistent with the learning principle that, in general, behavior that is not reinforced will be extinguished, a parent or the aunt put S to bed in a leisurely and relaxed fashion. After bedtime pleasantries, the parent left the bedroom and closed the door. S screamed and raged, but the parent did not re-enter the room. The duration of screaming and crying was obtained from the time the door was closed.

The results are shown in Figure 1. It can be seen that S continued screaming for 45 min. the first time he was put to bed in the first extinction series. S did not cry at all the second time he was put to bed. This is perhaps attributable to his fatigue from the crying of Occasion 1. By the tenth occasion, S no longer whimpered, or cried when the parent left the room. Rather, he smiled as they left. The parents felt that he made happy sounds until he dropped off to sleep.

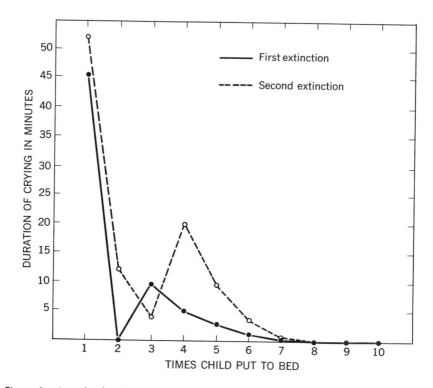

Figure 1. Length of crying in two extinction series as a function of successive occasions of being put to bed

About a week later, S screamed and fussed after the aunt put him to bed, probably reflecting spontaneous recovery of the tantrum behavior. The aunt then reinforced the tantrum behavior by returning to S's bedroom and remaining there until he went to sleep. It was then necessary to extinguish his behavior a second time.

Figure 1 shows that the second extinction curve is similar to the first. Both curves are generally similar to extinction curves obtained with subhuman subjects. The second extinction series reached zero by the ninth occasion. No further tantrums at bedtime were reported during the next two years.

It should be emphasized that the treatment in this case did not involve aversive punishment. All that was done was to remove the reinforcement. Extinction of the tyrant-like tantrum behavior then occurred.

No unfortunate side or aftereffects of this treatment were observed. At three and three-quarters years of age, S appeared to be a friendly, expressive, outgoing child.

# 14

# Effects of Adult Social Reinforcement on Child Behavior

*Florence R. Harris, Montrose M. Wolf, and Donald M. Baer*

## EDITORS' COMMENTS

Carl Williams, in the preceding brief paper, has shown us how the rudiments of social control may operate in the home for as everyday a problem as mild tantrum behavior. The next article extends this demonstration along a number of dimensions. It centers on the nursery school setting, an increasingly common preschool experience for American children (especially since the advent of Headstart programs across the nation). It adds applications of positive reinforcement procedures and utilizes the extinction procedure described in the William's study. It deals with a range of potential problem behaviors in young children: regressed crawling, inadequate social interaction with peers, passivity, and excessive crying and whining. (Later studies of the same type extended the application of these techniques in the same kind of settings to the modification of aggression, excessive fantasy play, fear of climbing, restricted playmate choice, underdeveloped speech, hyperactivity, nastiness to peers, and baby-like behaviors.) And, finally, the study involves a professional, the nursery school teacher, part of whose job is the dispensing of social reinforcers to young children to further many aspects of their behavioral development. As might be expected, this series of investigations led to revisions of the staff's previous practices in carrying out their program of nursery school guidance.

Florence R. Harris, Montrose M. Wolf, and Donald M. Baer, "Effects of Adult Social Reinforcement on Child Behavior." Reprinted from Vol. 20, No. 1, *Young Children*, 1964.

These studies were supported in part by research grants from the National Institute of Mental Health (MH-02208-07) and the University of Washington Graduate School Research Fund (11-1873).

The authors are also indebted to Sidney W. Bijou for his generous counsel and assistance.

It may be instructive to note the method of investigation employed in these studies and compare it with laboratory studies such as by Azrin and Lindsley, and Moore and Goldiamond. The method might also be compared to other field studies such as by R. G. Barker and H. F. Wright on the total behavior of one boy for a day,[1] and by Faigan on the social behavior of young children in the Kibbutz.[2]

There is general agreement among educators that one of the primary functions of a nursery school is to foster in each child social behaviors that contribute toward more pleasant and productive living for all. However, there is no similar consensus of opinion as to precisely how this objective is to be attained. Many writers subscribe to practices based on a combination of psychoanalytic theory and client-centered therapy principles, usually referred to as a mental hygiene approach. Yet there is considerable variation and vagueness in procedures recommended, particularly those dealing with such problem behaviors as the child's hitting people, breaking valuable things, or withdrawing from both people and things. Read (1955), for example, recommends accepting the child's feelings, verbalizing them for him, and draining them off through vigorous activities. Landreth (1942) advises keeping adult contacts with the child at a minimum based on his needs, backing up verbal suggestions by an implicit assumption that the suggestion will be carried out and, when in doubt, doing nothing unless the child's physical safety is involved. In addition to some of the above precepts, Taylor (1954) counsels parents and teachers to support both desirable and undesirable behaviors and to give non-emotional punishment. According to Standing (1959), Montessori advocates that teachers pursue a process of non-intervention, following careful preparation of a specified environment aimed at "canalizing the energy" and developing "inner command." Non-intervention does not preclude the "minimum dose" of instruction and correction.

Using some combination of such guidance precepts, teachers have reported success in helping some nursery school children who showed problem behaviors; but sometimes adherence to the same teaching principles has not been helpful in modifying the behavior of concern. Indeed, it was usually not at all clear what conditions and principles may or may not have been operative. All of these precepts have in common the adult behaviors of approaching and attending to a child. Therefore, it seemed to the staff of the Laboratory Preschool at the University of Washington that a first step in developing possible explicit criteria for judging

[1] *One Boy's Day,* New York: Harper & Row, 1951.
[2] Helen Faigan, "Social Behavior of Young Children in the *Kibbutz,*" *J. abnorm. soc. Psychol.,* 1958, *56,* 117–129.

when and when not to attend was to study the precise effects that adult attention can have on some problem behaviors.

This paper presents an account of the procedures and results of five such studies. Two groups of normal nursery school children provided the subjects studied. One group enrolled 12 three-year-olds and the other, 16 four-year-olds. The two teachers of the younger group and the three teachers of the older group conducted the studies as they carried out their regular teaching duties. The general methodology of these studies was developed in the course of dealing with a particularly pressing problem behavior, shown by one child at the beginning of the school year. It is worth considering this case before describing the procedures which evolved from it.

The study dealt with a three-year-old girl who had regressed to an excessive amount of crawling (Harris, Johnston, Kelley, & Wolf, 1964). By "excessive" is meant that after three weeks of school she was spending most of her morning crawling or in a crouched position with her face hidden. The parents reported that for some months the behavior had been occurring whenever they took her to visit or when friends came to their home. The teachers had used the conventional techniques, as outlined above, for building the child's "security."

Observations recorded in the third week at school showed, however, that more than 80% of the child's time was spent in off-feet positions. The records also showed that the crawling behavior frequently drew the attention of teachers. On-feet behaviors, such as standing and walking, which occurred infrequently, seldom drew such notice.

A program was instituted in which the teachers no longer attended to the child whenever she was crawling or crouching, but gave her continuous warm attention as long as she was engaging in behavior in which she was standing, running, or walking. Initially the only upright behaviors that the teachers were able to attend to occurred when the child pulled herself almost to her feet in order to hang up or take down her coat from her locker, and when she pulled herself up to wash her hands in the wash basin. Within a week of the initiation of the new attention-giving procedure, the child acquired a close-to-normal pattern of on-feet behavior.

In order to see whether the change from off- to on-feet behavior was related to the differential attention given by the teachers, they reversed their procedure, making attention once again contingent only upon crawling and other off-feet behavior. They waited for occasions of such off-feet behavior to "reinforce" with attention, while not attending to any on-feet behavior. By the second day the child had reverted to her old pattern of play and locomotion. The observational records showed the child was off her feet 80% of the class session.

To see whether on-feet behavior could be re-established, the teachers again reversed their procedure, giving attention to the child only when she was engaging in behaviors involving upright positions. On-feet behavior rose markedly during the first session. By the fourth day, the child again spent about 62% of the time on her feet.

Once the child was not spending the greater portion of her day crawling about, she quickly became a well-integrated member of the group. Evidently she already had well-developed social play skills.

As a result of this demonstration that either walking or crawling could be maintained and that the child's responses depended largely upon the teachers' attending behaviors, the teachers began a series of further experimental analyses of the relationship between teacher attention and nursery school child behavior.

## PROCEDURES

A specified set of procedures common to the next studies was followed. First, a child showing problem behavior was selected and records were secured. An observer recorded all of the child's behavior, the environmental conditions under which it occurred, and its immediate consequences under conventional teacher guidance. This was done throughout the 2½-hour school session, daily, and for several days. The records gave detailed pictures of the behavior under study. In each case, it became apparent that the problem behavior almost always succeeded in attracting adult attention.

As soon as these records, technically termed "baseline" records, of the typical behavior of the child and teachers were obtained, teachers instituted a program of systematically giving differential attention to the child. When the undesired behavior occurred, they did not in any way attend to him but remained absorbed in one of the many necessary activities of teachers with other children or with equipment. If the behavior occurred while a teacher was attending to the child, she at once turned to another child or task in a matter-of-fact and nonrejecting manner. Concurrently, teachers gave immediate attention to other behaviors of the child which were considered to be more desirable than the problem behavior. The net effect of these procedures was that the child could gain a great deal of adult attention if he refrained from engaging in "problem behavior." If under this regime of differential attention the problem behavior diminished to a stable low level at which it was no longer considered a problem, a second procedure was inaugurated to check out the functional relationship between changes in the child's behavior and the guidance procedures followed.

The second procedure was simply to reverse the first procedure. That is, when the problem behavior occurred, the teacher went immediately to the child and gave him her full, solicitous attention. If the behavior stopped, she turned to other children and tasks, remaining thus occupied until the behavior recurred. In effect, one sure way for the child to secure adult attention was to exhibit the problem behavior. This procedure was used to secure reasonably reliable information on whether the teachers' special program had indeed brought about the changes noted in the child's behavior. If adult attention was the critical factor in maintaining the behavior, the problem behavior should recur in stable form under these conditions. If it did so, this was evidence that adult attention was, technically speaking, a positive social reinforcer for the child's behavior.

The final stage of a study was, of course, to return to procedures in which attention was given at once and continuously for behaviors considered desirable. Concurrently, adult attention was again withheld or withdrawn as an immediate consequence of the problem behavior. As the problem disappeared and appropriate behaviors increased, the intense program of differential adult attention was gradually diminished until the child was receiving attention at times and in amounts normal for the teachers in the group. However, attention was given only on occasions of desirable behavior, and never (or very seldom) for the undesirable behavior.

## CRYING AND WHINING

Following the above procedures, a study was conducted on a four-year-old boy who cried a great deal after mild frustrations (Hart, Allen, Buell, Harris, & Wolf, 1964). This child averaged about eight full-fledged crying episodes each school morning. The baseline observations showed that this crying behavior consistently brought attention from the teachers, in the form of going to him and showing solicitous concern. During the following days, this behavior was simply ignored. (The only exceptions to this were to have been incidents in which the child had hurt himself considerably and was judged to have genuine grounds for crying. Naturally, his hurts were to be attended to. Such incidents, however, did not occur.) Ten days of ignoring the outcries, but giving approving attention for verbal and self-help behaviors, produced a steady weakening of the crying response to a nearly zero level. In the final five days of the interval, only one crying response was recorded. The number of crying episodes on successive days is graphed in cumulative form in Figure 1.

During the next ten days, crying was again reinforced whenever it occurred, the teachers attending to the boy on these occasions without fail. At first, it was necessary to give attention for mere grimaces that might follow a bump. The daily crying episodes quickly rose to a rate almost as high as formerly. A second ten-day period of ignoring the out-cries again produced a quick weakening of the response to a near-zero level, as is apparent in the figure. Crying remained at this low level there-after, according to the informal judgment of the teachers.

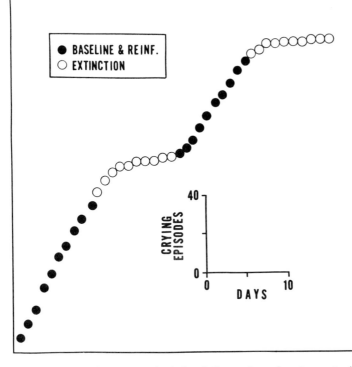

Figure 1.  Cumulative record of the daily number of crying episodes

The same procedures were used in another study of "operant crying" of a four-year-old boy, with the same general results.

## ISOLATE PLAY

Two studies involved children who exhibited markedly solitary play behavior. Extremely little of their morning at nursery school was spent in any interaction with other children. Instead, these children typically played alone in a quiet area of the school room or the play yard, or interacted only with the teachers. For present purposes, both of these response patterns will be called "isolate play." Systematic observation showed that isolate play usually attracted or maintained the attention of a teacher, whereas social play with other children did so comparatively seldom.

A plan was initiated in which the teacher was to attend regularly if the child approached other children and interacted with them. On the other hand, the teacher was not to attend to the child so long as he engaged in solitary play. To begin with, attention was given when the child merely stood nearby, watching other children; then when he played beside another child; and finally, only when he interacted with the other child. Teachers had to take special precautions that their attending behaviors did not result in drawing the child away from children and into interaction solely with the teacher. Two techniques were found particularly effective. The teacher directed her looks and comments to the other child or children, including the subject only as a participant in the play project. For example, "That's a big building you three boys are making; Bill and Tom and Jim (subject) are all working hard." Accessory materials were also kept at hand so that the teacher could bring a relevant item for the subject to add to the play: "Here's another plate for your tea party, Ann." In both isolate cases this new routine for giving adult attention produced the desired result: isolate play declined markedly in strength while social play increased two or three fold.

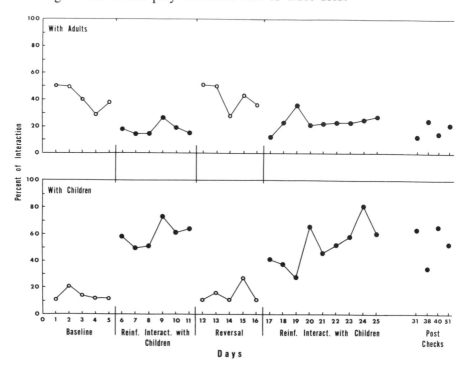

Figure 2.   Daily percentages of time spent in social interaction with adults and with children during approximately two hours of each morning session

After about a week of the above procedure, the consequences of non-isolate and isolate play were reversed. The teachers no longer attended to the child's interactions with other children, but instead gave continuous attention to the child when he was alone. Within a week, or less, isolate play became the dominant form of activity in both cases.

The former contingencies were then reinstated: the teachers attended to social interactions by the child, and ignored isolate play as completely as they could. Again, isolate play declined sharply while social interaction increased as before. The results of one of these studies (Allen, Hart, Buell, Harris, & Wolf, 1964) are summarized in Figure 2.

Figure 2 shows the changes in behavior of a 4½-year-old girl under the different guidance conditions. The graph shows the percentage of play time that she spent in interaction with other children and the percentage of time spent with an adult. The remainder of her time was spent alone. It is apparent that only about 15% of this child's play time was spent in social play as long as the teachers attended primarily to her solitary play. But interacting behaviors rose to about 60% of total play time when the teachers attended only to her social play. At the same time, her interactions solely with teachers, not being reinforced, fell from their usual 40% of the child's play time to about 20%. These were considered reasonable percentages for this nursery school child. During Days 17 through 25 the schedule of adult reinforcement of social play was gradually reduced to the usual amount of attention, given at the usual irregular intervals. Nevertheless, the social behavior maintained its strength, evidently becoming largely self-maintaining.

After Day 25, the teachers took care not to attend too often to the child when she was alone, but otherwise planned no special contingencies for attending. Four checks were made at later dates to see if the pattern of social behavior persisted. It is apparent (Figure 2, Post Checks) that the change was durable, at least until Day 51. Further checks were not possible because of the termination of the school year.

A parallel study, of a three-year-old isolate boy (Johnston, Kelley, Harris, Wolf, & Baer, 1964) yielded similar results showing the same pattern of rapid behavioral change in response to changing contingencies for adult attention. In the case of this boy, post-checks were made on three days during the early months of the school year following the summer vacation period. The data showed that on those days his interaction with children averaged 55% of his play time. Apparently his social play was well established. Teachers reported that throughout the remainder of the year he continued to develop ease and skills in playing with his peers.

The immediate shifts in these children's play behavior may be partly due to the fact that they had already developed skills readily adapted to play with peers at school. Similar studies in progress are showing that, for some children, development of social play behaviors may require much longer periods of reinforcement.

## EXCESSIVE PASSIVITY

A fifth case (Johnston, Kelley, Harris, & Wolf, 1966) involved a boy noted for his thorough-going lack of any sort of vigorous play activity. The teachers reported that this child consistently stood quietly about the play yard while other children ran, rode tricycles, and climbed on special climbing frames, trees, fences, and playhouses. Teachers also reported that they frequently attempted to encourage him, through suggestions or invitations, to engage in the more vigorous forms of play available. Teachers expressed concern over his apparent lack of strength and motor skills. It was decided to select a particular form of active play to attempt to strengthen. A wooden frame with ladders and platforms, called a climbing frame, was chosen as the vehicle for establishing this activity. The teachers attended at first to the child's mere proximity to the frame. As he came closer, they progressed to attending only to his touching it, climbing up a little, and finally to extensive climbing. Technically, this was reinforcement of successive approximations to climbing behavior. Figure 3 shows the results of nine days of this pro-

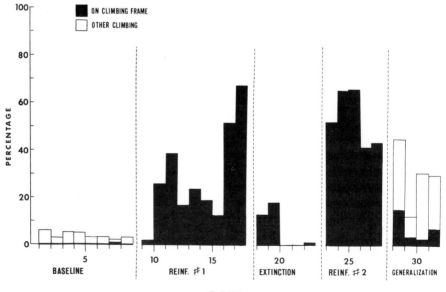

Figure 3.   Daily percentages of time spent in using a climbing-frame apparatus. Open bars indicate time spent in climbing on other equipment.

cedure, compared to a baseline of the preceding nine days. In this figure, black bars represent climbing on the climbing frame, and white bars represent climbing on any other equipment in the play yard. The height of the bars shows the percentage of the child's play time spent in such activities. It is clear that during the baseline period less than 10% of the child's time was spent in any sort of climbing activity, but that during the course of reinforcement with pleased adult attention for climbing on the frame, this behavior greatly increased, finally exceeding 50% of the child's morning. (Climbing on other objects was not scored during this period.) There then followed five days during which the teachers ignored any climbing on the frame, but attended to all other appropriate activities. The rate of climbing on the frame promptly fell virtually to zero, though the child climbed on other apparatus and was consistently given attention for this. Another five days of reinforcement of use of the climbing frame immediately restored the climbing-frame behavior to a high stable level, always in excess of 40% of the boy's play time. After this, the teachers began an intermittent program of reinforcement for climbing on any other suitable objects, as well as vigorous active play of all sorts, in an effort to generalize the increased vigorous activity. Frame-climbing weakened considerably, being largely replaced by other climbing activities, which were now scored again as data. Activities such as tricycle-riding and running were not systematically recorded due to difficulties in reliably scoring them. It is clear from the data obtained, however, that climbing activities were thoroughly generalized by this final procedure. Checks made the following school year in another play yard indicated that vigorous climbing had become a stable part of his behavior repertoire.

## SUMMARY AND DISCUSSION

The above studies systematically examined effects of adult attention on some problem behaviors of normal preschool children. The findings in each case clearly indicated that for these children adult attention was a strong positive reinforcer. That is, the behavior which was immediately followed by a teacher's giving the child attention rose rapidly to a high rate, and the rate fell markedly when adult attention was withheld from that behavior and concurrently given to an incompatible behavior. While it seems reasonable that for most young children adult attention may be a positive reinforcer, it is also conceivable that for some children adult attention may be a negative reinforcer. That is, the rate of a behavior may decrease when it is immediately followed by the attention of an adult, and rise again as soon as the adult withdraws. Actually, for a few children observed at the preschool, it has been thought that adult attention was a negative reinforcer. This seemed to be true, for instance, in the case of the climbing-frame child. Before the study was initiated, the teachers spent several weeks attempting to make themselves positively reinforcing to the child. This they did by staying at a little distance from him and avoiding attending directly to him until he came to them for something. At first, his approaches were only for routine help, such as buttoning his coat. On each of these occasions they took care to be smilingly friendly and helpful. In time, he began making approaches of other kinds; for instance, to show a toy. Finally, when a teacher approached him and commented with interest on what he was doing, he continued his play instead of stopping, hitting out, or running off. However, since his play remained lethargic and sedentary, it was decided that special measures were necessary to help him progress more rapidly. It was the use and effects of these special measures that constituted the study. Clearly, however, adult attention must be or become positively reinforcing to a child before it can be successfully used to help him achieve more desirably effective behaviors.

Studies such as those reported here seem to imply that teachers may help many children rapidly through systematic programming of their adult social reinforcements. However, further research in this area seems necessary. Some of our own studies now in progress suggest that guidance on the basis of reinforcement principles may perhaps bring rapidly into use only behaviors which are already available within the repertory of the child. If the desired behavior requires skills not yet in the child's repertory, then the process of developing those skills from such behaviors as the child has may require weeks or months. For example, a four-year-old child who could verbalize but who very rarely spoke was helped to speak freely within several days. On the other hand, a child of the same age who had never verbalized required a lengthy shaping process that involved reinforcing first any vocalization, and then gradually more appropriate sounds and combinations of sounds. The latter study was still incomplete at the close of a year of work. The time required to develop social behaviors in isolate children has likewise varied considerably, presumably for the same reasons.

Although the teachers conducted these studies in the course of carrying out their regular teaching duties, personnel in excess of the usual number were necessary. The laboratory school was staffed with one teacher to no more than six children, making it possible to assign one teacher the role of principal "reinforcer teacher" in a study. This teacher was responsible for giving the child immediate attention whenever he behaved in specified ways. In addition, observers were hired and trained to record the behavior of each child studied. Each observer kept a record in ten-second intervals of his subject's behavior throughout each morning at school. Only with such staffing could reinforcement contingencies be precisely and consistently administered and their effects recorded.

Unless the effects are recorded, it is easy to make incorrect judgments about them. Two instances illustrate such fallibility. A boy in the laboratory preschool frequently pinched adults. Attempts by the teachers to ignore the behavior proved ineffective, since the pinches were hard enough to produce at least an involuntary startle. Teachers next decided to try to develop a substitute behavior. They selected patting as a logical substitute. Whenever the child reached toward a teacher, she attempted to forestall a pinch by saying, "Pat, Davey," sometimes adding, "Not pinch," and then strongly approving his patting, when it occurred. Patting behavior increased rapidly to a high level. The teachers agreed that they had indeed succeeded in reducing the pinching behavior through substituting patting. Then they were shown the recorded data. It showed clearly that although patting behavior was indeed high, pinching behavior continued at the previous level. Apparently, the teachers were so focused on the rise in patting behavior that, without the objective data, they would have erroneously concluded that development of a substitute behavior was in this case a successful technique. A second example illustrates a different, but equally undersirable kind of erroneous assumption. A preschool child who had to wear glasses (Wolf, Risley, & Mees, 1964) developed a pattern of throwing them two or three times per day. Since this proved expensive, it was decided that the attendants should put him in his room for ten minutes following each glasses-throw. When the attendants were asked a few days later how the procedure was working, they said that the glasses-throwing had not diminished at all. A check of the records, however, showed that there was actually a marked decrease. The throwing dropped to zero within five days. Presumably, the additional effort involved in carrying out the procedure had given the attendants an exaggerated impression of the rate of the behavior. Recorded data, therefore, seem essential to accurate objective assessments of what has occurred.

The findings in the studies presented here accord generally with results of laboratory research on social development, reviewed in this journal by Horowitz (1963). The importance of social reinforcement was also noted by Bandura (1963) in his investigations of imitation. Gallwey (1964) has replicated the study of an isolate child discussed here, with results "clearly confirmatory of the effectiveness of the technique." Further studies in school situations that can combine the function of research with that of service seem highly desirable.

## REFERENCES

Allen, K. Eileen, Hart, Betty M., Buell, Joan S., Harris, Florence R., & Wolf, M. M. Effects of social reinforcement on isolate behavior of a nursery school child. *Child Develpm.*, 1964, *35*, 511–518.

Bandura, Albert. The role of imitation in personality development. *J. Nursery Educ.*, 1963, *18*, 207–215.

Gallwey, Mary, Director of the Nursery School, Washington State University, Pullman, Wash., 1964. Personal communication.

Harris, Florence R., Johnston, Margaret K., Kelley, C. Susan, & Wolf, M. M. Effects of positive social reinforcement on regressed crawling of a nursery school child. *J. educ. Psychol.*, 1964, *55*, 35–41.

Hart, Betty M., Allen, K. Eileen, Buell, Joan S., Harris, Florence R., & Wolf, M. M. Effects of social reinforcement on operant crying. *J. exp. child Psychol.*, 1964, *1*, 145–153.

Horowitz, Frances Degen. Social reinforcement effects on child behavior. *J. Nursery Educ.*, 1963, *18*, 276–284.

Johnston, Margaret K., Kelley, C. Susan, Harris, Florence R., Wolf, M. M., & Baer, D. M. Effects of positive social reinforcement on isolate behavior of a nursery school child. 1964. Unpublished manuscript.

Johnston, Margaret K., Kelley, C. Susan, Harris, Florence R., & Wolf, M. M. An application of reinforcement principles to development of motor skills of a young child. *Child Develpm.*, 1966, *37*, 379–387.

Landreth, Catherine. *Education of the young child.* New York: Wiley, 1942.

Read, Katherine H. *The nursery school.* (2nd ed.) Philadelphia: Saunders, 1955.

Standing, E. M. *Maria Montessori, her life and work.* Fresno: American Library Guild, 1959.

Taylor, Katherine W. *Parent cooperative nursery schools.* New York: Teachers College, 1954.

Wolf, M. M., Risley, T. R., & Mees, H. L. Application of operant conditioning procedures to the behavior problems of an autistic child. *Behav. Res. Ther.*, 1964, *1*, 305–312.

# To Deviant Behavior

There is no need for an explanation of a section devoted to applications to deviant development. Instead, we point with some pleasure to the range of readings available for this section. The functional analysis of child development has come a long way indeed, and must be a healthy and viable undertaking, if, so few years after Keller's prophecy, we may reprint studies of effective work ranging from autism through self-destructive behavior to rehabilitation problems, and including the training of parents to produce and continue therapeutic modification of their children's behaviors.

# 15

# A Method for the Experimental Analysis
# of the Behavior of Autistic Children

## C. B. Ferster and Marian K. DeMyer

### EDITORS' COMMENTS

The following is an account of a pioneering study which applied
operant principles to modify the behavior of extremely disturbed
young children. The children in this investigation showed a far
greater degree of maladjustment than those reported by Williams
and by Harris, Wolf, and Baer. They are referred to as autistic
children. Autism is a psychiatric diagnosis which has created a great
deal of controversy with respect to its definition and its symptoms,
its subtypes, and its relationships to other categories such as childhood schizophrenia. Of this disturbance, Rimland writes:

> Two decades have passed since Kanner (1943) published his classic
> paper describing the paradoxical and bewildering disturbance of
> behavior in children which he called "early infantile autism." The
> presence of the disturbance in early infancy, the strange pattern
> of motor and language behavior which is reproduced with incred-
> ible accuracy in case after case, the occurrence in the same child
> of behavior typical of both genius and idiocy, and the complete
> absence of any evidence of physical or neurological defect have
> led many investigators to consider early infantile autism the most
> baffling of the behavior disorders.[1]

The reader who wishes to learn more about early infantile emotional disturbances should start with Rimland's *Infantile Autism*
and with the following study by Ferster and DeMyer. One may gain
a great deal from this report without being concerned about the
"autism" label ascribed to the children in this study or the vague-

Charles B. Ferster and Marian K. DeMyer, "A Method for the Experimental Analysis of the Behavior of Autistic Children," *American Journal of Ortho-
psychiatry,* 1962, *32*(1), 89–98. Copyright, the American Orthopsychiatric Association, Inc. Reproduced by permission.
[1] Bernard Rimland, *Infantile Autism,* New York: Appleton-Century-Crofts,
1964, p. 1.

ness of its meaning. The important fact is that these are among the most disturbed children who come to the attention of clinics and hospitals, and these investigators (Ferster being an experimental psychologist and DeMyer a research psychiatrist) were among the first to attempt to modify such behavior by applying principles derived mainly from experimental studies with infrahuman subjects.

Until this study was reported, the analysis and treatment of severely disturbed children was based on psychotherapeutic procedures derived from psychoanalytic theory. Since this report, other behaviorally oriented investigators have applied learning principles to such severely disturbed children. Examples are reported in the next three studies by Wolf, Risley, and Mees; Risley and Wolf; and Lovaas, Freitag, Gold, and Kassorla.

A prominent feature of the autistic child's repertoire is a narrow range of activity and a small amount of behavior controlled by its effect on the environment. Whatever the causes or antecedent conditions of the narrow range of the autistic child's activities, it might be possible to deal with them experimentally by building a new behavioral repertoire beginning with activities already in the child's repertoire, finding a method of sustaining them, and then gradually widening their range. This paper describes such a method.

The general framework of the experiment is that of operant reinforcement (Ferster, 1958; Skinner, 1953). The focus of the experimental method is on the consequence of the behavior as the factor which maintains it. Reinforcement is the major concept and refers to a technique for increasing the frequency of an activity by following it with a special consequence. The organism acts and the subsequent frequency of this activity increases because of the past effect on the environment. In this experiment simple performances of the autistic children are experimentally developed and maintained because of the specific effects they have on the child's environment. As a result, the behavior being studied is, at least potentially, under close and manipulative control by the experimenter. These methods have been in wide use in the study of animal behavior, where they have provided a behavioral technology in respect to phylogenetically general behavioral processes. Experiments using the techniques of operant reinforcement with normal and feebleminded and psychotic children have already demonstrated the feasibility of the technical application and the generality of some behavioral processes (Azrin & Lindsley, 1956; Bijou, 1958a; Bijou, 1958b; Lindsley, 1954; Long, Hammack, May, & Campbell, 1958). In general, the paradigm of these experiments has been to select a simple response such as pressing an electrical switch (key) and sustaining it by arranging some consequence relevant to the particular organism's repertoire and its current level of deprivation. The reinforcers used have included trinkets with nursery school children (Bijou); pennies with grade school children (Azrin); and candy with feebleminded and psychotic children (Lindsley and Azrin). In many of these experiments, the authors report large satiation effects, inability to sustain the performance of every subject, necessity of using brief experimental sessions and frequently weak performances, all presumably arising from a reinforcer than is not sufficiently durable.

## SUBJECTS

Three subjects have been studied in the experiment. Thomas, aged 10 and hospitalized 3 years, has been studied for 12 months. He had a normal motor and speech development, speaking short sentences until he was 2½, when he developed severe rage reactions, wandering away from home, gradual loss of speech, and excessive reaction to changes in his daily routine, and withdrawing to a corner where he would remain for weeks. The second child, Margie, 11 years old and hospitalized 4 years, had been studied for 6 months. Margie has a slower than normal motor development. The parents cannot recall with sureness any motor development milestones except her walking at 19 months. Her speech was definitely advanced, beginning before her first birthday and proceeding quickly to well-formed sentences with good diction. Speech began regressing when she was 3 years old, gradually dropping off until she was mute. When speech was regained, it was not used socially but as a means of entertaining herself. At 3 years she was cutting with scissors but lost this skill, lost bowel and bladder training, and control over her affect. She has never developed any peer relationships. Patrick, the third child, aged 3½, was hospitalized 14 months. He has been studied for 4 months. In his first year he showed normal motor development but abnormal emotional development. He didn't like to be held by his mother, would not look her in the eye, would not respond to his name, and shunned the approaches of his sibling. Changes in routine brought rage reactions. He has never developed speech.

Each of these three children shows the common characteristics of an extremely narrow range of behavioral repertoire, disorders in speech ranging from muteness to atypical speech with reversal of pronouns and echolalia, lack of control or capricious control over affectual expressing, and rage reactions with a change in routine. The boys have good physical development with no detectable neurological damage. Margie had a congenital breast tumor removed by radium shortly after birth and has a reduplicated left kidney and ureter. However, she has excellent fine neuromuscular coordination and a negative neurological examination. All three children have normal electroencephalograms. Tommy and Margie had severe emotional traumata in their first three years of life, living in homes where the mothers were depressed, the parents in extreme discord, and their handling of the children inconsistent. Patrick's home situation was much better.

All three children are part of a special therapeutic program for autistic children in a children's psychiatric hospital unit.

## SPECIFIC FRAMEWORK OF THIS EXPERIMENT

The present experiment extends the work in this field by developing techniques for achieving a more durable reinforcer as well as methods for generating more complex activities. The two goals—developing a strong reinforcer and a complex repertoire—are closely interrelated. To develop complex forms of behavior it is necessary to have a durable reinforcer because of the intermittent reinforcement inevitably occurring whenever complex performances are developed. The ability of a given environmental consequence (reinforcer) to sustain an activity declines as the behavior is less and less frequently reinforced. As the reinforcement becomes more infrequent a durable reinforcer is necessary to continue to sustain the activity. A reinforcer able to sustain an activity when each response is reinforced might prove to be a very weak reinforcer when only occasional responses are reinforced. Such a weakening of behavior by infrequent reinforcement might occur when we attempt to bring a given activity under the control of a specific stimulus; for example, when we follow the key press of the child with food only in a green light and allow key presses to go unreinforced in the red light. During the early stages of training, before the colors come to control the child's behavior, the child emits many responses (in the red light) which go unreinforced and which may produce a cessation of responding.

In general, it is difficult to determine the durability of a reinforcer unless the behavior is maintained by intermittent reinforcement. Activities which have a high frequency of reinforcement will often be normally sustained even with weak reinforcers. Performances sustained under intermittent reinforcement, however, provide baselines which emphasize the frequency of occurrence of the activity as datum and give a continuous measurement of the strength of the behavior and the durability of the reinforcer. Under most conditions a response occurs less frequently as its frequency of reinforcement becomes less. An intermittently reinforced baseline also minimizes satiation effects, permitting longer sessions in which to experiment with the performances.

As a first stage in the experiment we therefore maintained performances of the children under intermittent reinforcement to provide a baseline for evaluating and developing durable reinforcers. If we could sustain the child's performance under intermittent reinforcement, then we would have achieved a reinforcer which could also maintain the child's activity during the development of complex behavior.

## EXPERIMENTAL TECHNIQUE

The experimental room contains a large number of devices which when operated either by a coin or direct key provide some rewarding consequence for the child. These devices include: a pinball machine; a pigeon and trained monkey both trained to perform only when the animals' compartments are lighted; a color wheel giving a kaleidoscopic effect; a television set; a phonograph; an electric train whose speed and direction the child can vary; an eight-column candy vending machine with a separate light and coin slot in each column so that the child can choose the particular candy; a second vending machine which can deliver small trinkets or small packages containing parts of the child's lunch (both the trinkets and the food were varied from day to day and from subject to subject depending upon the subject's preference); a telephone handset with music through the earpiece; an electric organ, and a 35 mm. slide viewer. Figure 1 is a schematized drawing of the experimental room. The room contains a one-way vision screen on the wall facing the experimental devices.

During the first phase of the experiment we measured the frequency with which the subject pressed a key. This activity was sustained because it delivered a coin (from an automatic coin dispenser) which, in turn, could be used to operate any of the reinforcing devices in the room. The major advantage of the generalized reinforcer, aside from the possibility of the summation of reinforcing effects, is the wide variety of devices contributing to the reinforcing effect of the coin to ensure that at least one of the reinforcing devices would be relevant to the current deprivation condition of the child. We do not know whether coins derive their reinforcing effect from a sum of the various uses of the coins or from the device currently relevant to the child's deprivation. The hospitalized subjects were deprived of all food between meals. One of the hospitalized patients, Tommy, received his lunch during the course of the experimental session (11:15 A.M. to 2:15 P.M.). The second subject's session was 90 minutes long, and the third subject's 60 minutes. In general the maximum length of the session was related to the level of deprivation and the rate of the child's satiation by the reinforcing devices in the room.

The entire experiment was programmed and recorded automatically through automatic vending machines, relay, electronic devices, and electrical recorders. Except during the first few days in the experiment, the child was alone in the experimental room during the entire experimental procedure. With few exceptions there were no interventions even during the most severe tantrums. There was an explicit attempt to minimize tantrums or other emotional upsets caused by sudden shifts in the frequency of reinforcement by arranging the changes of schedules of rein-

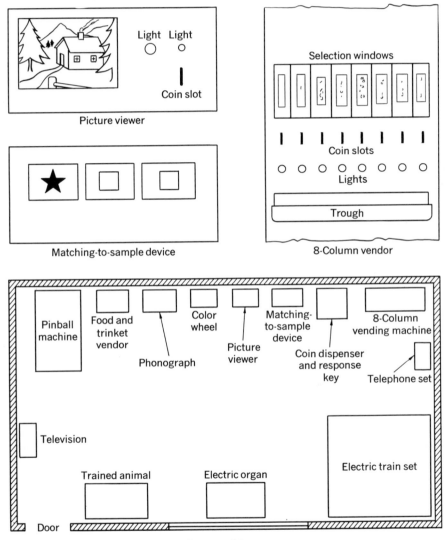

Figure 1. Schematic diagram of the experimental room. Each device had a coin slot, coin light and light which was on whenever the device was operating. The detail of the picture viewer illustrates the typical arrangement. Also shown in detail are the matching-to-sample device and coin slot, coin light arrangement on the 8-column vendor.

forcement as gradually as possible so that the child's behavior would be maintained strongly throughout. In general the frequency of tantrums declined continuously during the course of the experiment.

## THE EARLY DEVELOPMENT OF A PERFORMANCE

Food and candy appear to be the major reinforcers available, and candy was therefore the reinforcer used during the child's first introduction to the experimental procedures. Thereafter, the candy vending machine was supplemented by the gradual addition of the different reinforcing devices. Reinforcement conditions were manipulated during the early part of the experiment to give an estimate of how much activity might be controlled by the coin reinforcement and to demonstrate how much of the child's activity in the room was under the control of the specific parts of the environment that were manipulated.

When coins were delivered by pressing a simple key the pattern of emission of the child's behavior was like that normally occurring under similar reinforcement conditions in other species. Figure 2, Record A,

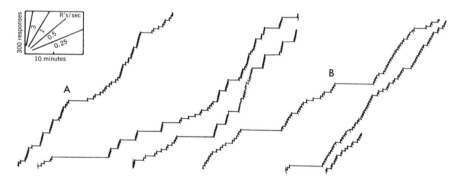

Figure 2. Graphic record of the subject's responses cumulated against time. The delivery of coins is indicated by the marks oblique to the curve and the scale is given by the grid. For more compact presentation, the records have been "collapsed" by removing the space between the excursions of the recording pen. Record A is for Thomas; Record B for Margie.

shows a record of the performance of the boy when every 15th operation of the key produced a coin (fixed ratio schedule of reinforcement), and when most of the coin-operated reinforcing devices were already present in the room. Following the delivery of each coin (the oblique marks on the record) there is frequently a slight pause ranging from a few seconds to several minutes. Once responding begins, the boy presses the key

Table 1
Summary of Distribution of Earned Coins in the Various Reinforcing Devices

| | | Total Coins | Candy Vendor | Record Player | White Vendor | Color Wheel | Organ | T.V. | Toy Car | 35 mm. Viewer | Telephone | Monkey |
|---|---|---|---|---|---|---|---|---|---|---|---|---|
| FR 15 | Tommy | 208 | 161 | 12 | 17 | 8 | | | | 4 | 4 | |
| | Margie | 158 | 55 | 6 | 75 | 1 | 1 | 1 | 13 | 2 | | |
| Matching | Tommy | 257 | 175 | 12 | 18 | 8 | 6 | 6 | | 4 | 12 | 5 |
| | Margie | 110 | 81 | 3 | 13 | 1 | | 2 | | 2 | | |

rapidly (3 or 4 presses per second) and continues until the reinforcement. The boy is continuously active throughout the two hours of the experimental session, either pressing the key for coins or using the coins in the various devices. During the two-hour session, 208 coins were delivered. Record B of Figure 2 shows a performance recorded for the 10-year-old girl under almost identical conditions. The performances are similar although this subject deposited coins into different reinforcing devices than did the first subject. Table 1 gives the distribution of each subject's coins in the various devices. Occasionally coins are not used because the child drops them into inaccessible places such as behind a vending machine. Limited data are available for the third subject, who has been in the experiment only a brief period of time. His performance corroborates the weak and narrow repertoires of the other children, however. In spite of the availability of a wide variety of reinforcing devices, all of this child's activities are restricted to the food vendor. As more and more behavior occurs under the control of the reinforcements of the experimental room, it may be possible to begin to widen this child's repertoire.

## DEVELOPMENT OF COMPLEX FORMS

Once it proved possible to sustain a simple activity for substantial periods of time and under conditions of infrequent reinforcement, we begin to develop more complex forms of activity. The general plan here was to choose a variation in the child's activities in the direction of the desired repertoire and shift the reinforcement contingency in that direction. We attempted to choose slight variations so that reinforcement would not occur too infrequently. Once the child's performance changed to conform with the new contingencies of reinforcement, reinforcements were delivered only for further variations in the direction of the required performance. The same process was continued until the required performance was achieved, often over a period of many weeks. The rate at which the complex performance is developed cannot be predicted in advance, is tailored to the individual child, and depends upon how rapidly the child's performance conforms to the new conditions of reinforcement. Too rapid a development of the repertoire may result in too low a frequency of reinforcement to continue to sustain the child's activity. In the extreme case, too rapid a change in the forms of activity required for reinforcement may result in an environment that does not make contact with any performances currently in the child's repertoire. In almost every case we changed the experimental procedures too rapidly, erring by assuming that the child's repertoire was larger than it proved to be. As a result the conditions of reinforcement had to be returned closer to the original ones and the progression made more gradual.

In a first procedure, the child's behavior was placed under the control of the lights behind the plastic panel where the key was mounted, by delivering coins only when the panel was lighted. This control was developed without difficulty in all of the subjects with whom it was attempted. A second kind of stimulus control, developed by making the coin slots and associated lights inoperative whenever the coin slot was not lighted, was developed with more difficulty. This control was carried out by lighting the coin slots after the delivery of every (2nd to 5th) coin. Coins deposited as soon as they were received in unlighted coin slots would be wasted. The result was a "coin saving." The child worked at the key, accumulating coins, until the coin slots on the various devices were lighted, and then cashed in the accumulated coins. The development of this discriminative repertoire also made it possible to study how the reinforcing value of the coin depends on the number and kinds of machines in which the coin could be used. This could be done simply by turning off the appropriate coin lights. A second by-product of this technique was a sample of activity unaffected by the intercurrent eating or the use of the nonfood machines.

A further extension of the discriminative repertoire was provided by the 8-column vending machine containing a light and coin slot for each column. When a column became empty its coin light went out and further coins in that column were wasted. This arrangement permitted the coin to be exchanged for the particular kind of candy relevant to the child's current deprivation. The slow development of the control by the lights on the 8-column vendor illustrated the minimal perceptual repertoire of these children. Even though one child's behavior had come under almost perfect control of the coin lights during the previous coin-saving procedure, the more complex matrix of lights and slots of the 8-column vending machine totally disrupted the previously acquired repertoire. The control was re-established only by the addition of many procedures and some two months of training.

The further development of more complex repertoires was carried out by reinforcing "matching to sample" (Skinner, 1950). Instead of a simple key, the child faced three windows (see Figure 1), each producing an electrical connection when pushed. A device behind the windows programmed a strip of paper on which could be painted or pasted any kind of visual material. The subject was first trained to respond to the sample appearing in the center window. Touching the sample in the center window tended to force the child to attend to the stimulus and produced the second frame. The sample reappeared in the center window with a matching figure either to the left or to the right and a nonmatching figure in the remaining position. If the child touched the matching figure, a coin was delivered. If he touched a nonmatching window, the apparatus was disconnected electrically (time out) for a period variously ranging from 1 to 20 seconds. During the time out, the device was inoperative and no further coins could be earned. The matching procedure was established gradually by first giving the child a coin when he touched any window, and gradually approximating the final procedure over a period of several months. Once the child matched simple figures (for example, colored dots) the complexity of the material was gradually increased. Here again, introducing stimuli too rapidly would result in many mistakes, an increase in the amount of activity per reinforcement, and a low frequency of reinforcement. We have recorded several large changes in procedure precipitating severe tantrums. On the other hand, procedural changes sometimes of an unusual sort had little effect when they did not change the frequency or amount of activity per reinforcement.

Figure 3 contains performances recorded on the matching-to-sample procedure where the stimuli being matched were large bold drawings of a circle, star, rectangle, square, and a triangle. Each time the child matched correctly, the device moved to the next problem, but every incorrect match interrupted the procedure for 6 seconds by disconnecting all of the circuits. Every 2nd correct match delivered a coin. Figure 3,

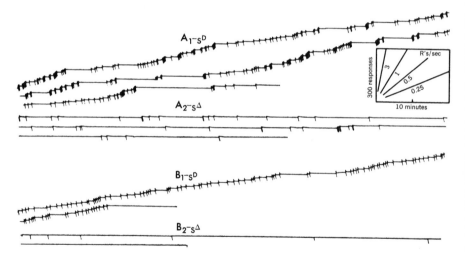

Figure 3. Graphic record of the matching procedure. Each matching sequence is recorded as a response and cumulated against time. Records A₁ and A₂ give the correct and incorrect matches respectively for Thomas. Both recorders ran concurrently. Each segment is a 1-hour portion. Records B₁ and B₂ give the records for Margie on the same procedures. The scale of the records is as in Figure 2.

Record A-1, is a record for the boy of the correct matches during a typical 170-minute experimental session. The recording pen moves one step for each correct match and the delivery of coins is indicated by the oblique mark. As in the record shown in Figure 2 with simple key press-ing, the boy is performing almost continuously during the entire experi-mental session with most of his behavior conforming to the requirements of the automatic environment. During this session 257 coins were de-livered and used. The stimulus material is controlling the boy's perform-ance closely with only 44 inappropriate responses out of a total of 1512 correct matching sequences. The incorrect matches are recorded on a separate recorder running concurrently. This record is shown in Record A-2 where the incorrect responses are emphasized by deflecting the pen obliquely as was done in the upper curve for reinforcements. Records B-1 and B-2 contain a similar performance for the girl for a 90-minute session. Again the performance is sustained almost continuously through-out the 90 minutes of the experimental session and the level of mistakes is about the same as for the previous subject, 6 mistakes out of 220 correct matching sequences. Table 1 also gives the distribution of coins in the various devices for the matching procedure.

## DISCUSSION

The early results of this experiment, using the techniques of operant reinforcement to sustain and widen the repertoire of autistic children, show that it is possible to bring the behavior of these children under the close control of an artificial environment by means of a conditioned rein-forcer possibly generalized. After sustaining simple performances it was possible to widen the behavioral patterns of the child by the normal processes by which behavior is sustained and altered in normal humans and in other species. While the behavioral repertoires developed in these children are still not nearly as complex as those involved in a normal social repertoire, they indicate at least the existence of normal processes at a very basic level. To date the results of these techniques do not sug-gest any basic deficit except in the rate at which these children acquire new types of behavioral control. Failures to develop normal performances as we get to more complex procedures will be difficult to interpret, how-ever, because such failures might be due either to a basic deficit or to our inadequate development of behavioral techniques for affecting the children. It is difficult to equate the complexity of the various procedures to which the children are exposed, however.

We do not consider these techniques as attempts at rehabilitation but rather as experimental analyses of the actual and potential repertoires of these children. Perhaps these analyses can serve as guides for attempts to use the same processes of developing behavior in social situations where the performances sustained and altered would be activities in re-spect to other persons (social) and where the important consequences sustaining the activities would be the social effects of these performances. If it proves possible to develop and widen behavioral repertoires significantly in the experimental room, then this would seem to indicate the possibility that the same potential for behavioral change would exist in the social milieu if the proper conditions could be generated. In the same vein, systematic deficits in particular areas may indicate deficient areas of control which may be of use in determining techniques for handling these children.

It is not known, of course, to what extent the behavioral deficits observed in autistic children represent a basic constitutional or physiological deficit. The possibility of recording "lawful" activity in a situation where behavior of autistic children can be objectively recorded may open the way to techniques for evaluating the extent of focal physiological deficits, or whether in fact infantile autism represents a uniform condition. Once we can sustain the performance of the child and bring it under the control of arbitrary stimuli it should be possible to manipulate physiological conditions and record the effects on the behavioral baselines. Behavioral baselines could serve to evaluate the child's repertoire in terms of the performances ordinarily considered in intelligence tests, to test the effect of drugs, and to test the integrity of the central nervous system.

## REFERENCES

Azrin, N. H., & Lindsley, O. R. The reinforcement of cooperation between children. *J. abnorm. soc. Psychol.*, 1956, *52*, 100–102.

Bijou, S. W., A child study laboratory on wheels. *Child Develpm.*, 1958, *29*, 425–427. (a)

Bijou, S. W., Operant extinction after fixed-interval reinforcement with young children. *J. exp. Anal. Behav.*, 1958, *1*, 25–29. (b)

Ferster, C. B., Reinforcement and punishment in the control of human behavior by social agencies. *Psychiat. Res. Rep.*, 1958, *10*, 101–118.

Lindsley, O. R., Studies in behavior therapy. Metropolitan State Hospital, Waltham, Massachusetts. Status Report III, 1954.

Long, E. R., Hammack, J. T., May, F., & Campbell, B. F. Intermittent reinforcement of operant behavior in children. *J. exp. Anal. Behav.*, 1958, *1*, 315–339.

Skinner, B. F., Are theories of learning necessary? *Psychol. Rev.*, 1950, *57*, 193–216.

Skinner, B. F., *Science and human behavior*. New York: Macmillan, 1953.

# 16

# Application of Operant Conditioning Procedures to the Behavior Problems of an Autistic Child

## Montrose M. Wolf, Todd R. Risley, and Hayden L. Mees

### EDITORS' COMMENTS

This study is an exciting account of the application of operant principles to the hospital treatment of a severely disturbed three-year-old boy. The child showed ineffective relationships with people, self-destructive temper tantrums, and distressing problems in eating and sleeping. Furthermore, his vision was severely curtained by the removal of both of his lenses (necessitated by the growth of cataracts). Thus, in addition to instituting procedures to treat his emotional problems, it was urgent that he be trained to wear glasses.

It is to be noted that the rehabilitation and treatment procedures described, like those in the Ferster and DeMyer study, were not carried out directly by psychiatrists or clinical psychologists, but by attendants, nurses, and teachers. These workers were guided in each step of the treatment program by the authors. The demonstration that by such procedures, complex processes can be modified by the application of behavioral principles has broad implications for the future development of new child therapy techniques.

This account is all the more remarkable considering that these investigators had to pioneer on two frontiers simultaneously. They had to develop training procedures for the staff as well as plan

Montrose M. Wolf, Todd R. Risley, and Hayden L. Mees, "Application of Operant Conditioning Procedures to the Behavior Problems of an Autistic Child," *Behavior Research and Therapy*, 1964, *1*, 305–312.

This study was supported in part by a research grant (M-2232) from National Institutes of Health, United States Public Health Service. The authors are indebted to Sidney W. Bijou for his invaluable counsel throughout the course of this study. We were most fortunate in having the cooperation and encouragement of Jerome Rose, M.D., Clinical Director, and Daniel Kelleher, Ph.D., Senior Clinical Psychologist of the Child Study and Treatment Center, Ft. Steilacoom, Washington.

Special appreciation is due Dicky's attendants: Jim McCoy, Robbie Littles, Grant Schneider, and particularly Betty Kazda, whose skill and cooperation were necessary conditions for the success of this study.

The major portion of this paper was presented at the Western Psychological Association, Santa Monica, California, 1963.

strategies for applying behavioral principles to this particular case. One important feature of the staff training was the keeping of moment-to-moment records of the child's behavior in a form suitable for an experimental analysis.

## INTRODUCTION

During the past few decades an experimental analysis of behavior has produced several powerful and reliable techniques for controlling behavior (Holland & Skinner, 1961). Although these procedures were originally established with lower organisms, they are increasingly being applied in areas concerned with human behavior (Ayllon & Michel, 1959; Baer, 1962; Bijou, 1963; Ferster, 1961; Isaacs, Thomas, & Goldiamond, 1960; Lindsley, 1962; Williams, 1959; Zimmerman & Zimmerman, 1962). Even so, techniques developed for dealing with specific human anomalies are limited.

This case study is an example of the application of behavioral principles to psychopathology. We developed techniques for dealing with the behavior problems of a hospitalized preschool autistic boy. Each of the techniques was derived from procedures developed and studied in experimental laboratories, such as handshaping, extinction, food deprivation, time-out from positive reinforcement, and discrimination training.

Dicky, the subject, was 3½ years old when the study began. He is the son of middle socio-economic class parents and has one younger and two older apparently normal female siblings.

From hospital records it appears that Dicky progressed normally till his ninth month, when cataracts were discovered in the lenses of both eyes. At this time severe temper tantrums and sleeping problems began to develop. During his second year he had a series of eye operations which culminated with the removal of his occluded lenses. This made glasses-wearing necessary. For more than a year his parents tried, and failed, to make Dicky wear glasses. During this time Dicky was seen by a variety of specialists who diagnosed him, variously, as mentally retarded, diffuse and locally brain-damaged, and psychotic, with the possibility of such additional anomalies as phenylpyruvic oligophenia and hyperthyroidism. One recommendation was that he be placed in an institution for the retarded since his prognosis was so poor.

Dicky did not eat normally and lacked normal social and verbal repertoires. His tantrums included self-destructive behaviors such as head-banging, face-slapping, hair-pulling, and face-scratching. His mother reported that after a severe tantrum "he was a mess, all black and blue and bleeding." He would not sleep at night, forcing one or both parents to remain by his bed. Sedatives, tranquilizers, and restraints were tried, without success.

He was admitted to a children's mental hospital with the diagnosis of childhood schizophrenia at the age of 3. After three months' hospitalization the terminal report stated that there was some improvement in his schizophrenic condition but no progress in glasses-wearing. A few months later his ophthalmologist predicted that unless Dicky began wearing glasses within the next six months he would permanently lose his macular vision. At this point the authors were invited in as consultants by the hospital staff for the purpose of training Dicky to wear glasses.

After observing a twenty-minute interaction between Dicky and his mother, a period occupied by almost continuous tantrums, we recommended that he be readmitted to the hospital in order to separate him from his mother temporarily and to deal with his disruptive behaviors, while training him to wear glasses.

Our prescribed operations were carried out by the attendants and the parents both on the ward and in the home. In addition to general comments we carefully specified behaviors and environmental events to be recorded on Dicky's chart and in notes from the parents. As the specific events to be recorded were highly distinctive and cooperation by the attendants and parents was good, the data presented probably reflect actual events to a large but undetermined degree.

By manipulating the consequences of the behaviors, we concurrently developed techniques for dealing with Dicky's tantrums, sleeping and eating problems, and for establishing glasses-wearing, and appropriate verbal and social behavior.

## PROCEDURES, RESULTS AND DISCUSSION

### Temper Tantrums

There is some evidence that temper tantrums will succumb to extinction (Williams, 1959). However, under ward conditions, with personnel untrained in these procedures, it was far from certain that extinction would be reliably carried out. So the prescribed procedure was a combination of mild punishment and extinction. Dicky was placed in his room contingent upon each tantrum, the door remaining closed until the tantrum behavior ceased. Each occurrence was to be noted on his chart.

Such a procedure, although initially involving social contacts and thus possible reinforcement at the onset of a tantrum, eliminated the possibility of continuous contact throughout the undesired behavior. This procedure also provided for differential reinforcement of nontantrum behavior by the door being opened contingent upon such behavior. Such a contingency, involving the removal of all social reinforcers for a period of time, resembles Ferster and Appel's (1961) use of a time-out from positive reinforcement as an aversive stimulus.

A cumulative record showing the frequency with which Dicky was placed in his room for tantrums and self-destructive behavior is presented in the upper graph of Figure 1. The curve is, however, partially arti-

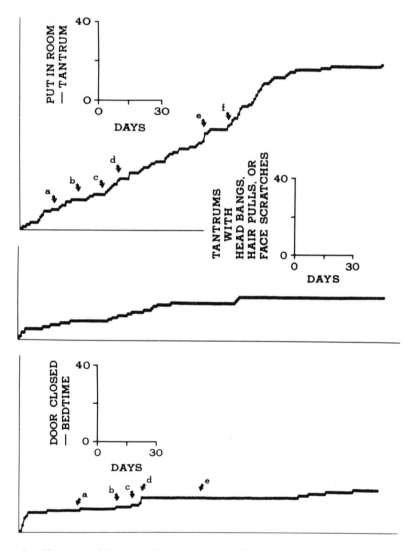

Figure 1. Three cumulative records showing the effects of extinction and mild punishment (time out from positive reinforcement) upon the tantrums, severe self-destructive episodes, and bedtime problems of a hospitalized preschool autistic boy

factual. The record shows a constant rate of being placed in his room for tantrums during the first four months, indicating a lack of change in behavior during this period which was contradictory to casual observation.

Several variables, each involving a sacrifice of experimental rigor, contributed to this discrepancy:

1. When Dicky was first admitted he whined, cried, and slapped himself frequently. The attendant was therefore instructed to place him in his room only when he was engaging in two or more of these behaviors simultaneously. As Dicky's behavior improved, the attendants lowered the original criterion finally to include any atavism. Since the author believed this was to the distinct advantage of the child, the criterion change was encouraged.

2. During the first few weeks the attendants' records contained reports of elaborate explanations offered Dicky as he was escorted to his room, and of tender, practically tearful apologies and fondling after the door was reopened. This pattern evolved to a perfunctory trip to the room with the door simply being reopened at the end of the tantrum, presenting a ward going on much as before.

3. By the beginning of the third month, tantrums lasting less than five minutes began to occur frequently, creating the likelihood that the trip to the room would become a socially reinforcing event. A minimum time of ten minutes in the room was therefore imposed.

4. Dicky's contact with his family and home progressively increased during this time. The major changes are indicated in the tantrum curve.

At (a) Dicky's parents were permitted their first one-hour visit. Subsequently they made several scheduled visits a week, during which an attendant observed and instructed them in their handling of Dicky.

At (b) the father put Dicky to bed on the ward for the first time.

At (c) Dicky began wearing his glasses.

At (d) the mother put Dicky to bed on the ward for the first time.

Midway between (d) and (e) Dicky began short home visits accompanied by the attendant.

At (e) Dicky spent his first night at home.

At (f) Dicky spent a second night at home.

After (f) he spent an average of three nights a week at home, increasing to five nights a week during the final month.

Some estimate of the decreasing severity of the tantrums is indicated in the middle cumulative record of Figure 1. Each step represents a tantrum, either during the day or at bedtime, involving head-banging, hair-pulling, or face-scratching. Such severe self-destructive behavior remained near zero after the first two and a half months. The remainder of the tantrum record consists of face-slapping, whining, and crying.

Conditions for handling tantrums at the home were made comparable to those on the ward. The attendants coached the parents to deal with Dicky's tantrums by putting him in his room both on the ward and at home. The descriptions of the parents' behavior by the attendants and by the parents themselves indicated that this training was effective.

## Bedtime Problems

The bedtime problem was handled in a manner similar to the tantrums. Dicky was bathed at a regular hour each night, cuddled for a short time, put to bed, and left with a door open. If he got up, he was told to go back to bed or the door would be closed. If he remained up, the door was closed. The door was reopened after a short time, or if a tantrum occurred, after it subsided. He was told again to get in his bed. If he stayed in bed the door was left open. Each door-closing at bedtime was recorded.

The lower graph in Figure 1 shows cumulative bedtime door-closings. The door was closed several times during the first five nights. The resulting tantrums were quite violent, one series totaling more than an hour. On the sixth night the attendant tucked Dicky in and said goodnight. Dicky remained in bed and soon went to sleep. Bedtime was seldom a problem again.

At (a) the father first put Dicky to bed on the ward.

At (b) the mother first put him to bed.

From (b) to (e) the parents put Dicky to bed once or twice a week.

At (c) and (d) the parents had to shut the door.

At (e) Dicky spent his first night at home. For a few weeks prior to this, he had been making short home visits accompanied by an attendant. Several days prior to (e) he was taken home in the evening, and after a few minutes of play, went through the routine of getting ready for bed with his siblings. The attendant then brought him back to the ward and put him to bed. Since this trial run was successful, he was sent home to spend the night several days later at (e). He was bathed and put in bed. After about thirty minutes he was heard humming to himself. The mother started to go in to Dicky but the attendant dissuaded her. Fifteen minutes later, Dicky was asleep.

Over the next three months, until his release from the hospital, Dicky spent a progressively greater proportion of his nights at home. One night a week an attendant went along to observe both Dicky and his parents.

The four times the door had to be shut after point (e) all occurred at home. These may have been the result of a certain amount of reshaping by the parents during a period when Dicky had chronic diarrhea.

## Glasses-Wearing

Shaping (Skinner, 1953) was the basic procedure used to get Dicky to wear his glasses. Our shaper, an attendant, was instructed to spend two or three twenty-minute sessions each day, with the subject in the subject's room.

During the first several sessions a conditioned reinforcer was established by having the clicks of a toy noisemaker followed by Dicky's receiving small bites of candy or fruit. The click soon became a discriminative stimulus and after each click Dicky would go to the bowl where the reinforcers were placed.

Since Dicky had worn the prescription glasses for a few seconds on at least one occasion and had not left them on, it was assumed that wearing them was not immediately reinforcing. The glasses might even have been mildly aversive, since they would drastically change all visual stimuli, as well as force the eyes into greater accommodation. Also, glasses with the full prescription had been paired in the past with attempts to physically force glasses-wearing.

For these reasons we decided not to begin with the actual prescription glasses. Instead, several empty glasses frames were placed around the room and Dicky was reinforced for picking them up, holding them, and carrying them about. Slowly, by successive approximations, he was reinforced for bringing the frames closer to his eyes.

The original plan was, after he was wearing the lenseless frames, to introduce plain glass and then prescription lenses in three steps of progressing severity. This was not the actual sequence of events, however, since our shaper met with considerable difficulty in getting Dicky to wear the glassless frames in the proper manner, i.e., with the ear pieces over instead of under the ears and the eye openings in line with the eyes. Furthermore, it was impossible to help place the frames correctly since Dicky became upset when anyone touched any part of his head.

The slow progress was probably attributable to two factors. First, the attendant, although cooperative, was inexperienced and imprecise with the shaping procedure. Secondly, due to the reluctance of the ward staff to deprive the child of food we began with reinforcers such as candy and fruit. It soon became obvious, however, that, at least for this child, these were rather weak reinforcers.

After the first two weeks we attempted to increase deprivational control by using breakfast as a shaping session, bites of breakfast now being dependent upon approximations to glasses-wearing. Two weeks later we added to the glasses larger adult ear pieces and a "roll bar" which would go over the top of his head and guide the ear pieces up and over the ears.

At the end of the fifth week Dicky was still not wearing the ear frames appropriately; so the authors, who had not previously spent any time shaping the subject themselves, spent the major portion of a day directing the shaping procedure.

A second bar was added to the back of the glasses. Now, they fit like a cap and would not slide off readily. As usual the breakfast session was not particularly effective. Lunch was also used as a session, but still there was no progress.

Later, at approximately two o'clock that afternoon, we had a third session. Dicky had received very little to eat all day, just a few pieces of dry cereal, and was most interested in the ice cream we brought to the session. We also decided to try the full prescription lenses. At the beginning of the session it was quite obvious that our reinforcers were much

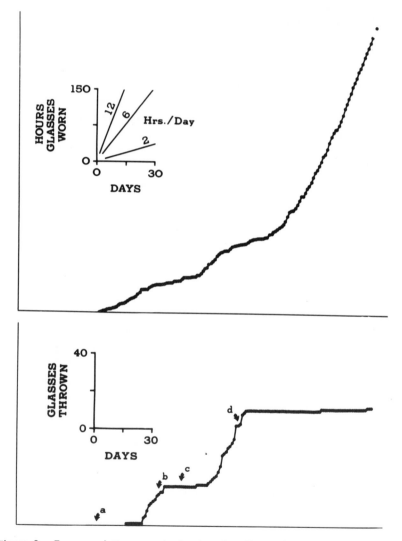

Figure 2. Two cumulative records showing the effects of positive reinforcement (bites of meals, etc.) upon glasses-wearing and the effects of extinction and mild punishment (time out from positive reinforcement) upon the glasses-throwing of a hospitalized preschool autistic boy

more powerful than earlier in the day. He carried the glasses at all times, often putting them up to his face, although not in the desired manner. However, since there was a great deal of the approximate kind of behavior it was easy to differentially reinforce the two aspects of wearing we wanted, placing the ear pieces straight over the ears, and looking through the lenses. At the end of approximately thirty minutes Dicky was holding the ear pieces properly over his ears, and the nose piece at the tip of his nose. He was looking through the lenses at such objects as a ring, a clicker, etc., that were displayed in the hopes of maintaining his looking behavior. After this, progress was rapid and he was soon wearing his glasses continuously during the meal session in his room.

After glasses-wearing was established in these sessions, it could be maintained with other, less manipulatable reinforcers. For example, the attendant would tell Dicky, "Put your glasses on and let's go for a walk." Dicky was usually required to wear the glasses during meals, snacks, automobile rides, walks, outdoor play, etc. If he removed the glasses, the activity was terminated.

The progress of glasses-wearing is presented cumulatively in the upper graph of Figure 2. At the time of Dicky's release from the hospital he had worn the glasses for more than 600 hours and was wearing them about 12 hours a day.

### Glasses-Throwing

The lower cumulative record in Figure 2 depicts the course of a problem that grew out of glasses-wearing—namely, glasses-throwing. Glasses-wearing began at (a). Two weeks later Dicky threw his glasses for the first time. A week later he began throwing them about twice a day. Although this in itself was not a serious behavior problem, it was moderately expensive due to breakage, and there was the danger that, once home, it would be reinforced by the mother's ineffectual fussing and thereby increase the frequency of throwing to a degree incompatible with glasses-wearing. We therefore attempted to develop a technique to control it. Beginning at (b) Dicky was put in his room for ten minutes following each glasses-throw, or if a tantrum developed, until it ceased. Glasses-throwing decreased to zero in five days. At (c) the conditions were reversed: he was no longer to be put in his room for throws. After about three weeks the rate of glasses-throwing resumed its earlier high level. At (d) he was again put in his room for throwing his glasses, and six days later the rate reached and remained near zero.

### Verbal Behavior

After glasses-wearing was established we developed a technique for generating a verbal repertoire. The technique also aimed at maintaining glasses-wearing and reinforcing visual attending. Like the glasses training, the verbal training consisted of sessions in which an attendant administered food reinforcers. Initially, we tried candy and fruit but these were unsuccessful. Only when we began using breakfast and lunch as training sessions did we have rapid and dramatic effects.

Dicky had no socially appropriate verbal behavior and, according to his parents, neither his verbal nor nonverbal behavior was under their verbal control. However, Dicky was far from mute. He had some long and complex verbal chains such as songs (*Chicago,* for example) and occasionally he would mimic quite clearly, but the mimicking could not be evoked under normal conditions.

Our training began with the attendant presenting, one at a time, five pictures (a Santa Claus, a cat, etc.). The attendant would say, "This is a cat," "Now, say cat," and so on, until Dicky mimicked her, whereupon she would say, "Good," or "That's right" and give him a bite of his meal. After several more days of differential reinforcement the attendant gradually omitted saying the word first and Dicky would usually say the word in the presence of each picture without a prompt. In three weeks he did this in the presence of about ten pictures. We then progressed to picture books, common household objects, and finally to remote events, for example, "Where are you going tonight," "What did you do outside?"

The more powerful food reinforcers were evidently necessary for initial strengthening, but weaker conditioned reinforcers, such as adult attention and approval, were effective for maintaining and expanding the original repertoire. The parents, although reluctant at first, were trained by the attendant to use the same technique at home. They have expanded his repertoire to include, for instance, the correct usage of personal pronouns, and Dicky now initiates requests and comments without adult prompting. However, his present verbal behavior is by no means comparable to that of a normal five-year-old child.

Dicky's ability to mimic entire phrases and sentences was apparently crucial to the rapid progress in verbal training. The authors' current work with other children indicates that without this mimicking behavior a long and arduous handshaping procedure would have been necessary to establish responses of the required topography (words, phrases, and sentences) prior to the discrimination training described above.

## Eating Problems

During those meals which Dicky ate with the rest of the children in the dining room, he would not use silverware, would snatch food from the other children's plates and would throw food around the room. We attempted to deal with these behaviors by having the attendant remove Dicky's plate for a few minutes whenever he would eat with his fingers and, after a warning, remove Dicky from the dining room (and the remainder of his meal) whenever he would throw food or take food from others' plates. Dicky spent an average of 55% of the mealtime inappropriately eating with his fingers. During one meal his plate was removed several times, and he was told to use his spoon after this, and in all subsequent meals he used a spoon for all appropriate foods. It was only necessary to warn Dicky and send him from the dining room a few times to completely eliminate food-stealing and food-throwing.

Probably as the result of being consistently paired with the aversive consequence of being put in his room, such verbal stimuli as "No," "Stop that," or "If you do that again you'll have to go to your room," came to suppress much undesirable nonverbal behavior. This type of control also seems important for normal child development.

According to a report from the mother six months after the child's return home, Dicky continues to wear his glasses, does not have tantrums, has no sleeping problems, is becoming increasingly verbal, and is a new source of joy to the members of his family.

## REFERENCES

Ayllon, T., & Michael, J. The psychiatric nurse as a behavioral engineer. *J. exp. Anal. Behav.*, 1959, *2*, 323–334.

Baer, D. M. Laboratory control of thumbsucking by withdrawal and representation of reinforcement. *J. exp. Anal. Behav.*, 1962, *5*, 525–528.

Bijou, S. W. Theory and research in mental (developmental) retardation. *Psychol. Rec.*, 1963, *13*, 95–110.

Ferster, C. B. Positive reinforcement and behavioral defects of autistic children. *Child Develpm.*, 1961, *32*, 437–456.

Ferster, C. B., & Appel, J. B. Punishment of $S^\Delta$ responding in match to sample by time out from positive reinforcement. *J. exp. Anal. Behav.*, 1961, *4*, 45–56.

Holland, J. G., & Skinner, B. F. *The analysis of behavior.* New York: McGraw-Hill, 1961.

Isaacs W., Thomas, J., & Goldiamond, I. Application of operant conditioning to reinstate verbal behavior in psychotics. *J. spec. hear. Dis.*, 1960, *25*, 8–12.

Lindsley, O. R. Operant conditioning methods in diagnosis. In *The first Hahnemann symposium on psychosomatic medicine.* New York: Lea & Febiger, 1962.

Skinner, B. F. *Science and human behavior.* New York: Macmillan, 1953.

Williams, C. D. The elimination of tantrum behavior by extinction procedures. *J. abnorm. soc. Psychol.*, 1959, *59*, 269.

Zimmerman, E. H., & Zimmerman, J. The alteration of behavior in a special classroom situation. *J. exp. Anal. Behav.*, 1962, *5*, 59–60.

# 17

# Experimental Manipulation
# of Autistic Behaviors
# and Generalization into the Home

## Todd R. Risley and Montrose M. Wolf

EDITORS' COMMENTS

The following paper by Risley and Wolf shows that in at least some cases, the mothers of children who have behavior problems can be trained to deal effectively with the problem. We shall see other examples in a different setting in the paper by Wahler, Winkel, Peterson, and Morrison. In the instances reported in this paper, the problem is one of shaping discriminated verbal operants, a task involving both discrimination and differentiation contingencies. The method of training the parents includes demonstration, imitation by the parents, and reinforcement by the experimenter of correct imitations. This is just the kind of training which most of the parents will in turn provide for their children.

It may well be noted that to train parents (or other adults) is itself an exercise in behavior modification. The fact that the parents have been living with the child whose behavior they have allowed to remain seriously deficient or deviant indicates that their everyday repertoires of behavior do not include effective instructional techniques; thus, they too may well require training. The fact that they are adults and (presumably) normal does not guarantee that a simple description of new procedures will suffice to change them into successful shapers of their child's behavior. Indeed, it should be assumed that the parent's behavior, like the child's, will change only if it is connected with appropriate discriminative stimuli (cues) and contin-

Todd R. Risley and Montrose M. Wolf, "Experimental Manipulation of Autistic Behaviors and Generalization into the Home." Paper delivered at the American Psychological Association Convention, Los Angeles, 1964.

This investigation was partially supported by NIMH Grant (M-2232), U.S. Public Health, S. W. Bijou, principal investigator.

gencies. Reliance merely on instructions will often prove ineffective. Thus, attention to the reinforcers appropriate to the parent's behavior is also an essential part of the process of effective modification or development of the child's behavior. Fortunately, most parents will be reinforced by seeing their child improve as a consequence of their own efforts. However, this feedback comes about only after the program of child training has been successfully initiated. Prior reinforcement will have to be provided by the experimenter. His remarks of approval and disapproval should have effective reinforcing functions for those parents who respect him and his work.

A previous study by Wolf, Risley and Mees (1964) described operant procedures which were used to reinstate normal behaviors in an institutionalized autistic child. Subsequent investigations have extended the use of behavioral techniques to two additional problem areas: speech training for the autistic child and instruction of the child's parents in employing similar procedures in the home.

The case of a six-year-old autistic child who attended the Developmental Psychology Laboratory at the University of Washington is reported here. The child exhibited bizarre mannerisms and echolalia. He was withdrawn, inactive and lacked appropriate verbal behavior.

## SPEECH TRAINING PROCEDURE

Each weekday the child was brought by the mother to the Laboratory in a state of mild food deprivation. During the training sessions, spoons of ice cream were used as a reinforcer for establishing mimicking behavior, labeling of pictures, and verbal utterances in the form of phrases and sentences.

### Mimicking

In the first session the experimenter said the word "ice cream" several times a minute and the child was reinforced for imitating the word. The child began mimicking the word within the first minute of the session and mimicking continued at a low, stable rate throughout this session. Following each correct response the experimenter said "very good" and gave the child a spoon of ice cream. The procedure of pairing the words with the reinforcer, however, had the effect of producing a high rate of saying, "very good, very good" by the subject, an inappropriate response which persisted beyond the first session. It is possible that this paradigm

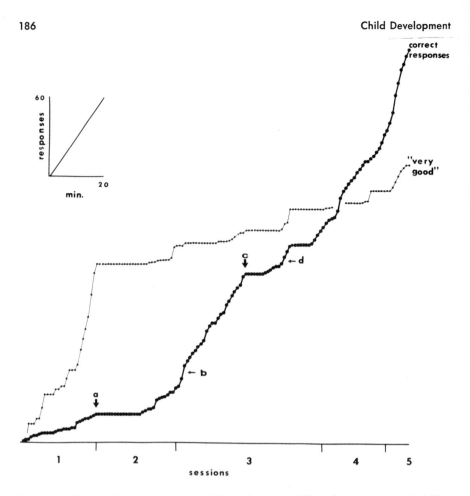

Figure 1.   Rates of inappropriate mimicking ("very good") and appropriate mimicking under form conditions indicated by "a," "b," "c," and "d"

of increasing the probability that the child would produce a sound, simply by pairing that sound with reinforcement, was functional in maintaining the child's echolalia. Rate of imitative verbal responding, both appropriate and inappropriate, is represented from the start to point "a" in Figure 1.

In the next session (beginning at a point "a" in Figure 1) a picture of a train was introduced and the word "train" was repeated by the experimenter. The subject mimicked this novel word once and was reinforced as before with "very good" and a spoon of ice cream. After a long delay during which the subject began repeating "ice cream, ice cream," and tantruming, he again mimicked "train." After this, the rate of mimicking the word rapidly increased.

Three new words, "flower," "car," and "airplane" and their pictures were introduced at the point shown by "b" in Figure 1. In each case, the picture was held out and the subject was required to look at it before the experimenter said the name. The immediate attention which was given when the picture was presented would indicate that the experimenter's *saying* the word (which was discriminative for the subject to mimic and be reinforced) had itself become a reinforcer.

Each of the new words was appropriately mimicked on the first presentation and on each subsequent presentation. Thus the general behavior class of appropriate mimicking had been established, with total training time only slightly more than one hour.

## Non-Imitative Labeling

The established behavior of mimicking a verbal stimulus could give no indication of whether the child was associating his own verbal response with the particular object pictured. To increase the probability that the subject would name the object in the picture instead of mimicking the experimenter, a delay procedure was introduced in which progressively longer periods of attending by the child were required before the name was given. This procedure was begun at the end of the third session (just before "c" Figure 1). During an especially long delay (point "c") the subject began to tantrum. The experimenter merely sat quietly holding the picture toward the subject. The tantrum gradually subsided and the subject again attended to the picture—and promptly named it. This was the first instance of spontaneous, unprompted naming of the object pictured. The same picture was repeatedly presented, and each time he named it with decreasing delay.

Beginning at point "d" in Figure 1, the picture of the airplane was reintroduced. The subject immediately said "car" which was corrected with, "No, airplane." The subject mimicked "airplane" and then correctly named the picture on the next presentation. The other pictures were reintroduced and the subject correctly named each after a single prompt. After this he correctly named the four pictures without prompting when each was presented. Thus the general behavior class of naming objects was established during the second hour of training.

## Effectiveness of the Reinforcer

After a high rate of naming the four pictures had been established, the procedures were altered to isolate experimentally the function of contingent delivery of ice cream. Noncontingent, random delivery of ice cream (an occasional spoon following a naming response) was instituted at the point indicated by the first arrow in Figure 2. Continuous verbal reinforcement ("very good") was maintained, contingent upon the correct

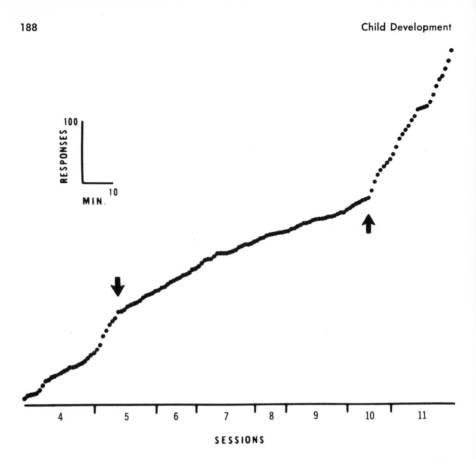

Figure 2. Rate of naming four pictures under conditions of contingent and random (solid line) delivery of ice cream. Performance during random delivery is shown between the arrows.

verbal response. A decrease in rate of naming from 7.5 to 3.1 responses per minute occurred immediately, and the rate had declined to 1.9 responses per minute by the end of the random-reinforcement period.

Resumption of contingent delivery of ice cream, accompanied with the usual "very good" (second arrow in Figure 2) resulted in a rapid increase to the rate of 9.8 responses per minute. The dramatic reversal shown in Figure 2 demonstrates that the child's naming behavior was maximally maintained by the contingent delivery of ice cream reinforcement and was only incidentally affected by verbal reinforcement and other situational variables.

### Use of Phrases and Sentences

Previously conditioned mimicking behavior, now firmly established in the child's behavioral repertoire and subject to adequate experimental control, was utilized to instigate the use of more complex verbal behavior in other situations.

For example, opening a door was used to reinforce mimicking the phrase, "... out (or in) the door." After several instances on successive days of reinforcing an appropriately mimicked response by opening the door, the experimenter began fading out his verbal prompt, saying only, "... out the _____," and the subject continued to say, "... out the door." This progressed until the subject responded to a hand put on the doorknob and a glance in his direction with the appropriate, "... out the door." A question: "Where are you going?" was then faded in as the discriminative stimulus for the phrase "... out (in) the door." If the child mimicked the question, it was repeated at a lower volume and followed with a louder prompt for the appropriate response: "Where are you going? OUT ...";  this would usually generate the appropriate response "... out the door." All prompting was eventually faded out until the subject responded consistently to the closed door and the question, "Where are you going?" with the statement, "... out the door."

The same procedure was used to established appropriate answers to the question, "Where are you going?" in each of the steps of going to and from the experimental room, e.g.: "... up the stairs ... in the door ... down the hall ... in the room," and "... out the door, ... down the hall ... out the door ... down the stairs ... in the car." In each case, being allowed to proceed out the door and down the hall, etc., was treated as the reinforcer.

This technique of giving a prompt for the subject to imitate and then fading out the prompt was used to establish appropriate responses to many other questions such as: "What's your name?" "My name is (name).";  "What do you want?" "I want some ice cream.";  "Hello (name)." "Hello, Mr. Risley."

An essential feature of this technique was the child's ability to detect subtle differences in inflection and volume as an aid in discriminating the stimulus to which he was to respond from the phrase he was to mimic, The increasing speed with which new responses were established indicated that the child was using such discriminative cues effectively.

## PARENT TRAINING

The mother was trained to assume the job of rehabilitating her child after the experimental program had progressed to the point where the imitative paradigm was effective in establishing new verbal behavior. The mother had periodically observed experimental sessions from behind a one-way screen, so that she had become minimally familiar with the experimental procedures. Training sessions were held in the home in late afternoon, again using ice cream as the reinforcer. The mother was instructed on the general procedure and was coached intermittently during sessions thereafter.

### Practice in General Procedure

The mother's first task was to teach the child to put together a puzzle, after which she was to record the number of puzzle pieces completed and the total time of each session. A series of large plywood puzzles each with four or five isolated figures was used.

During the initial sessions the mother showed a predominant tendency to prompt and assist the child continuously in order to evoke responses which she could reinforce. After the sixth session she was instructed to stop all urging and assistance and to do nothing except reinforce each successful fitting of a puzzle piece. In Figure 3, it can be seen that rate

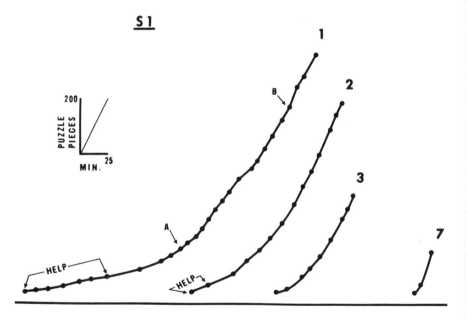

Figure 3. Rate of completing puzzles in the first, second, third, and seventh (last) sessions. "Help" refers to the assistance given by the mother in the first and second seconds. Reinforcements were delivered on a continuous puzzle piece basis up to "A" in the first session, on an increasing ratio between "A" and "B," and on a puzzle completion basis after "B."

of piece-fitting began to increase after all forms of assistance by the mother were terminated. At the point "A" in Figure 3, the mother was instructed in instituting a fixed-ratio schedule (reinforcement following every two correct responses). Between points "A" and "B" in Figure 3, the ratio was progressively increased; this interval shows a marked increase in response rate. Beyond point "B" reinforcement was contingent only upon assembling the complete puzzle. This reinforcement-upon-completion schedule was used with all subsequent puzzles. Rate of completion increased steadily from session to session.

When the second puzzle was introduced the mother assisted the child for the first pieces and then stopped on her own initiative, and no further assistance was given or required on subsequent puzzles. Responses on the second puzzle are represented in curve 2 in Figure 3. Work on the third and the seventh (final) puzzle is also represented by curves in the figure. By the seventh puzzle the child's behavior showed almost no decrement when a new puzzle was introduced and a new puzzle could be assembled nearly as fast as an old one. At about this time the child also began fitting puzzles together by himself during play.

Through this experience the mother learned to rely on the reinforcer to increase the child's rate of behavior, and to deemphasize verbal prompting or urging. She gained insight into the effectiveness of the procedure for establishing general behavioral classes as well as those specific behaviors which were reinforced, and of their generalizability to new tasks and new situations.

## Vocabulary Expansion

The same reinforcement procedures were used by the mother in teaching the child to recognize and name pictures. Pictures of objects were paired with their names as before, and the criterion for learning was the emission of an unprompted correct name for the picture on its first presentation each day for three days in succession. Once a picture was learned to this criterion, it was retired until ten subsequent pictures had been learned, at which time it was re-presented as a test for recall. New pictures were introduced in a session if the subject was consistently giving correct names for all pictures used during that session.

During the home vocabulary training program a modification in the reinforcement was introduced as a test of the relative effectiveness of the mother's verbal reinforcement as compared with the now-standard spoon of ice cream. Initial training in this program included two separate sets of pictures, each of which was used during only one of the two daily training sessions. Responses to the first set of pictures were reinforced with praise ("That's right, very good.") and a spoon of ice cream. Responses to the second set of pictures were reinforced with praise alone.

The results of this comparison, both rate of learning and percent of recall, are shown in Figure 4. While praise alone was an effective reinforcer (dashed line in Figure 4), praise plus ice cream resulted in 50 percent greater rate of learning (solid line in Figure 4). However, words learned under both conditions were equally well recalled (bar graph in Figure 4). Thus the value of ice cream as a reinforcer was again demonstrated, and all subsequent sessions were carried out using ice cream as reinforcer. As the dotted line in the figure shows, the child learned approximately one new word per session during the experimental period, and the mother has continued this training on her own beyond any formal connection with the experiment.

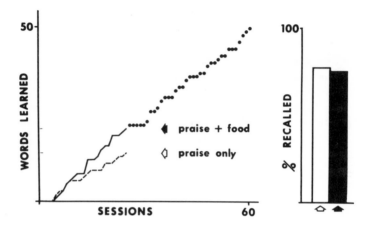

Figure 4. Rate of learning words under conditions praise plus food (solid line) and praise only (dashed line), and percentage of recall under both conditions

In addition to simply expanding the child's naming vocabulary, this procedure was designed to establish the general skill of attending to small differences in printed matter—a step in preparing him for academic materials.

**Behavior Modification**

Concurrent with the training procedures, the parents had been systematically recording instances of stereotyped chanting, a routine which had occupied much of the child's past verbal behavior. The child would repeat a word or phrase over and over, with increasing volume, and terminate in shrieks and crying. The parents habitually "turned off" this sequence at some point simply by attending to the child. For example, the child would stand by the couch and repeat "sit down, sit down," etc., which would terminate when the parents responded in any way (e.g., "Yes, son"; "O.K., sit down"; "You can sit down if you want to").

As a first step in eliminating this well-established and often reinforced operant chain, the positive reinforcement of parental attention was withdrawn and the child was sent to his room contingent upon the shrieking and crying at the end of the chanting routine. Occurrences of shrieking decreased but the rate of stereotyped chanting was unaffected. (See Figure 5.)

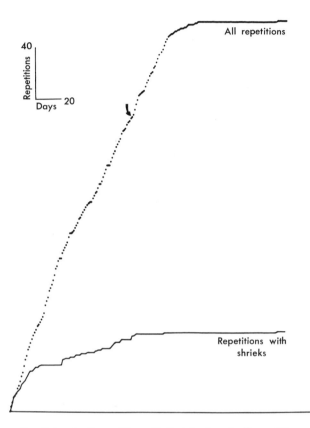

Figure 5.   Rate of all repetitions (dotted line) and all repetitions with shrieks (solid line) under conditions withdrawal of parental attention and sending to room contingent on shrieking and crying at end of chanting routine. Arrow on the curve showing all repetitions indicates the beginning of withdrawal of parental attention and the use of mimics to prompt and reinforce appropriate behavior.

Since elements of appropriate social behavior often occurred within the chanting routine, an attempt was made to modify the form of these occurrences rather than to eliminate them altogether. On each occurrence of stereotypic chanting, both parents would turn away from the child. One parent (e.g., the father) would call out the name of the other parent, "Mommy." The well-established mimic response again found its place as an instrument in dealing with a new class of behavior. The child would mimic the call, and the parent thus addressed would respond by saying, "Yes, son?" The first parent would then say a complete sentence such as,

"I want to sit down, please," which the child would again mimic. The parent addressed would again reinforce the mimic by responding accordingly, "Oh, you want to sit down. Well you can sit down right here." On subsequent occasions the verbal prompts were faded out and the parents would withhold reinforcement by looking away until the child called their names. They would then look at the child until he emitted the complete sentence, and would then respond appropriately to his request.

This procedure was begun at the arrow in Figure 5. The stereotyped chanting decreased to zero, as the child began to initiate more appropriate requests such as, "Mommy, I want to sit down, please."

The explicitness and effectiveness of operant conditioning procedures enables parents to contribute significantly to the rehabilitation of their deviant children after only a minimum of training. Similar programs of parent training were instituted with seven sets of parents, all of whom conducted the major part of the rehabilitation program with their children in the home.

It is apparent that the child's initial echolalic behavior was crucial to the rapid establishment of appropriate verbal behavior. Similar work by the authors and others (e.g., Sherman, 1965) indicates that it is much more difficult to establish a mimicking repertoire in a mute individual than to bring already-present mimicking behavior under the controls of appropriate discriminative stimuli, as was done in this study.

## REFERENCES

Sherman, J. A. Use of reinforcement and imitation to reinstate verbal behavior in psychotics. *J. abnorm. Psychol.,* 1965, *70,* 155–164.

Wolf, M. M., Risley, T. R., & Mees, H. L. Application of operant conditioning procedures to the behavior problems of an autistic child. *Behav. Res. Ther.,* 1964, *1,* 305–312.

# 18

# Experimental Studies in Childhood Schizophrenia. I. Analysis of Self-Destructive Behavior

## O. Ivar Lovaas, Gilbert Freitag, Vivian J. Gold, and Irene C. Kassorla

## EDITORS' COMMENTS

In the following article, the reader will find an effective analysis of one of the tragic forms of child behavior: personal destruction through physical self attack. A moment's consideration will bring to mind that the common characteristics of operant behavior changes are that (1) behavior occurs, and (2) the consequences of the behavior are arranged so as to produce the desired change. But if the behavior is self-destructive, and if it is such intense behavior that it threatens the health or life of the behaver, and, finally, if that behaver is a child: Can an experimental analysis be considered?

Perhaps the best answer is a counter-question: Can we fail to apply what we know? The usual way of containing self-destructive behavior is almost literally containment: the child is placed in a strait-jacket, sometimes for the extent of his life, to protect him against his own attack. A modern alternative is the heavy use of tranquilizers to produce a state in which the child is not self-destructive—but is only minimally awake. Either technique marks virtually an end to any further development and restricts the child's institutional life to a small fraction of what it might be in such surroundings.

To avoid those alternatives will require some analysis of the fundamental nature of self-destructive behavior, leading to an understanding of the variables which can reduce it virtually to zero. Such an analysis requires scientific expertness, a deep humane concern

O. Ivar Lovaas, Gilbert Freitag, Vivian J. Gold, and Irene C. Kassorla, "Experimental Studies in Childhood Schizophrenia. I. Analysis of Self-Destructive Behavior," *Journal of Experimental Child Psychology*, 1965, 2, 67–84. Reprinted by permission of Academic Press Inc.

This study was supported by a grant from the National Institute of Health (M-6241).

for the child's welfare, and a good deal of dedication and courage. The following report is an excellent example of the work of investigators who meet this description.

Dr. Lovaas and his co-workers have published a series of papers on their work with severely disturbed young children. A paper preceding this one is a description of the recording apparatus and procedure for observation of children in free play settings,[1] and several following this one describe further findings using aversive stimulation. Also, an excellent description of Dr. Lovaas' work is presented in a film produced by Smith, Kline, and French entitled "Reinforcement Therapy."

This paper will report on three studies concerned with investigating variables which controlled the self-destructive behavior of a schizophrenic child. The self-destructive behavior included head- and arm-banging against sharp corners of the furniture. This behavior was usually so intense that the child's skin was discolored, bruised and swollen.

The self-destructive behavior of this child will be viewed as learned (operant or instrumental) behavior; the strength of self-destructive behavior will be considered functionally related to the presentation and the withdrawal of social reinforcement.

In considering self-destructive behavior as similar to other learned social behaviors, one probably is working with the simplest and most easily testable notion designed to account for such behavior. Most alternative conceptual systems (to be presented subsequently) appear based on mechanisms other than social reinforcement as the explanation of self-destructive behavior. These other mechanisms might center on the assumption that the negatively reinforcing pain-inducing consequences of the behavior outweighs the positively reinforcing consequences from such sources as the social environment might provide, such as sympathy or attention. This is not to say that such an assumption excludes the possibility of positively reinforcing consequences, but that such consequences are deemphasized and subordinated to the role of "secondary" gains.

Conceptualizations involving guilt, and the reduction of guilt consequent upon self-inflicted pain, have become familiar through psychoanalytic writings. Equally familiar notions center on self-destructive behavior as a form of aggression. This aggression, instigated by frustration, is turned against the self, in so far as punishment had previously been associated with outward expression of aggression (Dollard et al., 1939). Somewhat more circumscribed conceptualizations, formulated primarily with young children in mind, consider destructive behavior towards one's own person

[1] O. Ivar Lovaas, Gilbert Freitag, Vivian J. Gold, and Irene C. Kassorla, "Recording Apparatus and Procedure for Observation of Behaviors of Children in Free Play Situations," *J. exp. child Psychol.*, 1965, 2, 108–120.

as serving to establish a "bodily reality" (Freud, 1954) and a "solidification" of the body image (Greenacre, 1954). Similarly, Bychowski (1954), in comparing the head-banging of adult schizophrenics to that of infants, maintains such behaviors are attempts to delimit the "self" from external reality. It has also been argued that aggression might be directed toward one's own person because of a *failure* to distinguish one's self from the external world (Hartmann, Kris, & Loewenstein, 1949). Some writers (Levy & Patrick, 1928) have considered head-banging to be autoerotic, hence self-reinforcing. Others (Goldfarb, 1945) consider it to provide compensatory stimulation in otherwise non-stimulated (e.g., institutionalized) children.

Cain (1961) has brought together several observational reports regarding self-destructive behavior in animals and young children. As far as the authors of this study are aware, there appears to be no study in print in which self-destructive behavior has been investigated systematically, i.e., where the investigator has attempted control over self-destruction by systematically manipulating the variables of which it might be a function.

There were three studies in which self-destructive behavior was investigated. Two concerned observation of self-destructive behavior which occurred while appropriate social behaviors were reinforced and subsequently extinguished. The third concerned changes in self-destructive behavior under a variety of conditions.

In all studies, observation centered on one *S,* a nine-year-old schizophrenic girl.[1] It is relevant to know that her history of self-destructive behavior dates back to her third year of life. This behavior was primarily "head-banging" (against walls and furniture, at times with great force), "arm-banging" (against sharp corners), pinching and slapping herself, setting her hair on fire by sticking her head into the electric wall heater, etc. It is also relevant that social approval (smiles, verbal praise, etc.) was a positively reinforcing event to her, a fact which was experimentally established in our laboratory. Her "appropriate" social behaviors were minimal (e.g., her speech was largely echolalic), and she engaged in considerable self-stimulatory behavior (fondling herself, and moving her arms and hands in repetitive, stereotyped manners). Similarly, her interaction with physical objects (play with toys, etc.) was stereotyped and restricted.

All experiments were conducted in sparsely furnished rooms which contained only tables and chairs. Adjoining observation rooms were connected by one-way mirrors and sound equipment which permitted observation and recording of the child's behavior. *S*'s behavior was recorded on an Esterline Angus pen recorder by equipment and procedures which have been more fully described in an earlier paper (Lovaas *et al.,* 1964). In

---

[1] *S* was diagnosed as Schizophrenic, with autistic and symbiotic features, at the Neuropsychiatric Institute and the Psychology Clinic, U. C. L. A., 1962, and had been so diagnosed previously at other clinics in the Los Angeles area.

short, the observer could, with a panel of button-switches, reliably record both the frequency and duration of several behaviors simultaneously.

# STUDY 1

### The First Acquisition

During this phase of the study, S acquired a repertoire of appropriate behavior to music. The repertoire consisted of clapping her hands and rocking in rhythm with the music, making correct gestures to the songs as were indicated by the words (e.g., "clap your hands"), and saying or singing some words of the songs at appropriate times. She reinforced this behavior with approval. Smiles and comments such as "that's a good girl" were used. The acquisition was carried out somewhat informally over a two-month interval. No accurate recording was made of the first acquisition.

### The First Extinction

The only difference between the extinction and acquisition sessions was that *the reinforcement, social approval, was not given contingent upon any behavior of S.* The S's appropriate musical behavior now ceased to have an effect on Es. However, Es maintained the same amount of friendly behavior, i.e., they smiled continuously and looked pleasant. Each session lasted for ten minutes and occurred once a day, five days a week, for 41 days. The songs and dance were the same as in the acquisition: the order and duration of their presentation was held constant.

During the music sessions S's behavior in general had been unusually appropriate compared to sessions with S in other settings such as the playroom. The importance of the effect of music *per se,* relating to the appropriateness of S's behavior, was assessed by omitting the guitar from the music sessions on alternate days. During these sessions the words of the songs were not sung, but spoken. Otherwise conditions were the same as on the days when the guitar was included. Although this operation appears to be irrelevant in understanding the variables involved in this study, mention is made of it since it accounts for certain fluctuations in her behavior. These alternations, of music and no music, occurred only during the first extinction of Study 1.

### The Second Acquisition

The second acquisition started 48 days after termination of the first extinction and lasted for 27 sessions. A new set of three songs and a dance were employed. Singing with the guitar (i.e., music) was present on every session. Whenever *S* emitted appropriate music behavior, she was again socially reinforced with verbal comments and smiles.

In other respects the sessions were the same as during the extinction; they lasted for 10 minutes, occurred once a day, 5 days a week. *E*s were pleasant and smiling, etc.

## The Second Extinction

The second extinction lasted for five sessions and was identical to the first extinction except that music was present each time.

In short, the first step consisted of reinforcing *S* for appropriate behaviors in the music sessions with social approval. The second step consisted of withholding social approval for these behaviors. The third and fourth steps were replications of the first and second, respectively.

Starting with the first extinction, an observer in the adjoining room recorded the following behaviors of *S*:

1. *Appropriate Music Behavior* was defined as: clapping hands or rocking in time to the music; singing or saying the words to the songs at the correct time (as they appeared in the lyrics and were sung or spoken by the *E*s); making suitable gestures in conjunction with parts of the songs (such as wiggling the body during the phrase, "the children in the bus go 'wiggle-wiggle-wiggle' ").

2. *Self-destructive Behavior* was defined as: hitting head, elbows, wrists, or other parts of the body against the wall, sharp corners of the furniture, the light switch, etc.

When *S* initiated any one of the defined behaviors, the observer pressed the button on the operating panel assigned to that behavior. The button was pressed at the time the behavior occurred and was kept down until the behavior terminated. If more than two seconds separated two responses (e.g., two words, or two head-bangs) these were recorded as separate responses. In this way, the apparatus kept a running account of both frequency and duration of each behavior.

# RESULTS OF STUDY 1

The data from Study 1 are presented in Figure 1. The abscissa gives the sessions, numbered from the first extinction. The ordinate gives the percent of total session time *S* engaged in the two behaviors, self-destructive and appropriate music behavior. The frequencies of self-destructive behaviors over the various sessions are given directly below the session numbers on the abscissa.

The percentage of appropriate music behavior alternated from high to low from one session to the next, the alternations becoming less marked

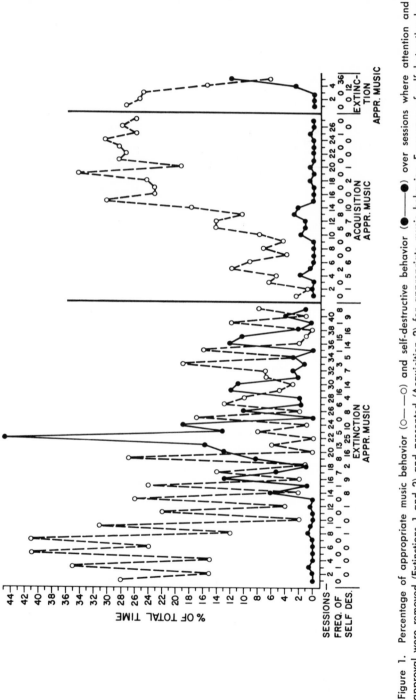
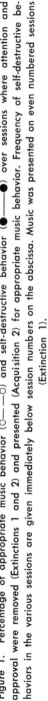

Figure 1. Percentage of appropriate music behavior (O——O) and self-destructive behavior (●——●) over sessions where attention and approval were removed (Extinctions 1 and 2) and presented (Acquisition 2) for appropriate music behavior. Frequency of self-destructive behaviors in the various sessions are given immediately below session numbers on the abscissa. Music was presented on even numbered sessions (Extinction 1).

200

by the 28th session. These alternations correlate with and probably are a function of the presence and absence of music (music was present on even-numbered sessions). These noticeable alternations in the record, if considered a function of music *per se,* are irrelevant in understanding the main variables involved in this study.

*The first extinction* (reinforcement withheld for appropriate music behavior) is accompanied by an initial increase in appropriate music behavior. By the 7th session, however, this behavior decreased. On the other hand, self-destructive behavior, which stayed at almost zero level during the first part of the extinction, increased. By the 20th session the percentage of self-destructive behavior exceeded that of appropriate music behavior, and by the 22nd session reached the level previously attained by appropriate music behavior. Self-destructive behavior then decreased. From the 25th session on, very systematic alternations of the relative magnitude of the two behaviors occurred. On days when self-destructive behavior was high, appropriate music behavior was low, and *vice versa.* It is to be noted that there was no correlation between the amount of self-destructive behavior in the music room and other places such as the playroom or home. In fact, on the day of the 22nd session, when she peaked on self-destructive behavior, S had no self-destructive behavior in any other setting. So far as Es know, S was not treated differently, in the clinic or the home, on the days when she was self-destructive in the music room as compared to other days. It is concluded, therefore, that variations in her self-destructive behavior were due to the experimental manipulations.

*The second acquisition* (reinforcement delivered for appropriate music behavior) showed a gradual increase in appropriate music behavoir over the 27 sessions, while self-destructive behavior decreased to a near-zero level. The sudden drop in self-destructive behavior during the second acquisition was probably due to the introduction of a new set of songs and dances (which had not been associated with reinforcement withdrawal). A further discussion of this point will be presented in Study 3, when a similar reduction was observed.

*The second extinction* (reinforcement withheld for appropriate music behavior) showed a relatively rapid decrease in appropriate music behaviors, accompanied by a similarly rapid increase in self-destructive behaviors. By the 5th session the percentage of self-destructive behaviors exceeded appropriate music behavior. The study was terminated at that point so as to prevent S from further self-inflicted damage.

In summary, then, the data indicate that the occurrence and magnitude of self-destructive behavior is a function of the reinforcement and subsequent extinction of another behavior in that same situation. The data also show that when one of these behaviors is high, the other is low, the behaviors systematically alternating in relative magnitude. The inference that the two behaviors are members of the same response class, i.e., that they are both social responses or responses controlled by social stimuli, will be discussed after additional data are examined.

## STUDY 2

A replication of Study 1, involving acquisition and extinction of another social response, was made with the same $S$ in another experimental setting. $S$ was brought into another room, similar to the one in Study 1. Study 2 was initiated immediately after the completion of Study 3, but is presented here because of its similarity to Study 1. On a table was a bar-pressing apparatus which consisted of a wooden box, about one foot on a side, with a 6-inch bar extending in front. The bar-pressing apparatus was placed on a table between $E$ and $S$ who were both seated on opposite sides of the table facing each other.

When $S$ first entered the room, she was told by $E$ to press the bar, and praised when she did so. After this initial prompted response $E$ maintained an inattentive position, i.e., looking down in her lap and not conversing, unless $S$ pressed the bar. When $S$ did press the bar, $E$ would look up at $S$, smile, and provide five seconds of "pleasant talk": "That's a good girl, I love you very much, you are a sweetheart," etc. $E$ would then resume her original inattentive position until $S$ again pressed the bar. With a stable and high rate of bar-pressing, it was possible for $S$ to keep $E$ delivering attention and approval at a continuous, almost non-interrupted level. The sessions had lasted for ten minutes daily, five days a week, for 30 days. $S$ reached a relatively stable rate of responding by the 14th day, only the last 16 days of this training will be presented (in Figure 2).

Once a steady rate of bar-pressing had been acquired, extinction began. $E$ no longer attended to $S$ contingent upon bar-press responses, but remained in an inattentive position throughout the sessions. The extinction for bar-pressing behavior lasted for 7 days. The end of these 7 extinction sessions was followed by a second acquisition period, with $E$ reintroducing attention and approval contingent upon $S$'s bar-press for another 4 days.

Each response on the bar activated a cumulative recorder located in an adjacent observation room. The observer in this room kept recordings of $S$'s self-destructive behavior in the same manner as in Study 1.

## RESULTS OF STUDY 2

The data of Study 2 are presented in Figure 2. The abscissa gives the acquisition and extinction sessions. The ordinate gives the frequency of self-destructive behaviors during the 10 minute session. (Since there was a high correlation between frequency and duration of self-destructive behaviors (see Study 1, Figure 1), and in order to avoid the time-consuming task of deriving the duration measures, only frequency of self-destructive behavior will be presented in Studies 2 and 3.) Total numbers of bar-pressings for the social reinforcer over the various sessions are presented on the abscissa, immediately below the session numbers.

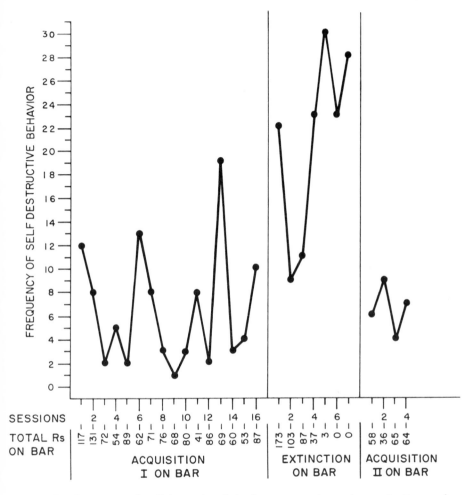

Figure 2. Frequency of self-destructive behavior over sessions where attention and approval were presented (Acquisitions 1 and 2) and removed (Extinction 1) for bar-pressing behavior. Frequency of bar-pressing in the various sessions is given immediately below session numbers on the abscissa.

As can be observed, extinction of the bar-pressing response shows an immediate increase in frequency of that response which is accompanied by an increase in self-destructive behavior over the level maintained while the bar-press was reinforced. The figure also shows a decrease in self-destructive behavior and a reinstatement of the bar-pressing response upon reintroduction of reinforcement for bar-pressing (the second acquisition).

E considered it unnecessary to repeat the extinction operations for the bar-press in lieu of the similarity of these data to Study 1. A further consideration for termination of the study at this time was based on protecting S from additional self-inflicted injury.

In summary, Study 2 supports the findings of Study 1. Frequency of self-destructive behavior appears to be a function of the presentation and withdrawal of reinforcement for other behaviors in the same situation. The behaviors alternate in relative magnitude with the alternation of conditions of reinforcement for the other response.

## STUDY 3

This study was undertaken to investigate the affect of three variables involved in self-destructive behavior. First, an attempt was made to investigate the effect of verbal comments made contingent upon S's self-destructive behavior. The question asked was whether or not this kind of social consequence would change the frequency of that behavior. To test this effect, the comment "I don't think you are bad" was expressed by E in an emphatic and reassuring manner after S engaged in self-destructive behavior. The rationale underlying the choice of this comment rather than any other comment will be discussed later. Secondly, an attempt was made to investigate the effect upon S's self-destructive behavior of E's "ignoring" her. To test the effect of ignoring, Es would not smile and attend to S for the duration of entire sessions. Thirdly, an attempt was made to investigate the effect upon self-destruction of a change in the particular stimulus events which had been associated with reinforcement withdrawal. The concern here was the extent to which the songs with which withdrawal of reinforcement had been associated in the recent past (within the last month) had acquired stimulus control over the occurrence of self-destructive behavior in the music situation. In order to accomplish this test, a set of new songs with which S had had no previous reinforcement history (hence no history of reinforcement withdrawal) was introduced.

The experimental design consisted of introducing these experimental variables, i.e., comments, "ignoring," and new songs, during certain sessions (experimental sessions), interspersed with sessions when no experimental variables were introduced (control sessions). The criterion for alternations of these sessions was that S's self-destructive behavior in control sessions should fall within the level of the pre-experimental sessions before the experimental variables were introduced. Essentially, then, the pattern follows a single subject, "baseline" design.

Study 3 took place in the same room as Study 1. Study 3 was started immediately after the completion of Study 1, and before the initiation of Study 2. Except for the experimental variables the procedure was identical to that of the *second extinction* of Study 1. S was not reinforced for appropriate music behavior, Es maintained friendly and attentive behavior throughout, the sessions lasted for 10 minutes, S's behavior was recorded in the same manner, etc.

The experimental variables became distributed over the sessions in the following manner: (1) The comment "I don't think you're bad" followed every self-destructive response during sessions 16 through 19 (FR:1). During sessions 20, 24, 25, 26, 33, and 38 a comment was made on the average of every 5th self-destructive response (VR:5). No comments were given during the remaining sessions. (2) During sessions 30 through 38, Es, who had been smiling and attentive to S throughout the sessions, did not smile and became inattentive. During sessions 33 and 38, E smiled and attended to S only while commenting, and continued to "ignore" when not commenting. (3) On sessions 44, 46, and 48, Es introduced a set of new nursery school songs with which S had had no prior experience and therefore no history of reinforcement withdrawal. All other sessions (1–15, 21–23, 27–29, 39–43, 45, 47) were control, or "baseline" sessions. The experimental operations are given in Figure 3 to facilitate their presentation.

# RESULTS OF STUDY 3

The data are presented in Figure 3. The abscissa indicates the various experimental manipulations in abbreviated form below their respective sessions. The ordinate gives the frequency of self-destructive behaviors in the 10 minute music session.

### Effect of the Comment

Examination of the frequency of self-destructive behaviors on the sessions where E commented upon that behavior (sessions 16 through 20, 24 through 26, 33, and 38) shows a definite increase in the behavior over the frequency of self-destruction on control days. This increase is attributed to the comments, i.e., the comments served to increase the frequency of S's self-destructive behavior. No attempt was made to separately evaluate the effect of the two schedules of comment delivery.

### Effect of Attention and Smile Withdrawal

There was no change in self-destructive behavior when E's smiles and attention were withdrawn from the sessions (sessions 30 through 37). Self-

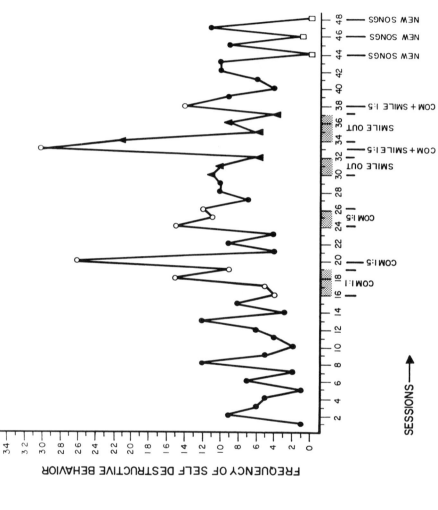

Figure 3. Frequency of self-destructive behavior over sessions when E commented (○) upon the behavior (16–19, 20, 24–26, 33, 38), when Es withdrew smiles and attention (▲) from entire sessions (30–38), and when new songs were introduced (□) (44, 46, 48). All other ses-

206

destructive behavior was not effected by a change in *Es'* smiles and attention *per se:* "ignoring" when presented continuously during a session did not increase self-destructive behavior. However, these same social stimuli presented and withdrawn *in relationship to S's behavior* did effect self-destruction. That is, the presentation and removal of smiles and attention, contingent upon appropriate music behavior, effected her self-destructive behavior (conf. Studies 1 and 2). Similarly, the comment, which involved attention and smiles, when delivered contingent upon her self-destructive behavior, altered that behavior. It is possible that the withdrawal of smiles and attention functioned as a deprivation operation, thereby increasing the effectiveness of such stimuli as reinforcers. This operation might account for the peak in self-destructive behaviors in session 33 when they are again presented contingent upon that behavior.

### Effect of the New Songs

During sessions 44, 46, and 48, when new songs were introduced, the level of self-destructive behavior fell to zero or near-zero level. A similar drop in self-destructive behavior with the introduction of new songs was observed during the second acquisition in Study 1. In the case of the new songs *S* does not have a history of reinforcement-withdrawal since reinforcement had not been delivered previously. Thus, *S's* self-destructive behavior appears to be functionally related to the kinds of history she has had with the stimulus situation presented to her.

The data of Study 3 can be summarized by saying that (1) the effect of verbal comments contingent upon self-destruction served to increase the frequency of that behavior, (2) the effect of ignoring *per se* was not enough to produce any changes in self-destructive behavior (although the same operation, in specific behavioral contingencies, was effective), and (3) the removal of a stimulus previously associated with reinforcement withdrawal decreases the frequency of self-destructive behavior.

# DISCUSSION

The results illustrate the lawfulness and regularity which characterize the self-destructive behavior of this child. The data show the functional relationships between very specific environmental operations and the self-destruction: reinforcement and extinction of other behaviors in a given setting controls the frequency and magnitude of self-destructive behavior; delivery of social reinforcement contingent upon the occurrence of self-destructive behavior increases its frequency and magnitude. The data also show a systematic reversal of self-destructive responses with appropriate social behaviors which argues for their membership in the same response class, as social behaviors. Conceptually, the system which best fits these functional relationships involves a consideration of self-destructive behavior as learned, operant, or instrumental, behavior. An attempt will be made to relate the behavioral observations as evidenced in this study to this system.

The occurrence of operant behavior is controlled by two kinds of stimuli, discriminative and reinforcing. We shall label those stimuli discriminative which "set the occasion" for self-destructive behavior because they signalled reinforcement for such behavior. In other words, they "cued" the self-destructive behavior. A stimulus is called a reinforcing stimulus when, produced by self-destructive behavior, it strengthens that behavior. In a sense, it served as a "reward" or "pay-off" for that behavior. Since both these kinds of stimuli were social (i.e., provided by another person) the self-destructive behavior will be labelled as social behavior. The two kinds of control (reinforcing and discriminative) over the self-destructive behavior will be discussed separately.

**Reinforcement Control**

The effect of social reinforcement upon self-destructive behavior is shown in Study 3. A social event ("I don't think you are bad"), when delivered contingent upon self-destructive behavior, increases the frequency of that behavior. By definition, then, the comment serves as a social reinforcer, and the behavior follows the laws of operant behavior. No attempt was made to analyze the particular stimulus aspect which was reinforcing in this comment, but $E$s consider it reasonable to expect that almost any comment, delivering attention, would have had a similar effect.

The reinforcement control is also apparent when reinforcement is withheld for the self-destructive behavior, in which case the self-destructive behavior should decrease in strength, as did appropriate music behavior. The first extinction of Study 1 shows this effect—the self-destructive behavior was "cued off" by the reinforcement withdrawal, but since self-destructive behavior is not reinforced, it decreases in strength and thereby has the form of operant behavior. In the last part of the first extinction the two behaviors (appropriate music and self-destruction) alternate in relative magnitude from one session to another. In a sense, the two behaviors compete for social reinforcement. They have the same history of non-reinforcement in this particular setting, hence they have about equal (and low) probability of occurrence, or strength. The self-destructive behavior appears, then, to have the same relationships to consequential environmental events as does appropriate music behavior.

## Discriminative Stimulus Control

The discriminative stimulus control over self-destructive behavior is evident in the sudden reduction of this behavior to zero level when the new stimuli (songs) were introduced. Conceptually, the new songs were not discriminative for self-destruction. The argument supporting this statement would be based on the different reinforcement history $S$ has had with the two sets of songs. The old songs have been associated with withdrawal of reinforcement for appropriate musical behavior. The new songs have not been associated with reinforcement withdrawal, since no reinforcement had been given for music behavior appropriate to these songs. Thus, introduction of new songs reduced self-destructive behavior rather than maintaining it at the level at which it occurred in the presence of the old songs. It is considered, therefore, that withdrawal of reinforcement *from a previously reinforced response* is the discriminative stimulus for self-destructive behavior. The establishment of this event as discriminative for self-destruction would indicate that in the past this event has signalled reinstatement of reinforcement, should $S$ behave self-destructively. In popular terms, it can be said that whenever reinforcement was withheld (as in a demand situation) $S$ could obtain reinforcement (the demand would be withdrawn and reinforcement produced) provided she hurt herself. This self-destruction, therefore, had an immediate "pay-off," the reinstatement of the desired reinforcement.

The same kind of discriminative stimulus control is present in Studies 1 and 2, the effects shown particularly well in Study 2. When a response (appropriate music behavior) fails to bring reinforcement during extinction as it has previously during acquisition, this marks the occasion for $S$ to engage in self-destructive behavior. That is, the self-destructive behaviors in Studies 1 and 2 were controlled by reinforcement withdrawal for another response, namely the appropriate music behavior to the songs.

Theoretically, the operation of withholding reinforcement should be discriminative for any response which could serve to "reinstate" the reinforcement, and not only for self-destructive behavior. Both in Study 1 (first extinction) and in Study 2 (extinction), the withdrawal of reinforcement is accompanied by an increase in the magnitude of the response being extinguished (music behavior and bar-press) before the increase of self-destructive behavior occurs. We also observed, but were unable to replicate, an increase in appropriate and acceptable verbal behavior during the first seven days of Study 1 (first extinction). From a reinforcement theory point of view, the withholding of reinforcement is discriminative for a number of behaviors, some more socially acceptable than others. One might state that when a response, previously effective in bringing about reinforcement, ceases to bring on these effects, this signals the person to either increase the magnitude of this same behavior or to switch to some other behavior, however acceptable, which in the past has been operative in obtaining reinforcement. Predicting what specific response will be emitted, and at what times, involves a detailed knowledge of the person's past reinforcement history which most often is unavailable. It can be considered that S exhausted her repertoire of social behaviors in a hierarchal manner during the extinction sessions: the first behaviors to appear and the first to extinguish were those most recently acquired in the laboratory (e.g., appropriate music behavior, bar-pressing, appropriate verbal behavior) and the last behaviors to appear and the last to extinguish were those brought into the laboratory from home and other situations (e.g., self-destructive behaviors).

Further support for discriminative stimulus control is given by two additional considerations which show how highly discriminating S was in the very specific times and explicit circumstances during which she was self-destructive. A physically rather gross operation, such as Es' removal of smiles and attention from entire sessions 30 through 37 of Study 3, did not alter S's behavior. Yet the removal of attention and smiles for responding in Study 1, an operation which was physically so small that a casual observer would not have been able to discern it in Es' behavior, did produce major changes in S's behavior.

A second observation, this time in another setting, supports the notion of S's ability to discriminate the highly specific circumstances in which to be self-destructive. The day of session 22 of the first extinction in Study 1, when she peaked on self-destruction in the music room, was her "best" day in another setting, the preschool room. Concurrent recordings of her acceptable social behaviors in the preschool room, to which she returned immediately following the music sessions, show a steady rise in these behaviors, completely unrelated to her self-destructive behavior in the music room.

The data, then, supports the notion of very specific environmental control over her self-destruction rather than control from internal "states" (such as guilt and "hostile introjects"). A discussion of the effects of the comment "I do not think you are bad" is particularly related to this point. The choice of the comment was made after consulting several professional people, who in agreement, concluded S's self-destructive behavior to be a function of internal states, predominantly guilt. The comment, they hypothesized, might reduce her self-destruction by reducing her guilt-level (or the magnitude of the "hostile introject"). It was shown in Study 3 that, on the contrary, this comment when made contingent upon self-destructive behavior increased such behavior. According to the considerations already mentioned in this paper any verbal response by E delivering attention contingent upon self-destructive behavior would serve to positively reinforce that behavior. An implication of this finding is that when one responds to a patient—even with a minor comment to a "socially insulated" (i.e., autistic) child—one may cause considerable harm rather than good, unless one is aware of several possible stimulus aspects of one's response and their *temporal relationships* to the patient's behavior.

Although the findings in these studies indicate that social stimuli controlled the self-destructive behavior, we have no evidence that *only* social stimuli control self-destruction. Furthermore, the authors do not intend the data, presented here on a single child, to be explanatory of self-destructive behavior in children in general. Rather, the findings demonstrate a phenomenon (certain reliable relationships between self-destructive behavior and social stimuli), but its generality over Ss has not been established. However, the findings we have presented are consistent with those obtained by other investigators. In Cain's descriptions (1961, p. 183–185) of self-destructive behaviors in children, almost every instigation to self-destruction appears to involve reinforcement withdrawal: ". . . when things 'went wrong' . . . whenever he was cross. . . . when isolated . . . put in crib against her wishes . . . thwarted in any way . . . touch a toy in her possession. . . . not get his own way . . . not allowed to go out . . ." etc. Although there are no studies in which self-destructive behavior has been systematically reinforced, several studies report extinction of self-destructive behavior when social stimuli have been withheld contingent upon such behavior. For example, Wolf *et al.,* (1963) extinguished self-destructive behavior in a 6-year-old autistic boy by isolating him from interpersonal contact whenever he was self-destructive. In a similar manner, Ball *et al.,* (1964) reduced self-destructive behavior in a 12-year-old psychotic retarded boy. His self-destruction had been so severe and prolonged that it had necessitated physical restraints (both arms and feet) for 24 hours a day, for most of the seven years he had been hospitalized. Williams (1959) also reports extinction in the case of children's tantrum behavior.

Although self-destructive behavior will extinguish, or at least reach very low magnitudes when not reinforced, this is a slow procedure requiring several sessions or days. Furthermore, in placing the child on extinction $E$ temporarily exposes the child to danger because of the apparent increase in self-destruction immediately accompanying the onset of extinction. To overcome these problems of the slow extinction and the temporary danger to the child, Lovaas *et al.,* (1964) delivered painful electric shock contingent upon such behaviors with two children who engaged in self-destructive (and tantrum) behaviors. The behaviors were suppressed within minutes, and remained suppressed for eleven months. One non-contingent shock re-suppressed the behavior for the remainder of the study (several months).

The beneficial effect of suppressing and/or extinguishing self-destructive behavior is probably obvious—when one is attempting to educate these children one invariably places demands on the child, i.e., reinforcement is withheld until the desired response is emitted. Ensuing tantrum and self-destructive behaviors of the child not only retards educational efforts of others, but interferes with the likelihood that the desired response would be emitted.

## SUMMARY

This paper reported on three studies concerned with investigating variables which controlled self-destructive behaviors in a schizophrenic child. The self-destructive behaviors included head- and arm-banging which was usually so intense that the child's skin was discolored, bruised and swollen.

Methodologically, the experimental procedure followed an intrasubject replication design which involved repeated presentations of the same experimental variables in order to insure reliability.

The results illustrate the lawfulness and regularity which characterized the self-destructive behavior. The data show the functional relationships between very specific environmental operations and the self-destruction: reinforcement and extinction of other behaviors in a given setting controlled the frequency and magnitude of self-destructive behavior; delivery of sympathetic comments, contingent upon the occurrence of self-destructive behavior increased its frequency and magnitude.

Conceptually, the system which best fits the observed relationships involves a consideration of self-destructive behavior as learned, operant or instrumental, social behavior.

## REFERENCES

Ball, T. S., Dameron, L. E., & Lovaas, O. I. Control of self-destructive behaviors in mentally retarded children, 1964. Unpublished manuscript.

Bychowski, G. Problems of infantile neurosis: a discussion. In *The psychoanalytic study of the child*. Vol. IX. New York: International Universities Press, 1954.

Cain, A. C. The presuperego turning inward of aggression. *Psychoanalyt. Quart.*, 1961, *30*, 171–208.

Dollard, J., Doob, L. W., Miller, N. E., Mowrer, O. H., & Sears, R. R. *Frustration and aggression*. New Haven: Yale, 1939.

Freud, A. Problems of infantile neurosis: a discussion. In *The psychoanalytic study of the child*. Vol. IX. New York: International Universities Press, 1954.

Goldfarb, W. Psychological privation in infancy. *Amer. J. Orthopsychiat.*, 1945, *15*, 247–255.

Greenacre, P. Problems of infantile neurosis: a discussion. In *The psychoanalytic study of the child*. Vol. IX. New York: International Universities Press, 1954.

Hartmann, H., Kris, E., & Loewenstein, R. M. Notes on the theory of aggression. In *The psychoanalytic study of the child*. Vols. III-IV. New York: International Universities Press, 1949.

Levy, D. M., & Patrick, H. T. Relations of infantile convulsions and head-banging to fainting and headache in parents. *Arch. Neurol. Psychiat.*, 1928, *19*, 864–887.

Lovaas, O. I., Freitag, G., Kinder, M. I., Rubenstein, D. B., Schaeffer, B., & Simmons, J. B. Experimental studies in childhood schizophrenia. Developing social behavior using electric shock. Paper read at *Amer. Psychol. Ass.* meetings, Los Angeles, September, 1964.

Williams, C. D. The elimination of tantrum behavior by extinction procedures. *J. abnorm. soc. Psychol.*, 1959, *59*, 269.

Wolf, M., Mees, H., & Risley, T. Application of operant conditioning procedures to the behavior problems of an autistic child. Paper delivered to *Western Psychol. Ass.*, Santa Monica, California, May, 1963.

# 19

# Behavior Modification in Rehabilitation

## Lee Meyerson, Nancy Kerr, and Jack L. Michael

### EDITORS' COMMENTS

This paper was written specifically for this volume. We are grateful to the authors for the preparation of this paper because we wanted to include at least one report of work from the area of "rehabilitation" rather than child therapy.

After reading this article and comparing it with the studies by Wolf *et al.,* and Lovaas *et al.,* the reader may wonder about the difference between child therapy and rehabilitation. In the study by Wolf *et al.,* the programming of glasses-wearing was obviously rehabilitative. On the other hand in the three studies by Lovaas *et al.,* self-destructive behavior was treated with child therapy. Yet the same principles were used in all of these studies. It is apparent that the distinction is a practical one and that there are frequent instances of overlapping. If rehabilitation has as its main core the application of psychological principles to problems with physical origins, and child therapy is concerned with problems with interactional-historical factors, obviously no clear-cut distinctions can be made. The causal conditions in one category can apply to the other. To force a distinction is to ignore what is known about child behavior and development.

This paper should be particularly instructive in addition, because the authors are skilled in giving an easily understandable account of what they do, of the differences between their procedures and others, and of some of the common objections to their approach.

The treatment of handicapped persons in rehabilitation centers often

Edward Hanley, William Heard, Brian Jacobson, Karl Minke, Albert Neal, and Larry Sayre, graduate students at Arizona State University, were the experimenters in the studies reported in this paper. Their collaboration is acknowledged with appreciation and thanks.

The research training program of which this work was a part was supported by National Institute of Mental Health Grant MH-7818 and by Vocational Rehabilitation Administration Grant 344-T.

We are grateful to our colleagues at the Valley of the Sun School and the Gompers Memorial Rehabilitation Center for their many courtesies.

requires them to engage in activities that are difficult, effortful, or un-
pleasant to perform. It is not surprising, in view of this factor alone and
without consideration of other possible influential variables, that many
rehabilitation clients resist rehabilitative efforts. Nor is it surprising that
rehabilitation personnel complain frequently of "lack of motivation" in
their clients or that the proportion of cases discharged from rehabilitation
centers for this reason is relatively high.

Characteristically, the patient whose behavior fails to conform to
the expectations of the rehabilitation staff is referred to the psychologist
for "evaluation." Much of the work of the psychologist in rehabilitation
is at present devoted to the routine evaluation of client intelligence, personality, and achievement, in the belief that these data are "good things"
to know and that they may help the staff do better work. Most of the
data obtained, however, seem strikingly unrelated to the behavior required in the rehabilitation center. They may lead the psychologist to
believe that he "understands" better why a client acts as he does, but the
data lend little aid in changing unacceptable behavior to more-acceptable
behavior. Most often the psychologist confirms the observation of others
that the client is unmotivated, and he assigns a reason for it. This reason
is usually some inaccessible trait of the client: "He hasn't accepted his
disability." "He isn't bright enough or mature enough to understand what
is best for him." "He is overly dependent." "His super-ego is weak."

Sometimes such evaluations are accompanied by vague directions
to give the client "psychological support," to coax him more, or counsel
him so that he will understand himself better. More often they seem to
result in a decision to discharge the client as unmotivated or as having
reached the maximum medical benefit that is possible without long-term
psychotherapy which may or may not change the underlying or "real"
personality problems.

This kind of approach to rehabilitation not only places an over-
whelming, needless, and often unfulfillable responsibilty on the client to
be the architect of his own rehabilitation, but also neglects two other
basic variables that can be manipulated for the client's benefit: his
environment and, as a result of the manipulation of his environment, his
behavior.

Most rehabilitation psychologists will accept the formula $B=f(P, E)$,
or behavior is a function of a person's interaction with his environment.
In concentrating on the P term in the formula, however, it is easy to
neglect the fact that the formula has three terms and that B and E can
be independent variables also. Among psychologists who strive to do more
than measure and categorize the traits of disabled persons, present practice is to attempt direct changes in the person by counseling and verbal
psychotherapeutic procedures. It is not generally perceived that equally
indirect changes of the psychological situation by manipulation of the

environment may be equally valuable and far more feasible. It may be better, for example, to assist a physical therapist in achieving his goal of restoring functional use of an arm or leg than to attempt to deal with the inferiority feelings or dependency status that may be engendered in a person because he lacks such functional use. Counseling and psychotherapy were developed in an attempt to modify abnormal reactions to normal situations. It is by no means clear that they are the treatments of choice for normal reactions to abnormal situations.

Following the pattern of previous experimentation (Meyerson & Kerr, in press,) in which operant conditioning techniques were used to obtain striking behavioral changes in rehabilitation clients, we accepted at face value the behavioral problems referred to us by other members of a rehabilitation-center team. We gave no tests; we made no evaluations; we held no interviews; we took no history. In fact, we generally knew nothing at all about the person referred to us except that he was not engaging in some behavior that was desirable for his rehabilitation. In addition, almost all of the experimental work was conducted by first-year graduate students who had had no previous experience in clinical psychology or rehabilitation, but who did know learning theory.

We were guided in this work by the theoretical formulations of the Workgroup on Learning of the Miami Conference on Psychological Research and Rehabilitation (Meyerson, Michael, Mowrer, Osgood, & Staats, 1963). In particular, we took seriously the following statements:

Motivation may be considered the task of specifying adequate reinforcers (p. 91).

If an individual "should" do something . . . you must provide strong reinforcers contingent upon his behavior . . . (p. 92).

One of the most important things that we can offer . . . is a frame of reference which induces (psychologists in rehabilitation) to look for adequate reinforcers and to apply them correctly, skillfully and subtly . . . if this approach were followed, many presently difficult problems might become readily amenable to solution (p. 101).

Psychologists in rehabilitation (should) look for causal, manipulable variables in a situation which they would then use to facilitate the generally accepted goals of rehabilitation workers (p. 78).

Some of the problems referred to us were remarkably simple ones that could be solved immediately by the application of a single behavioral principle. Others were much more complex, and the results reported here can be considered only a beginning in the application of behavioral principles to some rehabilitation problems. As in other beginnings, our initial experiments have been crude, lacking in the precision and elegance of design, the data collecting, and the reporting that are desirable, but a start has been made, and the fruitfulness of the approach may be apparent.

## CASE 1. LACK OF MOTIVATION IN A TRAUMATIC QUADRIPLEGIC ADOLESCENT

### Background

John K. was in an automobile accident when he was 16 years old. After he had spent four months in what was medically diagnosed as a decerebrate condition, recovery of function began to occur. At the time he was first seen by us, at the age of 18, he was unable to walk, and tremors in the upper extremities were severe. Binocular vision, speech, memory, attention span, and muscular coordination were reported to be impaired.

### Problem

The occupational therapist had selected the task of learning to type, by hunt and peck, as an intrinsically interesting and useful one which would also improve the client's hand-eye coordination. Although the client verbally expressed interest in learning to type, in practice, he did not attend to the task. He would type a few letters, stop, and then call the therapist with a complaint or a question or simply wait for her to approach him and ask why he was not working. He did this with a frequency that allowed little time for actual typing behavior, and hand-eye coordination did not improve. In addition, his "need" for attention made it difficult for the occupational therapist to function effectively with other patients. In view of the client's behavior and his failure to make progress, the therapist believed that maximum functional benefit had been reached and the client should be discharged.

### Observation

The client never worked for longer than 5 to 7 minutes at a time. He would then stop or call for the therapist's attention. The therapist invariably responded by coming over to where he was working, answering his question or complaint, and talking with him for a few moments before coaxing him to return to work.

### Behavioral Analysis

The occupational therapist was reinforcing the disrupting behavior. The client "liked" to talk and receive attention from the therapist more than he liked to engage in the difficult typing task, and he controlled the situation because the therapist invariably responded to his demands.

In this case, as in others, there were four basic questions to be answered:

1. What is the "desirable" behavior? This question must be answered with precision in terms of objectively observable actions. An answer that the client should "do more," or "show more interest and spunk" is insufficient unless *what* he should do more of or what he should show more interest in is specified. In this case it was desired that the client engage in more typing behavior.

2. What is the criterion for success? This question must be answered in terms of frequency of specified actions, time spent at the task, speed or accuracy or adequacy of the performance, or some combination of these. Under automated conditions it would have been possible to use the increase in the number of letters typed as a criterion. Since automated equipment was not available, however, a more global set of criteria were specified as follows: (a) The client should attend to the typing task for at least 30 minutes. (b) During this period he should not demand the therapist's attention. (c) The work output in terms of lines typed should increase. (d) Accuracy of typing should improve. Of course, only the first two of these criteria were the focus of the experiment. The latter two criteria ordinarily would be met, in some degree, if the first two were met; although great improvement in speed and accuracy undoubtedly would require a separate analysis and special attention.

3. What behavior must be generated, extinguished, or altered? If desirable and undesirable behavior are incompatible, one might expect that reinforcing the desirable behavior would be sufficient to maintain it in strength. This question deserves attention, however, because the training of rehabilitation personnel to be responsive to "human needs" may lead them to reinforce undesirable behaviors concurrently with their reinforcement of desirable behaviors without being aware of what they are doing. They may not perceive that the undesirable behaviors must never be reinforced. In the present instance, for example, the occupational therapist did give moderate attention to the client for typing while he was typing, but she was also responsive to his demands for attention and was rather incredulous that paying no attention to the latter might have positive effects on the former. Extinguishing incompatible behaviors is especially important in cases of relearning, where the desired behaviors are usually present in at least minimal strength. In cases of new learning, where the desired behaviors are absent, altering behavior by means other than extinction is more important.

4. What will serve as a reinforcer? In the absence of knowledge of what has been reinforcing to the client in the past, the behavioral engineer may attempt to use an extrinsic reinforcer such as money, trading stamps, trinkets, food delicacies, or any activity of consumption that therapists

may report the client engages in. Apparatus for programming and reinforcement delivery usually is required for effective extrinsic reinforcement. Social reinforcement is also possible. The latter is particularly effective with many rehabilitation clients since much of their behavior appears to be under aversive social control, and they have been deprived, sometimes for long periods of time, of the positive social reinforcement they experienced prior to disablement. It also has the advantage of not requiring programming apparatus. In general, a good reinforcer often is that reinforcing stimulus that has been maintaining undesired behavior. In the present case, it was social reinforcement which was maintaining the client's disruptive behaviors and which could be used just as easily to reinforce behavior.

## Behavioral Treatment

Treatment in this situation consisted of making two changes: (1) Moving the typewriter and the client from the large occupational-therapy room where non-typewriting behavior had been reinforced to a smaller, more-isolated room. This was done partly to help weaken the past behavior by introducing new discriminative stimuli and partly to decrease the response alternatives that were presented by the presence, activities, and conversation of other people. (2) Making social reinforcement contingent upon engaging in typing behavior. The client was given 5 minutes of social interaction, on a "man to man" basis, at the end of each 30-minute therapy session in which the client typed more lines than in the previous session. (Sessions were held semi-weekly.) The talk during the break was of cars, sports, and other topics of masculine interest which were not otherwise available to the client within the institution. Although he was 18 years old, his slight physique and unsophisticated manner had led the staff to treat him as a child.

The task was sufficiently difficult for John so that if he stopped typing for several minutes during the session, he could not possibly exceed his previous output; in that event, of course, no social reinforcement was given. In addition, the experimenter attempted to avoid demands for attention by giving reinforcement for smaller units of work. He did this by walking into the room about every 5 minutes and, without interrupting the client, estimating the number of words typed. If output per minute of time appeared roughly to have increased over the previous period, he would make some positive remark such as "You're doing very well," and then walk out.

## Results

After a single 30-minute session in which variable-interval reinforcement was given but demands for attention were ignored, the client no longer attempted to engage the experimenter in conversation during the working period. After the ninth session, the client asked the experimenter not to dispense the variable-interval reinforcements because they slowed down his output. Three additional 30-minute sessions were then held without the variable-interval reinforcement contingency.

During each session from the second to the twelfth, John attended to the typing task for the entire 30 minutes. He neither stopped work nor demanded the therapist's attention. In addition, his typing output increased from 5 lines in the first session to 12 lines in the twelfth session, and his error rate decreased from 3 errors per line to ½ per line.

From the thirteenth through the fifteenth experimental periods, the duration of typing activity was increased to one hour with only a 5-minute reinforcement break at the half-way point. The client's close attention to the typing task was maintained without decreasing the production rate or increasing the error rate. He now appeared to be "well-motivated," and it was clear that further gains were possible if the regular therapist, to whose care he was now returned, gained skill in maintaining the reinforcement contingencies.

## CASE 2. FEAR OF FALLING IN A CEREBRAL-PALSIED CHILD

### Background

Tom was born with multiple congenital anomalies. In addition to nystagmus, ptosis, scoliosis, and three-fingered hands without thumbs, he was diagnosed as a "mild spastic with left hemiplegia." He was one of several seven-year-old cerebral-palsied children participating in an experiment concerned with investigating the process by which tokens (poker chips) might be established as generalized conditioned reinforcers.

In rehabilitating handicapped children, it is often necessary to generate new behavior or to strengthen weak behavior. Since these children are not deprived of primary reinforcers, and since it is usually impossible, for social and administrative reasons, to place them under such deprivation, it is not easy to find conditioned reinforcers of powerful and continuing effectiveness. The ideal reinforcer should be of the kind which can be easily dispensed by the experimenter or therapist and delivered immediately contingent upon the appropriate behavior; it should be non-satiating or low in satiation so that many can be dispensed in a short period of time; it should be non-distracting or low in distraction by reason of its own intrinsic reinforcing properties; it should be appropriate for the many different deprivations which may exist in any subject and be capable of use in a variety of situations. Money has these characteristics for adults. Tokens exchangeable after the experimental or therapeutic sessions for a wide variety of social and material reinforcers may be equally effective for handicapped children who are given some experience in a "token culture."

The main experiment, in which Tom participated, showed that tokens which were exchangeable for toys were effective generalized conditioned reinforcers in shaping increased attention span, speed, and accuracy in two behaviors: (1) hand-eye coordination in coloring and (2) manipulation in a nut-bolt-washer assembly.

### Problem

Tom would not stand unless he had something to hold on to, and he would not walk unless he held someone's hand. It was believed by the child's physician and physical therapist that he could walk alone, and recurrent but unsuccessful efforts had been made in the past to induce him to do so. It was said that he had an extreme fear of falling, but the child refused to attempt the exercise that would teach him to fall without discomfort or injury.

### Observation

Observation confirmed the fact that Tom never stood or walked unassisted. Attempts were sometimes made to coax him or goad him into walking. He smiled shyly and was good humored in these situations until ultimately someone took him by the hand and walked with him. Tom had "insight" and "acceptance" of his disability. He talked freely and at some length to many people about his inability to walk alone.

### Behavioral Analysis

The adults in the environment were reinforcing the non-walking behavior. The child was at the center of the stage and received a great deal of attention, which he seemed to enjoy, for not walking and for refusing to fall.

The terminal behaviors, their criteria, and the conditions for their occurrence were as follows: (1) Desired Behaviors: The child should stand and walk independently, and he should learn how to fall safely. (2) Criteria for Success: He should walk unassisted to and from the experimental room, and he should fall, in the approved way, on command. (3) Behavior to be generated, extinguished, or altered: The problem appeared to be one of overcoming the fear of falling and having the child experience the freedom of unassisted walking—to get him over the hump so that the naturally reinforcing contingencies in the environment that are available to one who walks alone could exert their effects. It was decided that these behaviors could be generated by reinforcement more powerful than the child was receiving for not walking. However, the social reinforcement given for not walking was so widespread within the rehabilitation center, and of such long standing, that it was not considered feasible to try to extinguish this behavior in the staff. (4) Reinforcer: Tom came strongly under the control of tokens in the main experiment mentioned earlier, and there was evidence that they would serve for him as generalized conditioned reinforcers.

## Behavioral Treatment

Treatment was begun by reinforcing with tokens successive approximations to independent walking. First, while engaged in a coloring task, Tom was given two extra tokens if he scooted in his chair from his work table to the experimenter's correction desk and pulled himself up to a standing position. If he chose not to come to the desk to have his paper corrected, the experimenter went to his table, but he received no extra tokens. After one reinforcement for coming to the desk, Tom refused to let the experimenter come to him. After a dozen reinforcements for this behavior, Tom was offered extra tokens for standing at the desk without holding on. He met this contingency in one 20-minute session and thereafter would stand unassisted. During the shaping process, the child's verbal behavior changed from comments about being unable to walk, to statements such as "Look, I can stand by myself."

The next step was to place two chairs back to back close enough so that Tom could hold onto one chair, turn, and grasp the other chair without letting go of the first chair. He was reinforced with tokens for this behavior. The chairs were then gradually moved apart until it was necessary to take one or more steps without support to get from one chair to the other. At the end of the first 20-minute session, Tom was walking three unsupported, unassisted, consecutive steps from one chair to the other.

At the next session five days later, Tom walked into the experimental room unassisted, and it was obvious from his verbal behavior that walking, in itself, was now reinforcing. It was not possible to trace what had occurred in the institution during those five days. It seems probable that some unassisted walking occurred which provided the opportunity for the physical therapist, who was also working on this behavior, to give massive, positive, social reinforcement. Combined with the intrinsically reinforcing effects of walking itself, the consequences were sufficient to maintain the strength of the behavior. It was evident that the child was now walking freely all over the institution, and although it was believed that the experimental effort provided the catalyst, we could not be sure that it was the behavioral treatment and not some adventitious occurrence that was responsible for the result.

Accordingly, attention then turned to a behavior that was non-existent in the subject's repertory—falling on command, correctly and safely. The physical therapist had given up trying to teach this behavior, and she agreed not to attempt to teach it again during the period of the experiment. The physical therapist stated that the ability to fall voluntarily was an important behavior to develop inasmuch as incoordination resulting from the spastic paralysis probably would result in the child's falling from time to time. It would be beneficial if he would learn to fall correctly and safely. However, she had been unable to induce Tom to engage in falling exercises under any circumstances.

In accord with the physical therapist's instructions to the experimenters, falling was broken down into three phases: (1) Placing the subject's hands and knees on the mat and having him roll his body to one side. (2) Placing the subject on his knees with his body in an erect position and having him fall forward on his hands and then roll to his side. (3) Standing the subject beside the mat and having him fall to his knees, then to his hands, and then having him roll his body to one side.

Tom was told and shown the successive approximations to falling behavior outlined above. Tokens were then dispensed contingent upon his performing the required behavior upon command.

## Results

The results are shown in Table 1. It will be seen that after the rolling response was well established, it was possible to proceed quickly to the behaviors of falling from the kneeling position and falling from an upright position. More rapid acquisition of the desired response might

Table 1
Frequency of the Component Parts of the Falling
Sequence during Four Sessions of Training

| Sessions (20 minutes) | Rolling to side | *Responses* Falling from knees to hands and rolling | Falling from upright to knees, hands and rolling |
|---|---|---|---|
| 1 | 8 | 3 | --- |
| 2 | 2 | 2 | 7 |
| 3 | 3 | --- | 4 |
| 4 | --- | 5 | 6 |

have been possible. At the end of the first session, Tom was reluctant to stop and asked the experimenters if he might try, "for tokens," the falling from an upright position exercise. This was not permitted because of the complexity of the response and the inexperience of the investigators in physical-therapy activities. It is perhaps sufficiently noteworthy that an important behavior that had been unobtainable previously by traditional physical-therapy methods was obtained in just four sessions of 20 minutes each by utilizing principles of behavior theory. Moreover, the behavior was engaged in willingly, almost eagerly, and with little or none of the emotionalism that the subject was reported to have shown in previous attempts to teach him to fall.

The rapidity with which the falling behavior was obtained lends some support to the belief that the tokens functioned as strong, generalized conditioned reinforcers. As in the walking study, the desired behavior was manifested immediately after token reinforcement was put into effect.

## CASE 3. INABILITY TO WALK IN A MENTALLY RETARDED CHILD

### Background

Mary was a nine-year-old girl who, in addition to having other behavioral deficits, didn't walk, didn't talk, and wasn't toilet trained. She was classified by the residential institution in which she lived as "congenitally mentally retarded." She was reported to have crawled when she was two years old, but she never walked. At the time of first observation, she would not stand on her feet unless someone lifted her by the hands or arms and supported most of her weight.

It wasn't clear why Mary didn't walk. She was somewhat bow-legged, as if she had had rickets at the age when most children begin to walk, but there were no other physical abnormalities now that would tend to interfere with walking or standing unsupported.

To the institution, however, it was an old and familiar story. Many mentally retarded children do not walk. It is believed to be one of the "characteristics" of severely mentally retarded children that is related not to their muscular strength but to their not being smart enough or sufficiently coordinated to learn to walk. An inquiry sometimes follows this pattern:

"Why doesn't Mary walk?"
"Well, she's severely mentally retarded, and it is not uncommon among
   the severely mentally retarded that they don't walk."

"I see, but what is the reason for it?"

"She's slow in development."

"I see. And what is it that is responsible for her slow development?"

"It is the fact that she is mentally retarded."

"I see. And how do you know that she is mentally retarded?"

"Why you can see for yourself. She doesn't walk, she doesn't talk, she isn't toilet trained and doesn't do many other things like a mentally normal child."

There may be many reasons for the impoverished behavioral repertory of long-institutionalized children. Not the least of these variables are the impoverished environmental contingencies to which the child must respond appropriately either to receive reinforcement or to avoid punishment. A diagnosis of mental retardation, however, which by definition is an "incurable" disorder, tends to lead to the easy acceptance of the inevitability of behavioral deviance and behavioral deficits and to choke off some simple rearrangements of the environment which might lead to the generation of more adequate behavior.

## Observation

Mary, except for her very thin, bowed legs and lack of muscular development in the calf, seemed physically capable of walking. Her primary mode of locomotion, however, was scooting across the floor on her buttocks by pushing with her feet and hands. She could be pulled to a standing position if the experimenter supported most of her weight, but she could not be induced to move her legs, and she would drop to the floor as soon as support was removed or relaxed.

## Behavioral Analysis

For physical reasons, Mary may not have had the capacity to walk when she was younger. The acceptance of her as "a child who doesn't walk," however, led to neglect in providing environmental contingencies which would shape up and maintain walking. At present there were no important positive consequences contingent upon walking, or aversive consequences contingent upon not walking. She was carried or wheeled in a chair wherever it was necessary for her to go.

The behavior desired from Mary was that she should stand unsupported and walk independently; first, upon request of the experimenter in the experimental room and, later, in response to the naturally reinforcing contingencies of the ward. The task here, as with Tom, was to get her over the hump of initiating the strange and strenuous effort of walking so that this ultimately less effortful mode of locomotion could be experienced and so that the naturally reinforcing contingencies in the environment that are available to one who walks could exert their effects. No attempt was to be made to induce the ward attendants not to carry Mary or not to push her in a wheelchair, since these efforts would introduce uncontrolled variables. Since Mary was highly reinforceable with edibles such as popcorn, raisins, crackers, nuts, and ice cream, it was believed that these reinforcers would be sufficient to generate walking behavior and that the reinforcing effects of walking itself would maintain the behavior on the ward.

## Behavioral Treatment

Mary was seen twice a week in experimental sessions usually lasting 20 to 45 minutes. In the initial sessions, resting periods of 5 to 15 minutes were as long as or longer than working periods; but later, as her muscles became stronger, the walking periods were about twice as long as the resting periods.

In Phase 1, lasting one session, Mary was lifted to her feet and given a reinforcer while she was standing. Gradually the experimenter released his support. In the beginning, when the child supported on her own legs even a small portion of her weight for a fraction of a second, she was reinforced with an edible. Later, the contingencies were modified to require higher degrees of weight-bearing over longer periods of time, until at the end of the first session she would stand unsupported for 5 to 15 seconds at a time. Detailed records were not kept of this session.

In Phase 2, two folding chairs were placed approximately 30 inches apart, back to back. Mary was placed on the floor between the chairs while an experimenter stood behind each chair. She was told and shown how to pull herself to her feet by grasping the back of one chair, then turn around and grasp the back of the other chair first with one hand and then with both hands. When Mary was standing, the experimenter behind her would say, "Mary, come over here." If the command was followed, she was reinforced with an edible. If it was not followed, or if she dropped to the floor and scooted on her buttocks to the other chair, a reinforcer was not dispensed.

When Mary was effectively making the transfer from chair to chair upon command, the distance between the chairs was very gradually increased until it was impossible for her to move from one chair to the other while holding on to either of them. Initially she was able to release one chair with one hand and, standing unsupported, lean over until she could grasp the second chair with the other hand. As the distance between the chairs increased, however, it was necessary for her at first to take one unsupported step and later several, before she was reinforced. In the seven sessions of Phase 2, the greatest distance between the chairs was 45 inches.

In Phase 3, the chairs were removed and the procedure was as follows: One experimenter would hold Mary's hand while the other experimenter, a few feet away, would hold out a reinforcer. When she had taken a few steps toward the reinforcer, the first experimenter would release her hand while the second experimenter walked backwards away from her. Initially, Mary was given a reinforcer after taking three or four steps, but this requirement was gradually increased at each session. By Session 12, for example, reinforcement was contingent upon taking at least 25 steps. The number of steps taken was recorded as "Steps from Supported Start." In addition, an attempt was made to keep Mary walking for additional reinforcements as the experimenter moved away from her. The steps taken under this contingency were recorded as "Steps from Unsupported Start." These categories were not really meaningful after Session 11, as by that time it was Mary who released her hand from the experimenter's hand rather than vice versa.

In Sessions 13, 14 and 15, the procedure was modified further by placing the second experimenter across the room rather than having him lead the child by a few steps. If, when she was called, Mary walked across the room without sinking to the floor, she received a reinforcer. If she sat down, no reinforcement was given, she was walked back to the starting point, and the command was given again. The same attempt was made as before to keep Mary walking for additional reinforcements as the experimenter moved across the room.

## Results

The results are shown in Tables 2 and 3 and in Figures 1 and 2. It will be seen in Table 2 that there was a gradual but consistent shift from transferring from one chair while holding on to the other, to standing unsupported between the chairs, to taking unsupported steps between the chairs. By the end of Session 8 of Phase 2, and after the expenditure of less than 200 minutes of experimental time, Mary had taken 28 unsupported steps in one session. The cumulative performances under the Phase 2 contingency are shown in Figure 1.

Table 3 shows that a gradually increasing total number of steps was obtained in each succeeding 45-minute session. Session 11 lasted for more than an hour and resulted in an unusually large number of steps, while Session 15 was terminated after 30 minutes. The table also shows the gradually increasing number of steps obtained per reinforcer as the reinforcement contingency was raised, from six steps in Session 9 to 40 consecutive steps in Session 15. Figure 2 presents the same data in cumulative record form.

By the end of the last session, the institutional attendants reported that Mary was taking unsupported steps in the ward. No attempt was made, as would ordinarily be desirable, to generalize the walking behavior to the ward or to fade out gradually the food reinforcers and replace them with other reinforcers. At the present writing, however, six months after the training sessions were completed, Mary is walking freely and frequently throughout the institution. Less than 9 hours of experimental effort had removed a behavioral deficit of 9 years' standing.

## Table 2
### Progression in Alternating Between Chairs During Phase 2 Training

| Session | Commands* | Reinforced Transfers Between Chairs | Standing Unsupported Between Chairs | No. of Unsupported Steps Between Chairs |
|---|---|---|---|---|
| 1+ | | | | |
| 2 | 66 | 34 | 6 | |
| 3 | 64 | 39 | 18 | |
| 4 | 23 | 18 | 1 | |
| 5 | 57 | 32 | 24 | |
| 6 | 68 | 32 | 25 | 17 |
| 7 | 20 | 7 | 3 | 3 |
| 8 | 39 | 9 | 0= | 28 |

*The number of commands given provides a rough index to the length of a working session. Sessions 4, 7, and 8 were shorter than others.
+Session 1 was part of Phase 1 and consisted only of reinforcement for standing unsupported for a short time. Records were not kept.
=The chairs were separated by a distance that required one or more steps for completion of the task.

## Table 3
### Steps Reinforced with Supported and Unsupported Starts in Phase 3 of Training

| Cumulative Session* | Steps from Supported Start | Steps from Unsupported Start | Total Steps | Reinforcements | Steps/Reinf. |
|---|---|---|---|---|---|
| 9 | 190 | | 190 | 31 | 6.1 |
| 10 | 560 | | 560 | 36 | 15.5 |
| 11* | 790 | 223 | 1013 | 61 | 16.6 |
| 12 | 414 | 249 | 663 | 20 | 33.1 |
| 13 | 422 | 391 | 813 | 29 | 28.0 |
| 14 | 806 | 111 | 917 | 22 | 41.7 |
| 15* | 445 | 40 | 485 | 10 | 48.5 |

*Each session was 45 minutes long except Session 11, which ran for 70 minutes, and Session 15, which was interrupted after 30 minutes.

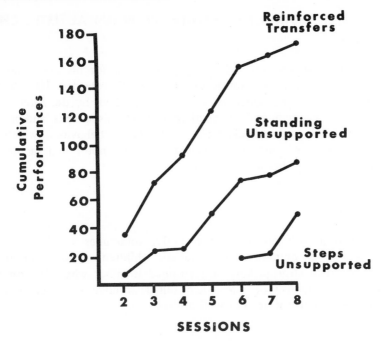

Figure 1. Alternations between chairs by Mary in Phase 2

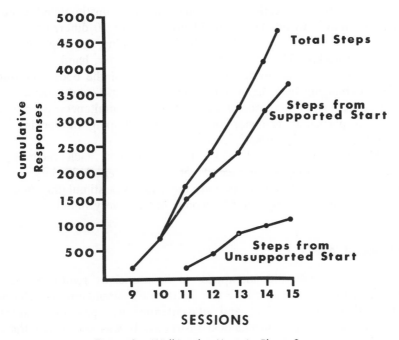

Figure 2. Walking by Mary in Phase 3

## CASE 4. SELF-DESTRUCTIVE BEHAVIOR IN AN AUTISTIC CHILD

### Background

Phil was a 4-year-old child, physically small for his age, who was confined to a crib in an institution for the mentally retarded. He attracted the attention of visitors, when he was not restrained, by the forcefulness with which he slapped and punched himself on his cheeks and mouth, banged his head, and scratched his body. These behaviors, which left visible injuries, were part of his almost ceaseless motor and tactual activity during most of his waking hours.

### Problem

Physical assault on one's own body, sometimes to the point of injury, is not uncommon among autistic children. Such children are often confined in strait-jackets or restrained in other ways. It would be desirable to extinguish or alter such self-destructive behavior, but the variables that control it are not well understood.

### Observation

Systematic observation of the unrestrained, unstimulated child for three 10-minute periods led to the identification of 20 different motor and tactual behaviors. These included hitting, slapping, kicking, scratching, biting, and rocking himself; sucking on thumb, finger, hand, arm; rubbing or flipping fingers against teeth and other parts of the body, chewing on bedsheet, banging head against the bars of the crib, and others. Several of these behaviors were sometimes manifested simultaneously, and once begun, a particular behavior such as finger-flipping or rocking might continue for several hours.

Simultaneous observation by four observers, each recording the frequency and duration in seconds of five different behaviors, revealed that during three 10-minute periods the child was stimulating himself in some way for an average of 44 seconds out of every minute.

### Behavioral Analysis

Phil's behavior did not appear to be a socially reinforced operant. His behavior was accepted by the institution's attendants as "characteristic of that kind of child," and little attention was paid to it except for periodic imposition of mechanical restraints. It was speculated that sensory deprivation in this child was of such a degree that tactual stimulation, even of a painful kind, was reinforcing in itself; and self-destructive behavior might be reduced if an external source of tactual stimulation were available.

It was desirable in this case to reduce the frequency of self-destructive behaviors and to determine the functional relationship between such a reduction, if it occurred, and two kinds of tactile stimulation which would be applied for brief periods. As in other behavioral alteration experiments in which the stimuli controlling the undesired behavior are not known and extinction procedures, therefore, are not possible, the

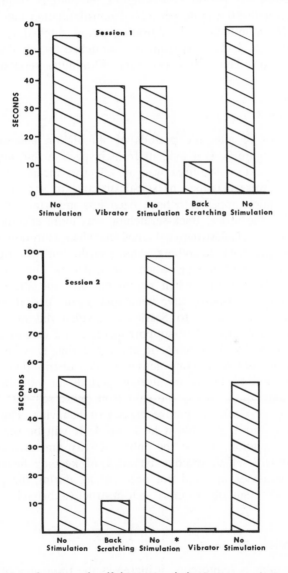

Figure 3. Average duration of self-destructive behaviors per minute under natural and tactually stimulating conditions

intent here was to generate a behavior that was incompatible with self-destruction—namely, lying quietly.

## Experimentation, Phase 1

Four observers gathered around the child's crib. Each observer was responsible for recording the frequency and duration of five of the 20 self-destructive behaviors that the child had exhibited in the past. A 50-minute experimental period consisting of alternating 10-minute periods of stimulation with 10-minute periods of nonstimulation had the following format: 1. No stimulation. 2. Vibrating pillow applied to child's back. 3. No stimulation. 4. The experimenter scratched the child's back gently. 5. No stimulation. There were two such 50-minutes sessions spaced one week apart.

## Results, Phase 1

The results of alternate periods of stimulation and no stimulation are shown in Figure 3. It is evident from inspection that applying stimulation from an external source was an effective means of reducing the behaviors that were classified as self-destructive in various degrees. The kind of stimulation appears to have been less important than its ordinal position within the series. Back-scratching was more effective than vibration in reducing self-destructive behaviors when vibration came second in the series and back-scratching came fourth, but vibration was more effective than back-scratching when the order of the stimuli was reversed. This phenomenon, when combined with the striking reductions in the duration of self-destructive behaviors during periods of stimulation in Session 2 as compared to Session 1 (which did not occur during periods of no stimulation) lent support to the belief that external stimulation was intrinsically reinforcing, in the sense that it reduced some and eliminated other self-stimulating activities. The distributions of the durations of the several behaviors during periods of no stimulation and stimulation show quite clearly the shift from more self-destructive classes of behavior to less self-destructive classes of behavior. The distributions for Sessions 1 and 2 are shown in Table 4. It will be seen that during periods of stimulation, almost the entire activity time was accounted for by the minimally self-destructive behavior of keeping fingers in mouth. This was a behavior that did not occur at all during the periods of no stimulation, although other, more self-destructive behaviors were manifested.

## Experimentation, Phase 2

If a stimulus is reinforcing, it increases the frequency of the behavior that was emitted immediately prior to its presentation. It seemed impor-

## Table 4

### Distribution and Duration in Seconds of Self-Destructive Behaviors Observed Under Two Conditions in Alternating Ten Minute Trials

| Condition | Finger Flipping | Ear Pulling | Slapping Hitting | Kicking | Scratching | Chewing on Sheet | Rocking | Sucking | Tooth Rubbing | Fingers in Mouth | Total Mouth Secs. | Average Per Min. |
|---|---|---|---|---|---|---|---|---|---|---|---|---|
| **Session 1** | | | | | | | | | | | | |
| No Stim. | 7 | 0 | 0 | 12 | 90 | 0 | 392 | 45 | 5 | 0 | 551 | 55.1 |
| Vibrator | 0 | 0 | 0 | 0 | 0 | 0 | 0 | 0 | 0 | 385 | 385 | 38.5 |
| No Stim. | 9 | 0 | 40 | 96 | 19 | 0 | 82 | 120 | 22 | 0 | 388 | 38.8 |
| Back Scratch | 15 | 0 | 0 | 8 | 20 | 0 | 0 | 20 | 0 | 52 | 115 | 11.5 |
| No Stim. | 0 | 0 | 0 | 5 | 0 | 0 | 520 | 18 | 0 | 0 | 543 | 54.3 |
| **Session 2** | | | | | | | | | | | | |
| No Stim. | 41 | 0 | 76 | 37 | 34 | 32 | 97 | 215 | 9 | 0 | 541 | 54.1 |
| Back Scratch | 0 | 0 | 0 | 0 | 0 | 0 | 0 | 0 | 0 | 106 | 108 | 10.8 |
| No Stim. | 0 | 133 | 0 | 34 | 0 | 0 | 390 | 407 | 0 | 0 | 964 | 96.4 |
| Vibrator | 0 | 0 | 0 | 0 | 1 | 1 | 0 | 0 | 0 | 2 | 3 | .3 |
| No Stim. | 0 | 0 | 0 | 0 | 20 | 20 | 511 | 5 | 0 | 0 | 536 | 53.6 |

tant, for two reasons, to know if external tactual stimulation was intrinsically reinforcing. First, tactual stimulation is not presently included in the list of known primary reinforcers, although some reports of sensory-deprivation phenomena indicate that it might well be one. Second, if tactual stimulation is a primary reinforcer, it offers a powerful tool for altering the self-destructive behaviors of children like Phil, and it becomes potentially possible to modify and improve a tremendous range of behaviors in children for whom tactual deprivation may be a naturally occurring phenomenon.

Back-scratching does not lend itself very well to precise programming or automation, but a vibratory stimulus does. Inasmuch as the results of Phase 1 did not indicate compelling reasons for preferring one kind of tactual stimulation to the other, experimentation was continued with vibration.

To assess the reinforcing properties of vibratory stimuli, a vibrator imbedded in a pillow (Sears catalogue #2858) was sewn immediately beneath the surface of the mattress in the child's crib. The vibrator was controlled by automated programming equipment which turned it on for 10 seconds of vibratory stimulation after each light pressing of a foam-rubber-padded, leather-covered, oblong lever, 8½ inches by 5½ inches in size, that was mounted on the side of the child's crib. The lever was mounted a few inches away from one of Phil's arms so that he would be likely to hit it by chance while engaging in the gross motor activity that he frequently exhibited, but his hand would have to turn at a sharp angle in order to strike the lever with his fingers or palm.

The vibration was contingent on pressing the lever; so if vibratory stimulation was reinforcing, after a few reinforcements resulting from adventitious lever pressing, Phil would be expected to strike the lever with increasing frequency. Two one-hour sessions, spaced one week apart, were run.

### Results, Phase 2

The cumulative records are shown in Figure 4. It will be seen that the results of Session 1 were strikingly successful. It appeared evident that vibratory stimulation was reinforcing. Temporary satiation seemed to occur after 5 or 10 minutes of stimulation, but recovery was rapid. Records of the topography of the lever-pressing response showed that all except the first few presses were made by hand and fingers and were clearly not accidental.

Figure 4 also shows the cumulative record of the first 20 minutes of Session 2. The lever-pressing behavior that was so evident in Session 1 was no longer present. Moreover, attempts to hand-shape the response by delivering vibratory stimulation for successive approximations to lever

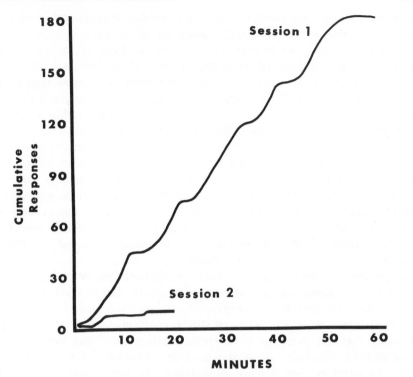

Figure 4.  Cumulative record of lever-pressing for vibratory stimulation by an autistic child

pressing were unsuccessful. No progress toward reinstating the lever-pressing response was evident after 60 minutes of experimental effort.

## DISCUSSION

Case 4 was included in this paper to indicate that behavioral experimentation is not always, or even usually, a hop, skip, and jump from isolating a problem, to devising a procedure, to successful outcome. In every case reported, there were some false starts and some difficulties of greater or lesser degree that had to be solved. In Case 4, we may or may not be on the track of important phenomena. It is clearly evident, however, that the problem has not been solved; nor is there a clear interpretation for the data obtained. Additional experimentation is necessary. It is now planned to place the lever and the automatically recording vibratory apparatus in Phil's crib on a 24-hour-per-day basis over a period of several weeks to determine if a longer period of experimentation will yield more interpretable data. The reader may conceive of other procedures that would be equally promising or better.

The responses of behavioral scientists, medical personnel, parents, and others to the kind of experimentation and applied psychology that is exemplified by the cases reported have been very encouraging. The psychologist in rehabilitation who tests, evaluates, classifies, and describes the strengths and weaknesses of candidates for rehabilitation services is not uniformly valued by his colleagues or those he serves. There appears to be an increasing demand for psychologists who have the knowledge and the ability to modify behavior—to generate desirable behavior when it is not present, to maintain good behavior in strength, and to extinguish or alter undesirable behavior. The role of the psychologist in rehabilitation of the future clearly requires a specialist in behavioral engineering who by open, clearly specifiable, non-esoteric, and non-subjective procedures can alter human behavior and thereby contribute more fully to the improved functioning of disabled persons.

Helping a child learn to work productively in activities that will improve his hand-eye coordination, to fall safely, and to walk, when these behaviors were not present previously, is surely beneficial. Some individuals, however, appear to have strong emotional reactions to the procedures that are used in the experimentation that was described and doubts about the value of what was done. It may be of value to discuss two spontaneous, but perhaps unthinking, objections that are most frequently made:

1. "I don't believe in bribing children." Critics who make this comment appear to be expressing the belief that children should "voluntarily" engage in certain behaviors because "it is for their own good," or "it is the right thing to do," and that it is somehow dishonest, evil, ineffective, or contrary to some immutable moral law to offer them extrinsic inducements to behave as they "should" behave.

Such critics appear to forget that infants and children learn to behave in ways that the significant others in their lives consider right and good—they are not born with such behaviors. The learning is accomplished as a consequence of thousands and thousands of materially and socially reinforced responses and exposure to the naturally reinforcing or punishing contingencies of the environment.

For various reasons, some children do not receive the kind or frequency of reinforcement that shapes the behavior of most children to the ordinary demands of the social environment. Other children, because of the physical or social effects of disabilities, or other fortuitous circumstances that are presently relatively unexplored, do not come under the control of the naturally occurring contingencies in the environment. The critical choice for those who work with children whose behavior is maladaptive is whether to view the problem as a scientific, valuatively neutral task of facilitating the learning of more adaptive behavior—even though the behavior "should have" been learned earlier—or to view it as a moral problem of the childrens' own making which requires that they be consigned to limbo in preference to "bribing" them to behave more adaptively. The scientifically oriented psychologist should experience no conflict in making this choice.

The student-psychologist, perhaps because of his own moral training, may sympathize initially with the rehabilitation therapist who resolutely refuses to permit extrinsic reinforcement to be given in his clinic on the grounds that "these children are here to work and to improve themselves. If they won't work, we'll discharge them." The sympathy is considerably diluted when, on further inquiry, it becomes clear that the therapist himself would not show up for work if *his* reinforcements (money, social approval, accomplishment) were terminated; and he apparently expects that the behavior of his clients "should be" controlled by principles of behavior that are markedly different from those that control his own.

Some further clarification may be obtained by considering the appropriateness of an emotionally loaded term such as "bribe." To bribe means to influence dishonestly, to pervert the judgment or to corrupt the conduct of a person in a position of trust by means of some reward. It refers to inducing a person by some payment or promised action to violate a trust, and sometimes it is extended metaphorically to include payment for some *undesirable* behavior that the person would not engage in were it not for the payment.

The therapeutic effort is not of this nature. It is aimed at generating, maintaining, or strengthening desirable behavior and altering undesirable behavior. It is the same kind of social control that is exerted by the employer who says, "I will pay you $2 an hour to come to work in my pickle factory," by the professor who indicates that if you learn the material in his course, he will give you a good grade, or by the parent who praises a child for polite and unselfish behavior. We do not designate such reinforcements as "bribery."

One may attempt to distinguish the behavior required of rehabilitation clients from these examples on the grounds that rehabilitative therapy is for the client's own good and "should be" engaged in without payment, but this is not tenable. It is for their own good that college students "should" acquire as much knowledge as possible, and children "should be" polite and unselfish without the aid of symbolic or social payment. But these behaviors must be learned, and it is necessary in the learning process to reinforce them.

One real difference between college students, children, and rehabilitation clients who behave appropriately and those who do not may be that the desirable behaviors of the former have already come under the control of a wide variety of secondary reinforcers. A good grade, for example, is simply a mark on paper which has acquired significance be-

cause in the past it has repeatedly been closely followed by more powerful, primary reinforcers. The individuals who are not under the control
of the secondary reinforcers that our culture values as "good" become
school dropouts, delinquents, and "unmotivated" rehabilitation clients.
Effective rehabilitative therapy in such cases may require the use of
primary reinforcement or relatively crude extrinsic reinforcement such
as is common with infants and young children. It may be that it is this
necessary use of overtly seductive rather than more subtle reinforcement
that leads to the unwarranted judgment of "bribery." However, as Michael
(1964) has remarked, "If behavior which 'should' be engaged in without
extrinsic reinforcement is not, in fact, occurring, a program of extrinsic
reinforcement must be evaluated, not in an absolute sense, but in comparison with the common alternative approaches: increased aversive control, or simply accepting failure."

On a similarly practical level, some professional persons are not
so much concerned with the moral implications of dispensing extrinsic
reinforcements as they are with the likelihood that the behavior obtained
will be temporary or cease abruptly when the reinforcement is discontinued.

It is not possible here to describe the processes by which behavior
comes under the control of secondary and so-called intrinsic reinforcement, but the transition to secondary reinforcement is often necessary for
long-term persistence of behavior under natural conditions. If such additional learning does not occur, and the behavior does not come under
the control of naturally occurring reinforcement in the environment, it
is true that the behavior developed and maintained by experimentally
manipulated, extrinsic reinforcement will cease. We deceive ourselves if
we believe that any behavior that is without consequences will be maintained indefinitely. "All experimental evidence indicates that when behavior is no longer followed by positive reinforcement and when it no
longer escapes or avoids aversive consequences, it ceases" (Michael, 1964).
It is probably to our advantage that it does, for otherwise we would be
greatly impeded in learning new and more-adaptive behavior that environmental changes may require. The transience of much behavior is
both inevitable and desirable.

When long-term persistence is desired for some behavior that does
not receive primary reinforcement from the environment, it is necessary
for the behavioral engineer to ensure that the behavior comes under
the control of readily available secondary reinforcement. To ensure the
maintenance of some behaviors in handicapped persons, it may be necessary to construct prosthetic environments. There are no approaches to
learning that are free of these requirements, although the terminology employed may be different.

2. "What is the value of changing one or two discrete bits of behavior? The children are still physically handicapped or mentally retarded,

aren't they?" It would be delightful if varied, complex, and poorly under-stood disorders could be put completely right at one blow, but that process is called a miracle, and people who believe in it generally resort to prayer. The scientific process tends to proceed by slow accretion and the step-by-step solution of discrete problems.

From an immediate, practical standpoint, when one compares the time, effort, and resources that are necessary to care for ambulant and non-ambulant, toilet-trained and non-toilet-trained, self-destructive and non-self-destructive, or hyperactive and non-hyperactive children, it seems clear that changing one or two bits of discrete behavior should not be despised.

In addition, the objection quoted neglects the fact that no learned behavior appears in full bloom. It is learned bit by bit from the moment of birth, or earlier, and refined by thousands and thousands of repetitions. The learning of congenitally physically handicapped or retarded persons may be obstructed or impeded by insuperable physical barriers, chance exposure to conditions that are detrimental to learning, lack of knowledge of how to facilitate learning under unusual conditions, or perhaps more frequently, lack of skilled application of the learning principles that are already known.

In the rehabilitation setting, one or more behavioral deficits of a sensory, motor, or discriminative nature may be evident in handicapped persons when comparison is made with non-handicapped individuals of similar age. There is presently no alternative to treating such deficits one by one; and the outcome, in terms of the total person or total behavior, depends on how many and how severe the deficits are and the degree to which generalization of newly learned behavior may be possible. As progress is made in overcoming behavioral deficits that are presently beyond rehabilitative knowledge, and as increased behavioral engineering skill is gained in reducing or removing other deficits, we may expect that the behavioral deficits that are presently associated with some physical disabilities will disappear, and some kinds of so-called mental retardation will be remediable.

## REFERENCES

Meyerson, L., & Kerr, Nancy. *Learning theory and rehabilitation*. New York: Random House. In press.

Meyerson, L., Michael, J. L., Mowrer, O. H. Osgood, C. E., & Staats, A. W. Learning, behavior, and rehabilitation. In *Psychological research and re-habilitation*. Washington D.C.: American Psychological Association, 1963.

Michael, J. L. Guidance and counseling as the control of behavior. In *Guid-ance in American education: backgrounds and prospects*. Cambridge: Harvard Graduate School of Education, 1964. (Distributed by Harvard University Press.)

# 20

# Mothers as Behavior Therapists
# for Their Own Children

## *Robert G. Wahler, Gary H. Winkel, Robert F. Peterson, and Delmont C. Morrison*

### EDITORS' COMMENTS

The next paper is presented to reiterate one point and to make another for the first time. The point already discussed is that much of a child's deviant behavior is traceable to practices of his parents, who unwittingly provide reinforcement that maintains the behavior. The other point is that the parents may serve *entirely* as the remediators of the child's behavior, once modification of their own behavior has been made.

Two additional factors are to be considered. One is to note that the authors studied parent-child interactions in their own laboratory, the playroom of a child development clinic. They might have done nothing more than is usually done: advise the parents about correct home behaviors and rely upon them to do as advised. Under the circumstances they would then have been forced to rely on the parents' reports to determine whether their advice had been correct and effective. But by observing the interactions between the parents and their children directly, the investigators were able to confirm with corresponding directness that their analysis was sound. Subsequent discussion of modification of parental practices in the home, even if not directly observed, could then be made with greater confidence.

The second factor may be raised as a question: What if the parents could not do as advised; that is, What if they continued to reinforce undesirable behavior, despite their protestations that they were really trying hard but "just couldn't help it"? Clearly, the counselors would then have been forced to devise a program for reinforcing parents for reinforcing desirable behaviors in their chil-

Robert G. Wahler, Gary H. Winkel, Robert F. Peterson, and Delmont C. Morrison, "Mothers as Behavior Therapists for Their Own Children," *Behavior Research and Therapy,* 1965 *3*, 113–134.

dren. In short, behavioral techniques would be applied to the users of the same techniques. The devising of such a program of parent training should, by this stage of these readings, be no mystery; it is left, therefore, as an exercise for the reader. Some hints might be provided in a paper by Hawkins *et al.*, in the *Journal of Experimental Child Psychology*.[1]

## SUMMARY

An attempt was made to modify the deviant behavior of three children by producing specific changes in the behavior of their mothers. It was demonstrated that a mother's social behavior may function as a powerful class of reinforcers for her child's deviant as well as normal behavior. It was also demonstrated that a mother's reactions to her child's behavior may be systematically modified, at least within the confines of an experimental setting, and these modifications may produce marked changes in her child's deviant behavior.

Two reviews of the literature on behavior therapy (Bandura, 1961; Grossberg, 1964) reveal a large number of systematic attempts to apply principles of learning theory to psychotherapy. It would appear that many investigators, working within the conceptual frameworks of respondent and operant learning, have produced practical changes in the deviant behavior of both adults and children.

Typically, these investigators have implied that stimuli making up the adult's or child's natural environments are responsible for development and maintenance of the deviant behaviors involved. That is, through unfortunate contingencies between stimuli, or between stimuli and behavior, deviant behavior is produced and maintained. However, while most investigators have assumed that this is true, few have accepted the full implications of this position. Instead of changing "faulty" contingencies involving the natural environment, most research therapists have placed their subjects in artificial environments, designed to modify the deviant behavior through extinction, punishment, and/or reinforcement of responses which are incompatible with the deviant behavior. Although these techniques have produced some remarkable changes in the deviant behavior within the artificial environments—and in some cases within the natural environments—one wonders about the effect that the unmodified natural environments would eventually have on the behavior changes; logically, it would be expected that the deviant behavior would again be

[1] R. P. Hawkins, R. F. Peterson, Edda Schweid, & S. W. Bijou, "Behavior Therapy in the Home: Amelioration of Problem Parent-Child Relations with the Parent in a Therapeutic Role," *J. exp. child Psychol.*, 1966, *4*, 99–107.

strengthened, and behavior developed in the artificial environments would be weakened.

From the standpoint of methodology there is good reason for the behavior of therapists' failure to deal with the natural environment. Since the efficacy of their techniques depends upon control of specific contingencies between stimuli, or between stimuli and behavior, they have typically chosen to work in settings that are highly contrived. However, the extent of this methodological problem is, in large part, correlated with the patient's age. Undoubtedly, the natural environment of the young child is far less complex than that of an adolescent or an adult, and it therefore should present fewer difficulties in systematic control. One might conclude that attempts to develop therapeutic techniques for the control of natural environments should initially utilize children as patient-subjects.

Most psychotherapists assume that a child's parents compose the most influential part of his natural environment. It is likely, from a learning theory viewpoint, that their behaviors serve a large variety of stimulus functions, controlling both the respondent and operant behaviors of their children. It then follows that if some of the child's behavior is considered to be deviant at a particular time in his early years, his parents are probably the source of eliciting stimuli and reinforcers which have produced, and are currently maintaining this behavior. A logical procedure for the modification of the child's deviant behavior would involve changing the parents' behavior. These changes would be aimed at training them both to eliminate the contingencies which currently support their child's deviant behavior, and to provide new contingencies to produce and maintain more normal behaviors which would compete with the deviant behavior.

Techniques of parent-child psychotherapy have been investigated by several researchers (Prince, 1961; Russo, 1964; Straughan, 1964). However, the procedures used in these studies did not permit assessment of variables which were maintaining the children's deviant behavior, nor did they permit analyses of those variables which were responsible for changing the deviant behavior. While the investigators concluded that changes in the children's deviant behavior were probably a function of changes in the parents' behavior, these conclusions could not be clearly supported. Thus, in the further study of parent-child therapeutic techniques it would be of value to utilize procedures which will provide information concerning those stimulus events provided by the parents which function to maintain deviant classes of the child's behavior. Once these controlling stimulus events are detected, it might prove feasible to modify the occurrence of these events in ways which will produce predictable and clinically significant changes in the child's behavior.

The present experiment was an attempt to modify the deviant behavior of three children by producing specific changes in the behavior of their mothers. The major purposes of the study were: (1) to experimentally analyze the mother-child interbehaviors in an effort to specify those variables (i.e., reinforcement contingencies) which may function to maintain the deviant behavior of children; (2) to eliminate these variables in an effort to modify the children's deviant behavior. Therefore, the focus of the study was not on producing long term changes in the children, but rather to discover how their deviant behavior is maintained and how appropriate changes may be brought about.

# METHOD

## Subjects and Apparatus

Subjects were three boys varying in age from four to six years and their respective mothers. While the children's behavior problems would probably be considered moderate by most clinical standards, all had exhibited behavior which was sufficiently deviant to motivate their parents to seek psychological help. More detailed information on the children and their mothers will be presented in a later section.

The apparatus was located in the Gatzert Child Development Clinic of the University of Washington. The equipment consisted of a playroom with two adjoining observation rooms which were equipped for visual and auditory monitoring of behavior in the playroom. Each observation room contained a panel with three microswitches which were connected to a Gerbrand six-channel event recorder; depression of the microswitches by observers activated selected channels of the event recorder. In addition, the playroom was equipped with a signal light which could be illuminated by the experimenter in one of the observation rooms.

## General Procedure

Prior to the behavior therapy sessions, the parents of each child were seen in interviews aimed at obtaining descriptions of the behavior which created problems at home and/or at school. The interviewer also asked the parents to describe their typical reactions to these behavior patterns whenever they occurred.

All mother-child cases were seen separately for approximately twenty-minute sessions, held once or twice weekly in the playroom. The mother and her child were always the sole occupants of the playroom.

### Classification of Mother-Child Interbehavior

For the first two sessions, the mother was instructed, "Just play with_____as you might at home." These instructions were modified for one of the cases when a later analysis of the data revealed little or no evidence of what the parents had earlier described as deviant behavior. In this case the mother was given other instructions, based on her description of her typical behavior at home.

During these sessions, two observers, working in separate observation rooms, obtained complete written records of the child's and the mother's behavior. Analysis of these records began with a selection of the child's deviant behavior. This selection was based upon similarities between the recorded behavior and the behavior which the parents reported to create problems at home. A second classification of the child's behavior was made to establish a class of behavior which the experimenter regarded as incompatible with the deviant behavior. Later, strengthening of this class was used in eliminating the deviant behavior.

A second analysis of the written records involved a description of the mother's ways of reacting to her child's deviant behavior, and to his incompatible behavior. Essentially, this analysis provided a description of possible reinforcers provided by the mother for the two classes of the child's behavior.

### Observer Reliability and Baseline Measures of Behavior

Following the classification sessions, instructions to the mother were the same; however, the observers now recorded only three classes of behavior—two for the child (deviant behavior and incompatible behavior) and one for the mother (her reactions to her child's behavior classes). This was done by depressing selected microswitches every five seconds for any of the previously classified deviant or incompatible behavior patterns which occurred during the five-second intervals. Another microswitch was reserved for any behavior of the mother's which occurred immediately after the child's two classes of behavior. Essentially, this system was a time-saving device which eliminated the laborious procedure of writing down behavior and then classifying it. Thus, once the child's deviant and incompatible behaviors, and the mother's reactions to them were defined and labeled by the experimenter, the observer's attention in further sessions was focused only on these behavior patterns.

The observational records obtained from the above sessions were also analysed for observer reliability. For each behavior class an agreement or disagreement was tallied for every five-second interval. The percentage of agreements for observers was then computed for each behavior class, for each session. Observer agreement of ninety per cent or better was considered to be adequate; once this agreement was obtained on all behavior classes the baseline sessions were begun. Essentially, the baseline sessions provided a measure of the strength or rate of occurrence of the child's deviant or incompatible behavior, and a measure of how frequently the mother responded to them. These sessions were continued until both mother and child showed fairly stable behavioral rates.

Before the baseline sessions were begun, one of the observers was arbitrarily chosen to record the data, and the other observer served only as a reliability check. In all cases reliability checks showed observer agreement of ninety per cent or better.

### Behavior Modification Procedures

Following the baseline sessions, E made systematic attempts to change the mother's reactions to her child's behavior. These attempts involved the use of instructions to the mother before and after the playroom sessions, plus signal light communications to her during the sessions. During initial sessions, E used the signal light as a cueing system, essentially to tell the mother when and how to behave in response to her child's behavior. As the mother improved in her ability to follow instructions, E eventually changed the function of the signal light from cueing system to reinforcement system. The mother was now required to discriminate and respond appropriately to her child's behavior without E's cueing. E used the signal light to provide immediate feedback to the mother concerning her correct and incorrect discriminations, thus teaching her appropriate discrimination responses.

Instructions and the coded significance of the signal light were determined from the baseline data and principles of operant learning theory. In general, the aim was to eliminate possible reinforcers provided by the mother for her child's deviant behavior, but to have her produce them following the child's incompatible behavior. It was thus hoped to train the mother to weaken her child's deviant behavior through a combination of extinction, and by reinforcement of behavior which would compete with the deviant behavior. To accomplish these goals, the mother was first shown the baseline data and given a complete explanation of it; she was also given numerous examples of her child's deviant behavior and his incompatible behavior. She was then told that in further sessions she must completely ignore her child's deviant behavior and respond in any approving way only to his incompatible behavior. The signal light was described to her as an aid which would help her to carry out the instructions. She was told to keep an eye on the light and to respond to her child *only* if it was illuminated; otherwise she was to sit in a chair, ostensibly reading a book and make no verbal or non-verbal contact with her child. E, of course, illuminated the light only following the child's incompatible behavior. In one case, where the child's deviant behavior proved to be unusually resistant to extinction, the mother was trained in the use of a punishment technique as well as the differential reinforcement procedure.

When the observational data revealed that the mother was responding appropriately to the signal light, she was told that in later sessions she must make her own decisions to respond or not respond to her child. She was again told to keep an eye on the light, since it would now be illuminated following her correct decisions.

### Experimental Demonstration of Mother's Control

As later results will indicate, the behavior modification procedures appeared to be effective in producing expected changes in the behavior of the mothers and their children. However, there yet remained the task of demonstrating that modification of the child's behavior was solely a function of the mother's ways of reacting to him. In further sessions the mother was instructed to react to her child as she had done during the baseline sessions; that is, to again be responsive to the deviant behavior. If the mother's reactions to her child during the behavior modification sessions had been responsible for weakening his deviant behavior, one would expect that this procedure would strengthen the deviant behavior. Once this test for control had been made, the mother was instructed to again make her reinforcement contingent only upon the incompatible behavior, thus resuming her "therapeutic" ways of reacting to him.

# RESULTS

### Case Number One

Danny was a six-year-old boy who was brought to the Child Development Clinic by his parents, because of his frequent attempts to force them to comply with his wishes. According to the parents, he virtually determined his own bedtime, foods he would eat, when the parents would play with him and other household activities. In addition, he frequently attempted, with less success, to manipulate his teacher and peers. His parents reported they were simply "unable" to refuse his demands, and had rarely attempted to ignore or punish him. On the few occasions when they had refused him, they quickly relented when he began to shout or cry.

During the classification and baseline sessions, Danny's mother reported that she was extremely uncomfortable, because of Danny's behavior and her knowledge that she was being observed. Figure 1 shows cumulative records of Danny's deviant and incompatible behaviors during all therapy sessions. His deviant behavior was labelled as "commanding behavior" during the classification sessions, and was defined as any verbal or non-verbal instructions to his mother (e.g., pushes his mother into a chair; "Now we'll play this"; "You go over there and I'll stay here"; "No, that's wrong. Do it this way."). The incompatible behavior, labelled as

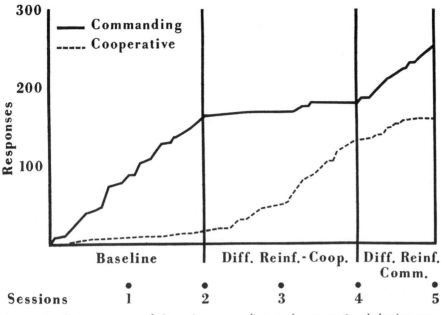

Figure 1. Rate measures of Danny's commanding and cooperative behavior over baseline and therapy sessions

"cooperative behavior," was defined as non-imperative statements or actions or by questions. Note the marked difference in rate between the deviant and incompatible behaviors during the two baseline sessions. Figure 2 shows cumulative records of the mother's general reactions to Danny's two behavior classes during the therapy sessions. Her reactions usually consisted of following Danny's instructions and such verbal comments as "Okay, if that's what you think; am I doing it right now?"

Following the baseline sessions the mother was instructed to be responsive to Danny's cooperative behavior but to completely ignore his commanding behavior. Reference to Figure 2 indicates that she was successful in following these instructions. During the first two differential reinforcement sessions her rate of response to his commanding behavior dropped to zero, while her response to his cooperative behavior increased steadily in rate. (Use of the signal light as a cueing system was discontinued for the second differential reinforcement session.) Danny's behavior during the differential reinforcement sessions is shown in Figure 1. Note that his rate of commanding behavior dropped considerably compared to the baseline sessions, while his cooperative behavior increased sharply in rate. Interestingly enough, Danny's mother reported that she was much more comfortable with him during the last of these sessions.

The test of Mother's control was performed following the first two differential reinforcement sessions. This one session demonstration in-

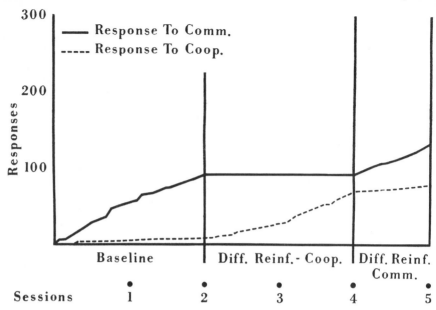

Figure 2.  Rate measures of Mother's general responses to Danny's commanding and
cooperative behavior over baseline and therapy sessions

volved instructing the mother to behave as she had done during the base-line sessions. As the rate of response curves in Figures 1 and 2 indicates, change in the mother's behavior was again correlated with the expected change in Danny's behavior; his rate of commanding behavior increased compared to the previous two sessions, and his cooperative behavior declined in rate. Thus, the finding that Danny's commanding and cooperative behaviors could be weakened when his mother's reactions to these classes were eliminated, and strengthened when they were replaced, points with some certainty to the fact that her behavior changes were responsible for the changes in Danny's behavior.

Further sessions were planned to reinstate the contingencies of the first differential reinforcement sessions. Again the mother was instructed to reinforce only the cooperative behavior; unfortunately, administrative problems made it necessary to terminate this case before the sessions could be conducted.

**Case Number Two**

Johnny, age four, was brought to the Clinic by his parents because of what they termed "very dependent" behavior. In addition, they were concerned about a nursery-school teacher's report that he frequently hit or kicked his peers and teacher when they were inattentive to him. According to his mother, Johnny rarely showed this behavior at home, but instead tended to follow her around the house much of the day, asking questions and requesting her help for various tasks. She, in turn, tended to be very responsive to this behavior and also tended to interrupt him when he played alone or with his peers. When asked why she behaved in these ways, she reported that she was quite concerned about the possibility that he might break things in the house or get into trouble with his playmates; she felt much more comfortable when he was at her side or at least within sight.

Johnny's teachers felt that his aggressive behavior in nursery school was related to his "dependence on others for direction and support." They stated that if he was told what to do, or if a teacher watched him or played with him, the hitting and kicking were not likely to occur. However, it was also apparent from the teacher's report that, inadvertently, they may have been providing social reinforcement for his aggressive behavior.

Following an analysis of the classification session, two classes of Johnny's behavior were defined; the deviant class was labeled "dependent behavior," which included such behavior as questions and non-verbal requests for help (e.g., bringing a toy to her following a request for her to play with it or to show him how it works). Aggressive behavior, such as hitting or kicking did not occur. Behavior considered incompatible with the deviant class was labeled "independent behavior." This class included any behavior in which he played alone, with no verbal comment to his mother.

Figure 3 shows cumulative records of Johnny's dependent and independent behaviors during all therapy sessions. Note that the response rates for his two behavior classes during the baseline sessions are roughly comparable. Figure 4 shows cumulative records of mother's general reactions to Johnny's two behavior classes during the therapy sessions. Her reactions to his dependent behavior usually involved answering his questions or granting his requests for help. Consistent with her self observations, Mother's reactions to Johnny's independent behavior almost always involved interrupting his play with imperative statements or non-verbal interference such as taking a toy away from him.

During the differential reinforcement sessions, Johnny's mother was instructed to ignore his dependency behavior and respond approvingly to his independent behavior. Reference to the differential reinforcement sessions shown in Figure 4 indicate that she was successful in following these instructions, even following elimination of the cueing system after the first session. As the rate of response curves shows, her rate of response to his independent behavior increased, and for his dependent behavior it dropped to zero. Correlated with his mother's behavior changes, Johnny's behavior changed in the expected ways. The rate of response curve for his dependent behavior, seen in Figure 3, dropped compared to the baseline session, while his independent behavior increased in rate.

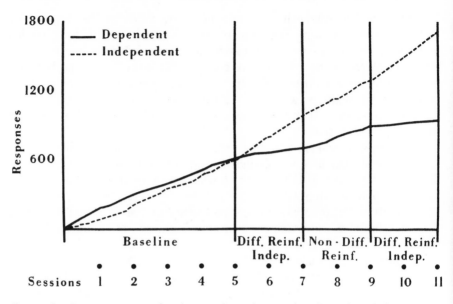

Figure 3. Rate measures of Johnny's dependent and independent behavior over baseline and therapy sessions

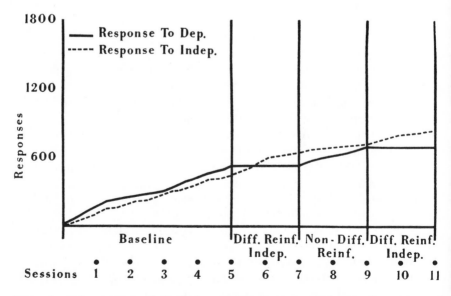

Figure 4. Rate measures of Mother's general responses to Johnny's dependent and independent behavior over baseline and therapy sessions

Following the two differential reinforcement sessions, the test of mother's control was performed. She was now instructed to resume her baseline behavior, and as the data indicate, she was successful in following these instructions; her response rates shown in the non-differential reinforcement sessions in Figure 4, were roughly similar, and comparable to her baseline rates.

Again, correlated with these changes in Mother's behavior, Johnny's behavior changed in the expected ways. Reference to the non-differential reinforcement sessions of Figure 3 shows that his response rates for the two behavior classes are comparable to his baseline rates.

The final two sessions involved reinstatement of Mother's differential reinforcement contingencies without use of the cueing system. The response rates shown in the last two sessions of Figures 3 and 4 indicate that this procedure was effective. Therefore, as was true in case number one, the finding that Johnny's deviant and incompatible behavior patterns could be weakened when his mother's reactions to these classes were eliminated, and strengthened when they were replaced, supports the contention that her behavior changes were responsible for the changes in Johnny's behavior.

## Case Number Three

Eddie, age four, was brought to the Clinic because of what his parents referred to as "extreme stubbornness." According to the parents, this behavior occurred only in the presence of Eddie's mother. Essentially, this "stubbornness" involved ignoring her commands and requests or doing the opposite of what he was told or asked to do.

She reported that her reactions to this behavior usually involved pleas, threats, and spankings, none of which appeared to be effective. It also became clear that most of her interactions with him were restricted to his oppositional behavior; she rarely played games with him, read to him, or talked to him. She did however, attempt to respond approvingly to his infrequent cooperative behavior. When asked why she was so selective in her interactions with him, she reported that because of his opposition, she felt "frustrated with him" and "angry with him" most of the time. She was convinced that he opposed her because he "liked" to get her angry.

During the classification sessions it became necessary to modify the instructions to Eddie's mother. Initially she was told to "just play with Eddie as you would at home." However, as might have been expected, mother and child ignored each other. The instructions were then changed to require Mother to ask Eddie to play with a different toy every sixty seconds. These instructions were in effect throughout all therapy sessions.

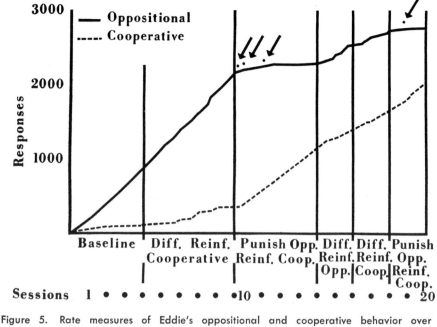

Figure 5. Rate measures of Eddie's oppositional and cooperative behavior over baseline and therapy sessions

Eddie's behavior was classified as either oppositional (not complying with Mother's request) or cooperative (complying).

Figure 5 shows cumulative records of Eddie's oppositional and cooperative behaviors during all therapy sessions. Note that his rate of oppositional behavior during the baseline sessions is far greater than his rate of cooperative behavior. Figure 6 shows cumulative records of Mother's general reactions to Eddie's two behavior classes. Her reactions to his oppositional behavior almost always involved threats or repetition of her request. Following his few cooperative responses, she either ignored him or stated her approval in a low voice without smiling.

During the differential reinforcement sessions, Eddie's mother was instructed to ignore his oppositional behavior and respond enthusiastically and with a smile to his cooperative behavior. As the differential reinforcement sessions shown in Figure 6 indicate, she was successful in following the instructions and use of the cueing system was discontinued after the second session. Reference to the same sessions in Figure 5 indicates that the expected changes in Eddie's behavior occurred gradually as the sessions progressed. However, note that the increase in his rate of cooperative behavior was not marked, and it declined during the fourth and fifth differential reinforcement sessions. Because of this problem, E decided to instruct Mother in the use of a punishment procedure which could be

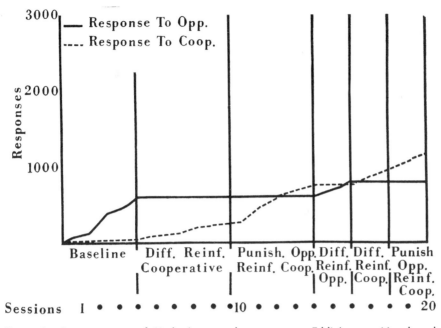

Figure 6. Rate measures of Mother's general responses to Eddie's oppositional and cooperative behavior over baseline and therapy sessions

combined with the differential reinforcement technique. She was instructed to isolate Eddie in an empty room (adjacent to the playroom) immediately following any of his oppositional responses. She was also told to leave him alone in this room for five minutes, unless he exhibited other undesirable behavior such as temper tantrums; if this type of behavior occurred, he remained in the room until it terminated.

Eddie's behavior during the punishment-reinforcement sessions is shown in Figure 5. The arrows indicate those instances in which Mother was signaled via the cueing system, to initiate the punishment procedure. Note the marked change in Eddie's oppositional and cooperative behavior; his oppositional behavior declined sharply in rate while his rate of cooperative behavior increased markedly. As these records also indicate, modifications in Eddie's behavior were maintained during the last two punishment-reinforcement sessions by Mother's use of differential reinforcement alone. Interestingly enough, Eddie's mother reported, following one of these latter sessions, that she "actually enjoyed being with him."

The test of Mother's control of Eddie's behavior was complicated by the fact that she had used two procedures in the course of the therapy sessions. As a result, two questions had to be answered: (1) Was Mother responsible for the changes in Eddie's behavior? (2) Was one of her procedures more important than the other in producing these changes? To answer these questions, Mother was first instructed to respond only to Eddie's oppositional behavior. The differential-reinforcement-oppositional sessions of Figure 6 revealed that she was successful in following these instructions. Correlated with these changes in Mother's behavior, Eddie's oppositional behavior (Figure 5) increased in rate, while his cooperative behavior declined in rate. Thus, it seemed certain that Mother was responsible for the earlier changes in Eddie's behavior. To determine whether Mother's differential reinforcement or differential reinforcement *plus* punishment had produced these changes, she was instructed in one set of sessions to resume her differential reinforcement of Eddie's cooperative behavior; in another set of sessions she was instructed to differentially reinforce the cooperative behavior and punish the oppositional behavior. Mother's success in following these instructions is shown in the last two sessions of Figure 6 and by the arrow in the last session of Figure 5. As Figure 5 also indicates, the expected changes in Eddie's behavior occurred only during the last set of sessions, thus demonstrating that Mother's combined use of differential reinforcement and punishment was responsible for the modification in Eddie's behavior.

## DISCUSSION

The data from two of the cases reported in this study indicate that a mother's social behavior may function as a powerful class of positive reinforcers for her child's deviant as well as his normal behavior. Experimental analysis of case number one revealed that Danny's mother was maintaining his commanding and cooperative behavior patterns through her reactions to these two response classes. A similar experimental analysis of case number two showed that Johnny's mother was maintaining his dependent and independent behavior through her reactions to these response classes. In both of these cases the response rates of the children's deviant and incompatible behavior patterns were weakened when their mothers' contingent behavior was eliminated, and strengthened when they were replaced. It would thus seem beyond a reasonable possibility of coincidence that the children's behavior classes were under the control of their respective mothers. However, this conclusion could not be supported by the data from case number three. It will be recalled that little rate change occurred in Eddie's oppositional and cooperative behavior following manipulation of the contingencies between these response classes and his mother's behavior; not until his mother utilized a punishment procedure did dramatic rate changes occur. Thus, little can be said concerning variables in Eddie's natural environment which were responsible for maintaining his deviant and incompatible behavior.

The data reported in this study are also of interest in terms of the modification of deviant child behavior. In all cases it proved possible to train the mothers in the effective use of behavior modification techniques based upon principles of operant learning theory. In two of the cases (Danny and Johnny) the techniques simply involved instructing the mothers to change the usual contingencies between their behavior and their children's deviant and incompatible behavior. Since it had been experimentally demonstrated with these cases that the mothers were providing social reinforcement for their children's deviant behavior, the next logical step would involve training the mothers to ignore these behavior patterns and to provide their reinforcers for behavior which was incompatible with the deviant behavior. As the data indicate, this differential reinforcement procedure was quite effective within the confines of the experimental setting.

Selection of the behavior modification technique used for the third case (Eddie) required more reliance on past research findings than on information gained from an analysis of mother-child interbehavior. Since E was unable after five sessions to determine the source of control of Eddie's deviant behavior, it was decided to stop the search for controlling stimulus events and concentrate on finding the most practical means of eliminating his deviant behavior. Past research (Wolf *et al.,* 1964) has shown that social isolation may function as a highly effective punishment technique for deviant child behavior. As the data indicate, Eddie's mother made very effective use of this technique.

The design of this study did not permit assessment of the generality of the changes in the children's behavior. One would expect that since the mothers were responsible for the changes which were produced, the question of generality would in part be a question of how well the mothers' "therapeutic" behaviors were maintained outside the experimental setting. That is, were their newly learned reactions to their children effective in obtaining reinforcement from the natural environment as well as from the experimental setting? Further research is planned to provide answers to this question.

## REFERENCES

Bandura, A. Psychotherapy as a learning process. *Psychol. Bull.,* 1961, *58,* 143–149.

Grossberg, J. N. Behavior therapy: a review. *Psychol. Bull.,* 1964, *62,* 73–88.

Prince, G. S. A clinical approach to parent-child interaction. *J. child Psychol. Psychiat.,* 1961, *2,* 169–184.

Russo, S. Adaptations in behavioral therapy with children. *Behav. Res. Ther.,* 1964, *2,* 43–47.

Straughan, J. H. Treatment with child and mother in the playroom. *Behav. Res. Ther.,* 1964, *2,* 37–41.

Wolf, M. M., Risley, T., & Mees, H. Application of operant conditioning procedures to the behavior problems of an autistic child. *Behav. Res. Ther.,* 1964, *1,* 305–312.

# 21

# Theory and Research
# in Mental (Developmental) Retardation

## Sidney W. Bijou

### EDITORS' COMMENTS

This paper makes a case for an analysis of retardation from a functional point of view. It offers a theory of retardation and, as is true of most theories, especially those closely related to empirical facts, presents implications for research and applications to practices in the home, clinic, and school.

Retardation is to be viewed as deviation in psychological development, and hence there is a preference for the term developmental rather than mental retardation. The differences between normal and retarded development lie in the nature of the conditions and interactions of development, past and present. Normal development—progressive changes in interactions between the individual and the environment—comes about through the action of biological, social, and physical conditions that are "within normal limits." Retarded development evolves through the action of biological, social, and physical conditions which deviate from the so-called normal in extreme degrees—the more extreme the deviations in conditions, the more retarded the development. Thus the retarded child's structural makeup or his physiological functioning may be incomplete or damaged; similarly, his history of interactions with people and things may not have provided essential experiences or may have developed behaviors which interfere with normal progressions in learning.

This paper also touches upon the larger issue of the relationship between the "mind" and the "body" in theorizing about retardation in particular, and in psychopathology in general. A unitary rather than a dualistic model of the mind-body relationship is followed.

Sidney W. Bijou, "Theory and Research in Mental (Developmental) Retardation," *The Psychological Record*, 1963, *13*, 95–110.

A good deal of the stimulation for this paper has come from the research supported by a grant (M-2232) from the National Institute of Mental Health, Public Health Service, and the Gatzert Foundation.

Thanks are due Jay S. Birnbrauer for his many helpful criticisms and comments.

"Mental" in this formulation would refer to the behavioral interactions of the individual and environmental events. Anatomical features of the body and its physiological functioning are conceived of as a part of such environmental events, in that they provide determining conditions, along with social and physical conditions outside the body wall. In other words, biological, social, and physical conditions interrelate and combine to determine the course of behavior change, progressive and regressive.

In the preface of a volume entitled *Strategies for Behavioral Research in Mental Retardation: A Seminar Report,* Wilcox writes:

> Research progress in the behavioral aspects of mental retardation has been quite slow. It has been criticized for its unimaginativeness, its methodological inadequacies, its lack of conceptual clarity, its lack of integration with the behavioral sciences, and its focus upon certain areas to the neglect of others. More specifically, according to its critics, it has lacked a sense or plan or direction (1961, p. ix).

There is much to support Wilcox's evaluation. Whether he overstates the case is not of importance. What is of significance is that his survey has led him to conclude that current research is not producing principles and techniques which enhance the understanding of retardation and generating new ways of dealing with it. Though many complex conditions contribute to this state of affairs, a prime factor is the currently accepted theory of psychological retardation. The objective of this paper is to evaluate the contemporary theory and to present an alternate approach.

It should be emphasized at the outset that concern here is with an analysis of mental (more meaningful substitutes would be "psychological," "developmental," or "behavioral") retardation and not with biological retardation, i.e., retardation in anatomical and physiological growth. Analysis of the conditions producing such anomalies is, of course, the special province of the biological sciences.

To assert that this approach is not concerned with an analysis of biological phenomena does not mean that biological factors are excluded from an account of the conditions that influence retarded psychological development. In the formulation to follow, biological variables are regarded as one of several classes given the status of independent variables along with nonbiological variables, that limit the range of psychological behavior at any given point in the developmental sequence.

## CURRENT THEORY OF PSYCHOLOGICAL RETARDATION

It is not accurate to talk about the current theory of psychological retardation, since, in actuality, there are many theories of retardation. In addition to proliferations from differing viewpoints, the variety is augmented by the fact that some are concerned only with one aspect of retardation (personal, social, educational, emotional, or vocational) while others attempt to encompass all aspects of retardation. Rather than describe and classify the variations, it will be more in keeping with the task of this paper to discuss the current concepts regarding the nature of retardation, and its causes.

## Nature of Retardation

Most frequently retardation is thought of as an impairment of intellectual functioning. It is also conceived of as incomplete development or as a state of social or intellectual incompetence. These words usually refer to behavior. The treatment of the term given by Cameron and Margaret (1951) is an example. They define retardation as behavior which is more appropriate for younger age levels than for the individual's own life age.

## Causes of Retardation

Retardation is usually thought to be caused by a hypothetical construct like defective intellect or mentality. Defective intellect or mentality is in turn said to be caused by faulty hereditary processes, deleterious environmental influences, or both. (See Figure 1.)

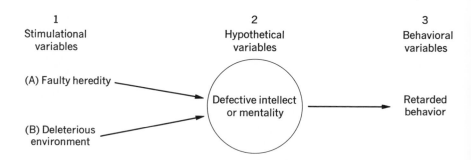

Figure 1. The relationships among stimulational, hypothetical, and behavioral variables

Let us first consider the implications of attributing retardation to a hypothetical construct. The serviceability of a hypothetical construct for the advancement of a scientific analysis of behavior rests heavily on how the term is defined. It is common practice in psychology to define a concept of this type on the basis of *observed behavior alone* (Number 3 in Figure 1), or on a *combination of antecedent conditions* and *observed be-*

*havior* (Numbers 1 and 3 in Figure 1). Judging the amount of intellect from observed behavior *alone* usually follows this procedure: A sequence of behavior is observed, measured, or described, then a verbal statement is made, giving the estimated level of intelligence that must be present to account for the observed behavior. Nothing is gained. An additional word or phrase is attached to a description of behavior. Skinner (1953) describes the process of inferring causes from observed behavior as follows:

> Trait-names usually begin as adjective—"intelligent," "aggressive," "disorganized," "angry," "introverted," "ravenous," and so on, but the almost inevitable linguistic result is that adjectives give birth to nouns. The things to which these nouns refer are then taken to be the active causes of the aspects. We begin with "intelligent behavior," pass first to "behavior which shows intelligence," and then to "behavior" which is the effect of intelligence." . . . But at no point in such a series do we make contact with any event outside the behavior itself which justifies the claim of a causal connection (p. 202).

Let us now turn to a consideration of defining a hypothetical construct in terms involving *both antecedent conditions and observed behavior*. This mode of procedure which attempts to avoid the pitfalls of the response-inferred method described above has been employed mostly by theorists interested in formulating a general behavior theory. In such systems theoretical terms form a hypothetical linkage between measures of behavior (frequency, latency, or amplitude) on one hand (Number 3 in Figure 1), and genetic, physical, and social variables on the other (Number 1 in Figure 1). In other words, hypothetical concepts *bridge the gap* between measures of behavior as dependent variables or output variables and independent genetic and environmental variables.

Hunt (1961), in a volume devoted exclusively to the relationship between intelligence and experience, attempts to make a case for defining intelligence this way. In a sense he suggests that this procedure is feasible for formulating a limited or miniature system.

> In view of the conceptual developments and the evidence coming from animals learning to learn, from neuropsychology, from the programming of electronic computers to solve problems, and from the development of intelligence in children, it would appear that intelligence should be conceived as intellectual capacities based on central processes hierarchically arranged within the instrinsic portions of the cerebrum. These central processes are approximately analogous to the strategies for information processing and action with which electronic computers are programmed (p. 362).

The "bridging the gap" method of defining a term like intelligence has at least two limitations. First, it suggests that an analysis of environmental conditions and behavioral changes serves as a means of getting at internal processes, that environmental and behavioral concepts are "symptoms" or "surface terms" and that the "more fundamental ones" are located inside the organism, correlated or uncorrelated with physiological processes. It stands to reason that such an orientation discourages a minute search for observable physical and social events which *might* play a role in retarding psychological growth, especially in the very early phases. Only recently, for example, it has been deemed profitable to analyze specific and subtle relationships between the infant and mother. Reference here is to studies on smiling behavior by Brackbill (1958), on vocalization by Rheingold, Gewirtz, and Ross (1959), and on exploratory behavior by Rheingold, Stanley, and Cooley (1962).

The second limitation of the "gap" type of definition of a causal variable is that it runs the danger of contributing little or no new knowledge to retarded development as such. This fact evolves from an explicit point of view which suggests that basic research should be aimed at extending the system of hypothetical terms and determining the exact relationships among them. It is surely true that much research on retarded children has evolved from this orientation but since the interest has been focused, for the most part, on the properties of relationships among intervening variables (or on theory testing), little data are provided on the magnitude of conditions, past and present, that may limit the range of behavior development. Although this practice is not indigenous to the approach, it is, however, descriptive of what has happened thus far.

Let us now discuss the antecedents (Number 1 in Figure 1) of defective intellect or mentality. Usually the literature states that defective intellect has a two-fold causation: (A) hereditary, familial, constitutional, intrinsic, and endogenous; and (B) environmental, extrinsic, or exogenous.

The first set of conditions is said to come about through genetic processes or some other transmissional mechanism not fully understood at present. The second are external physical and social events which impair or lower the level of mentality established by the first set. The typical view is that an individual inherits a level (with a range) of intellect. If, on one hand, environmental factors are disadvantageous because of injuries, diseases, toxic conditions, physical and social neglects, his "native ability" will not be fully expressed in his behavior. If, on the other hand, the environment is normal or advantageous because of "good" physical care and social stimulation, his "native level" will be fully or almost fully manifested in his behavior. The following combinations are therefore possible:

1. Low native ability and a favorable environment resulting in mild manifest retardation.
2. Low native ability and an unfavorable environment resulting in marked manifest retardation.

3. Normal to high native ability and an unfavorable environment resulting in mild retardation or lowered manifest ability, but within borderline or normal ranges.
4. Normal to high native ability and a favorable environment resulting in normal or accelerated manifest development.

The concept that *native ability of mentality* may be weakened, strengthened, or uninfluenced by environmental conditions is an aspect of the nature-nurture controversy which assumes that one can determine for an observed sample of psychological behavior what proportion of its determination can be attributed to heredity and what to environment. As the literature will attest, psychologists have lost enthusiasm for trying to determine whether heredity or environment is more important in determining a level of intellectual functioning. It has become apparent over the years that (1) the amount of "native ability" existing at birth or at any other point in development cannot be known independent of behavior, (2) heredity and environment are generic terms pertaining to locus of variables and not fixed forces in oppositional struggle (Beach, 1955; Verplanck, 1955), and (3) the interaction among variables within the organism and between the organism and environmental events produces continual change of behavior. Anastasi and Foley (1949) give an excellent discussion of the relationship between hereditary and environmental variables and behavior recorded in intelligence tests and in other psychometric data.

To take another tack, a convincing case could be made against attributing level of mentality (defined as a hypothetical term) to the genetic process. Anatomical and physiological variations are at issue in the genetic processes, and these should be viewed in terms of the interactions prior to fertilization, and the interactions of the new biological unit in relation to the circumstances with which they make contact. Species and individual characteristics observed at a specified moment in the prenatal cycle are a *product of such interactions,* and psychological behavior evolves from the interaction of the uniquely constituted organism with physical and social events.

In some writings psychological retardation is not defined as a hypothetical term but rather as an impairment of some system of the body, usually the brain. A typical contention is that mental retardation is a condition in which the brain is prevented from attaining full development, thus limiting the ability to learn and putting learning to use. From this point of view research should be directed toward exploring brain processes. To understand brain activity is to understand the basis of psychological behavior. Direct study of retarded behavior and the possible determining environmental conditions that may produce it are reduced to subordinate considerations.

There is no question that physiological psychologists and psychobiologists have made and will continue to make contributions to the understanding of the conditions that generate retardation. The only point at issue here is the expediency of reducing psychological variables to biological terms, and of conceptualizing psychological retardation in such a way as to encourage an all-out research effort on physiological variables on the assumption that they are the ones that will eventually yield all of the desired information on psychological phenomena. The view advanced here, and expressed explicitly in the writings of Kantor (1959) and Skinner (1953), is that psychological or behavioral retardation can profitably be defined in terms of the interaction of an organism behaving as a unified system in an inseparable context of environmental events. This approach describes the domain of the behavioral scientist in terms of making observation of behavior-environmental interactions, effecting stimulational changes, formulating constructs, and making statements about constructs.

## A NATURAL SCIENCE APPROACH TO RETARDATION

It is suggested that retardation be conceptualized in observable, functionally defined relationships without appealing to hypothetical constructs or without reducing the causes of psychological events to biological events. "In such cases as have been traditionally called idiocy, imbecility, and moronity the basic principle is the failure of the individual to build up response equipment to certain things. There is failure to coordinate certain stimulus-response functions" (Kantor, 1959, p. 176). In other words, a retarded individual is one who has a limited repertory of behavior evolving from interactions of the individual with his environmental contacts which constitute his history.

From this point of view the task of behavioral research is to investigate the observable or potentially observable conditions that may produce retarded behavior, not retarded mentality. The conditions subjected to investigation are the biological, physical, and social interactions, past and current. These, of course, are the same conditions that are analyzed in studying normal development. The difference in studying retarded versus normal children is in the values or magnitudes of the antecedent conditions. It is contended that retarded development is generated by extreme variations in biological, physical, and social factors.

It may be noted that the three sets of conditions referred to are similar to those under discussion in the current literature on retardation (Jervis, 1954, for example). The difference lies *in the way* in which these variables are said to interact, or in the role attributed to each. In the view presented here, retarded behavior is a function of observable biological, physical, and social conditions, all conceived as independent variables. In the typical view presented in the literature, retarded behavior is caused by hypothetic or biological variables which *in turn* are determined by heredity but which are modifiable, within limits, by physical and social environmental events.

Since an analysis of retarded behavior does not involve special sets of environmental conditions (or unique responses) it follows that the concepts and principles of a general theory of psychological development might be applied with advantage. The recognition of a continuity between retarded and normal development suggests that findings and formulations emanating from animal and human experimental laboratories during the past 50 years might be applied advantageously to an analysis of retardation. The remainder of this paper will deal with variables of which retarded development may be a function and will make reference to behavioral concepts and principles that seem pertinent.

## Biological and Physiological Factors

In discussing the role of biological and physiological factors we shall use "organismic" as a general term. Extreme variations in organismic conditions and anomalies may limit the development of behavior repertories in three interrelated ways: (1) Essential response equipment may be impaired; (2) certain classes of environmental stimuli may be unavailable or restricted; and (3) stimuli presented by an impaired person might reduce social interactions essential to the execution of later behaviors. Organismic anomalies or organismic pathology includes defects in gross-anatomy, structure and functioning of the sense organs, the musculo-skeletal system, the neurological and endocrine systems, and other systems and glands of the body. Organismic flaws may originate in genetic processes or in injurious chemical and mechanical actions during the prenatal period, during birth, or after birth. Since the extent of the anomaly or damage may vary from mild to severe, the effect on psychological development may range from mild or inconsequential to severe or devastating. Medical practice uses such diagnostic categories as microcephaly, mongolism, and cretinism suggesting that such categories of organismic malformation are correlated with retarded psychological development.

As to the first point, the impairment of essential response equipment, it is obvious that certain kinds of impairment could have a profound influence on retarding psychological development. Clearly a child cannot perform tasks requiring responses impossible for him to execute, i.e., he does not have the necessary anatomical parts and/or physiological functioning to make the required response. If he cannot perform the task on organismic grounds, no amount of stimulation, exposure, or training in the home, school, or community will enable him to do so. (He may learn other responses that may serve the same function. He may compensate.

Whether or not he does depends to a considerable extent upon the "guidance" received from others.)

The second way in which the organismically atypical child may develop a limited repertory is through the restriction of stimuli that ordinarily becomes available with more control over the physical and social environmental events. If body control, manual and locomotor skills are inadequately developed, the number and kind of physical and social stimuli available for contact are curtailed. A child who can lie only on his back can have commerce only with stimuli that are naturally above his body (e.g., the ceiling), or are brought into his line of vision, while the child who can roll from side to side and can remain in a sitting position can interact with stimuli over a wider range. Similarly, a child who can reach, grasp, and retrieve an object can have infinitely more experiences than a child who has yet to develop such coordination and skill. The child who can move from place to place can get into all sorts of novel situations compared to one who must depend upon the "good will" of others for his locomotion. Depending on the locus and extent or organismic impairment, some stimuli will always be inaccessible to a child; others will become available on a delayed schedule.

A third way in which an organismically impaired child might be restricted in developmental opportunities is related to the way he appears to others as a social person. His appearance of status might be aversive or nonreinforcing to others, causing them to avoid him, to leave his presence as quickly as possible, or to behave toward him in an altogether indifferent manner. For example, a physically-disabled youngster may not get "his share of attention" because his parents are "too busy" looking after the other children; his siblings are "bogged down" with school work and have no time for him; the children in the neighborhood do not include him in their play because he cannot keep up with them, and the school principal does not enroll him in the kindergarten because he is not "ready." Abbreviated and dutiful relationships do not provide the child with foundational experiences which only people can supply. High levels of conceptualizing and abstracting performances require people to arrange and rearrange stimuli and to reinforce responses differentially (pointing out similarities and differences, assisting in grouping stimuli on the basis of several criteria, etc.). Many activities of this sort occur informally (and almost on an "unconscious level") in the home, neighborhood, and preschool. Likewise, appropriate emotional behavior in adolescence and adulthood evidently requires early social relationships based on positive reinforcement, on support under conditions of aversive stimulation (consolation following a nasty fall or an immunization shot), and on relative freedom from conflict-arousing environment.

To summarize: Organismic factors may constitute one set of conditions generating retarded psychological development. These independent variables participate with other nonbiological independent variables to produce retardation. Impairment of the organism does not imply impairment of a central causal condition called "mentality," whether theoretically or biologically defined. Insofar as hereditary processes participate in determining retardation, they may do so in the production of anomalies in the anatomy and physiology of the individual. A child with organismic damage or anomaly may be excluded from, or seriously delayed in, having contacts with things and people because (1) his *biological equipment* is impaired, (2) his underdeveloped *psychological equipment* limits the range of available stimuli, and (3) his appearance and status might *prevent* him from social interactions essential for later learning.

Since a certain proportion of children will always have organismic impairment through hereditary processes, diseases, injuries, or toxic conditions, it is expected that a certain segment of these individuals will, as a consequence, have limited behavior repertories and therefore be considered by society as psychologically retarded. In those cases in which the organismic conditions are not preventable or medically remediable, the task of devising special training techniques and of preparing special psychological environments falls on the shoulders of the behavioral scientists.

## Intermittent Reinforcement and Extinction

Positive reinforcement refers to the procedure of following a response with a stimulus which increases the probability of the occurrence of a response of the same class on the next occasion. Reinforcement can be continuous in that it follows every response of a given class or intermittent in that it follows such reaction on a sporadic basis, contrived or otherwise. Extinction concerns the reduction of the probability of a response of a given class through the operation of a consequence neutral stimulus. These processes may operate to delay or decelerate progressive changes in behavior in at least two ways. First, it is possible that for some parents, seeing their child remain helpless, ineffective, and infantile is reinforcing, and contrariwise seeing him resourceful, effective, efficient and mature is irritating or aversive. Under these circumstances they are likely (whether they can talk about this tendency or not) to reinforce dependent behavior (behaviors that stimulate the parents to perform so as to make reinforcing stimuli immediately available to the child), and systematically extinguish (or even punish) independent behaviors (behaviors that make reinforcing stimuli available directly through the activity of the child).

The second way in which these processes may delay development is clearly and succinctly given by Ferster (1961) in his discussion of performance deficits in the early development of the autistic child.

Intermittent reinforcement and extinction are the major techniques for removing or weakening behavior in a repertoire. The most fundamental way to eliminate a kind of behavior from an organism's repertoire is to discontinue the effect the behavior has on the environment (extinction). A performance may also be weakened if its maintaining effect on the environment occurs intermittently (intermittent reinforcement). Behaviors occurring because of their effects on the parent are especially likely to be weakened by intermittent reinforcement and extinction, because the parental reinforcements are a function of other variables and behavioral processes usually not directly under the control of the child (pp. 443–444).

He goes on to point out that speech and social behavior are the segments of the young child's developments most likely to be affected by these processes because at this stage the parents' behaviors constitute the most important source of reinforcers for the development of these behaviors.

A question might be raised about the relevance of the causes of autistic behavior for an analysis of retarded development. It is likely that the frequencies and range of behaviors of the retarded and autistic child overlap and at the same time differ. It is clear that both have limited repertories. What is claimed, however, is that similar processes may operate to produce both patterns of behavior. The differences in the behavior observed in each may come about through differences in the permutations and combinations of organismic and historically defined interactional events.

To summarize: Intermittent reinforcement and extinction or nonreinforcement may operate to retard development. Child rearing practices may be of such a nature that parents selectively reinforce dependent behavior and nonreinforce or extinguish independent. The behavior of both classes are, of course, related to the developmental stage of the child. Another possibility is that intermittent reinforcement and extinction under the control of parents may operate to weaken the development of behavior. These "schedule" effects could come about through the disruption of the repertories of the parents and prepotency of other performance inside and outside of the home.

### Inadequate Reinforcement History

When the environment is dull, routine, unvaried, and limited in range, interactions are restricted. Circumstances of this sort would be expected to limit repertories in self-care, "manners," emotional-social reactions, and preacademic and academic skills. Ferster (1958) describes this condition as follows:

Under this category belong individuals who are not making contact with important parts of their environment simply because their history did not include a set of experiences (educational) which could develop these performances during the normal maturation of the individual. Especially in the area of everyday social contacts, considerable skill is necessary for producing social reinforcements, and the absence of this skill either results in an individual without a social repertoire or one who achieves affects on his social environment by indirect means, as, for example, using aversive stimulation to gain attention.

Inadequate reinforcement histories may be expected to occur in several social situations. They might include (1) children reared in isolated communities and under barely adequate economic means, (2) infants and children reared in institutions in which the social-emotional contacts possible in family living are absent, and (3) children in families with emotionally-disturbed parents who prevent their offspring, for idiosyncratic reasons, from having the usual interactions with things and people.

The classical case of Kaspar Hauser exemplifies the possible developmental effects of inadequate reinforcement history generated by isolated living under marginal economic conditions. One may argue that because of economic abundance at the present time this type of conditions no longer play a significant role in contributing to developmental retardation. It should not be overlooked, however, that in many of the undeveloped countries that extreme inadequacies still exist and that in nations with high standards of living there are substantial minority groups whose children must be reared under marked physical, geographical, and economic deprivations.

In regard to inadequate reinforcement histories for children reared in institutional settings, Dennis' study (1957) has a bearing. He observed the behavior of children, ages one to four, and the rearing practices in three Iranian institutions. In two of the three, the children were markedly retarded in motor development; in the other, little retardation of this sort was evident. He summarized his findings as follows:

The extreme retardation in Institutions I and II was probably due to the paucity of handling, including the failure of attendants to place the children in the sitting position and the prone position. The absence of experience in these positions is believed to have retarded the children in regard to sitting alone and also in regard to the onset of locomotion. The lack of experience in the prone positions seems in most cases to have prevented children from learning to creep; instead of creeping, the majority of the children in Institutions I and II, prior to walking, locomoted by scooting. In Institution III, in which children were frequently handled, propped in the sitting position, and placed prone, motor development resembled that of most home-reared children. The retardation of subjects in Institutions I and II is believed to be due to the restriction of specific kinds of learning opportunities.

Children exposed to only limited sectors of the normal environment because of the idiosyncratic behavior of their disturbed parents might be said to suffer from inadequate reinforcement histories. Davis' (1947) report of Isabelle provides an interesting example. Because she was illegitimate, Isabelle was kept in isolation by her deaf-mute mother. The child and her mother spent most of the time together in a dark room shut off from the rest of the family. When discovered, Isabelle was six-and-a-half years old. She communicated with her mother by gestures and made only "strange croaking sounds." At first it could not be determined whether she could hear; later it was established that she could. She showed fear and hostility toward others, especially men. Her reactions to objects were unusual. For example, when presented with a ball she used it to stroke the interviewer's face. Her mental age on the Stanford-Binet was one year and seven months and her social age on the Vineland was two years six months. Physically she was underdeveloped and had rickets.

To summarize: An inadequate reinforcement history may produce retarded or a limited repertory of behavior. A child may fail to be exposed to the physical and social stimulation ordinarily provided children in the culture because of isolated geographical living conditions, marginal economic conditions, or because of the practices in certain kinds of group rearing institutions, or because of the disturbed behavior of parents. (As we shall see, the disturbed behavior of parents also influence the occasions and frequencies with which aversive stimulations and positive reinforcements are made available to the child).

### Severe Punishment

A third factor that could retard development and one that generates from interactions between the individual and his environmental contacts, is *severe* punishment. Skinner (1953) defines punishment as follows: the process of following a response with a negative reinforcer (e.g., hitting) or the withdrawal of a positive reinforcer (removing food from a hungry organism). Punishment may, of course, be meted out by the physical environment (getting caught in a bear trap) or by the social environment (the "naughty" child ordered to leave the dining room table).

The consequences of severe punishment on the behavior producing it are several. We shall briefly describe only the three that seem most apparent in delaying development. First, such stimulation may *modify* a serviceable response (i.e., one that produced reinforcers) to the point at which it no longer does so. Ferster (1958) describes this consequence in these words "The absence of adequate repertoires in the individual could

result from the distortion of the form of the behavior so that the performance does not have its customary effect" (p. 104). A simple example
would be as follows: A child is punished by his parents for saying certain
words about his younger sibling. After a few experiences of this sort,
he may garble words so that what is uttered is not reacted to in a punishing way. Such a change in the form of the behavior avoids punishment
but is not conducive to further growth in language behavior, at least in
regard to siblings and possibly other children. Second, punishment *stops
on-going behavior,* at least in situations in which it is administered. If
the punishment is moderate or mild, it is likely that the behavior would
be readily reinstituted. If, however, the punishment is severe, it is likely
that the suppression effects would be extremely resistive to change. The
action of intense aversive stimulation is more impressive when stimulus
and response inductive processes are taken into account. That is, stimuli
resembling those present at the time of punishment could have similar
suppressive effects, and responses similar to or "chained in" with the
punished responses could also be curtailed. Third, situations or settings
in which punishment occurs acquire aversive properties; formerly neutral
conditions in the punishing situation become, through pairing, conditioned
aversive stimuli (having been thrown by a horse, the child thereafter may
be afraid of that horse, and perhaps horses in general). Behaviors which
*avoid stimuli* present during punishment, as well as stimuli which resemble them, are strengthened. The removal of aversive stimuli (in this
case they are conditioned aversive stimuli) is reinforcing, negatively reinforcing. Responses such as getting out of an aversive situation, getting
away from it, avoiding getting in or near it, as well as being inactive
will be strengthened. Thus, punishment terminates on-going behavior—
sensory, manual, locomotor, linguistic, and emotional—and sets up situations that strengthen those behaviors which keep "clear of them." When
the punishment is strong, either traumatic or severe and frequent, and
the behavior terminated is pertinent to further psychological development
(e.g., language, speech, verbal behavior), and when the evaded situations
constitute a good share of the environment (e.g., those which involve
Father) and generalize to other essential aspects of the environment (from
Father to all adults), the punishing interaction could have extensive retarding consequences.

To summarize: Severe punishment mediated by physical or social
events may retard the development of a behavioral repertory. Intensive
or traumatic aversive stimulation contingent upon behavior may operate
to distort the form and intensity of a response so as to reduce its functional value, may suppress behavior to the point of virtual nonrecoverabil-
ity, and may lead to avoidant behavior, preventing experiences essential
to later learning. These interactions may have magnified effects on retarding development through the operation of stimulus and response induction.

Stimuli not directly involved may have similar consequences and responses associated with those in the contingencies may also become affected.

### Other Processes

Undoubtedly other processes contribute to retarded psychological development, such as satiations and deprivations for reinforcers and emotionalizing stimuli. Findings from objective field and laboratory studies are as yet unavailable to indicate their specific roles in a functional analysis.

## PSYCHOLOGICAL RESEARCH

The number of studies dealing with retardation from a functional, or antecedent-consequent, point of view is in the minority. Most investigations are correlational in nature. That is to say, most correlate responses on tests with other responses on tests, or with physiological measures, or with other behavior criteria such as performance on learning tasks.

Studies analyzing functional relationships fall into two categories— those concerned with hypothetical constructs and those dealing with direct relationships between environmental and response variables.

As stated earlier, hypothetical construct type of functional studies are rarely concerned with an analysis of the interactional history or the environmental conditions of retardation. Typical concern is with whether the properties of hypothetical constructs inferred from infrahuman young adults or subjects also hold for the retarded. Some are devoted to testing hypotheses relevant to properties and relationships among the hypothetical terms.

Let us turn briefly to the limited literature that deals with manipulatable conditions of which retarded repertories may be a function. Some studies in this group provide information on the construction of a laboratory to study retarded children, on the nature of reinforcers that have been found to sustain behavior for substantial periods and for many sessions, on the behavioral characteristics of the basic schedules of reinforcement, and on the orderliness of performances on simple learning and discrimination tasks.

A second cluster of functional-empirical studies attempt to analyze and control behavior frequently observed in the retarded. Typically, the concern of investigators in this group involve such terms as distractability, attending behavior, "rigidity," and "perseveration." Some of these studies attempt to demonstrate the action of conditions which produce the high frequencies of behavior observed in retarded as compared to other deviant growth patterns in children.

A third group which has emerged only recently consists of studies which apply learning principles to the development of other kinds of behavior. That is, studies have not as yet been launched which would bring retarded children into specially engineered environments to see what may be done to build, in a systematic fashion, skills and knowledge in communication behavior, and skills and knowledge involved in social activities. Concerted research on these problems would not only throw light on the conditions and processes unique to each, but would also be expected to enhance the behavioral repertories of retarded individuals and increase their satisfactions in general.

# SUMMARY

Instead of viewing the cause of psychological retardation as being a theoretical construct such as mentality, or as a biological phenomenon such as impairment of the brain, it is suggested that it be conceived as being generated by adverse histories or simply as failures of coordinations of stimulus and response functions. This position suggests a search for the specific conditions of which limited repertories may be a function. The ganismic variables—and the life history of the total organism interacting development, toward analyzing organismic variables—the role of the hereditary process and the environmental events influencing consequent organismic variables—and the life history of the total organism interacting with environmental events from fertilization on. A functional analysis suggests a search into interactions conceptualized as intermittent reinforcement and extinction, inadequate reinforcement history, severe punishment, and other factors, such as extreme satiation and deprivations, and emotional operations.

One advantage of this approach is that the variables suggested are all subject to objective definition and are all manipulatable or potentially manipulatable, a feature obviously desirable for both research and application. Another is that it does not appeal to special theory of retardation. The concepts and principles thus far developed on infrahuman and human subjects may be applied, as a general theory of behavior to the problem of retardation. This contention follows from the conditions and the behaviors observed in retarded development which do not differ qualitatively, but only quantitatively from normal and accelerated development. Thus, functional-analytic research on retardation can be the immediate heir of the empirical principles developed to date. On the other hand, future research on retardation can enrich general behavior theory, in particular, by analyzing the behavior that is generated by the operation of extreme conditions.

At present studies concerned with functional analyses which incidentally do not exceed those correlating response measures are either aimed at theory testing involving the properties of hypothetical constructs or at direct analysis of the relationship between independent environmental events and behavior measures. The latter may be conceived as constituting three subgroups. The first is concerned with exploring the situation and the basic conditions for conducting laboratory-experimental studies. The second, with an analysis of some of the behaviors that seem to occur with frequency among the retarded, and the third, with applying behavior principles to the education and training of the retarded individual.

## REFERENCES

Anastasi, Anne, & Foley, J. P. *Differential psychology*. New York: Macmillan, 1949.

Beach, F. A., The descent of instinct. *Psychol. Rev.*, 1955, *62*, 401–410.

Bijou, S. W., & Baer, D. M. *Child development*. Vol. 1. *A systematic and empirical theory*. New York: Appleton-Century-Crofts, 1961.

Brackbill, Yvonne. Extinction of the smiling response in infants as a function of reinforcement schedule. *Child Develpm.*, 1958 *29*, 115–124.

Cameron, N., & Margaret, Ann. *Behavior pathology*. New York: Houghton Mifflin, 1951.

Davis, K. Final note on a case of extreme isolation. *Amer. J. Sociol.*, 1947, *57*, 432–457.

Dennis, W. Infant development under environment handicaps. *Psychol. Monogr.*, 1957, *71*, No. 7 (Whole No. 436).

Dobzhansky, T. *The biological basis of human freedom*. New York: Columbia, 1956.

Ferster, C. B. Reinforcement and punishment in the control of human behavior by social agencies. *Psychiat. res. Reports*, 1958, *10*, 101–118.

Ferster, C. B. Positive reinforcement and behavioral deficits of autistic children. *Child Develpm.*, 1961, *32*, 437–456.

Gilbert, T. F. Fundamental dimensional properties of the operant. *Psychol. Rev.*, 1958, *65*, 272–282.

Hunt, J. McV. *Intelligence and experience*. New York: Ronald, 1961.

Jervis, G. A. Factors in mental retardation. *Children*, 1954, *1*, 27–211.

Kantor, J. R. *Interbehavioral psychology* (rev. ed.) Bloomington, Indiana: Principia Press, 1959.

Rheingold, Harriet L., Gewirtz, J. L., & Ross, Helen W. Social conditioning of vocalizations in the infant. *J. comp. physiol. Psychol.*, 1959, *52*, 68–73.

Rheingold, Harriet L., Stanley, W. C., & Cooley, J. A. Method for studying exploratory behavior in infants. *Science*, 1962, *136*, 1054–1055.

Skinner, B. F. *Science and human behavior*. New York: Macmillan, 1953.

Verplanck, W. S. Since learned behavior is innate and vice versa what now? *Psychol. Rev.*, 1955, *62*, 139–144.

Wilcox, R. (Ed.) *Strategies for behavioral research in mental retardation: A seminar report*. Madison, Wis.: Univer. of Wisconsin Press, 1961.

# To Education

Education is the massive modification of behavior. Extensive and diverse repertoires of behavior are to be developed, hopefully, in every individual of the culture. The problem is primarily one of adding new responses to one's current catalogue of skills; but it also involves the unlearning of incorrect prior teaching.

If the experimental analysis of child development at this point in its history had little or nothing to contribute to as basic an exercise in behavior change as education, it would be a dubious science indeed. These readings should by now have shown the reader that the problem of teaching a child is reasonably well understood. What is required for a successful application of this knowledge to modern education is an understanding of the learning process which will produce a massive enough contribution to match the dimensions of the problem. The following readings offer a sample of the possibilities so far developed. Note that the preceding articles have emphasized repeatedly that the essential elements of teaching are a one-to-one interaction between a responding child on the one hand and a response-judging, reinforcer-dispensing programmer on the other. In educational applications, that one-to-one relationship is embodied in the teaching machine, as a mass-produced instructor.

273

# 22

# Why We Need Teaching Machines

## B. F. Skinner

### EDITORS' COMMENTS

The experimental analysis point of view, expressed in most of the papers in this collection, instigated the renaissance of the programmed instruction and teaching machine movement, and provided much of the power of its forward thrust. It is ten years since B. F. Skinner delivered a paper, "The Science of Learning and the Art of Teaching,"[1] in which he pointed out that contemporary experimental psychology had accumulated many principles which could be applied effectively to pedagogy. Since then, the concepts of teaching machines and programmed instruction have received wide public notice and have been topics for spirited discussions by educators, industrialists, publishers, and filmmakers. Increasingly large numbers of psychologists and educators have been devoting time and resources to programming materials for use in schools, industry, and the armed services.

During this ten-year period, Skinner has continued to write on the topic, pointing out the potentialities of a sound technology of education, correcting misconceptions, and commenting on blind alleys as well as encouraging signs.

The two papers which follow have been selected because they contain so much about the implications of the science of behavior not only to the educational process but also to the strengthening of the society of which it is a part. It will be profitable to reflect on many of the ideas advanced.

Current suggestions for improving education are familiar to everyone. We need more and better schools and colleges. We must pay salaries which will attract and hold good teachers. We should group students according to ability. We must bring textbooks and other materials up to date, particularly in science and mathematics. And so on. It is significant that all

[1] *Harvard educ. Rev.,* 1954, *24,* 86–97.

this can be done without knowing much about teaching or learning. Those who are most actively concerned with improving education seldom discuss what is happening when a student reads a book, writes a paper, listens to a lecture, or solves a problem, and their proposals are only indirectly designed to make these activities more productive. In short, there is a general neglect of education method. (Television is no exception, for it is only a way of amplifying and extending *old* methods, together with their shortcomings.)

It is true that the psychology of learning has so far not been very helpful in education. Its learning curves and its theories of learning have not yielded greatly improved classroom practices. But it is too early to conclude that nothing useful is to be learned about the behavior of teacher and student. No enterprise can improve itself very effectively without examining its basic processes. Fortunately, recent advances in the experimental analysis of behavior suggest that a true technology of education is feasible. Improved techniques are available to carry out the two basic assignments of education: constructing extensive repertoires of verbal and nonverbal behavior and generating that high probability of action which is said to show interest, enthusiasm, or a strong "desire to learn."

The processes clarified by an experimental analysis of behavior have, of course. always played a part in education, but they have been used with little understanding of their effects, wanted or unwanted. Whether by intention or necessity, teachers have been less given to teaching than to holding students responsible for learning. Methods are still basically aversive. The student looks, listens, and answers questions (and, incidentally, sometimes learns) as a gesture of avoidance or escape. A good teacher can cite exceptions, but it is a mistake to call them typical. The birch rod and cane are gone, but their place has been taken by equally effective punishments (criticism, possibly ridicule, failure) used in the same way: the students must learn, or else!

By-products of aversive control in education range from truancy, early dropouts, and school-vandalism to inattention, "mental fatigue," forgetting, and apathy. It does not take a scientific analysis to trace these to their sources in educational practice. But more acceptable techniques have been hard to find. Erasmus tells of an English gentleman who tried to teach his son Greek and Latin without punishment. He taught the boy to use a bow and arrow and set up targets in the shape of Greek and Latin letters, rewarding each hit with a cherry. He also fed the boy letters cut from delicious biscuits. As a result, we may assume that the boy salivated slightly upon seeing a Greek or Latin text and that he was probably a better archer; but any effect on his knowledge of Greek and Latin is doubtful.

Current efforts to use rewards in education show the same indirection. Texts garnished with pictures in four colors, exciting episodes in a scientific film, interesting classroom activities—these will make a school interesting and even attractive (just as the boy probably liked his study of Greek and Latin), but to generate specific forms of behavior these things must be related to the student's behavior in special ways. Only then will they be truly rewarding or, technically speaking, "reinforcing."

We make a reinforcing event contingent on behavior when, for example, we design a piece of equipment in which a hungry rat or monkey or chimpanzee may press a lever and immediately obtain a bit of food. Such a piece of equipment gives us a powerful control over behavior. By scheduling reinforcements, we may maintain the behavior of pressing the lever in any given strength for long periods of time. By reinforcing special kinds of responses to the lever—for example, very light or very heavy presses or those made with one hand or the other—we "shape" different forms or topographies of behavior. By reinforcing only when particular stimuli or classes of stimuli are present, we bring the behavior under the control of the environment. All these processes have been thoroughly investigated, and they have already yielded standard laboratory practices in manipulating complex forms of behavior for experimental purposes. They are obviously appropriate to educational design.

In approaching the problem of the educator we may begin by surveying available reinforcers. What positive reasons can we give the student for studying? We can point to the ultimate advantages of an education—to the ways of life which are open only to educated men—and the student himself may cite these to explain why he wants an education, but ultimate advantages are not contingent on behavior in ways which generate action. Many a student can testify to the result. No matter how much he may *want* to become a doctor or an engineer, say, he cannot force himself to read and remember the page of text in front of him at the moment. All notions of ultimate utility (as, for example, in economics) suffer from the same shortcoming: they do not specify effective contingencies of reinforcement.

The gap between behavior and a distant consequence is sometimes bridged by a series of "conditioned reinforcers." In the laboratory experiment just described a delay of even a fraction of a second between the response to the lever and the appearance of food may reduce the effectiveness of the food by a measurable amount. It is standard practice to let the movement of a lever produce some visual stimulus, such as a change in the illumination in the apparatus, which is then followed by food. In this way the change in illumination becomes a conditioned reinforcer which can be made immediately contingent on the response. The marks, grades, and diplomas of education are conditioned reinforcers designed to bring ultimate consequences closer to the behavior reinforced. Like prizes and medals, they represent the approval of teachers, parents, and others, and they show competitive superiority, but they are mainly effective because they signalize progress through the system—toward some ultimate advantage of, or at least freedom from, education. To this extent they bridge the gap between behavior and its remote consequences; but they are still not contingent on behavior in a very effective way.

Progressive education tried to replace the birch rod, and at the same time avoid the artificiality of grades and prizes, by bringing the reinforcers of everyday life into the schools. Such natural contingencies have a kind of guaranteed effectiveness. But a school is only a small part of the student's world, and no matter how real it may seem, it cannot provide natural reinforcing consequences for all the kinds of behavior which education is to set up. The goals of progressive education were shifted to conform to this limitation, and many worthwhile assignments were simply abandoned.

Fortunately, we can solve the problem of education without discovering or inventing additional reinforcers. We merely need to make better use of those we have. Human behavior is distinguished by the fact that it is affected by small consequences. Describing something with the right word is often reinforcing. So is the clarification of a temporary puzzlement, or the solution of a complex problem, or simply the opportunity to move forward after completing one stage of an activity. We need not stop to explain *why* these things are reinforcing. It is enough that, when properly contingent upon behavior, they provide the control we need for successful educational design. Proper contingencies of reinforcement, however, are not always easily arranged. A modern laboratory for the study of behavior contains elaborate equipment designed to control the environment of individual organisms during many hours or days of continuous study. The required conditions and changes in conditions cannot be arranged by hand, not only because the experimenter does not have the time and energy, but because many contingencies are too subtle and precise to be arranged without instrumental help. The same problem arises in education.

Consider, for example, the temporal patterning of behavior called "rhythm." Behavior is often effective only if properly timed. Individual differences in timing, ranging from the most awkward to the most skillful performances, affect choice of career and of artistic interests and participation in sports and crafts. Presumably a "sense of rhythm" is worth teaching, yet practically nothing is now done to arrange the necessary contingencies of reinforcement. The skilled typist, tennis player, lathe operator, or musician is, of course, under the influence of reinforcing mechanisms which generate subtle timing, but many people never reach the point at which these natural contingencies can take over.

A relatively simple device supplies the necessary contingencies. The student taps a rhythmic pattern in unison with the device. "Unison" is specified very loosely at first (the student can be a little early or late at each tap) but the specifications are slowly sharpened. The process is repeated for various speeds and patterns. In another arrangement, the student echoes rhythmic patterns sounded by the machine, though not in unison, and again the specifications for an accurate reproduction are progressively sharpened. Rhythmic patterns can also be brought under the control of a printed score.

Another kind of teaching machine generates sensitivity to properties of the environment. We call an effective person "discriminating." He can tell the difference between the colors, shapes, and sizes of objects, he can identify three-dimensional forms seen from different aspects, he can find patterns concealed in other patterns, he can identify pitches, intervals, and musical themes and distinguish between different tempos and rhythms— and all of this in an almost infinite variety. Subtle discriminations of this sort are as important in science and industry and in everyday life as in identifying the school of a painter or the period of a composer.

The ability to make a given kind of discrimination can be taught. A pigeon, for example, can be *made* sensitive to the color, shape, and size of objects, to pitches, and rhythms, and so on—simply by reinforcing it when it responds in some arbitrary way to one set of stimuli and extinguishing responses to all others. The same kinds of contingencies of reinforcement are responsible for human discriminative behavior. *The remarkable fact is that they are quite rare in the environment of the average child.* True, children are encouraged to play with objects of different sizes, shapes, and colors, and are given a passing acquaintance with musical patterns; but they are seldom exposed to the precise contingencies needed to build subtle discriminations. It is not surprising that most of them move into adulthood with largely undeveloped "abilities."

The number of reinforcements required to build discriminative behavior in the population as a whole is far beyond the capacity of teachers. Too many teachers would be needed, and many contingencies are too subtle to be mediated by even the most skillful. *Yet relatively simple machines will suffice.* The apparatus shown in Figure 1 is adapted from research on lower organisms. It teaches an organism to discriminate selected properties of stimuli while "matching to sample." Pictures or words are projected on translucent windows which respond to a touch by closing circuits. A child can be made to "look at the sample" by reinforcing him for pressing the top window. An adequate reinforcement for this response is simply the appearance of material in the lower windows, from which a choice is to be made.

The child identifies the material which corresponds to the sample in some prescribed way by pressing one of the lower windows, and he is then reinforced again—possibly simply because a new set of materials now appears on the windows. If he presses the wrong window, all three choices disappear until the top window has been pressed again—which means until he has again looked at the sample. Many other arrangements of responses and reinforcements are, of course, possible. In an auditory version, the child listens to a sample pattern of tones and then explores other samples to find a match.

Figure 1. A machine to teach the matching of colors, shapes, sizes, as well as correspondences between pictures and words, words and other words, and so on

If devices similar to these were generally available in our nursery schools and kindergartens, our children would be far more skillful in dealing with their environments. They would be more productive in their work, more sensitive to art and music, better at sports, and so on. They would lead more effective lives. We cannot assert all this with complete confidence on the present evidence, but there is no doubt whatsoever *that the conditions needed to produce such a state of affairs are now lacking.* In the light of what we know about differential contingencies of reinforcement, the world of the young child is shamefully impoverished. And only machines will remedy this, for the required frequency and subtlety of reinforcement cannot otherwise be arranged.

The teacher is, of course, at a disadvantage in teaching skilled and discriminative behavior because such instruction is largely nonverbal. It may be that the methods of the classroom, in which the teacher is said to "communicate" with the student, to "impart information," and to build "verbal abilities," are better adapted to standard subjects matters, the learning of which is usually regarded as more than the acquisition of forms of behavior or of environmental control. Yet a second look may be worthwhile. Traditional characterizations of verbal behavior raise almost insuperable problems for the teacher, and a more rigorous analysis suggests another possibility. We can define terms like "information," "knowledge," and "verbal ability" by reference to the behavior from which we infer their presence. *We may then teach the behavior directly*. Instead of "transmitting information to the student" we may simply set up the behavior which is taken as a sign that he possesses information. Instead of teaching a "knowledge of French" we may teach the behavior from which we infer such knowledge. Instead of teaching "an ability to read" we may set up the behavioral repertoire which distinguishes the child who knows how to read from one who does not.

To take the last example, a child reads or "shows that he knows how to read" by exhibiting a behavioral repertoire of great complexity. He finds a letter or word in a list on demand; he reads aloud; he finds or identifies objects described in a text; he rephrases sentences; he obeys written instructions; he behaves appropriately to described situations; he reacts emotionally to described events; and so on, in a long list. He does none of this before learning to read and all of it afterwards. To bring about such a change is an extensive assignment, and it is tempting to try to circumvent it by teaching something called "an ability to read" from which all these specific behaviors will flow. But this has never actually been done. "Teaching reading" is always directed toward setting up specific items in such a repertoire.

It is true that parts of the repertoire are not independent. A student may acquire some kinds of responses more readily for having acquired others, and he may for a time use some in place of others (for example, he may follow written directions not by responding directly to a text but by following his own spoken instructions as he reads the text aloud). In the long run all parts of the repertoire tend to be filled in, not because the student is rounding out an ability to read, but simply because all parts are in their several ways useful. They all continue to be reinforced by the world at large after the explicit teaching of reading has ceased.

Viewed in this way, reading can also be most effectively taught with instrumental help. A pupil can learn to distinguish among letters and groups of letters in an alphabet simply as visual patterns in using the device and procedures just described. He can be taught to identify arbitrary correspondences (for example, between capitals and lower-case letters, or between handwritten and printed letters) in a more complex type of stimulus control which is within reach of the same device. With a phonographic attachment, correspondences between printed letters and sounds, between sounds and letters, between words and sounds, between sounds and printed words, and so on, can be set up. (The student could be taught all of this without pronouncing a word, and it is possible that he would learn good pronunciation more quickly if he had first done so.)

The same device can teach correspondences between words and the properties of objects. The pupil selects a printed or spoken word which corresponds in the language to, say, a pictured object or another printed or spoken word. These semantic correspondences differ in important respects from formal matches, but the same processes of programming and reinforcement can—indeed, must—be used. Traditional ways of teaching reading establish all these repertoires, but they do so indirectly and, alas, inefficiently. In "building a child's need to read," in motivating "his mental readiness," in "sharing information," and so on, the teacher arranges, sometimes almost surreptitiously, many of the contingencies just listed, and these are responsible for whatever is learned. An explicit treatment clarifies the program, suggests effective procedures, and guarantees a coverage which is often lacking with traditional methods. Much of what is called reading has not been covered, of course, but it may not need to be taught, for once these basic repertoires have been established, the child begins to receive automatic reinforcement in responding to textual material.

The same need for a behavioral definition arises in teaching other verbal skills (for example, a second language) as well as the traditional subjects of education. In advancing to that level, however, we must transcend a limitation of the device in Figure 1. The student can *select* a response without being able to speak or write, but we want him to learn to *emit* the response, since this is the kind of behavior which he will later find most useful. The emission of verbal behavior is taught by another kind of machine. A frame of textual material appearing in the square opening is incomplete: in place of certain letters or figures there are holes. Letters or figures can be made to appear in these holes by moving sliders (a keyboard would be an obvious improvement). When the material has been completed, the student checks his response by turning a crank. The machine senses the settings of the sliders, and, if they are correct, moves a new frame of material into place, the sliders returning to their home position. If the response is wrong, the sliders return home, and a second setting must be made.

The machine can tell the student he is wrong without telling him what is right. This is an advantage, but it is relatively costly. Moreover, correct behavior is rather rigidly specified. Such a machine is probably suitable only for the lower grades. A simpler and cheaper procedure, with greater flexibility, is to allow the student to compare his written response with a revealed text. The device shown in Figure 2 uses this principle. It is suitable for verbal instruction beyond the lower primary grades—that is, through junior high school, high school, and college, and in industrial and professional education. Programmed material is stored on fan-folded paper tapes. One frame of material, the size of which may be varied with the nature of the material, is exposed at a time. The student writes on a separate paper strip. He cannot look at unauthorized parts of the material without recording the fact that he has done so, because when the machine has been loaded and closed, it can be opened only by punching the strip of paper.

Figure 2.   A machine to teach "verbal knowledge"

The student sees printed material in the large window at the left. This may be a sentence to be completed, a question to be answered, or a problem to be solved. He writes his response in an uncovered portion of a paper strip at the right. He then moves a slider which covers the response he has written with a transparent mask and uncovers additional material in the larger opening. This may tell him that his response is wrong without telling him what is right. For example, it may list a few of the commonest errors. If the response he wrote is among them, he can try again on a newly uncovered portion of the paper strip. A further operation of the machine covers his second attempt and uncovers the correct response. The student records a wrong response by punching a hole alongside it, leaving a record for the instructor who may wish to review a student's performance, and operating a counter which becomes visible at the end of the set. Then the student records the number of mistakes he has made and may compare it with a par score for the set.

Exploratory research in schools and colleges indicates that what is now taught by teacher, textbook, lecture, or film can be taught in half the time with half the effort by a machine of this general type.[1] One has only to see students at work to understand why this is a conservative estimate. The student remains active. If he stops, the program stops (in marked contrast with classroom practice and educational television); but there is no compulsion for he is not inclined to stop. Immediate and frequent reinforcement sustains a lively interest. (The interest, incidentally, outlasts any effect of novelty. Novelty may be relevant to interest, but the material in the machine is always novel.) Where current instructional procedures are highly efficient, the gain may not be so great. In one experiment[2] involving industrial education there was approximately a 25% saving in the time required for instruction, something of the order of a 10% increase in retention, and about 90% of the students preferred to study by machine. In general, the student generally likes what he is doing; he makes no effort to escape—for example, by letting his attention wander. He need not force himself to work and is usually free of the feeling of effort generated by aversive control. He has no reason to be anxious about impending examinations, for none are required. Both he and his instructor know where he stands at all times.

No less important in explaining the success of teaching machines is the fact that each student is free to proceed at his own rate. Holding students together for instructional purposes in a class is probably the greatest source of inefficiency in education. Some efforts to mechanize instruction have missed this point. A language laboratory controlled from a central console presupposes a group of students advancing at about the same rate, even though some choice of material is permitted.

---

[1] Under the direction of Allen Calvin of Hollands College, an 8th grade class in the Roanoke School System completed all the work of a 9th grade class in algebra in one term. Test scores were comparable with a normal 9th grade performance, and a test nine months later showed a retention of at least 90% of the material learned.

[2] More recent results with the same material improved in the light of the earlier experiment were reported by J. L. Hughes and W. J. McNamara at the Annual Meeting of the American Psychological Association in New York, September, 1961. Their work concerned the use of programmed texts in industrial education.

Television in education has made the same mistake on a colossal scale. A class of twenty or thirty students moving at the same pace is inefficient enough, but what must we say of all the students in half a dozen states marching in a similar lock step?

In trying to teach more than one student at once we harm both fast and slow learners. The plight of the good student has been recognized, but the slow learner suffers more disastrous consequences. The effect of pressure to move beyond one's natural speed is cumulative. The student who has not fully mastered a first lesson is less able to master a second. His ultimate failure may greatly exaggerate his shortcoming; a small difference in speed has grown to an immense difference in comprehension. Some of those most active in improving education have been tempted to dismiss slow students impatiently as a waste of time, but it is quite possible that many of them are capable of substantial, even extraordinary, achievements if permitted to move at their own pace. Many distinguished scientists, for example, have appeared to think slowly.

One advantage of individual instruction is that the student is able to follow a program without breaks or omissions. A member of a class moving at approximately the same rate cannot always make up for absences, and limitations of contact time between student and teacher make it necessary to abbreviate material to the point at which substantial gaps are inevitable. Working on a machine, the student can always take up where he left off or, if he wishes, review earlier work after a longer absence. The coherence of the program helps to maximize the student's success, for by thoroughly mastering one step he is optimally prepared for the next. Many years ago, in their *Elementary Principles of Education,*[3] Thorndike and Gates considered the possibility of a book "so arranged that only to him who had done what was directed on page one would page two become visible, and so on." With such a book, they felt, "much that now requires personal instruction could be managed by print." The teaching machine is, of course, such a book.

In summary, then, machine teaching is unusually efficient because (1) the student is frequently and immediately reinforced, (2) he is free to move at his natural rate, and (3) he follows a coherent sequence. These are the more obvious advantages, and they may well explain current successes. But there are more promising possibilities: the conditions arranged by a good teaching machine make it possible to apply to education what we have learned from laboratory research and to extend our knowledge through rigorous experiments in schools and colleges.

The conceptions of the learning process which underlie classroom practices have long been out of date. For example, teachers and textbooks are said to "impart information." They expose the student to verbal and

[3] Edward Thorndike & Arthur Gates, *Elementary Principles of Education.* New York: Macmillan, 1929.

nonverbal material and call attention to particular features of it, and in so doing they are said to "tell the student something." In spite of discouraging evidence to the contrary, it is still supposed that if you tell a student something, he then knows it. In this scheme, teaching is the transmission of information, a notion which, through a false analogy, has acquired undue prestige from communication engineering. Something is undoubtedly transmitted by teacher to student, for if communication is interrupted, instruction ceases; but the teacher is not merely a source from which knowledge flows into the student. We cannot necessarily improve instruction by altering the conditions of transmission—as, for example, by changing to a different sensory modality. This is a mistake made by some so-called teaching machines which, accepting our failure to teach reading, have tried to restore communication by using recorded speech. The student no longer pores over a book, as in the traditional portrait; he stares into space with earphones on his head. For the same reasons improvements in the coding of information may not be immediately relevant.

The student is more than a receiver of information. He must take some kind of action. The traditional view is that he must "associate." The stream of information flowing from teacher to student contains pairs of items which, being close together or otherwise related, become connected in the student's mind. This is the old doctrine of the association of ideas, now strengthened by a scientific, if uncritical, appeal to conditioned reflexes: two things occurring together in experience somehow become connected so that one of them later reminds the student of the other. The teacher has little control over the process except to make sure that things occur together often and that the student pays attention to them— for example, by making the experiences vivid or, as we say, memorable. Some devices called teaching machines are simply ways of presenting things together in ways which attract attention. The student listens to recorded speech, for example, while looking at pictures. The theory is that he will associate these auditory and visual presentations.

But the action demanded of the student is not some sort of mental association of contiguous experiences. It is more objective and, fortunately, more controllable than that. To acquire behavior, *the student must engage in behavior*. This has long been known. The principle is implied in any philosophy of "learning by doing." But it is not enough simply to acknowledge its validity. Teaching machines provide the conditions needed to apply the principle effectively.

Only in the early stages of education are we mainly interested in establishing *forms* of behavior. In the verbal field, for example, we teach a child to speak, eventually with acceptable accent and pronunciation, and later to write and spell. After that, topography of behavior is assumed; the student can speak and write and must now learn to do so appropriately—that is, he must speak or write in given ways under given circumstances. How he comes to do so is widely misunderstood. Education usually begins by establishing so-called formal repertoires. The young child is taught to "echo" verbal behavior in the sense of repeating verbal stimuli with reasonable accuracy. A little later he is taught to read —to emit verbal behavior under the control of textual stimuli. These and other formal repertoires are used in later stages of instruction to evoke new responses without "shaping" them.

In an important case of what we call instruction, control is simply transferred from so-called formal to thematic stimuli. When a student learns to memorize a poem, for example, it is clearly inadequate to say that by reading the poem he presents to himself its various parts contiguously and then associates them. He does not simply read the poem again and again until he knows it. (It is possible that he could never learn the poem in that way.) Something else must be done, as anyone knows who has memorized a poem from the text. The student must make tentative responses while looking away from the text. He must glance at the text from time to time to provide fragmentary help in emitting a partially learned response. If a recalled passage makes sense, it may provide its own automatic confirmation, but if the passage is fragmentary or obscure, the student must confirm the correctness of an emitted response by referring to the text after he has emitted it.

A teaching machine facilitates this process. It presents the poem line by line and asks the student to read it. The text is then "vanished"— that is, it becomes less and less clear or less and less complete in subsequent presentations. Other stimuli (arising from the student's own behavior in this case) take over. In one procedure a few unimportant letters are omitted in the first presentation. The student reads the line without their help and indicates his success by writing down the omitted letters, which are confirmed by the machine. More of the line is missing when it again appears, but because he has recently responded to a fuller text, the student can nevertheless read it correctly. Eventually, no textual stimulus remains, and he can "recite" the poem.

(If the reader wishes to try this method on a friend or member of his family without a machine, he may do so by writing the poem on a chalk board in a clear hand, omitting a few unimportant letters. He should ask his subject to read the poem aloud but to make no effort to memorize it. He should then erase another selection of letters. He will have to guess at how far he can go without interfering with his subject's success on the next reading, but under controlled conditions this could be determined for the average student quite accurately. Again the subject reads the poem aloud, making no effort to memorize, though he may have to make some effort to recall. Other letters are then erased and the process repeated. For a dozen lines of average material, four or five readings should suffice to eliminate the text altogether. The poem can still be "read.")

Memorized verbal behavior is a valuable form of knowledge which has played an important role in classical education. There are other, and generally more useful, forms in which the same processes are involved. Consider, for example, a labeled picture. To say that such an instructional device "tells the student the name of the pictured object" is highly elliptical—and dangerous if we are trying to understand the processes involved. Simply showing a student a labeled picture is no more effective than letting him read a poem. He must take some sort of action. As a formal stimulus, the label evokes a verbal response, not in this case in the presence of other verbal behavior on the part of the student, but in the presence of the picture. The control of the response is to pass from the label to the picture; the student is to give the name of the pictured object without reading it.

The steps taken in teaching with labeled pictures can also be arranged particularly well with a machine. Suppose we are teaching medical-school anatomy at the textbook level. Certain labeled charts represent what is to be learned in the sense that the student will eventually (1) give the names of indicated parts and describe relations among them and (2) be able to point to, draw, or construct models of parts, or relations among them, given their names. To teach the first of these, we induce the student to describe relations among the parts shown on a fully labeled chart. One effect of this is that he executes the verbal behavior at issue —he writes the names of the parts. More important, he does this while, or just after, looking at corresponding pictured details. He will be able to write the names again while looking at a chart which shows only incomplete names, possibly only initial letters. Finally, he will be able to supply the complete names of parts identified only by number on still another chart. His verbal responses have passed from the control of textual stimuli to that of pictured anatomical details. Eventually, as he studies a cadaver, the control will pass to the actual anatomy of the human body. In this sense he then "knows the names of the parts of the body and can describe relations among them."

(The device shown in Figure 2 is designed to skip one or two steps in "vanishing" textual stimuli. A fully labeled chart may be followed by a merely numbered one. The student writes the name corresponding to a number in the first space. If he cannot do this, he operates the machine to uncover, not merely some indication that he is right or wrong, but additional help—say, a few letters of the correct response.)

Learning a poem or the names of pictured objects is a relatively straightforward task. More complex forms of knowledge require other procedures. At an early point, the main problem becomes that of analyzing knowledge. Traditionally, for example, something called a "knowledge of French" is said to permit the student who possesses it to do many things. One who possesses it can (1) repeat a French phrase with a good accent, (2) read a French text in all the senses of reading listed above, (3) take dictation in French, (4) find a word spoken in French on a printed list, (5) obey instructions spoken in French, (6) comment in French upon objects or events, (7) give orders in French, and so on. If he also "knows English," he can give the English equivalents of French words or phrases or the French equivalents of English words or phrases.

The concept of "a knowledge of French" offers very little help to the would-be teacher. As in the case of reading, we must turn to the behavioral repertoires themselves, for these are all that have ever been taught when education has been effective. The definition of a subject matter in such terms may be extraordinarily difficult. Students who are "competent in first-year college physics," for example, obviously differ from those who are not—but in what way? Even a tentative answer to that question should clarify the problem of teaching physics. It may well do more. In the not-too-distant future much more general issues in epistemology may be approached from the same direction. It is possible that we shall fully understand the nature of knowledge only after having solved the practical problems of imparting it.

Until we can define subject matters more accurately and until we have improved our techniques of building verbal repertoires, writing programs for teaching machines will remain something of an art. This is not wholly satisfactory, but there is some consolation in the fact that an impeccable authority on the excellence of a program is available. The student himself can tell the programmer where he has failed. By analyzing the errors made by even a small number of students in a pilot study, it is usually possible to work a great improvement in an early version of a program. (The machine shown in Figure 2 is designed to supply the necessary feedback to the programmer in a convenient form. When a student punches an error, he marks the back of the printed material, which eventually carries an item-by-item record of the success or failure of the programmer. This is obviously valuable during the experimental stages of programming, but it will also be desirable when machines are widely used in schools and colleges, since publishers can then periodically call in programs to be studied and improved by their authors. The information supplied might be compared to a record showing the percentage of students who have misunderstood each sentence in a text.)

The teaching machine shown in Figure 2 falls far short of the "electronic classrooms" often visualized for the schools and colleges of the future. Many of these, often incorporating small computers, are based on misunderstandings of the learning process. They are designed to duplicate current classroom conditions. When instruction is badly programmed, a student often goes astray, and a teacher must come to his rescue His mistakes must be analyzed and corrected. This may give the impression that instruction is largely a matter of correcting errors. If this were the case, an effective machine would, indeed, have to follow the student into many unprofitable paths and take remedial action. But under proper programming nothing of this sort is required. It is true that a relatively important function of the teacher will be to follow the progress of each student and to suggest collateral material which may be of interest, as well as to outline further studies, to recommend changes to programs of different levels of difficulty, and so on, and to this extent a student's course of study will show "branching." But changes in level of difficulty or in the character of the subject need not be frequent and can be made as the student moves from one set of material to another.

Teaching machines based on the principle of "multiple choice" also often show a misunderstanding of the learning process. When multiple-choice apparatuses were first used, the organism was left to proceed by "trial and error." The term does not refer to a behavioral process but simply to the fact that contingencies of reinforcement were left to chance: some responses happened to be successful and others not. Learning was not facilitated or accelerated by procedures which increased the probability of successful responses. The results, like those of much classroom instruction, suggested that errors were essential to the learning process. But when material is carefully programmed, both subhuman and human subjects can learn while making few errors or even none at all. Recent research by Herbert S. Terrace,[4] for example, has shown that a pigeon can learn to discriminate colors practically without making mistakes. The control exerted by color may be passed, *via* a vanishing technique, to more difficult properties of stimuli—again without error. Of course we learn something from our mistakes—for one thing, we learn not to make them again—but we *acquire* behavior in other ways.

The teaching machines of S. J. Pressey,[5] the first psychologist to see the "coming industrial revolution in education," were mechanical versions of self-scoring test forms, which Pressey and his students also pioneered. They were not designed for programmed instruction in the present sense. The student was presumed to have studied a subject before coming to the machine. By testing himself, he consolidated what he had already partially learned. For this purpose a device which evaluated the student's selection from an array of multiple-choice items was appropriate. For the same purpose multiple-choice material can, of course, be

[4] Herbert S. Terrace, Discrimination Learning With and Without Errors. Unpublished Ph.D. Dissertation, Department of Psychology, Harvard University, 1961.

[5] S. J. Pressey, "A Simple Apparatus Which Gives Tests and Scores—and Teaches," *Sch. & Soc.*, 1926, *23*, 373–376. (This article and other articles concerning teaching machines by S. J. Pressey are included in A. A. Lumsdaine & R. Glaser (Eds.), *Teaching Machines and Programmed Learning: A Source Book*. Washington, D.C.: National Education Association, 1960.)

used in all the machines described above. But several advantages of programmed instruction are lost when such material is used in straightforward instruction.

In the first place, the student should *construct* rather than *select* a response, since this is the behavior he will later find useful. Secondly, he should advance to the level of being able to emit a response rather than merely recognize a given response as correct. This represents a much more considerable achievement, as the difference between the sizes of reading and writing vocabularies in a foreign language demonstrates. Thirdly, and more important, multiple-choice material violates a basic principle of good programming by inducing the student to engage in erroneous behavior. Those who have written multiple-choice tests know how much time, energy, and ingenuity are needed to construct plausible wrong answers. (They must be plausible or the test will be of little value.) In a multiple-choice *test,* they may do no harm, since a student who has already learned the right answer may reject wrong answers with ease and possibly with no undesirable side-effects. The student who is *learning,* however, can scarcely avoid trouble. Traces of erroneous responses survive in spite of the correction of errors or the confirmation of a right answer. In multiple-choice material designed to teach "literary appreciation," for example, the student is asked to consider three or four plausible paraphrases of a passage in a poem and to identify the most acceptable. But as the student reads and considers inacceptable paraphrases, the very processes which the poet himself used in making his poem effective are at work to destroy it. Neither the vigorous correction of wrong choices nor the confirmation of a right choice will free the student of the verbal and nonverbal associations thus generated.

Scientific subjects offer more specific examples. Consider an item such as the following, which might be part of a course in high school physics:

As the pressure of a gas increases, volume decreases. This is because:
1. the space between the molecules grows smaller
2. the molecules are flattened
3. etc. . . .

Unless the student is as industrious and as ingenious as the multiple-choice programmer, it will probably not have occurred to him that molecules may be flattened as a gas is compressed (within the limits under consideration). If he chooses item 2 and is corrected by the machine, we may say that he "has learned that it is wrong," but this does not mean that the sentence will never occur to him again. And if he is unlucky enough to select the right answer first, his reading of the plausible but erroneous answer will be corrected only "by implication"—an equally vague and presumably less effective process. In either case, he may later find himself recalling that "somewhere he has read that molecules are flattened when a gas is compressed." And, of course, somewhere he has.

Multiple-choice techniques are appropriate when the student is to learn to compare and choose. In forming a discrimination (as with the device shown in Figure 1), an organism must be exposed to at least two stimuli, one of which may be said to be wrong. Similarly, in learning to "troubleshoot" equipment there may be several almost equally plausible ways of correcting a malfunction. Games offer other examples. A given hand at bridge may justify several bids or plays, no one of which is wholly right and all the others wrong. In such cases, the student is to learn the most expedient course to be taken among a natural array of possibilities. This is not true in the simple acquisition of knowledge—particularly verbal knowledge—where the task is only rarely to discriminate among responses in an array. In solving an equation, reporting a fact of history, restating the meaning of a sentence, or engaging in almost any of the other behavior which is the main concern of education, the student is to *generate* responses. He may generate and reject, but only rarely will he generate a set of responses from which he must then make a choice.

It may be argued that machines which provide for branching and decision-making are designed to teach more than verbal repertoires—in particular, that they will teach thinking. There are strategies in choosing from an array, for example, which require kinds of behavior beyond the mere emission of correct responses. We may agree to this without questioning the value of knowledge in the sense of a verbal repertoire. (The distinction is not between rote and insightful learning, for programmed instruction is especially free of rote memorizing in the etymological sense of wearing down a path through repetition.) If an "idea" or "proposition" is defined as something which can be expressed in many ways, then it may be taught by teaching many of these "ways." What is learned is more likely to generalize to comparable situations than a single syntactical form, and generalization is what distinguishes so-called deeper understanding.

But not all thinking is verbal. There are, first of all, alternative, parallel nonverbal repertoires. The mathematician begins with a verbal problem and ends with a verbal solution, but much of his intervening behavior may be of a different nature. The student who learns to follow or construct a proof entirely by manipulating symbols may not engage in this kind of thinking. Similarly, a merely verbal knowledge of physics, as often seen in the student who has "memorized the text," is of little interest to the serious educator. Laboratories and demonstrations sometimes supply contingencies which build some nonverbal knowledge of physics. Special kinds of teaching machines could help, for machines are not only not confined to verbal instruction, they may well make it possible to reduce the emphasis on verbal communication between teacher and student.

A more clear-cut example of the distinction between verbal and nonverbal thinking is musical composition. The composer who "thinks musically" does more than perform on an instrument or enjoy music. He also does more than use musical notation. In some sense he "thinks" pitches, intervals, melodies, harmonic progressions, and so on. It should not surprise us that individuals differ greatly in their "abilities" to do this, since the necessary contingencies are in very short supply. One might attack the problem by setting up an explicit kinesthetic repertoire in which "thinking a pitch" takes the form of identifying a position on a keyboard. A device which arranges the necessary contingencies is under development. With its help we may discover the extent to which students can in general learn (and at what ages they can learn most effectively) to strike a key which produces a tone which has just been heard. Similar devices might generate important forms of nonverbal mathematical behavior or the behavior exhibited, say, by an inventor conceiving of a device in three dimensions, as well as creative repertoires in other forms of art. Here is an extraordinary challenge to the technology of instrumentation.

There is another sense in which the student must learn to think. Verbal and nonverbal repertoires may prepare him to behave in effective ways, but he will inevitably face novel situations in which he cannot at first respond appropriately. He may solve such problems, not by exercising some mental ability, but by altering either the external situation or the relative probabilities of parts of his own repertoire. In this way he may increase the probability of an adequate response.

In this sense, thinking consists of a special repertoire which we may call self-management. For example, the student may alter the extent to which the environment affects him by "attending" to it in different ways. As one step in teaching thinking we must teach effective attending. The phrase "Pay attention!" is as common on the lips of teachers as "Open, please" on those of dentists—and for much the same reason: both phrases set up working conditions. The student may pay attention to avoid punishment and in doing so may learn to pay attention, but where aversive sanctions have been given up, teachers have resorted to attracting and holding attention. The techniques of the publication and entertainment industries are extensively invoked. Primers are usually decorated with colored pictures, and high school textbooks are sometimes designed to resemble picture magazines. Films dramatize subject matters in competition with noneducational films and television.

Attention which is captured by attractive stimuli must be distinguished from attention which is "paid." Only the latter must be learned.

Looking and listening are forms of behavior, and they are strengthened by reinforcement. A pigeon can learn to match colors, for example, only if it "pays attention to them." The experimenter makes sure that it does so, not by attracting its attention, but by reinforcing it for looking. Similarly, a well-taught student pays attention to sentences, diagrams, samples of recorded speech and music, and so on, not because they are attractive but because something interesting occasionally happens *after* he has paid attention.

Most audio-visual devices fail to teach attention because they stimulate the student *before* he looks or listens closely. No matter how well a four-colored text or a dramatically filmed experiment in physics attracts attention, it prepares the student only for comics, advertising, picture magazines, television programs, and other material which *is interesting on its face*. What is wanted is an adult who, upon seeing a page of black-and-white text, will read it because it may *prove* interesting. Unfortunately, the techniques associated with captured and paid attention are incompatible. Whenever a teacher attracts the attention of a student, he deprives him of an opportunity to learn to pay attention. Teaching machines, with their control over the consequences of action, can make sure that paying attention will be effectively reinforced.

Another activity associated with thinking is studying—not merely looking at a text and reading it but looking and reading *for the sake of future action*. Suppose we show a child a picture and later, in the absence of the picture, reinforce him generously for correct answers to questions about it. If he has done nothing like this before, he will probably not be very successful. If we then show him another picture, he may begin to behave in a different way: he may engage in behavior which will increase the probability that he will later answer questions correctly. It will be to his advantage (and to ours as educators) if this kind of behavior is taught rather than left to chance. We teach a student "how to study" when we teach him to take notes, to rehearse his own behavior, to test himself, to organize, outline, and analyze, to look for or construct mnemonic patterns, and so on. Some of these behaviors are obvious, but others are of more subtle dimensions and admittedly hard to teach. Machines have an advantage in maintaining the contingencies required for indirect or mediated reinforcement.

Other aspects of thinking, including the solution of personal problems, can also be analyzed and directly programmed. This is not current practice, however. Students are most often "taught to think" simply by thrusting them into situations in which already established repertoires are inadequate. Some of them modify their behavior or the situation effectively and come up with solutions. They may have learned, but they have not necessarily been taught, how to think.

Logicians, mathematicians, and scientists have often tried to record and understand their own thinking processes, but we are still far from a satisfactory formulation of all relevant behaviors. Much remains to be learned about how a skillful thinker examines a situation, alters it, samples his own responses with respect to it, carries out specific verbal manipulations appropriate to it, and so on. It is quite possible that we cannot teach thinking adequately until all this has been analyzed. Once we have specified the behavior, however, we have no reason to suppose that it will then be any less adaptable to programmed instruction than simple verbal repertoires.

Teaching machines and the associated practices of programmed instruction will have proved too successful if their practical consequences are allowed to overshadow their promise for the future. We need teaching machines to help solve a very pressing problem, but we also need them to utilize our basic knowledge of human behavior in the design of entirely new educational practices.

Teaching machines are an example of the technological application of basic science. It is true that current machines might have been designed in the light of classroom experience and common sense, and that explanations of why they are effective can be paraphrased in traditional terms. The fact remains that more than half a century of the self-conscious examination of instructional processes had worked only moderate changes in educational practices. The laboratory study of learning provided the confidence, if not all the knowledge, needed for a successful instrumental attack on the *status quo*. Traditional views may not have been actually wrong, but they were vague and were not entertained with sufficient commitment to work substantial technological changes.

As a technology, however, education is still immature, as we may see from the fact that it defines its goals in terms of traditional achievements. Teachers are usually concerned with reproducing the characteristics and achievements of already educated men. When the nature of the human organism is better understood, we may begin to consider not only what man has already shown himself to be, but what he may become under carefully designed conditions. The goal of education should be nothing short of the fullest possible development of the human organism. An experimental analysis of behavior, carried out under the advantageous conditions of the laboratory, will contribute to progress toward that goal. So will practical experiments conducted in schools and colleges with the help of adequate instrumentation.

# 23

# Reflections on a Decade of Teaching Machines

*B. F. Skinner*

To the general public, and to many educators as well, the nature and scope of teaching machines are by no means clear. There is an extraordinary need for more and better teaching, and any enterprise which may help to meet it will not be left to develop normally. The demand for information about teaching machines has been excessive. Articles and books have been published and lectures given; symposia have been arranged, and conferences and workshops have been held and courses taught. Those who have had anything useful to say have said it far too often, and those who have had nothing to say have been no more reticent.

Education is big business. Teaching machines were soon heralded as a growth industry, and fantastic predictions of the sales of programed texts were circulated. Devices have been sold as teaching machines which were not well built or designed with any understanding of their function or the practical exigencies of their use. No author was ever more warmly received by a publisher than the author of a programed text. Many programs, to be used either with machines or in textbook form, have been marketed without adequate evaluation.

## TEACHERS AND DEVICES

The "mechanizing of education" has been taken literally in the sense of doing by machine what was formerly done by people. Some of the so-called computer-based teaching machines are designed simply to duplicate the behavior of teachers. To automate education with mechanical teachers is like automating banking with mechanical tellers and bookkeepers. What is needed in both cases is an analysis of the functions to be served, followed by the design of appropriate equipment. Nothing we now know about the learning process calls for very elaborate instrumentation.

B. F. Skinner, "Reflections on a Decade of Teaching Machines," *Teachers College Record*, 1963, *65*, 168–177.

Educational specialists have added to the confusion by trying to assimilate the principles upon which teaching machines are based to older theories of learning and teaching.

In the broadest sense, teaching machines are simply devices which make it possible to apply our technical knowledge of human behavior to the practical field of education (Skinner, 1954). Teaching is the expediting of learning. Students learn without teaching, but the teacher arranges conditions under which they learn more rapidly and effectively. In recent years, the experimental analysis of behavior has revealed many new facts about relevant conditions. The growing effectiveness of an experimental analysis is still not widely recognized, even within the behavioral sciences themselves, but the implications of some of its achievements for education can no longer be ignored.

An important condition is the relation between behavior and its consequences; learning occurs when behavior is "reinforced." The power of reinforcement is not easily appreciated by those who have not had firsthand experience in its use or have not at least seen some sort of experimental demonstration. Extensive changes in behavior can be brought about by arranging so-called contingencies of reinforcement. Various kinds of contingencies are concealed in the teacher's discussions with his students, in the books he gives them to read, in the charts and other materials he shows them, in the questions he asks them, and in the comments he makes on their answers. An experimental analysis clarifies these contingencies and suggests many improvements.

## SHAPING BY PROGRAM

An important contribution has been the so-called "programming" of knowledge and skills—the construction of carefully arranged sequences of contingencies leading to the terminal performances which are the object of education. The teacher begins with whatever behavior the student brings to the instructional situation; by selective reinforcement, he changes that behavior so that a given terminal performance is more and more closely approximated. Even with lower organisms, quite complex behaviors can be "shaped" in this way with surprising speed; the human organism is presumably far more sensitive. So important is the principle of programming that it is often regarded as the main contribution of the teaching machine movement, but the experimental analysis of behavior has much more to contribute to a technology of education.

The direct contact which often exists between teacher and student favors the construction of programed sequences, and the teacher who understands the process can profit from the opportunity to improvise programs as he goes. Programs can be constructed in advance, however, which will successfully shape the behavior of most students without local modifications, and many of them can conveniently be mediated by mechanical devices. Laboratory studies have shown that contingencies emphasizing subtle properties of behavior can often be arranged *only* through instrumentation. There are potentially as many different kinds of teaching machines as there are kinds of contingencies of reinforcement.

Teaching machines which present material to the student and differentially reinforce his responses in well constructed programs differ in several ways from self-testing devices and self-scoring test forms, as well as from the training devices which have long been used by industry and the armed services. As Pressey (1926) pointed out many years ago, a student will learn while taking a multiple-choice test if he is told immediately whether his answers are right or wrong. He learns not to give wrong answers again and his right answers are strengthened. But testing has traditionally been distinguished from teaching for good reason. Before using a self-testing device, the student must already have studied the subject and, presumably, learned most of what he is to learn about it. Tests usually occupy only a small part of his time. Their main effect is motivational: A poor score induces him to study harder and possibly more effectively. Materials designed to be used in self-testing devices have recently been programed, but the contingencies which prevail during a test are not favorable to the shaping and maintaining of behavior.

Conventional training devices arrange conditions under which students learn, usually by simulating the conditions under which they eventually perform. Their original purpose was to prevent injury or waste during early stages of learning, but attention has recently been given to programing the actual behaviors they are designed to teach. To the extent that they expedite learning, they are teaching machines. Terminal performances have usually been selected for practical reasons, but a more promising possibility is the analysis and programing of basic motor and perceptual skills—a goal which should have an important place in any statement of educational policy.

In arranging contingencies of reinforcement, machines do many of the things teachers do; in that sense, they teach. The resulting instruction is not impersonal, however. A machine presents a program designed by someone who knew what was to be taught and could prepare an appropriate series of contingencies. It is most effective if used by a teacher who knows the student, has followed his progress, and can adapt available machines and materials to his needs. Instrumentation simply makes it possible for programer and teacher to provide conditions which maximally expedite learning. Instrumentation is thus secondary, but it is nevertheless inevitable if what is now known about behavior is to be used in an effective technology.

# THE NEW PEDAGOGY

Any practical application of basic knowledge about teaching and learning is, of course, pedagogy. In the United States at least, the term is now discredited, but by emphasizing an analysis of learning processes, teaching machines and programed instruction have been responsible for some improvement in its status. The significance of the teaching machine movement can be indicated by noting the astonishing lack of interest which other proposals for the improvement of education show in the teaching process.

### Find Better Teachers

In his *Talks to Teachers,* William James (1899) insisted that there was nothing wrong with the American school system which could not be corrected by "impregnating it with geniuses." It is an old formula: If you cannot solve a problem, find someone who can. If you do not know how to teach, find someone who knows or can find out for himself. But geniuses are in short supply, and good teachers do not come ready-made. Education would no doubt be improved if, as Conant (1963) has repeatedly pointed out, good teachers who know and like the subjects they teach could be attracted and retained. But something more is needed. It is not true that "the two essentials of a good teacher are (a) enthusiasm and (b) thorough knowledge of and interest in his subject" (Helwig, 1960, p. 845). A third essential is knowing how to teach.

### Emulate Model Schools

Rickover's (1959) criticism of the present American school system is well known. His only important positive suggestion is to set up model schools, staffed by model teachers. The implication is that we already have, or at least can have for the asking, schools which need no improvement and whose methods can be widely copied. This is a dangerous assumption if it discourages further inquiry into instruction.

### Simplify What Is To Be Learned

Unsuccessful instruction is often blamed on refractory subject matters. Difficulties in teaching the verbal arts are often attributed to the inconsistencies and unnecessary complexities of a language. The pupil is taught manuscript handwriting because it more closely resembles printed forms. He is taught to spell only those words he is likely to use. Phonetic alphabets are devised to help him learn to read. It may be easier to teach such materials, but teaching itself is not thereby improved. Effective teaching would correct these pessimistic estimates of available instructional power.

## Reorganize What Is To Be Learned

The proper structuring of a subject matter is perhaps a part of pedagogy, but it can also serve as a mode of escape. Proposals for improving education by reorganizing what is to be learned usually contain an implicit assumption that students will automatically perceive and remember anything which has "good form"—a doctrine probably traceable to Gestalt psychology. Current revisions of high school curricula often seem to lean heavily on the belief that if what the student is to be taught has been "structured," he cannot help understanding and remembering it (Bruner, 1960). Other purposes of such revisions cannot be questioned: Materials should be up to date and well organized. But a high school presentation acceptable to a current physicist is no more easily taught or easily remembered than the out-of-date and erroneous material to be found in texts of a decade or more ago. Similarly, the accent of a native speaker encountered in a language laboratory is no more easily learned than a bad accent. No matter how well structured a subject matter may be, it must still be taught.

## Improve Presentation

Pedagogy can also be avoided if what is to be learned can be made memorable. Audio-visual devices are often recommended for this purpose. Many of their other purposes are easily defended. It is not always easy to bring the student into contact with the things he is to learn about. Words are easily imported into the classroom, and books, lectures, and discussions are therefore staples of education; but this is often an unfortunate bias. Audio-visual devices can enlarge the student's nonverbal experience. They can also serve to present material clearly and conveniently. Their use in attracting and holding the student's attention and in dramatizing a subject matter in such a way that it is almost automatically remembered must be questioned, however. It is especially tempting to turn to them for these purposes when the teacher does not use punitive methods to "make students study." But the result is not the same. When a student observes or attends to something in order to see it more clearly or remember it more effectively, his behavior must have been shaped and maintained by reinforcement. The temporal order was important. Certain reinforcing events must have occurred *after* the student looked at, read, and perhaps tested himself on the material. But when colored displays, attractive objects, filmed episodes, and other potentially reinforcing materials are used to attract attention, they must occur *before* the student engages in these activities. Nothing can reinforce a student for *paying* attention if it has already been used to *attract* his attention. Material which attracts attention fails to prepare the student to attend to material which is not interesting on its face, and material which is naturally memorable fails to prepare him to study and recall things which are not, in themselves, unforgettable. A well prepared instructional film may appear to be successful in arousing interest in a given subject, and parts of it may be remembered without effort, but it has not taught the student that a subject may *become* interesting when more closely examined or that intensive study of something which is likely to be overlooked may have reinforcing consequences.

## Multiply Contacts Between Teacher and Students

Audio-visual devices, particularly when adapted to television, are also used to improve education by bringing one teacher into contact with an indefinitely large number of students. This can be done, of course, without analyzing how the teacher teaches, and it emphasizes a mode of communication which has two serious disadvantages: The teacher cannot see the effect he is having on his students, and large numbers of students must proceed at the same pace. Contributions to pedagogy may be made in designing programs for educational television, but the mere multiplication of contacts is not itself an improvement in teaching.

## Expand the Educational System

Inadequate education may be corrected by building more schools and recruiting more teachers so that the total quantity of education is increased, even though there is no change in efficiency.

## Raise Standards

Least effective in improving teaching are demands for higher standards. We may agree that students will be better educated when they learn more, but how are they to be induced to do so? Demands for higher standards usually come from critics who have least to offer in improving teaching itself.

The movement symbolized by the teaching machine differs from other proposals in two ways. It emphasizes the direct improvement of teaching on the principle that no enterprise can improve itself to the fullest extent without examining its basic processes. In the second place, it emphasizes the implementation of basic knowledge. If instructional practices violate many basic principles, it is only in part because these principles are not widely known. The teacher cannot put what he knows into practice in the classroom. Teaching machines and programed instruction constitute a direct attack on the problem of implementation. With appropriate administrative changes, they may bridge the gap between an effective pedagogical theory and actual practice.

## EDUCATIONAL GOALS

An effective technology of teaching calls for a re-examination of educational objectives. What is the teacher's actual assignment? Educational policy is usually stated in traditional terms: The teacher is to "impart knowledge," "improve skills," "develop rational faculties," and so on. That education is best, says Dr. Hutchins (1963), which develops "intellectual power." The task of the teacher is to change certain inner processes or states. He is to improve the mind.

The role of the teacher in fostering mental prowess has a certain prestige. It has always been held superior to the role of the trainer of motor skills. And it has the great advantage of being almost invulnerable to criticism. In reply to the complaint that he has not produced observable results, the teacher of the mind can lay claim to invisible achievements. His students may not be able to read, but he has only been trying to make sure they wanted to learn. They may not be able to solve problems, but he has been teaching them simply to think creatively. They may be ignorant of specific facts, but he has been primarily concerned with their general interest in a field.

Traditional specifications of the goals of education have never told the teacher what to do upon a given occasion. No one knows how to alter a mental process or strengthen a mental power, and no one can be sure that he has done so when he has tried. There have been many good teachers who have supposed themselves to be working on the minds of their students, but their actual practices and the results of those practices can be analyzed in other ways. The well educated student is distinguished by certain characteristics. What are they, and how can they be produced? Perhaps we could answer by redefining traditional goals: Instead of imparting knowledge, we could undertake to bring about those changes in behavior which are said to be the conspicuous manifestations of knowledge, or we could set up the behavior which is the mark of a man possessing well developed rational power. But mentalistic formulations are warped by irrelevant historical accidents. The behavior of the educated student is much more effectively analyzed directly as such.

Contrary to frequent assertions, a behavioristic formulation of human behavior is not a crude positivism which rejects mental processes because they are not accessible to the scientific public (Skinner, 1963a). It does not emphasize the rote learning of verbal responses. It does not neglect the complex systems of verbal behavior which are said to show that a student has had an idea, or developed a concept, or entertained a proposition. It does not ignore the behavior involved in the intellectual and ethical problem solving called "thinking." It does not overlook the value judgments said to be invoked when we decide to teach one thing rather than another or when we defend the time and effort given to education. It is merely an effective formulation of those activities of teacher and student which have always been the concern of educational specialists (Skinner, 1961).

Not all behavioristic theories of learning are relevant, however. A distinction is commonly drawn between learning and performance. Learning is said to be a change in some special part of the organism, possibly the nervous system, of which behavior is merely the external and often erratic sign. With modern techniques, however, behavior can be much more successfully studied and manipulated than any such inner system, even when inferences about the latter are drawn from the behavior with the help of sophisticated statistics. An analysis of learning which concentrates on the behavior applies most directly to a technology, for the task of the teacher is to bring about changes in the student's behavior. His methods are equally conspicuous: He makes changes in the environment. A teaching method is simply a way of arranging an environment which expedites learning.

## MANAGING CONTINGENCIES

Such a formulation is not easily assimilated to the traditional psychology of learning. The teacher may arrange contingencies of reinforcement to set up new *forms* of response, as in teaching handwriting and speech or nonverbal forms of behavior in the arts, crafts, and sports. He may arrange contingencies to bring responses under new kinds of *stimulus control,* as in teaching the student to read or draw from copy, or to behave effectively upon other kinds of occasions. Current instructional programs designed to fulfill such assignments are mainly verbal, but comparable contingencies generate nonverbal behavior, including perceptual and motor skills and various kinds of intellectual and ethical self-management.

A second kind of programing maintains the student's behavior in strength. The form of the response and the stimulus control may not change; the student is simply more likely to respond. Some relevant methods are traditionally discussed under the heading of motivation. For example, we can strengthen behavior by introducing new reinforcers or making old ones more effective, as in giving the student better reasons for getting an education. The experimental analysis of behavior suggests another important possibility: Schedule available reinforcers more effectively. Appropriate terminal schedules of reinforcement will maintain the student's interest, make him industrious and persevering, stimulate his curiosity, and so on; but less demanding schedules, carefully designed to maintain the behavior at every stage, must come first. The programing of schedules of reinforcement is a promising alternative to the aversive control which, in spite of repeated reforms, still prevails in educational practice.

In neglecting programing, teaching methods have merely followed the lead of the experimental psychology of learning, where the almost universal practice has been to submit an organism immediately to terminal contingencies of reinforcement (Skinner, 1963b). A maze or a discrimination problem, for example, is learned only if the subject acquires appropriate behavior before the behavior he brings to the experiment has extinguished. The intermediate contingencies are largely accidental. The differences in behavior and in rate of learning which appear under these conditions are often attributed to inherited differences in ability.

In maximizing the student's success, programed instruction differs from so-called trial-and-error learning where the student is said to learn from his mistakes. At best, he learns not to make mistakes again. A successful response may survive, but trial-and-error teaching makes little provision for actually strengthening it. The method seems inevitably committed to aversive control. For the same reason, programed instruction does not closely resemble teaching patterned on everyday communication. It is usually not enough simply to tell the student something or induce him to read a book; he must be told or must read and then be questioned. In this "tell-and-test" pattern, the test is not given to measure what he has learned, but to show him what he has not learned and thus induce him to listen and read more carefully in the future. A similar basically aversive pattern is widespread at the college level, where the instructor assigns material and then examines on it. The student may learn to read carefully, to make notes, to discover for himself how to study, and so on, because in doing so he avoids aversive consequences, but he has not necessarily been taught. Assigning-and-testing is not teaching. The aversive by-products, familiar to everyone in the field of education, can be avoided through the use of programmed positive reinforcement.

Many facts and principles derived from the experimental analysis of behavior are relevant to the construction of effective programs leading to terminal contingencies. The facts and principles are often difficult, but they make up an indispensable armamentarium of the effective teacher and educational specialist. We have long since passed the point at which our basic knowledge of human behavior can be applied to education through the use of a few general principles.

## PRINCIPLE AND PRACTICE

The difference between general principles and an effective technology can be seen in certain efforts to assimilate the principles of programed instruction to earlier theories. Programed instruction has, for example, been called "Socratic." It is true that Socrates proceeded by small steps and often led his students through an argument with a series of verbal prompts, but the example often cited to illustrate his method suggests that he was unaware of an important detail—namely, that prompts must eventually be "vanished" in order to put the student on his own. In the famous scene in the *Meno,* Socrates demonstrates his theory that learning is simply recollection by leading an uneducated slave boy through Pythagoras's Golden Theorem. The boy responds with the rather timid compliance to be expected under the circumstances and never without help. Although Socrates himself and some of those among his listeners who were already familiar with the theorem may have understood the proof better at the end of the scene, there is no evidence whatsoever that the boy understood it or could reconstruct it. In this example of Socratic instruction, at least, the student almost certainly learned nothing.[1]

A seventeenth-century anticipation of programed instruction has also been found in the work of Comenius, who advocated teaching in small steps, no step being too great for the student who was about to take it. Programing is sometimes described simply as breaking material into a large number of small pieces, arranged in a plausible genetic order. But size of step is not enough. Something must happen to help the student take each step, and something must happen as he takes it. An effective program is usually composed of small steps, but the whole story is not to be found in Comenius's philosophy of education.

Another venerable principle is that the student should not proceed until he has fully understood what he is to learn at a given stage. Several writers have quoted E. L. Thorndike to this effect, who wrote in 1912,

> If, by a miracle of mechanical ingenuity, a book could be so arranged that only to him who had done what was directed on page one would page two become visible, and so on, much that now requires personal instruction could be managed by print.

In commenting on this passage, Finn and Perrin (1962) have written, "... Here are the insights of a genius. History can very often teach us a lesson in humility—and it does here. The interesting question is: Why

---

[1] The program of the *Meno* episode constructed by Cohen (1962) is an improvement in that the student responds with less prompting.

couldn't we see it then?" We might also ask, why couldn't Thorndike see it then? He remained active in education for at least 30 years, but he turned from this extraordinarily promising principle to another and—as it proved—less profitable approach to educational psychology.

It is always tempting to argue that earlier ideas would have been effective if people had only paid attention to them. But a good idea must be more than right. It must command attention; it must make its own way because of what it does. Education does not need principles which will improve education as soon as people observe them; it needs a technology so powerful that it cannot be ignored. No matter how insightful the anticipation of modern principles in earlier writers may seem to have been, something was lacking or education would be much further advanced. We are on the threshold of a technology which will be not only right but effective (Skinner, in preparation).

## CRITERIA OF RESEARCH

A science of behavior makes its principal contribution to a technology of education through the analysis of useful contingencies of reinforcement. It also suggests a new kind of educational research. Thorndike never realized the potentialities of his early work on learning because he turned to the measurement of mental abilities and to matched-group comparisons of teaching practices. He pioneered in a kind of research which, with the encouragement offered by promising new statistical techniques, was to dominate educational psychology for decades. It led to a serious neglect of the process of instruction.

There are practical reasons why we want to know whether a given method or instruction is successful or whether it is more successful than another. We may want to know what changes it brings about in the student, possibly in addition to those it was designed to effect. The more reliable our answers to such questions, the better. But reliability is not enough. Correlations between test scores and significant differences between group means tell us less about the behavior of the student in the act of learning than results obtained when the investigator can manipulate variables and assess their effects in a manner characteristic of laboratory research. The practices evaluated in studies of groups of students have usually not been suggested by earlier research of a similar nature, but have been drawn from tradition, from the improvisations of skillful teachers, or from suggestions made by theorists working intuitively or with other kinds of facts. No matter how much they may have stimulated the insightful or inventive researcher, the evaluations have seldom led directly to the design of improved practices.

The contrast between statistical evaluation and the experimental analysis of teaching has an illuminating parallel in the field of medicine. Various drugs, regimens, surgical procedures, and so on, must be examined with respect to a very practical question: Does the health of the patient improve? But "health" is only a general description of specific physiological processes, and "improvement" is, so to speak, merely a by-product of the changes in these processes induced by a given treatment. Medicine has reached the point where research on specific processes is a much more fertile source of new kinds of therapy than evaluations in terms of improvement in health. Similarly, in education, no matter how important improvement in the student's performance may be, it remains a by-product of specific changes in behavior resulting from the specific changes in the environment wrought by the teacher. Educational research patterned on an experimental analysis of behavior leads to a much better understanding of these basic processes. Research directed toward the behavior of the individual student has, of course, a long history, but it can still profit greatly from the support supplied by an experimental analysis of behavior.

This distinction explains why those concerned with experimental analyses of learning are not likely to take matched-group evaluations of teaching machines and programed instruction very seriously. It is not possible, of course, to evaluate either machines or programs *in general* because only specific instances can be tested, and available examples by no means represent all the possibilities; but even the evaluation of a given machine or program in the traditional manner may not give an accurate account of its effects. For example, those who are concerned with improvement are likely to test the student's capacity to give right answers. Being right has, of course, practical importance, but it is only one result of instruction. It is a doubtful measure of "knowledge" in any useful sense. We say that a student "knows the answer" if he can select it from an array of choices, but this does not mean that he could have given it without help. The right answer to one question does not imply right answers to all questions said to show the "possession of the same fact." Instructional programs are often criticized as repetitious or redundant when they are actually designed to put the student in possession of a number of different responses "expressing the same proposition." Whether such instruction is successful is not shown by any one right answer.

## CORRECT OR EDUCATED?

A preoccupation with correct answers has led to a common misunderstanding of programed materials. Since a sentence with a blank to be filled in by the student resembles a test item, it is often supposed that the response demanded by the blank is what is learned. In that case, a student could not be learning much because he may respond correctly in 19 out of 20 frames and must therefore already have known 95 per cent of the answers. The instruction which occurs as he completes an item comes from having responded to other parts of it. The extent of this instruction cannot be estimated from the fact that he is right 19 out of 20 times, either while pursuing a program *or on a subsequent test*. Nor will this statistic tell us whether other conditions are important. Is it most profitable for the student to execute the response by writing it out, by speaking it aloud, by speaking it silently, or by reading it in some other way? These procedures may or may not have different effects on a selected "right-answer" statistic, but no one statistic will cover all their effects.

Research in teaching must not, of course, lose sight of its main objective—to make education more effective. But improvement as such is a questionable dimension of the behavior of either teacher or student. Dimensions which are much more intimately related to the conditions the teacher arranges to expedite learning must be studied even though they do not contribute to improvement or contribute to it in a way which is not immediately obvious.

The changes in the behavior of the individual student brought about by manipulating the environment are usually immediate and specific. The results of statisical comparisons of group performances usually are not. From his study of the behavior of the individual student, the investigator gains a special kind of confidence. He usually knows what he has done to get one effect and what he must do to get another.

Confidence *in* education is another possible result of an effective technology of teaching. Competition between the various cultures of the world, warlike or friendly, is now an accepted fact, and the role played by education in strengthening and perpetuating a given way of life is clear. No field is in greater need of our most powerful intellectual resources. An effective educational technology based upon an experimental analysis will bring it support commensurate with its importance in the world today.

## REFERENCES

Bruner, J. S. *The process of education.* Cambridge, Mass.: Harvard, 1960.

Cohen, I. S. Programed learning and the Socratic dialogue. *Amer. Psychologist,* 1962, *17*, 722–775.

Conant, J. B. *The education of American teachers.* New York: McGraw-Hill, 1963.

Finn, J. D., & Perrin, D. G. *Teaching machines and programmed learning: a survey of the industry, 1962.* Washington, D.C.: U.S. Office of Education, 1962.

Helwig, J. Training of college teachers. *Science,* 1960, *132*, 845.

Hutchins, R. M. *On education.* Santa Barbara: Center for the Study of Democratic Institutions, 1963.

James, W. *Talks to teachers.* New York: Holt, Rinehart and Winston, 1899.

Pressey, S. J. A simple device for teaching, testing and research in learning. *Sch. & Soc.,* 1926, *23,* 373–376.

Rickover, H. G. *Education and freedom.* New York: Dutton, 1959.

Skinner, B. F. The science of learning and the art of teaching. *Harvard educ. Rev.,* 1954, *24,* 86–97.

Skinner, B. F. Why we need teaching machines. *Harvard educ. Rev.,* 1961, *31,* 377–398.

Skinner, B. F. Behaviorism at fifty. *Science,* 1963, *140,* 951–958. (a)

Skinner, B. F. Operant behavior. *Amer. Psychologist,* 1963, *18,* 503–515. (b)

Skinner, B. F. *The technology of teaching.* In preparation.

Thorndike, E. L. *Education.* New York: Macmillan, 1912.

# 24

# Programmed Instruction as an Approach to Teaching of Reading, Writing, and Arithmetic to Retarded Children

*Sidney W. Bijou, Jay S. Birnbrauer, John D. Kidder, and Cecilia Tague*

## EDITORS' COMMENTS

The following paper is a report of a four-year project aimed exclusively at applying the principles of operant conditioning to teaching academic tool subjects to institutionalized retarded children. At the time of the writing, the project was in its third year of operation. The final report, therefore, is yet to be written.

The results of this study suggest that the academic future of the majority of retarded children is much brighter than had been forecast by the theorists who assume that abilities, capacities, and traits are largely fixed. Two decades ago textbooks claimed:

Sidney W. Bijou, Jay S. Birnbrauer, John D. Kidder, and Cecilia Tague, "Programmed Instruction as an Approach to Teaching of Reading, Writing, and Arithmetic to Retarded Children," *The Psychological Record*, 1966, *16*, 505–522.

The project was jointly sponsored by Rainier School (C. H. Martin, Superintendent), the White River School District, Buckley, Washington (Robert Johnsen, Superintendent), and the University of Washington. It was supported with funds from these organizations and the National Institute of Mental Health, U.S. Public Health Service Grants MH-01366 and MH-02232.

This paper is a revision and extension of a report prepared in 1963 by J. S. Birnbrauer, S. W. Bijou, M. M., Wolf, J. D. Kidder, and Cecilia Tague. We are deeply indebted to Montrose M. Wolf for his many stimulating ideas and suggestions for research and instructional techniques during the initial phases of the project; to Nancy Heid, William H. Heid and Judith Thoft for their assistance in preparing the initial stages of the academic programs; to Frances M. Greene for her contribution to every aspect of the project and especially for her stimulating efforts in redeveloping and extending the academic programs and reviewing this manuscript; to Richard F. Peterson, School Psychologist, Rainier School, for his aid in selecting and testing the pupils; to Clarence Youngberg, School Principal, Rainier School, for his full cooperation and support; and to Josephine Gatto, Eileen Argo, and Mary Jo Gregg for their work in programming materials, gathering and analysing data, and preparation of reports.

"The mentally retarded child is incapable of learning abstractions."
"The mentally retarded child has a short attention span."
"The mentally retarded child cannot generalize."
"The mentally retarded child with a mental age of six years (and, say, an IQ of 50) cannot learn academic subjects beyond first grade."

It will be no surprise at this stage in the readings to learn that these investigators had to devote considerable effort to motivating the children. This task was particularly difficult. The children had a history of failure in school, and their current living situation in no sense *required* proficiency in reading, writing, and arithmetic. To get them to display interest and enthusiasm for school work and thereby to learn academic skills, the investigators had to present efficient reinforcers.

Any kind of contrived learning cannot take place unless the subject "pays attention" to the critical components of the material to be presented. Thus programs were devised to strengthen good study habits of working alone for longer and longer time-spans, and to weaken behaviors which wasted time and disturbed the work of others. The principles applied to strengthen such study habits are the same as for teaching academic skills: consistent contingencies and reinforcement of successive approximations to the desired behavior.

Every detail of preparing and presenting the reading, writing, and arithmetic materials was considered in the light of operant principles and guided by results from repeated testing. The teaching machines, the physical structure of the classroom, and the classroom procedures were designed only to enhance the learning of individuals, even though the children attended class in a group.

This last point deserves further elaboration since it is easily misunderstood. The application of reinforcement contingencies to the modification of behavior requires a continuing program of alert responsiveness to changes in that behavior. One implication of this characteristic is that to develop a pattern of behavior in one person requires a considerable amount of behavior from another person. Reinforcement contingencies are very much one-to-one affairs: one student requires one teacher who is at least as throughly engrossed in the student as the student is in the subject matter. The essence of a technology based on reinforcement principles is the systematic attaching of stimulus consequences to behavior. When the task is the development of new patterns of behavior, then contingencies must change as the behavior changes, and whoever is responsible for changing the reinforcement contingencies must be attentive to the occurrences of desired changes in the student.

The requirement of one teacher to one student may give this technology an impractical appearance, in that it would require a large number of teachers. However, this technology cannot be set aside merely because it appears to be an expensive one; it is a fact of behavior change as we understand it today. Fortunately, the force of its implications may be reduced in a number of ways. At least one way is to reproduce some of the essential characteristics of the teacher mechanically. This, as you have read, was done. However, machine programming of stimulus contingencies often requires that the behaviors being developed fall within easily predicted limits, so that the machine may be constructed in advance to recognize all the responses which may arise and deal with them all effectively. Furthermore, the behavior being developed must be readily received by the machine as information: button-pushing may be integrated with machine circuitry easily; but the correct pronounciation of an "s" sound will be much more difficult to translate into machine stimulation, so that the machine will reinforce "s" but not "th." These limitations suggest that the teaching machines can be helpful but cannot, as of today, solve all the practical problems of behavior development.

An attractive supplement is the possibility of training other adults and children to become effective appliers of reinforcement techniques. This possibility remains attractive only if the training required can be accomplished both quickly and effectively, and if relatively restricted training will serve the purpose. The question of what is required to train other adults and children to be effective helpers is being investigated as part of this project. Should it prove necessary to equip every helper with the complete technology of operant and respondent conditioning, then the number of such individuals cannot increase rapidly enough.

## ABSTRACT

This is a report of three years of research in which behavior theory was applied to teaching reading, writing, and arithmetic to retarded children. The objectives of the study were: (1) to develop a motivational system that would be effective for each child, (2) to develop programmed procedures for the establishment of effective study behavior, and (3) to develop programmed instructional materials.

Although many children participated in the study since its inception, the core group consisted of 27 boys and girls ranging in chronological age from 8 years 7 months to 14 years 9 months. The average child was 11 years old and had a Peabody Picture Vocabulary mental age of 7 and an IQ of 63. The children had a variety of clinical diagnoses, were low in academic achievement and poorly motivated for academic achievement.

Initial efforts were devoted to developing a motivational system, the final form of which consisted of tokens exchangeable for candy, toys, and social outings. Tokens were paired with comments from the teacher to strengthen social reinforcers. Study behavior was made progressively more effective by reinforcing classroom behavior that would gradually approximate the ultimate kind of supporting behaviors necessary for efficient academic learning. The main effort during the second two years of the project was devoted to the construction of instructional programs in reading, writing, arithmetic, and correlated practical subjects. Programs began with pre-academic materials and became gradually more complex. Revisions were based on findings from the repeated performances of the children.

Instruction, whether aimed at developing academic skills in retarded children, increasing general knowledge in normal children, or advancing mathematical sophistication in gifted youngsters, may be conceived of as a process in which a teacher systematically and effectively arranges and rearranges an environment to bring about desired behavioral changes. Teaching on this basis, in whole or part, has been called programmed instruction (Green, 1962; Skinner, 1963). In its most promising form, programmed instruction is a budding technology based upon an experimental analysis of behavior (Skinner, 1953; 1961; 1964).

This paper is a report of research in which the principles of experimental analysis of behavior and programmed instruction (the latter developed primarily on normal adults and children) were applied to teaching reading, writing, and arithmetic to retarded children (Bijou, 1965; Birnbrauer, Bijou, Wolf, & Kidder, 1965). In a way, this study bears upon a technology of special education. Specifically the objectives of the investigation were: (1) to develop a motivational system for effectively strengthening academic and appropriate classroom conduct; (2) to develop programmed procedures which aim to strengthen cooperative and industrious behaviors in young retarded "educable" children who previously have shown little or no academic progress, and whose reactions to previous educational experience often range from apathy to rebellion; and (3) to develop programmed instructional materials (including teacher manuals) for reading, writing, arithmetic, telling time, handling money, and other correlated practical subjects.

This report, divided into six sections, describes (1) the children in the study; (2) the experimental classroom in which this study was conducted; (3) the motivational system developed for strengthening academic and appropriate social behaviors; (4) the programmed procedures for strengthening cooperative and industrious behaviors or prerequisite academic skills; (5) the current state of the programmed instructional materials; and (6) a brief recount and account of some principles employed in developing the programs and procedures.

## THE CHILDREN

Twenty-seven retarded boys and girls participated in the study to a major degree, 24 of whom resided at the Rainier School, the other 3 living at home in neighboring communities. All were subjects for a minimum of one school year, six participated for two years, and four for three years. The research objectives determined to a large measure which children would continue beyond the first year. Some children were retained as subjects so that the programs could be extended to more advanced levels; some were replaced so that revisions of procedures and programs could be still further refined on different children. In selecting new subjects, attempts were made to include children who: (1) had little or no prior formal education or had benefitted only minimally from previous educational experiences; (2) were a cross-sectional representation of the various clinical diagnostic categories; and (3) had no seriously limiting motor handicaps.

Table 1 gives the chronological ages and the Peabody Picture Vocabulary Test (PPVT) mental ages and IQ's for the 27 children. The data,

### Table 1
Chronological Age and Peabody (PPVT) Mental Age and IQ* of the Children Grouped According to the Year They Entered the Project

| | 1962-63 N = 8 | | 1963-64 N = 9 | | 1964-65 N = 10 | |
|---|---|---|---|---|---|---|
| | Range | Mean | Range | Mean | Range | Mean |
| CA | 9-4 to 14-9 | 12-1 | 8-7 to 12-0 | 10-4 | 8-10 to 11-4 | 10-2 |
| MA | 4-5 to 9-6 | 7-2 | 4-10 to 10-6 | 7-0 | 3-8 to 9-8 | 6-8 |
| IQ | 44 to 66 | 59 | 56 to 87 | 66 | 39 to 93 | 65 |

*Two of the scores were from the Wechsler Intelligence Test for Children, and one from the Stanford-Binet Intelligence Scale.

presented in ranges and means, are grouped according to the year of entry into the study. Thus the first-year group (1962–63) of 8 children ranged in age from 9 years 4 months to 14 years 9 months and with a mean age of 12 years 1 month. Their mental ages were from 4 years 5 months to 9 years 6 months with a mean of 7 years 2 months. Their IQ's ranged from 44 to 66 with a mean of 59. The entire group may be characterized as having a mean chronological age of 11 years, a mean mental age of 7 years, and a mean IQ of 63.

The academic achievement previous to participation in the study ranged from upper first grade (e.g., 1.8 reading) to "not measureable" on the standard scales employed.

Eleven children were diagnosed as brain-damaged, three as mongoloid, four as cultural-familial, and nine as "uncertain," unknown, or undifferentiated.

Upon enrollment the classroom behavior of the children was marked by refusal to study, temper-tantrums and pouting, and by apparent co-operation but little actual accomplishment in terms of independent work. None of the children could be relied upon to stay with even a short task, no matter how short, until it was satisfactorily completed. Indeed, it is doubtful that "completeness" or "correctness" were meaningful concepts to some of them.

From time to time, primarily to evaluate revisions and extensions of the programs, other children in the Institution and neighboring communities served as subjects.

## THE EXPERIMENTAL CLASSROOM

One of the characteristics of programmed instruction is that procedures, materials, and sequences are arranged to allow each child to proceed at his own rate and under conditions favorable for strengthening desired (terminal) behaviors. These requirements present one of the first practical problems in setting up the study—namely, how to have each child follow his own individual schedule in a productive manner and without interfering with the learning activities of the others. While this problem might be solved by utilizing a laboratory classroom similar to a university language laboratory in which each pupil studies in an individual study booth, such an arrangement would not contain the ingredients necessary for training children to study in a group setting, as in the typical classroom, the library, or the home. The plan of the classroom-laboratory shown schematically in Figure 1 was designed to provide a setting conducive to carrying out this objective. The classroom proper consists of six student desks, three tables for writing exercises, and two general-purpose or work tables for assignments requiring large working areas and for material and equipment storage. The three individual study rooms at the upper end of the diagram are separated from the classroom by curtains, providing observational space for visitors. Programs requiring considerable concentration and/or involving auditory stimuli, such as reading, are presented in these single rooms; work in writing and spelling, and practical exercises are conducted in the classroom proper. There is, in addition to the areas shown in the diagram, a room which serves as an office, a data processing room, and a place to prepare and store materials.

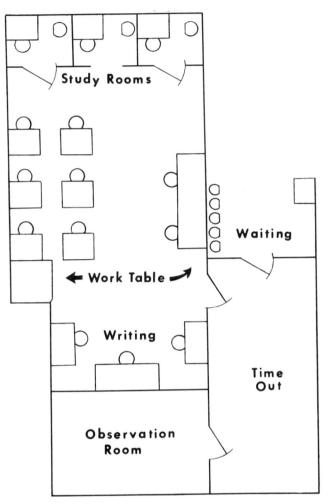

Figure 1.   The components of the Rainier School Experimental Classroom

The waiting area was used to help establish the classroom as a place for quiet, productive study. From the first day, the children were met in the waiting area by a teacher who instructed them to sit down, and reinforced them both socially and with tokens for sitting quietly and for engaging in "small talk." They remained in the waiting room until given permission to enter the classroom. If at any time a child entered the classroom without permission, he was reminded that he should be in the waiting room. If he behaved disruptively, he was placed in the "time-out" room. (An account of the general use of the "time-out" room is given in the section on the programmed procedure for strengthening "study habits.") The interval spent in the waiting area allowed the children to greet one another and the teachers, to talk about recent events, and in general, to "settle down" before entering the classroom. Under these circumstances it would be more probable that entering the classroom would come to serve as a cue for starting to work immediately on the assignment for the day.

## DEVELOPMENT OF A MOTIVATIONAL SYSTEM FOR STRENGTHENING ACADEMIC AND APPROPRIATE SOCIAL BEHAVIOR

Initially, the teachers attempted to strengthen desirable classroom behavior and correct answers to academic materials by following such behaviors with remarks of approval and by ignoring inappropriate responses. Little, if any, improvement in sustained studying behavior was obtained under these procedures. Evidently verbal remarks in the form of approval and praise did not have reinforcing functions for these children. Consequently, a token reinforcement system similar to that used by Staats, Staats, Schutz, & Wolf (1962) was added. This procedure did indeed establish and maintain higher rates of effective study and greater cooperation. It was also expected to increase the strength of teacher's comments of approval and praise as conditioned reinforcers since they were always given in conjunction with the delivery of tokens (Bijou & Baer, 1961; 1965; Skinner, 1953).

Colored gummed stars which served as tokens during the first year were subsequently replaced by "marks" (short diagonal strokes) entered by the teachers in squares in a three-page booklet which each child carried with him. "Marks," always preceded or accompanied by some comment of approval or praise, were given in proportion to the number of correct answers to items in the programs; bonus marks were given for especially cooperative behavior and error-free assignments. This system was decidedly less time-consuming to administer than stars and seemed just as effective.

When a page was filled with "marks" it could be exchanged for trinkets, candy, pencils, money, or for credit toward a larger sum of money and a privilege of spending it in town or on a special outing or trip. The number of "marks" on a completed page determined its value. Some children earned the equivalent of about one cent each day, while others averaged about a nickel every two days.

The reason for using a three-page booklet and entering marks on all pages concurrently was to reduce the likelihood that the child would lose "interest in school work" or even engage in disruptive behavior following the completion of a page. There was seldom a blank page in the booklet and the child could anticipate another full page within a short time if he continued to work. By this procedure, a relatively consistent and highly productive type of performance was achieved. This phenomenon—work stoppage after reinforcement—is often observed in the every day behavior of students and employees, and is well documented in the data from experimental laboratory studies (e.g., Ferster & Skinner, 1957).

Studies of the effects of eliminating the token system showed wide individual differences (Birnbrauer, Wolf, Kidder, & Tague, 1965). Some children continued to progress at their usual rate, some progressed at a reduced rate, and some regressed in their performance. Studies evaluating the consequences of taking away a mark contingent upon an incorrect academic response revealed that some pupils decreased their error rates and maintained more accurate study performances under these conditions. Others did not.

The next step in the development of the token procedure, undertaken only with the two-year veterans in the program, consisted of replacing the marks with numerical scores. The advantages of numerical scores are that they can be automatically dispensed, provide the children with additional experience in the use and meaning of numbers, and give them acquaintance with a system used frequently in traditional classrooms.

## DEVELOPMENT OF A PROGRAMMED PROCEDURE
## FOR STRENGTHENING PREREQUISITE
## ACADEMIC BEHAVIORS

The task of developing procedures for strengthening effective prerequisite academic behaviors (or "study habits") is two-fold. First, desirable behaviors such as sitting quietly, paying attention to instructions and contingencies, and working productivity for sustained periods require strengthening and gradual extensions. Second, the undesirable behaviors such as fighting, teasing, talking loudly, and losing personal control require weakening and gradual elimination. The following paragraphs give a brief account of how these ends were achieved.

The classroom situation was prepared so that a newly admitted child would receive almost constant attention from a teacher. Upon entering the classroom and taking a seat, he was given his first assignment which was to be carried out at his desk or in one of the individual study rooms. If the latter was the case, he would be reinforced for simply following the instructions to go to the designated study room. The teacher stayed with the child while he worked, giving instruction and reinforcing each correct response as it was made. When the assignment was completed, the child returned to his desk (if he had been in a study room) where he was given another assignment by the teacher. This routine continued until he had completed all of his work for that day. Before long, the child was able to complete some of the relatively simple, short assignments by himself. During this phase, the teacher remained nearby and waited until the child signaled that he had finished, at which time she responded by reinforcing him for each correct answer. Thus, independent study with delayed reinforcement was begun with an activity which the child could respond to with a high degree of success and which required sustained effort within a period of time in which he was likely to work continually. Delayed reinforcement for correct responses was introduced only when there was a high probability that the child would maintain his accuracy and complete the task. The length and number of assignments to be performed independently were then gradually increased.

Placing a child in a group learning situation naturally generates behavior incompatible with academic learning. The traditional procedure for dealing with such behavior was employed; however, it was systematically programmed. For example, a child was instructed to raise his hand to obtain permission to talk. Talking without permission was not responded to (extinction) unless the child was new to the class, in which case the teacher would prompt him into making the desired response by saying something like, "Raise your hand if you wish to ask a question." The teacher would then wait until the child responded as requested and then reinforce him with attention and perhaps an extra mark.

If the social situation of the classroom generated severe disruptive behavior other procedures were used. During the first year of the study attempts were made to weaken these behaviors by ignoring them (extinction). This plan proved effective only for some children, so another approach was explored and developed. Referred to as the "time-out" procedure, it involved removing the child from the classroom contingent upon inappropriate behavior. Specifically, the "time-out" procedure ("time-out" from positive reinforcement) was used if the child (1) engaged in aggressive behavior (hitting, biting, kicking, etc.) toward another pupil, teacher, or visitor, or (2) refused to comply with a teacher's instructions. If a child engaged in either of these behaviors he was given the choice of stopping immediately and returning to his work, or leaving the room. If he chose to persist in the disruptive behavior he was placed in the "time-out" room for ten minutes. At the end of this ten-minute period, if he had been quiet for the preceeding 30 seconds, he was told he could return to his work. In most instances, when a child was given the choice between returning to work or leaving the classroom he usually chose the former; hence the "time-out" room was used infrequently, i.e., about six times a month during the first year and about two times a month during the second year. At present it is rarely used. In agreement with research findings, the "time-out" procedure was found to be a faster and more permanent way of eliminating disruptive behaviors than extinction (Holz, Azrin, & Ayllon, 1963; Wolf, Risley, & Mees, 1964).

The terminal prerequisite academic behavior is best described in terms of the behavior of the advanced student. Instead of being given his assignment by the teacher, he obtained his own "work folder," set his own watch, and entered the date and starting time on his daily record sheet. He chose his first task, completed it, and went on to the next. Starting and finishing times were entered for each item. When all the work was completed, he called a teacher and together they checked his work. Marks were given at this time.

About one-third of the children studied reached the degree of independence described above. The amount of time required to achieve the terminal behavior varied. For example, three children were able to work independently in less than a year, one required a year-and-a-half. Because most of the children were in the program for only one year, it is impossible to say whether all could have reached the status of the "advanced students" and how long it would have taken each to do so.

## THE DEVELOPMENT OF INSTRUCTIONAL MATERIALS

The major concerns during the first year of the project were the development of an effective motivational system and a programmed procedure for strengthening prerequisite academic behaviors. These problems had to be solved, at least tentatively before concerted effort could be devoted to programming academic learning. However, in order to initiate the study it was essential to have at least tentative materials to make up a curriculum. Hence attempts were made from the start to prepare programmed academic material and procedures, but at times the research on motivation and on the shaping of "study habits" dictated the type of academic materials needed and the rate at which they would be introduced. This, then, is a brief description of the programmed materials developed in the first stage of the research. Currently they are being extensively revised and extended.

Three considerations influenced the development of materials and procedures for reading, writing, and arithmetic. First, all were planned to be serviceable for individual instruction. Second, new materials and new procedures were introduced as the child met certain necessary behavioral and academic prerequisites. Third, the work a child was given was planned to be as close as possible to his level of competence. An assignment and record sheet for each child was prepared every day. It listed the material to be covered and provided space for responses to the items and time spent on each task. The work sheet together with the necessary materials, made up each pupil's "work-folder." At the end of the day, data on the record sheet showing the number of correct and incorrect responses and the time required to complete a task served as a guide for the preparation of future assignments. For example, if a child's error rate on a particular task was low (e.g., below ten percent) the next set of related material would be placed in his folder for the next class. If his error rate remained high (e.g., above fifteen percent) over several sessions, the material would be revised and represented at the earliest time possible.

The major academic program—reading, writing, and arithmetic—consisted of several sequences which were presented concurrently, and each was designed not only to teach specific terminal behaviors but also to contribute to the child's progression in the other programs. For example, one program involved instruction in time-telling, a skill which involves number recognition, discrimination between the lengths of the clock hands, and writing and reading numbers. Therefore the arithmetic program began with recognition of the numbers zero to nine, and the introduction of the concepts of addition, subtraction, and discrimination of "greater than" and "less than." Computation was limited to numbers under 20. To relate the writing program to the others, training began with the writing of these numbers. The next step of the number recognition program presented only the "fives" through 60 so that the time-telling program could be started when this sequence was completed. Review of the "fives" and the numbers in-between was programmed to take place while the child was working on the "time-telling" sequence.

Each child started on a "discrimination program" which develops a discrimination repertory similar to reading and arithmetic "readiness" training (Holland, 1960; Skinner, 1961). The program required the pupil to select the letter group, geometric form, or numeral that matches a sample, from choices which increase in similarity to the correct answer. These materials were presented on a simple manually-operated teaching machine (Min/Max). When the child learned to operate the machine properly and had completed the discrimination program, he was introduced to the other program sequences, thus making program evaluation less complex.

**Reading**

There were three interrelated beginning reading programs. The first was a Sight Vocabulary Program (SVP) designed to teach the reading of words, phrases, and sentences. Two types of items were programmed: discrimination or choice items in which the child was required to circle the correct word in a four-choice situation, and construction items in which the youngster was expected to make vocal response. Initial correct responses were reinforced with a mark. Correct responses following incorrect responses on the same item were not so rewarded. The words used in the SVP were selected from all parts of speech, primarily on the basis of their assumed familiarity to children in a residential school and the ease with which they could be combined into sentences (Staats, Staats, Schutz, & Wolf, 1962).

The second reading sequence consisted of two Comprehension Programs intended to instruct the child in the meaning and use of the words in the Sight Vocabulary Program. The tasks consisted of (1) matching printed material with pictures, and (2) silent reading followed by answering questions or carrying out directions.

In the picture-matching sequence, the task for the child was to read silently a word, phrase, or sentence printed on a card and then to place the card on the appropriate picture. In one silent reading sequence the child read simple statements in a booklet and responded to multiple choice questions on the material. In another, he also read simple statements in a booklet and then followed the directions. This task was designed to be more complicated than the first in that it required integration of several previously learned skills. In this program the child was given a booklet, several containers with objects (e.g., circles, numbers, small plastic horses, boys, girls, cars, etc.), and a number of empty boxes. The booklet contained such statements as "Put 5 green cars and two black horses in box 4."

The third sequence consisted of a simple phonetic sequence designed to present a phonetic alphabet consisting of only short vowels, "hard" consonants, and blends. In this program the child was first required to respond to the visual presentation of each letter by vocally making the equivalent sound, and later to select the correct sound from a group when the letter name was presented vocally.

### Writing

At the outset, the writing program used an illuminated tracing box to initiate writing skills (Birnbrauer, Bijou, Wolf, & Kidder, 1965). This procedure, which presented or withdrew the model to be traced by light control, was introduced on the assumption that initial training in tracing lines, letters, and words provided the child with continuous and immediate information as long as the model was clear and the child could compare his strokes to the model. In addition to ensuring model clarity, the illuminated box permitted "weaning" of the child from tracing by gradually decreasing the proportion of time during which the model was illuminated. Simultaneously, the model increased in complexity, from the component strokes which make up cursive letters to complete words, and the error tolerance was decreased.

In the next stage of the research on writing, the illuminated tracing box was eliminated. Instead of starting with attempts to shape tracing skills, the program started with whatever copying behaviors the child displayed. The printing of letters was then introduced. Later in the program the child was required to use cursive writing when "copying" printed material or when doing any writing. There were several reasons for this revision in procedures, one being that transfer from tracing to copying frequently failed to occur. Some combination of tracing and copying from the outset seemed a more effective approach.

### Arithmetic

The arithmetic program began with matching dots or objects with numerals, counting aloud, and putting numbers in their proper order. (If a child could not discriminate, name, and write numbers, he was given training in the writing program designed to develop these responses.) Next, simple addition operations were introduced. An example from this sequence is shown in Figure 2. The next program consisted of material on

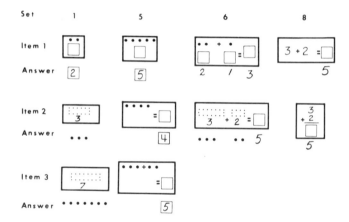

Figure 2. A sample of the arithmetic program

the concepts of "greater than," "less than," and "equal to," all of which were presented by the "dot-numeral" approach. After that came sequences on simple subtraction and addition facts. At the same time, another series was offered designed to teach ordering numbers from 1 through 60.

As soon as a child showed he could read simple instructions, sequences in arithmetical reasoning problems were presented. Carrying, multiplication, division, and more advanced arithmetical comprehension tasks were introduced in a similar gradual fashion in subsequent sets. Training in the discrimination of monetary values was given in a separate sequence after the child had learned the prerequisite knowledge. Training in telling time to the criterion of adequate oral and written responses also constituted a miniature program as was mentioned earlier.

## SOME PRINCIPLES

In this final section we shall attempt to make explicit the main principles which guided the development of the programmed procedures and materials. Two preliminary comments are in order: one pertains to the current status of the principles of programmed instruction; the other, to the research method we employed. With respect to principles, one can distill only a few reliable propositions from this decade's profusion of literature on programmed instruction. Many statements presented as principles turn out, on close scrutiny, to be assumptions, definitions, analogies, or only partially demonstrated functional relationships. In light of this state of affairs and the relative newness of applying behavioral principles to academic learning, it is more realistic to view this as summing up not so much a discussion of principles as a discussion of guidelines, or tentative formulations derived from our experiences with retarded children and from the writings of others working with normal subjects (e.g., Green, 1962; Holland, 1960; Skinner, 1961; 1963; 1965).

With respect to the research method used in this study, the strategy was not unlike that of constructing psychological tests. The essential difference was that instead of focussing on creating stimulus materials that would yield differences between groups, we attempted to prepare stimuli that would enable a child to acquire progressively more complex skills and knowledge. The method consisted of (1) preparing tentative procedures and programs based on general information from teaching experiences and the literature, (2) evaluating these materials on the performances of a small sample of children observed one-at-a-time and in a one-to-one situation, (3) revising them on the basis of the child's performance, (4) readministering the new versions to the same or a similar group, and (5) reevaluating and revising them again on the basis of the second administration. This format was continued until each child reached a criterion of progress set in terms of error rate, or a combination of error rate and another measure, such as performance on similar material (generalization).

### Guidelines for the Development of the Motivational System

There is good reason to believe that learning with positive reinforcement contingencies leads to better maintenance of learned behavior and avoids some of the undesirable behavioral consequences of contingent aversive stimulation. Therefore the major guideline adhered to in the development of the motivational system was that instruction be based on positive reinforcement. As we pointed out earlier, we quickly observed that the children in this study were not sensitive to the contingencies usually employed by the teacher (e.g., giving differential attention, praise, social recognition); consequently, it was necessary to contrive a workable motivational system. For several reasons, a token system was decided upon: first, "marks" can be dispensed rapidly and generously at very little cost; second, administering them does not interfere with studying behavior; third, they can be given on any time schedule; and finally, and most important, they allow each child to earn the kind of object or activity (the back-up reinforcers) most reinforcing for him personally. There are added advantages. By shifting schedules of reinforcement and the size of work unit required to earn a token, and by varying the number of tokens required for back-up reinforcers, the teacher can dispense tokens in quantities most effective at the different stages of mastering a program (Birnbrauer & Lawler, 1964). Furthermore, the teacher can dispense the reinforcers at the proper time and in the proper amounts by utilizing simple teaching machines and ingenious arrangements of teaching materials.

The system of giving "marks" entailed three components: (1) The marks must be given as soon as possible consequent to the specific behaviors to-be-strengthened. (2) They must be given for increasingly larger units of behavior. (3) They must be given simultaneously, or almost so, with social stimuli from the teacher.

1. *Giving "marks" as soon as possible consequent to the specific behaviors to be strengthened.* A functionally defined reinforcer has its greatest effect when it occurs close in time to the occurrence of the behavior to be reinforced. Hence simple teaching machines, such as the Min/Max, and other instructional techniques were employed to close the temporal gaps between response and stimulus occurrences at least in the initial stages of learning. As learning progressed delays of administering the reinforcers were gradually increased by employing techniques of constructing "bridges" of conditioned reinforcers spanning the time between the response to be reinforced and the occurrence of the token reinforcers.

2. *Giving "marks" for increasingly larger units of behavior.* Marks for appropriate social behavior were given first on a continuous reinforcement schedule, then at a pace set by the child on gradually increasing intermittent schedules. Marks for correct academic responses were given for correct responses to longer and longer sequences of academic material. These procedures of making contingencies systematically more infrequent not only prolong the effectiveness of reinforcers and increase resistances to extinction, but also contribute to developing the desired academic behaviors, e.g., reading words, phrases, sentences, and then paragraphs.

3. *Giving "marks" in close association with other stimuli.* One of the consequences of a reinforcing interaction is the emergence of new conditioned reinforcers. Thus, when a token is delivered by an individual, the

stimuli present at that moment (the appearance of the person, her facial expression, the words she utters, etc.) can acquire conditioned reinforcing properties. Thus "marks" were given with a smile or a comment such as "That's good," or "Yes, that's right." Effort was also made to make the products of learning, conditioned reinforcers (intrinsic reinforcers) by giving tokens and praise for concrete evidence of advancement in academic achievements such as a well-written word, sentence, or paragraph.

### Guidelines for Developing Prerequisite Academic Behaviors

As previously described the main guideline for the establishment of serviceable prerequisite academic or study behavior involved a two-pronged approach: (1) strengthening the desired classes of behavior, and at the same time, (2) weakening those behaviors which compete with the desired behavior. The main technique for strengthening appropriate study habit behavior was differential reinforcement of successive approximations to the criterion behavior.[1] In essence, this approach uses a shifting behavioral criterion for reinforcement, one that has the characteristic of gradually approximating the form of the desired behavior. Obviously, this shaping procedure cannot be carried out effectively unless the contingencies are meaningful to the child (i.e., are functionally defined), and the teacher is capable of discriminating the progressive succession of responses involved, beginning with the responses during initial training and ending with those that define the terminal behavior. If the teacher cannot discriminate the steps, she cannot deliver the reinforcers appropriately; as a consequence she will fail to build up the strength of the desired behavior beyond that of the undesired behavior.

Let us say that the study behavior of a child in this investigation consists of four segments. (1) Getting ready to start the day's assignments. To strengthen this sequence the child would be reinforced in turn for entering the classroom and walking directly to the table where the assignment folders are kept, picking up his folder, going to his desk, sitting down, setting his watch, opening the folder, obtaining the materials necessary for doing the first assignment, recording the starting time on the answer sheet, and starting to work on the first item. (2) Working on the first assignment. Here the youngster would be reinforced for carrying out the instructions, for paying attention to the confirmations, and for working more and more productively. He would also be reinforced for raising his hand when he requires assistance from the teacher. (3) Terminating an assignment and preparing for the next one. Rein-

---

[1] These procedures are elegantly illustrated in a paper by Wolf, Risley, and Mees (1964) describing the treatment of a preschool child diagnosed as retarded, brain-injured, emotionally disturbed and physically handicapped.

forcement would be forthcoming for recording the time at which he finished the assignment, putting away materials, and preparing for the next task. Preparation for the next task could consist of going to the "directions" table,[2] a writing table, or into one of the tutorial rooms, and gathering the materials he will need for working there. As in the first phase, reinforcements would be given for recording time and for starting promptly. (4) Increasing productivity during the class period. Extra reinforcers would be given for reduction in the number of errors and time required for a single assignment, then for several assignments, and then for all the assignments of the day. The criterion for determining when reinforcers should be given for increased productivity would be, of course, the child's previous performance.

The guideline involving the use of contingent "time-out" from positive reinforcement was predicated on the assumption that events in the classroom are in fact positive reinforcers for each child. If classroom events are not positively reinforcing, if the stimuli in the classroom have negative reinforcing properties for him, then removal of the child from this situation would seem to strengthen rather than weaken the preceding disruptive behavior (Skinner, 1953). In a study by Birnbrauer, Wolf, Kidder, and Tague (1965) on the effects of the token system, they found that when the token procedure was eliminated, not only was the "time-out" room used more frequently but two children overtly competed to go there. The authors state: "It appears that the removing of a child from a classroom is effective to the extent that it is, in fact, time-out from positive reinforcement. Complying with classroom expectations must be more reinforcing, one way or another, than the alternative" (p. 232).

Earlier we described the "time-out" procedure as being initiated by the teacher's comment to the child that continuation of his disruptive behavior would result in his removal from the classroom; disregard of this reminder was followed by his removal. Pairing of a verbal statement, "If you continue to behave like that you will have to go to the 'time-out' room," with the act of taking the child to the "time-out" room eventually gives such a statement the property of a conditioned aversive stimulus and as such becomes effective when used alone.

### Guidelines for the Development of Programmed Instructional Materials

The preparation of the programmed instructional materials was based on certain general assumptions which can be expressed in terms of the following general guidelines:

[2] The "directions table" was the work table to the right of the entrance to the classroom (see Figure 1) on which were materials used for following the directions in the reading booklets.

1. Reading, writing, arithmetic, and academic exercises based on these subjects are operant interactions. Therefore academic responses are strengthened, weakened, and elaborated in accordance with operant principles, and the educational environment should be engineered to provide for the appropriate arrangements of antecedent (cue, or discriminative) stimuli, contingencies, and setting events (Bijou & Baer, 1961).

2. Academic learning consists of changes in a child's performance in relation to events which make up his educational environment. Hence an academic environment should stimulate the child to react in an explicitly defined manner to the material to be learned. Therefore, attempts were made to arrange the learning situation so that reactions to cues, to instructions, and to contingencies were readily observable and recordable. This guideline does not imply the acceptance of a theoretical position which implies that academic learning takes place only when overt behaviors are in evidence. Obviously academic learning includes all sorts of unobservable behavior. The main reason for engineering the classroom situation so that responses were readily observable and recordable was to provide data for systematic evaluation of the materials and procedures.

3. Progress in academic learning depends upon the child's history with respect to previous academic interactions and the current academic environment functionally defined, i.e., defined in terms of the meaning of the environment as judged by the child's reactions to it. Hence extensive efforts were made to individualize the learning situation so that each child would work on tasks appropriate for him and fairly independent of teacher supervision.

4. Advancements in academic learning are achieved by systematically presenting materials which gradually require more and more complex behaviors. Therefore efforts were made to design programs which would allow each child to start at the level of his subject competence, as determined by pretests, and advance to materials requiring progressively more complex interactions. When we refer to progressively more complex interactions we are referring to responses to more complicated discriminative stimuli (words, phrases, and sentences), and to more subtle discriminative stimuli (the word "light" first has only one meaning, then different meanings depending on the context in which it appears). This term also refers to responses with increased differentiation (writing with greater ease and skill), and to larger repertories of responses to the same stimulus event (saying, writing, spelling, sounding-out and telling the meaning of the word "boat").

The discussion above covers the general guidelines which influenced the preparation of the academic programs and procedures. We turn now to some specific considerations.

1. Training in making discriminative responses should precede training in making constructed responses in sequencing programmed instruc-

tion material. For example, before a child is required to say or write a word, he is given training in discriminating that word from others which resemble it by pointing, touching, or marking the correct word, etc. Beside this requirement, attention was given to the position in which each item was presented, initially and on succeeding occurrences.

2. Training in the acquisition of knowledge (responding to textual material, naming objects, describing relationships, ordering stimulus material, etc.) should follow fading procedures. Basically such training involves bringing academic behavior under the control of substitute stimuli. Sometimes the surrogate cues are some aspect of the stimulus materials; sometimes they are produced by the behavior of the child. For example, a child is asked to say "house" when he is presented with a picture of a house, the written word "house," and the spoken word, "house" (given by the teacher directly or on a tape). The stimulus properties of the picture of the house and then spoken word are gradually reduced until the child says "house" when presented with only the written word. Discoveries of the most advantageous ways of systematically fading the stimulus supports constitute a large segment of the reading program.

3. Training in motor skills should follow shaping procedures. Shaping was the primary basis for teaching writing. In many instances training started with reinforcing the child for holding a pencil with the right amount of firmness (intensive characteristics), and for forming preletter strokes, then writing letters and numbers in crude forms. In the advanced stages a combination of shaping and fading procedures were involved. Fading procedures were used to remove cue support from tracing and copying from visual models, and in shifting from copying from models to writing from dictation.

4. Opportunities to use learned responses should be made available in increasingly complex situations within the program as well as in other related programs.

5. Since retarded children frequently have specific behavioral deficiencies that prevent consistent progress, supplementary short sequences, designed to produce the missing repertoires, should be made a part of programmed instruction. These special sequences should be constructed on diagnostic findings based on the child's actual performance.

6. The concept of stimulus-response chaining should play a central role in tasks involving serial learning. Guidelines on how chains are extended and strengthened and made into multiple systems were particularly influential in the arithmetical programs.

7. Training in the use of self-prompting techniques should be a part of programmed instruction. For example, after the child had acquired a sight vocabulary consisting of single words, simple phrases, and sentences, he was given training in discriminating the sounds of vowels, some consonants, and simple blends of consonants. This phonetic training was

included in the reading program in order to enable the child to "sound out" words he did not recognize on presentation.

## REFERENCES

Bijou, S. W. Application of operant principles to the teaching of reading, writing, and arithmetic to retarded children. *New Frontiers in Special Education,* NEA, 1965.

Bijou, S. W., & Baer, D. M. *Child development.* Vol. 1. *A systematic and empirical theory.* New York: Appleton-Century-Crofts, 1961.

Bijou, S. W., & Baer, D. M. *Child development.* Vol. 2. *Universal stage of infancy.* New York: Appleton-Century-Crofts, 1965.

Birnbrauer, J. S., Bijou, S. W., Wolf, M. M., & Kidder, J. D. Programmed instruction in the classroom. In L. P. Ullmann & L. Krasner (Eds.), *Case studies in behavior modification.* New York: Holt, Rinehart and Winston, 1965.

Birnbrauer, J. S., & Lawler, Julia. Token reinforcement for learning. *Ment. Retard.,* 1964, *2,* 275–279.

Birnbrauer, J. S., Wolf, M. M., Kidder, J. D., & Tague, Cecilia. Classroom behavior of retarded pupils with token reinforcement. *J. exp. child Psychol.,* 1965, *2,* 219–235.

Ferster, C. B., & Skinner, B. F. *Schedules of reinforcement.* New York: Appleton-Century-Crofts, 1957.

Green, E. J. *The learning process and programmed instruction.* New York: Holt, Rinehart and Winston, 1962.

Holland, J. G. Teaching machines: an application of principles from the laboratory. *J. exp. Anal. Beh.,* 1960, *3,* 275–287.

Holz, W. C., Azrin, N. H., & Ayllon, T. Elimination of behavior of mental patients by response-produced extinction. *J. exp. Anal. Beh.,* 1963, *4,* 407–412.

Skinner, B. F. *Science and human behavior.* New York: Macmillan, 1953.

Skinner, B. F. Why we need teaching machines. *Harvard educ. Rev.,* 1961, *31,* 377–398.

Skinner, B. F. Reflections on a decade of teaching machines. *Teachers Coll. Rec.,* 1963, *65,* 168–177.

Skinner, B. F. What is the experimental analysis of behavior? Address given at the 1964 meeting of the Amer. Psychol. Ass., Los Angeles, Calif.

Skinner, B. F. The technology of teaching. *Proceedings of the Royal Society.* B, 1965, *162,* 427–443.

Staats, A. W., Staats, Carolyn K., Schutz, R. E., & Wolf, M. M. The conditioning of textual responses using "extrinsic" reinforcers. *J. exp. Anal. Behav.,* 1962, *5,* 33–40.

Wolf, M. M., Risley, T. R., & Mees, H. L. Application of operant conditioning procedures to the behavior problems of an autistic child. *Behav. Res. Ther.,* 1964, *1,* 305–312.

# PART III

# Review and Overview

This section is a reprint of Chapter 17 in *Operant Behavior: Areas of Research and Application* edited by W. K. Honig (Appleton-Century-Crofts, 1966). Honig designed the volume to be "a handbook for the student who wants a summary of findings, for the experimentalist who wants a description of techniques, for the educator interested in teaching aids, and for the professor in need of illustrative materials to support the presentation of some of the theoretical concepts in the classroom."

Chapter 17 presents a survey of research and an analysis of research problems in the application of operant methods to child behavior and development. Hence it includes an account of the specific techniques developed in research to date (1964); it gives the context in which operant analyses should be considered; and it points out possible extensions, current limitations, and critical problem areas. In running the gamut from broad theoretical issues to mundane descriptions of specific research crafts and procedures, the discussion necessarily relies on both published and unpublished materials, and sometimes on the lore of the field.

Many of the theoretical ideas and studies presented in Parts I and II are referred to or abstracted in this section. These partial repetitions and restatements may help the student comprehend the topics more readily and afford an opportunity to view the separate readings in the light of a comprehensive context which constitutes a natural science approach to the science of human psychological development.

# 25

# Operant Methods in Child Behavior and Development

*Sidney W. Bijou and Donald M. Baer*

## INTRODUCTION

It is appropriate to begin with a quotation from a brief and prophetic paper by Keller (1950), in which he considered the future role of reinforcement theory in the analysis of child behavior and development:

> Its future will depend upon the ease with which it handles questions of social and verbal interaction. The experimental investigation of infant and child behavior presents itself as an alluring approach to this goal. It will be a pity if outmoded objections and extrascientific considerations stand in the way of its attainment (p. 12).

The future Keller spoke of in 1950 is now, in part, the present. Current research seems to be contributing three functions of operant principles and methods to developmental psychology: (1) It offers a basis for a positivistic approach to a developmental analysis of behavior. (2) It constitutes a segment of a theory of description and explanation of the development of child behavior, especially of social behaviors and "personality." (3) It provides techniques for measurement and experimentation relevant to general theories of the behavior of organisms young and old, human and infra-human.

The bulk of this chapter will deal with the third contribution—techniques of measurement and experimentation. However, the first and second contributions, a basis for a positivistic approach and a theory of behavior development, will constitute the essence of the initial discussion. These topics have obvious systematic significance and are thus appropriate as an

From *Operant Behavior: Areas of Research and Application*. Edited by Werner Honig. Copyright © 1966 by Meredith Publishing Company. Reprinted by permission of the publishers.

Many of the studies by the authors cited in this chapter and the preparation of the chapter per se, were supported in large measure from two grants (M-2208 and M-2232) from the National Institute of Mental Health, Public Health Service.

introduction to the application of operant techniques to developmental problems.

## A Basis for a Positivistic Approach

Those who follow a positivistic approach may be said to be devoted to the development of concepts which either are frankly tautological or else have operational definitions. Furthermore, they attempt to arrange their concepts into explanations of behavior which are testable at least in principle. A vivid description of this type of investigator is made by Stevens (1939). His account and ours suggest that the application of concepts of operant and respondent behavior developed by Skinner (1938; 1953) and by Keller and Schoenfeld (1950) to an analysis of the complex social behavior of humans will have the requisite appeal to many.

The positivistic approach is usually functional: an area of behavior is defined and then procedures are established to discover those variables which control it. As discoveries are made, responses are described as functions of certain experimental manipulations, usually of stimulus events in the past and present environments, and a set of empirical laws evolves. Concepts arise, not because of their imaginative, logical, or global characteristics, but only as they serve to describe and summarize the experimental stimulus operations which control behavior. Hence, such concepts are functional in that they pertain only to those procedures demonstrated to influence the behaviors in question.

The subject matter of child development has often been treated by virtually the reverse approach. Its concepts have had functional value mainly for the behavior of the theorist, not for the behavior of the child. This situation is probably related to the fact that, for the most part, these concepts have not been founded on experimental procedures. Instead, they have remained comfortably located in areas where no experimenter had the competence to manipulate processes: in the child's genes, for example, or in his state of neuro-muscular development, or in his intelligence, or in his ego.

Confronted with this tradition, a functionally-oriented investigator entering this area should find the concepts of operant and respondent behaviors and their controlling conditions appealing to him. These concepts emphasize the variety of environmental factors that may control a behavior through a sequence of development; they suggest the possibility of a response having an initial resemblance to a respondent, but with development showing operant characteristics; they tend to be free of non-operational definitions; and they tend to remain open to additions and revisions, since they contain no commitment to their own completeness.

## A Segment of Theory

The concepts of operant and respondent conditioning can be more than mere operational handles on which to hang environmentally controlled behavior. Owing to their number and scope, they can yield an account of the development of the human child's motor, perceptual, linguistic, intellectual, emotional, social, and motivational repertoires. Indeed, these concepts suggest that the foregoing list of traits is vague and overlapping. All of these presumed "faculties" can be described in their ontogenesis by combinations of the principles of operant and respondent behavior.

Such a theory, which has been presented by the authors elsewhere (Bijou & Baer, 1961), proceeds by the following chain of propositions:

1. The developing child is conceptualized as a source of responses and stimuli.

2. The responses are divided into two functional classes: *respondents,* which are controlled primarily by preceding stimulation and are largely insensitive to consequent stimulation; and *operants,* which are controlled primarily by consequent stimulation, their attachment to preceding (discriminative) stimuli being dependent upon the stimulus consequences of behavior made in the presence of these discriminative stimuli. Some responses may share attributes of both respondents and operants. Some responses may initially have only respondent properties, but with development may gain operant characteristics (and possibly lose their respondent features).

3. The stimuli are described as the child's environment (including the part within the body wall). Stated another way, the child's environment is conceptualized as a source of stimuli interacting with and controlling his respondent and operant responses. Some of these stimuli are identified as setting events (conditions that are identified as influencing specific stimulus-response relationships), such as satiation, deprivation, and level of biological maturity. Catalogues of classes of stimuli and setting events are required.

4. Subsequent analysis of the child's development proceeds by listing the ways in which respondents are attached to new stimuli and detached from old ones, through respondent conditioning and extinction. Similarly, a listing is made of the ways in which operants are strengthened or weakened through reinforcement contingencies, and discriminated to stimuli which mark occasions on which these contingencies hold. Many of these respondents are included in the category called *emotional;* some of their conditioned stimuli are provided by people, and hence are *social.* Some of the operants strengthened are manipulatory, and some of their $S^D$s (discriminative stimuli) are the size, distance, weight, and motion of objects; hence this development may be described as *perceptual-motor.* Some of

the operants are vocal, as are some of the respondents, and their discriminative stimuli, reinforcing stimuli, and conditioned stimuli typically are both objects and the behavior of people; hence this development is both *cultural* and *linguistic*.

5. Through discrimination and generalization the child's operants and respondents become attached to classes of eliciting and discriminative stimuli. These classes may vary in breadth, depending upon the history of conditioning and extinction procedures applied. Consequently, the child's manipulatory and verbal behaviors seem to deal in classes. This phenomenon, coupled with the complexity of $S^D$s possible in discriminating operants, and the use of verbal behavior to provide $S^D$s for self-control, gives the label *intellectual* to many of these behaviors.

6. The equation of discriminative stimuli to conditioned reinforcers (Keller & Schoenfeld, 1950, p. 236) suggests that many $S^D$s play a significant role in strengthening and weakening operants as the child develops. Some of these $S^D$s consist of the behavior of people (typically parents), and thus give rise to *social* reinforcers: attention, affection, approval, achievement, pride, status, and the like. Again, the preceding principles are applied, but now to social reinforcement for social behaviors, under social $S^D$s. Hence, the development described is social behavior or *personality*.

7. In all of these steps, the scheduling of eliciting, discriminative, and reinforcing stimuli has important consequences. The principles involved give some explanation of the characteristic modes of response which may distinguish children: typical rates, the use of steady responding or bursts of activity, resistance to extinction, likelihood of pausing after reinforcement, etc.

8. Setting events such as deprivation and satiation cycles would have similar application, especially in areas said to be *motivational*.

Even from this sketchy outline, it should be clear that, in number and range of application, the basic principles are adequate to describe much of the development discussed in child psychology. Indeed, it seems at this stage that enough conceptual equipment is available to raise programmatic questions such as: Is there any aspect of child development which might not be analyzed by these concepts? Is there any range of individual differences exhibited by children which cannot be covered by an appropriate combination of the degrees of freedom possible in these procedures?

A different question arises as well. Even if child development can be described in terms of operant and respondent conditioning principles, is it necessarily stated *correctly* in those terms? That is, of course, a matter to be decided only after completion of a large number of experiments. Unfortunately, many of these experiments will be extremely difficult or impossible to perform due to practical, legal, and moral considerations. However, the use of operant and respondent principles to construct a theory of human development is no more susceptible to such limitations than is the use of the principles of Hull, Freud, Lewin, Piaget, or Rogers. And in those instances in which practical, legal, or moral restraints do not apply or can be overcome, an operant-respondent theory of development will generate empirical laws and directly testable hypotheses.

## LABORATORIES AND PROCEDURES FOR FREE-OPERANT STUDIES OF CHILDREN

Except for a few studies published in the twenties and thirties on young infants (for example, those on sensory equipment and respondent conditioning in the neonate), experimental investigations with children have not been characterized by careful control over physical and social stimuli. This state of affairs continues despite general acceptance of the dictum that what is observed is, in part, a function of the procedures and circumstances of observation, and despite general recognition that the laboratory method has advantages because it permits direct control of behavior.

Many recent studies have been performed under makeshift conditions in the home, clinic, hospital, school, residential home, and recreational hall. Even in those conducted in specially designed laboratories, adequate control is not always exercised over non-experimental stimuli. Most often the interaction of investigator and $S$ (subject) is not adequately evaluated, controlled, or eliminated.

The question of social reinforcement of child behavior can often prove to be a fundamental one in the design or evaluation of research on child behavior. It is, of course, an important area in its own right and will be discussed as such later in this section. At this point, however, it is important to discuss the role of social reinforcers in situations where they are not the stimulus of primary interest to the experimenter $(E)$. Since children represent a species highly sensitive to social reinforcement, and indeed represent an age in which their parents and other members of society typically are striving to implant and develop this sensitivity, it is clear that unrecognized social reinforcement contingencies may abound in almost any experimental situation. For example, instructions that tell the child what he *may* do are sometimes responded to as if he had been told what he *must* do. Children are observed to give thousands of extinction responses after only modest reinforcement programs. (One child sat and responded with tears rolling down his cheeks. When asked what the trouble was, he replied, "I don't want to do this any more." When asked why he didn't stop, he said, "You didn't tell me I could stop!" While it is not wise to give complete credence to the verbal behavior of children as indicators of controlling variables, it is likely that a process like this has played a part in many experimental contingencies.)

No doubt because of distinctive past histories of reinforcement, some children respond to reinforcement contingencies themselves as a kind of instruction, which, for example, could make discrimination reversal difficult once the discrimination is established. Others respond to reinforcement as if it is aversive, and do not want to take anything from *E*. When offered a tray of toys from which they are to pick the one they want, they choose the smallest and least attractive, and if asked, "Is *that* the one you want?" may say, "I shouldn't take the best." Where *E* uses demonstration methods, the demonstration may act as a command, and *S* may not modify his behavior from imitation of the demonstration, even in the face of protracted changes in the discriminative stimulus or reinforcement schedule. Yet a simple re-demonstration of the new behavior pattern by *E* may produce an immediate (and appropriate) change in the behavior. Merely the statement by *E*, "You're not doing it right" or "You do not have to press the button all the time," may bring about a prompt change to the appropriate behavior, although thousands of inappropriate responses have been emitted previously.

Extensive work with the experimentally manipulated stimulus usually demonstrates to *E* when he does not in fact have control of the child's behavior, and may lead him to investigate what social reinforcers unwittingly have been dispensed (if any). In this instance, although the experiment will not have proceeded as planned, at least no erroneous conclusions will be drawn. However, in studies where stimulus operations are not used extensively to show the responsiveness of the child's behavior to them, it is easier to attribute a behavior pattern actually controlled by unsuspected social reinforcement to the experimentally manipulated stimulus, which may, in fact, have been ineffective.

An example of methods to show the role of uninvited social reinforcement in operant studies with children may be given in the context of the Robinsons' study (1961), which was designed to show the role of negative reinforcers in supporting avoidance behavior in preschool children. A stimulus consisting of a 50-db tone pitched at 2300 cycles per second was used as the negative reinforcer; it was introduced to the child as an interruption in an ongoing tape recording of children's music, stories, and songs. A plunger-pulling response terminated the sound or avoided its next presentation. A signal light was presented 1.5 seconds before the sound. The child received the following instructions: "A very loud, bad noise is going to come out of here; it's really a very bad noise, a terrible noise; it may even hurt your ears a little. I don't like to hear it and I'm sure you won't either. But you can turn off the noise, or keep it from ever coming on. First the lights will come on, and then the noise. You will have time to turn it off before it ever comes on. The way you do it is to pull this (demonstrating). Let's see you do it. Let it go back each time as soon as you pull it out, or else your hand will get tired." During the early trials, if the child did not respond by turning off or avoiding the sound, *E* said, "Oh, that awful, nasty noise," "Turn that awful noise off," or "You can keep that bad noise from ever coming on" (p. 21).

As the authors point out (pp. 22-23), there is considerable room in the procedure for social reinforcement to exert more control than the noise which is of primary interest. The following possibilities arise:

1. The noise does, indeed, act as a negative reinforcer, or as a loss of the positive reinforcers on the tape recording, and the rest of the procedure is perhaps helpful to prompt development of the avoidance behavior, but is not essential. Elimination of the instructions would constitute a condition, then, in which avoidance learning would still take place, perhaps more slowly. (But the authors say, ". . . it would soon become obvious that such comments were required by the children . . ." [p. 22].)

2. It is possible that neither the tone nor the interruption of the tape recording is negatively reinforcing, but that the child responds to prevent $E$ from receiving negative reinforcement. $E$ says, "I don't like to hear it." Many children have a history of reinforcement for "consideration" for the comfort of others. The instructions might be pared down to include only such statements from $E$, or they might be purged of such comments; $E$ might be removed from the situation entirely; a neutral tone might be substituted for the loud one; or any combination of these might be employed.

3. It is possible that the child responds simply to gain $E$'s approval and maintain it. $E$ has said that the noise is "bad" and "terrible." Again, instructions might be reduced to this kind of statement; this kind of statement might be eliminated from the instructions; a neutral tone might be substituted; or $E$ might be removed.

4. Perhaps the child responds on the basis of implied commands. $E$ says, "I don't like to hear it, and I'm sure you won't either" (speaking of the tone). This may constitute a command for some children. Or, $E$'s demonstration of how and when to respond may constitute a command for a child possibly unresponsive to what $E$ does not like to hear. Finally, there is the explicit command, "Turn that awful noise off." Each statement or demonstration might be tried alone or eliminated, in conjunction with $E$'s presence or absence, and tones known to be neutral or negatively reinforcing might be used in order to determine the controlling factors.

5. The most realistic possibility is that every one of the above processes (and others as well) will be exemplified in the behavior of *some* of the children. The logic of single-subject analysis which pervades operant conditioning with animal $S$s has at least equally compelling application in studies with children. This is clear when considering how variable are children's histories of social conditioning, and how many stimuli serve as $S^D$s for these social reinforcers, as the previous example shows. It is extremely difficult to guarantee that an experimental situation does not exemplify $S^D$s for social reinforcement for some children. $E$ must either turn his at-

tention explicitly to these social reinforcers and their cues, or engage in sufficient manipulation of the other stimuli of greater interest to show that they do indeed control the experimental behavior of some of his *S*s.

## Laboratories for the Study of Infants

Let us consider a laboratory situation for the free-operant study of infants. Because of the infrequent use of free-operant methods with neonates and young babies, it is difficult to cite a reference which contains a description of a laboratory entirely adequate for presenting stimuli, recording stimulus and response events, and controlling other extrinsic conditions for this age of development. It might, however, be of value to point out that enclosures and laboratory cribs designed for infant respondent conditioning have potential for free-operant studies. For example, the stabilimeter used in neonatal studies (e.g., Dockery & Valentine, 1939) could be appropriately modified. Also, fruitful suggestions might be found in the work of Crowell, Peterson, and Safely (1960), and especially Lipsitt and De-Lucia (1960), who devised cribs with associated control units for presenting stimuli such as shock, lights, and tones and for recording foot and leg responses and general bodily activity.

A laboratory or a method for studying infants from about three to six months has been developed by Rheingold, Stanley, and Cooley (1962). A diagram of the apparatus is given in Figure 1. The investigators describe the device in these words:

> An apparatus designed for use in studying the beginning of this behavior [exploratory behavior], especially in relation to feedback from the external environment, is also adaptable to the study of other kinds of early behavior, both human and animal. The apparatus holds the infant in a suitable position, permits measurement of certain behavior, and provides for sensory feedback from that behavior (1962, p. 1054).

A study situation for infants about eight months of age was built around a discrimination apparatus by Lipsitt (1960), and used in a discrimination study by Simmons and Lipsitt (1961). (The device and data obtained from it are described in the section on convenient responses studied in children.) The authors state that if the infant is placed in a steady seat, one that gives him ample support, and is situated so that he can reach and touch the two panels in front of him, he will sustain attention long enough to establish reasonably stable discriminations.

## Laboratories for the Study of Early and Middle Childhood Subjects

There have been several descriptions of free-operant laboratories and procedures for youngsters from two to five years. Bijou gives an ac-

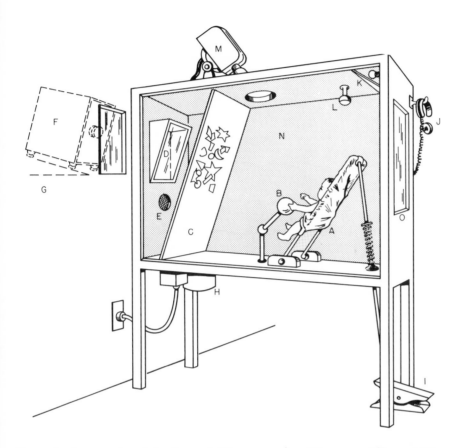

Figure 1. An experimental crib: seat (A), operandum (B), screen (C), projection opening (D), sound source (E), projector (F), control room (G), ventilator (H), rocker (I), intercom (J), crib lights (K), microphone (L), television camera (M), doors of crib (N), window (O). (From Rheingold, Stanley, & Cooley, 1962.)

count of one in a child development institute (1957a) and another in a mobile unit (1958b). Both are designed to produce a playroom atmosphere, to handle a wide variety of free-operant problems, to utilize automated devices for presenting stimuli and recording responses, and to control extraneous stimulations. One aspect of the procedure used in each is that the young lady who escorts the child to and from the laboratory remains behind an opaque screen while $E$ monitors the equipment in the control room and observes through a one-way screen. Figure 2 shows the mobile-laboratory floor plan, which is similar to the laboratory at the university.

A laboratory and methodology for children from about four to ten

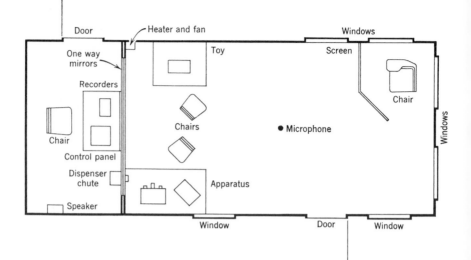

Figure 2. Floor plan of a mobile child-study laboratory. (From Bijou, 1958b.)

years of age has been described by Long, Hammack, May, and Campbell (1958b), and Long (1959a) (see Figure 3). Regarding the procedures, Long says:

> . . . a child sits at a console in a relatively isolated experimental cubicle. Before him [on the face of the console] are a manipulandum (an enclosed telegraph key), colored lights used as discriminative stimuli, a translucent screen on which pictures or other stimuli are projected, and a tray into which reinforcers are delivered. . . . Inside is a Gerbrands universal feeder for delivering reinforcers, an automatic projector, a buzzer, and additional lights (1959a, pp. 113-114).

Several free-operant laboratories for children with deviant behaviors are in operation. Some are for retarded *Ss* in residential institutions (Ellis, Barnett, & Pryer, 1960; House, Zeaman, Orlando, & Fischer, unpublished progress report, 1957; Orlando, Bijou, Tyler, & Marshall, 1961); others, for severely disturbed youngsters (Ferster & DeMyer, 1961; Lindsley, 1956). In all of these laboratories, *S* is alone in the experimental chamber, stimuli are manipulated and responses are recorded by switching circuits, the operanda are sturdy and harmless, extraneous conditions are controlled, and observing and communication devices are utilized. Figure 4 is a photograph of the experimental room devised by Ferster and DeMyer for autistic children. Coins may be deposited for candy, food, milk, motion pictures, and color-wheel movement in the vending machines shown.

It is apparent that advances have been made in preparing experimental situations for normal children between three and ten, and for retarded and

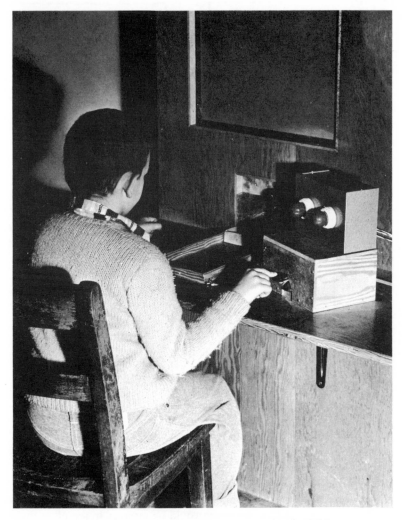

Figure 3. Experimental console for elementary school children. (From Long, 1959a.)

severely disturbed children in residential institutions. Exploratory work on the physical setting, equipment, and procedures for infants and for adolescents, normal and deviant, is yet to be accomplished in corresponding detail.

## PROCURING AND PREPARING SUBJECTS FOR PARTICIPATION IN STUDIES

In addition to sampling problems, the laboratory study of children poses problems of procuring and preparing children for participation in

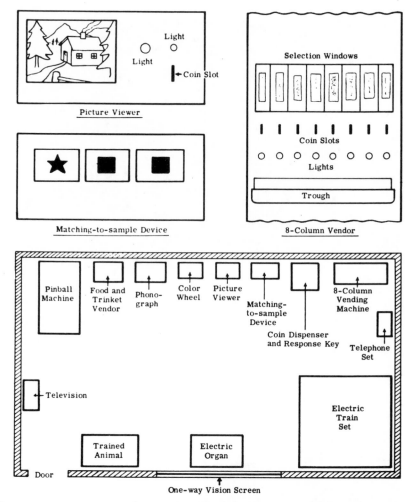

Figure 4. An experimental room for the study of autistic children. Operation of the coin dispenser produced coins, which could be inserted in the other machines pictured to produce other reinforcers. (From Ferster & De Meyer, 1961.)

studies. A corollary consideration relates to basic social and ethical practices naturally involved in working with children. Each topic will be discussed briefly with the view of orienting investigators new to the field.

## Procurement of Subjects

### Infants

Babies have been procured from practically all the agencies and institutions involved in child care. For example, out-patient research clinics with psychological laboratories are usually part of a medical school and frequently operate in conjunction with a child-care or a well-baby clinic in which mothers and infants are seen at regular intervals. Often mothers and babies receive professional services in exchange for their cooperation. The advantage of such a setting is the possibility of making repeated observations over weeks, months, or even years.

Most neonate and young-infant studies have been conducted in psychological laboratories attached to maternity wards. Procuring young Ss in this way presents problems such as finding and retaining adequate working space, establishing cooperative operating procedures with the medical and nursing staffs, and coordinating laboratory sessions with hospital routines. Also, investigations in maternity wards or hospital laboratories must necessarily be limited to the time from birth until mothers are discharged, a period which is continually shrinking, and which now seems to average four days.

Experimental studies in foundling homes, children's homes, and orphanages have been conducted with and without the advantages of a psychological laboratory. Establishing and operating a laboratory in a children's institution poses problems similar to those associated with working in a maternity ward. One major limitation is the possibility of loss of Ss at any time through adoption. Another limitation is the small probability of finding laboratory space within such institutions. One advantage of institutional laboratories is the opportunity to study infants at the different stages of development and for longer periods. Another is that many studies can be carried out with little disruption of living routines. Since the current practice is to place infants at the earliest age possible, infants and babies of this source are becoming scarce.

Infants might also be studied in a mobile laboratory which could be moved to an institution or even a private home and remain for the duration of the study. Under these conditions, it would be possible to conduct research under the constant conditions of a laboratory in a child center, without using institutional space. Studies conducted in a movable laboratory would probably be more disruptive to the baby's routines than those conducted in an institution laboratory, however.

### Young Children

Much of the research on young children has been made possible by the availability of Ss in nursery schools. An additional impetus was given by the establishment, in about 1920, of laboratory nursery schools in colleges or universities (Moustakas & Berson, 1955). One advantage of the laboratory nursery school is the interest of the staff in research; another is the stimulation that research derives from training college students in child behavior and development. On the other hand, a frequent disadvantage is the limited number of Ss, apparent particularly when teaching and research needs are heavy. Nevertheless, even then a sufficient number are usually available for pilot studies and intensive individual analyses. In most laboratory schools it is expected that the investigator give occasional talks to parents and teachers on the research and its implications.

Probably the second largest number of Ss have come from private nursery schools and from private and public day-care centers. Day-care centers (all-day schools for youngsters of working mothers) often pose the problem of finding adequate working space and conditions. When space limitations make it impractical to control experimental conditions adequately, children have been taken from school to a nearby research center or to a mobile laboratory. In this setting, too, the investigator is expected to discuss his research with parents and teachers.

Ss have also been procured through direct contacts with parents. Lists of parents with children of the required age have been obtained from pediatricians, teachers, clinic waiting lists, mothers' clubs, and students from university housing groups. In all instances, personal and written contacts are usually made, and in many situations, transportation is provided to a research center.

Residential institutions—orphanages or schools for exceptional children such as the retarded, blind, disturbed, and dependent—provide further opportunities for laboratory research. Some (especially those for the retarded and emotionally disturbed) already have research laboratories (as has been pointed out in the section on laboratory considerations). Many are more than willing to provide space and basic facilities on request.

### Older Children and Preadolescents

As would be expected, most Ss between six and twelve have been procured through public and private schools. The procedure for obtaining permission to work with elementary school children varies but basically consists of personal or written contact with the principal or superintendent, describing the nature, method, and implications of the investigation, the time required of each child, and the time needed for the entire study. Frequently, time problems arise, such as adjusting the time of experimental sessions so that it does not conflict with class schedules. When a study requires the children to return for a sequence of sessions, arrangements may have to be worked out for the children to compensate for lost time. It is a foregone conclusion that an adequate laboratory cannot at present be constructed in the schools. This means that studies have to be conducted in a mobile laboratory parked near the school, or in a nearby research center. The latter arrangement involves problems associated with transporting children.

Some investigators have obtained elementary school Ss through parent contacts. Long, for example, wrote a letter telling parents that he had received their child's name and address through the school office and asked permission to have their child serve in his research. He described the study and pointed out that it was part of a university project, indicating also what was not included. ("Lest you be concerned, let me assure you that the situation involves no competition between children, no psychological tests, or anything else that might be disturbing.") Finally, he gave basic information on appointments and transportation arrangements. Long's approach has particular merit for obtaining Ss during the summer.

Ss have also been obtained through organizations such as boys' clubs, community centers, Boy Scouts, and Campfire Girls. For example, a settlement house was the setting for a study by Azrin and Lindsley (1956) on cooperative behavior in pairs of children. Permission to conduct a study ordinarily is obtained from both the person in charge and the parents.

Finally, large numbers of elementary-school-age children living in schools and hospitals for the retarded and emotionally disturbed have been studied in laboratories in the institutions.

### Preparation for Participation

Most experimental child psychologists would agree that it is essential to prepare children for a study. Thus far, however, little attention has been given to this aspect of experimental procedure, and consequently practices vary from carefully planned and rigidly maintained routines to no explicit preparation at all.

A case might be made that a pre-experimental preparation procedure is even more essential in work with children than in work with infra-humans. A child, at the beginning of a study, is exposed not only to mild emotional stimuli (being separated from his group and accompanying a relative stranger to a new room with unusual furnishings) but also to stimuli which may have conditioned aversive influence. (This does not apply, of course, to certain groups such neonates, young infants, and children who are grossly disturbed or injured.) For example, it is commonplace to find a school child who believes he is going to the laboratory to take a test which will determine his class placement, or a preschool child who likes to "play the games" but who is reluctant to accept "gifts" from a stranger. Our discussion on the special problems of operant level in the next section also bears on the need for adequate preparation of Ss.

Without going into the details required for a specific study, the following general suggestions are offered for consideration. First, the child should be given an opportunity to become acquainted with the person who will take him to and from the laboratory. With nursery school children one practice is to have the young lady serving as research assistant spend several days in the classrooms and yards, taking the role of a teacher or observer. Second, when it is a child's turn to go to the laboratory, he should be told where he will go, what he will do ("play games," perhaps), and how long he will stay. Third, when he enters the laboratory he should be shown around the room and given an opportunity to explore and examine the situation. He should then be given instructions—the fewer, the better.

## Social and Ethical Practices in Research with Children

Throughout the discussions on procuring Ss and preparing them for participation, practices were advocated which bear on safeguarding the children, their parents, and others responsible for their care. Psychologists (field observers as well as laboratory workers) have long been aware of and have devoted much thought to the problem of doing reliable and meaningful research with children, and at the same time, preserving and promoting the welfare of all involved (e.g., Shakow, 1959). When E establishes appropriate working relationships with Ss and orients their caretakers to the nature and purpose of the study, the specific findings, and their ultimate implications, he not only helps to dispel misconceptions about psychological research, but also makes a positive contribution as a community teacher.

# OPERANT RESPONSES STUDIED IN CHILDREN

The operant resonses of the child studied thus far may be grouped into two classes: (1) The first includes those that are unremarkable in themselves but are taken as typical of the class of operants. These are selected because they are easy to emit, observe, record, and integrate with stimulus operations. They include bar pressing, button pushing, knob pulling, window pressing, and box opening. (2) The second includes those that are studied because they are intrinsically interesting. Examples are thumb-sucking, verbal and vocal behavior, hesitant speech, and smiling. Often studies involving such responses are concerned with the implicit question, "Is this an operant response?" An occasional study deals with one response which is intrinsically interesting and chains it to another response chosen for its convenience for study, e.g., chaining verbal behavior to bar-pressing behavior, as in the studies by Lovaas (1961a; 1961c).

Whatever the reasons dictating the choice of response, the response selected must have certain characteristics to be practical for free-operant techniques. These have been discussed by Ferster (1953), who points out that the optimal free operant is a response which results in a minimal displacement of the organism in both space and time, requires little muscular exertion, and can display a wide range of rates. Adherence to these criteria results in a measuring technique which can give accounts of behavior changes with slight environmental manipulations.

In studies with children, other characteristics of the response require attention as well. One is the stability of the operant level of the response. Some children are likely to respond to any response device as if it were a new toy. Performance is likely to be characterized by initial bursts of responding, which may be followed quickly by a zero level if they are free to explore other parts of the laboratory. Returns to the operandum are likely but may result in successively smaller bursts of output. The overall picture is reminiscent of the course of satiation, which very likely it is. The reinforcers supporting the initial response rate presumably are implicit in the action of the operandum and accompanying clicks, thuds, or bangs which are produced.

There is also the probability of extensive generalization from the child's own toys to the operandum. Indeed, a common technique in child studies is to paint the operandum and its housing unit so as to emphasize its toylike appearance. These additional stimuli are also subject to quick satiation effects (as most parents and baby sitters will testify). Hence, experimental reinforcement of responses to such devices may produce effects which are confounded with the satiation phenomenon. If the experimental reinforcers are of low value, or if the child is slow to respond to the operandum ("warm-up" is descriptive, not explanatory), erroneous conclusions may be drawn about the experimental reinforcer. Attention to these possibilities in pilot work can save considerable embarrassment. In general, a two-minute operant level, unsupported by pilot work on the course of the operant level over time, is not likely to produce easily interpreted data.

An opposite effect may result from the adaptation of some children to the laboratory, within the first session or over several sessions. As was pointed out in the discussion on preparing a child for participation, almost any new situation is aversive for some children. The salient condition may be the strange adult ($E$), the physical setting, or the discriminative function of the particular reinforcing stimulus. Many children have heard their parent repeat, "Never take candy from strangers." Many have also been told about the devastating effect of candy on their teeth. (One of the authors was once reproached by an $S$ on receiving the first candy reinforcement, "I have 11 cavities.") In instances such as these, the child's continued experience with the laboratory situation may eventually produce a weakening of avoidance behaviors, resulting possibly in increasing responding which would appear to be related to the experimental reinforcer. A judiciously inserted extinction period may show that the experimental reinforcer is not the controlling stimulus. Valuable information on this possibility would also be provided by fairly extensive observations of the operant level.

Unfortunately, it seems that the responses which qualify as representative of operant behavior in general, with the characteristics just described, are those most subject to satiation and adaptation effects. Since it has not as yet been demonstrated that a response situation can be engineered which has all of the characteristics important to a study of free operants, most $E$s accept the possibilities of satiation and adaptation effects, control for them, and design operanda in terms of the other criteria.

The following discussion deals with: (1) responses and response situations in which the aim is to develop a sensitive and convenient response measure, and (2) responses interesting in themselves. Sacrifices in technical advantages often required in studying the latter will also be noted.

### Convenient Responses

Bijou has designed a simple bar-pressing operandum suitable for $Ss$ of preschool age and above. This is a modification of a sponge-mop assembly which holds and squeezes the sponge (O'Cedar Mop). With the sponge and mop handle removed, the bright, chromed handle becames a bar (see Figure 5), and its spring loading provides satisfactory tension for a small child to press against. The part of the assembly to which the sponge is ordinarily

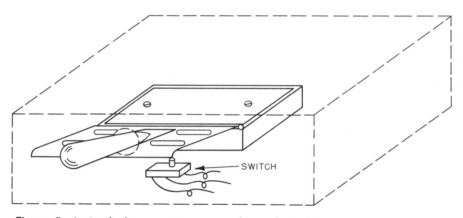

Figure 5. A simple bar-pressing operandum adapted from a sponge-mop assembly. (From Bijou, 1957a.)

attached may be screwed to a horizontal surface within a box housing all but the handle. The rest of the assembly offers a wealth of flat area moving with the bar which can operate several switches of various designs. The assembly is of heavy-gauge chromed metal and has so far resisted determined onslaughts from $Ss$ of various ages (Baer, 1960; 1961; Bijou, 1957a; 1958a; 1961; Bijou & Orlando, 1961; Lovaas, 1961a; 1961b; 1961c).

This type of bar defines a response which is easily emitted, even by very young $Ss$. Added springs may be employed to lighten or stiffen the action. The response requires very little time to emit, and it can be shaped readily by defining the lifting of the bar after depression as the response to be reinforced. Alternatively, the $E$ may define the maintenance of bar depression as the response, keeping positive reinforcement (like movies or music) present as long as the bar is held down. In either event, the response is simple to record. The child is not displaced while responding; the movement of the bar may be made as little as 1/16 inch, or as much as five inches.

Typically, the bar is worked by one hand; occasionally, response is accomplished with a finger, chin, forehead, foot, or fist. Rate is continuously flexible through a wide range. Satiation and adaptation phenomena are often seen, but typically they disappear by the second session.

Another response device largely sharing these characteristics is the Lindsley operandum. With this device, the response consists of pulling a plunger out from a panel. The plunger is a one-half-inch metal rod with a one-inch metal ball welded to its end as a handle. The spring tension and travel of the plunger are adjustable. Two notable advantages of the operandum are its ruggedness and the limited range of responses which can be used to pull the plunger. The second characteristic eliminates the variance in response rate apparent with other operanda when the child turns to using chin, forehead, or feet to effect the response. (However, in many such eventualities, it is not likely that much experimental control over the child's behavior has been achieved. A change in reinforcers or schedules may be more helpful than a change in response device.) The Lindsley operandum was designed to survive occasional attacks from psychotic adults or aggressive primates; thus, it has seen useful application in the study of developmentally retarded as well as normal children (Ellis, Barnett, & Pryer, 1960; Long, Hammack, May, & Campbell, 1958; Orlando, 1961a; 1961b; Orlando, Bijou, Tyler, & Marshall, 1961).

In his earlier work, Bijou (1955; 1957b; Bijou & Oblinger, 1960) made use of a response device which may be classified as a free operant, although the response did require more time than the bar and plunger described above. The child sat before a panel in which two holes appeared, one above the other. The response consisted of dropping a handball in the top hole; the ball returned out the bottom hole 3.3 seconds later, and could be picked up and dropped again. In its travels through the apparatus, the ball triggered switches which recorded the response and activated a reinforcement dispenser. Gewirtz and Baer (1958a; 1958b) used a somewhat similar technique which partially removed the restriction on response rate. In their situation, $S$ sat before a small toy. The toy had two holes in its top surface (allowing for response descrimination) and another hole near the base of its front surface. Directly below this was a tray holding marbles. The response was to take a marble from the tray and drop it down either of the two top holes. The child did not have to wait for the marble to return to the tray; he could immediately pick up another of the marbles in the tray and drop it down a hole (see Figure 6).

Again, internal switches tripped by the marble rolling through the apparatus allowed for recording the response, and could have been used to operate reinforcer dispensers as well. Similar techniques involving marble dropping in one or several holes have been used by Stevenson and his associates and others (Stevenson, 1961; Stevenson & Cruse, 1961; Stevenson & Fahel, 1961; Walters & Ray, 1960). Where more than one hole is used, response measures may include rate over time for each hole, the proportion of responses for each hole per unit of time, or the proportion of responses for each hole per block of total responses.

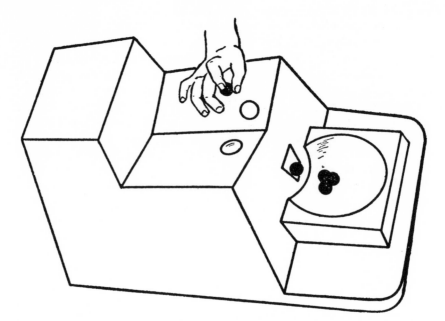

Figure 6. "Marble game" used as a free-operant response situation. (From Gewirtz & Baer, 1958b.)

A response device which is an anlogue to a pigeon apparatus has been developed by Ferster (1962) for a study of complex discrimination processes in children: matching to sample. The child sits or stands facing a panel on which appear three milk-glass screens. The central screen is stationary, but the screens on each side are attached to switch arms and may be pushed back a fraction of an inch. The child presses the center window to bring on the next set of stimuli. In a typical problem, stimulus A is projected on the middle screen, stimulus A on one side screen, and stimulus B on the other side screen. In some conditions the child is reinforced for pressing the screen matching the center screen (stimulus A); in other conditions, he is reinforced for pushing the screen differing from the center screen (stimulus B). The practice of presenting the next three stimuli as an immediate consequence of a correct response allows for a high rate and yields data in terms of both speed of pressing and accuracy of matching. The close integration of the response to the stimuli being discriminated and the fact that the response may be shaped without instruction (for example, by displaying stimulus A on the center and one side screen and leaving the other side screen blank during early trials) are important features of the method.

Variations on Ferster's device were developed by Hively (1962) and J. G. Holland (1963) for discrimination studies with elementary school children and retardates. Both involve a slide projector to present stimuli on windows in the front panel. The sample stimulus is projected on a window above the choice windows. Hively, in his studies on stimuli which differed systematically in shape, size, and color, limited his S to two choices, although it was possible to use as many as four. Holland, working with Long, programmed material on inductive reasoning, coin discrimination, and conceptualization. Their Ss made selections from five stimuli. In Hively's situation the correct response automatically presented the next problem, and an incorrect response did not produce a change, thereby permitting the S to respond again immediately. In Holland's procedure a correct response produced the sample for the next match, and a window-pressing response to the sample presented the five stimuli. An incorrect response blacked out the choices, and another press on the sample window was required to re-present them. A correct response after an incorrect response automatically backed up the slide magazine so that the previous slide was presented again. In other words, progress through the stimulus material was uninterrupted as long as the first response on each match was correct. The same apparatus and procedure was used by Bijou (Bijou & Baer, 1964) to study mirror-image concepts in young normal and retarded children.

A response device developed by Solomon, suitable for problems emphasizing work output, has been described by Lambert, Lambert, and Watson (1953). The response consists of turning a crank on the side of a vending machine which dispenses tokens and candy, and potentially, almost any other tangible reinforcer of reasonable size (see Figure 7). The response may be defined as any number of turns (or any fraction of a turn), and the crank may be made easy or difficult to turn. The device usually needs a ratchet arrangement so that the crank can be turned only in one direction. Even when the crank is easy to turn, the response is not as minimal a movement as bar pressing or plunger pulling. Screven (1954) has also reported data concerning the role of the effort required in a crank-turning response with preschool children.

Azrin and Lindsley (1956) have devised a response situation notable for the discriminability of the response to an onlooker who must cooperate to obtain reinforcers. In this situation, two children sit at opposite sides of a table, with a wire screen between them so that each may observe the other. In front of each child is a row of three small holes. Each child holds a metal stylus connected to a wire from the experimental programmer. The response which is reinforced requires that the children place their styli in corresponding holes within .04 seconds of each other. The wired metal styli are parts of the programmer circuit, as are the bottoms of the holes. (Naturally, low voltages are employed.)

When S is an infant, the design of a suitable response device must be

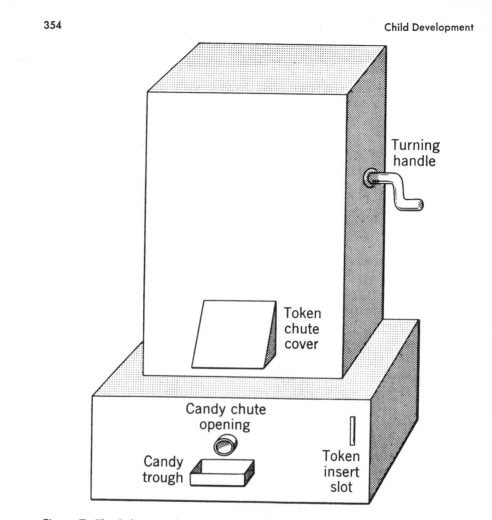

**Figure 7.** The Solomon token-reward vendor. (From Lambert, Lambert, & Watson, 1953.)

a compromise between the desirable characteristics of the free operant technique and the limited motor capabilities of the infant. Lipsitt (1960) has developed a practical solution for infants 8 to 12 months of age, and possibly younger.

A black box with two white panels is placed in a playpen. The two panels are hinged and each activates a microswitch when depressed. . . . In the middle of each panel is a stimulus aperture in which it is possible to produce any one of four different colored lights. . . . Inside the black box is a set of door chimes, which can be activated by either of the panels, under any present condition. Our procedure involves showing one color in one of the panels and another color in the other. Only one of the colors is associated with chimes. When the child pushes the panel of the appropriate color he hears (and presumably is reinforced by) chimes.

With this technique, Simmons and Lipsitt (1961) have shown color discrimination (red vs. pink) in their Ss.

Rheingold, Stanley, and Cooley (1962) have used an even more minimal response for studies of the reinforcement of hypothesized operant behavior in six-month-old infants. In their situation, the infant is seated in a special chair, half reclining and half sitting. He faces a screen on which can be projected brightly colored moving images for a brief period as reinforcement of the response. The response consists of the infant's merely touching a ball mounted in front of him near his hands. Responses may be scored by an observer, visually, or the ball may be made the antenna of an oscillator circuit serving as a capacity-sensitive relay, yielding automatic recording and programming. This device allows for shaping the desired response, since the circuit can be set to respond to the approach of the infant's hand in varying degrees of proximity, as well as to his touch. Since Rheingold has approached this as part of a study of the development of exploratory behavior in the human infant, it might well be included in the next section.

### Interesting Responses

The compromise with optimal design of the operandum involved in the study of infants and children is more apparent when the investigator wishes to study a response because of its intrinsic interest. Most of the preceding descriptions of response devices have come from studies concerned with stimulus operations that can be integrated with response operations. Hence, the response is engineered for the ease of such integration, because such responses can be readily shaped into a baseline. Given such a stable rate, the stimulus operations of interest can be evaluated by their effect on the baseline.

In the studies to be discussed here, the response in each is deemed to be significant in itself. The significance of a response may derive from the fact that it may be considered as an early behavior in social development, like smiling or vocalizing. Or it may seem to be the prototype of a class of behaviors which later will constitute certain personality characteristics. Sucking, for example, may be thought to be an initial behavior in the learning of "dependency." Again, a response class may be of interest because it is so pervasive, such as verbal behavior, and may come to coordinate still larger classes of behavior. Other behaviors are interesting because they constitute a "problem" in children, like stuttering or thumb-sucking.

Whatever the context from which such responses arise, their identification as operant behavior may have significance. Positive findings would relate the behavior to the known (and suspected) laws describing the acquisition, control, maintenance, and weakening of the behavior and thereby give the investigator specific and pointed hypotheses about the development of the behavior in the history of any child: what reinforcers have followed this response, on what schedules, under what $S^D$s, how often, with what delay, and under what deprivation states. Similarly, a reliable failure to identify a behavior as an operant suggests the irrelevance of all such questions, and points instead to an examination of the child's environment in terms of responses controlled by antecedent stimuli.

In general, it should be emphasized that contributions from studies of this category do not lie in the identification of another response, somewhat "cuter" than bar pressing, to be used for studying scheduling procedures. Instead, studies in this area represent a first step in the developmental analysis of the behavior in either a particular or a typical individual's history.

### Sucking

The youngest $S$s to be involved in what might be considered operant conditioning studies are probably those of Jensen (1932). These were newborn infants in some cases, and not more than three weeks old in others. His study incorporates a sensitive method of recording the natural sucking responses of the infants in feeding (and other) situations, and shows the control over this response exercised by the taste and temperature of the fluid ingested. Since these are stimulus consequences of the response, the control may testify to the reinforcing qualities of taste and temperature. However, stimuli are also close antecedents of the *next* response, given the usual rate of sucking. The control produced therefore may be related to their eliciting qualities in a respondent paradigm. These distinctions are absent from Jensen's report, and would not be easy to establish in any event. However, the close stimulus control achieved is intriguing, be it eliciting, discriminative, or reinforcing. Furthermore, sucking is a response which often excites the interest of the psychologist, in that it is a well-coordinated and differentiated response apparent in the first hours after birth. Hence, it is tempting to analyze sucking behavior for fundamental principles since it is uncomplicated by much prior experience. In addition, it is viewed by some as the infant's route to his first dependency relationships.

The method of recording sucking involved insertion of a tube into the nursing bottle. Pressure changes within the bottle resulting from sucking were transmitted through the tube to a series of manometers driving a pressure-sensitive metal bellows, which activated a pen writing on a moving tape of paper. (The apparatus is obviously a refined piece of engineering, incorporating solutions to a number of plumbing problems inherent in such recording, and Jensen's detailed description of his apparatus is recommended to the interested reader.) The recording system allowed graphic and instantaneous accounts of rate, magnitude, interresponse times, and the often increasing pressure differential built up during an unbroken chain of sucking.

Jensen's procedure was to establish a baseline of sucking behavior, using milk at 40°C for ten seconds. (This is a short operant level, but one collected at repeated intervals. Data indicated that the response was sufficiently stable for this purpose.) The bottle would be removed for 20 seconds and replaced for 20 seconds by another bottle holding the experimental mixture (which might be milk or formula, sterile water, or various concentrations of salt or glucose), at the same or different temperatures. After another 20-second delay, the baseline was remeasured, sometimes for 20 seconds. Procedure continued in this sequence of baseline-delay-experimental mixture-delay-baseline until six baseline periods had been established, which constituted a session for S. The method was adequate to show differential sucking to variations in the temperature and taste of the experimental mixtures, as is evident in Figure 8.

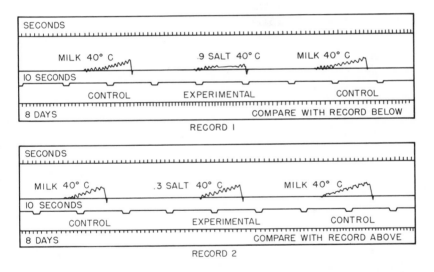

Figure 8. A typical record from Jensen's (1932) study of sucking in newborns. Curves show individual responses (non-cumulative) under various conditions of temperature and taste of the ingested formula, as indicated. (From Jensen, 1932.)

### Smiling

Brackbill's study of smiling (1958) in infants four months of age was generated by her interest in the response in relation to its presumed social nature and its early role in social learning. The infants were chosen as old enough to remain awake throughout the experimental sessions, young enough not to respond differentially to "mother" versus "others," placid enough not to cry too often during sessions and to lie on their backs for at least five minutes without struggling, and responsive enough to show an operant level of at least two smiles per five-minute session. Brackbill offers no verbal description of smiling, but reports that prior to the main study, she and another judge observed some 970 occasions of smiling or non-smiling in infants, and agreed in 97.5 percent of their judgments.

Clearly, smiling (like vocalization) can be a lingering response in infants, and for this reason can detract from the flexibility of its rate. Another factor in this study was the duration of the social reinforcement offered as a consequence of smiling: "Five seconds were required for picking $S$ up; 30 seconds for reinforcement; five seconds for putting $S$ down; and five seconds for recording. Therefore, no more than six responses could occur and be reinforced during any five-minute interval" (p. 117).

Despite these limitations, differences emerged between experimental conditions. These consisted of an operant level period, a conditioning period of either continuous or intermittent reinforcement, and an extinction period. The operant level was taken as the rate observed through at least eight separate five-minute intervals, during which $E$ stood motionless over the infant (who lay on his back in his crib), maintaining an expressionless face about 15 inches from the infant's. During conditioning sessions (consisting of 10 to 12 five-minute intervals), $E$ reinforced smiling by smiling and cuddling the infant, using continuous reinforcement (crf) with one group and working steadily from crf to variable ratios of 1, 2, 3, and 4 with another group. Extinction was similar to the operant level condition, and was observed over 15 or more five-minute intervals. The conditioning rate was reliably higher than operant level. During extinction, the intermittently reinforced group extinguished less rapidly; both groups fell in rate of smiling to below their previous operant level and displayed "protest" behavior to the unsmiling $E$, crying or turning away from her.

All $S$s were studied immediately after a meal following a nap. The mother phoned Brackbill when her infant awoke, and Brackbill would arrive at the infant's home in time for a freshly diapered infant just satiated with food. The mother cooperated to the extent of subjecting her infant to a period of social "deprivation," involving only minimal contact between her and the infant, prior to an experimental session. The study took place in the infant's own home and crib.

### Vocal and Verbal Behavior

Among the youngest children whose vocal behavior has been studied are the three-month-olds of Rheingold, Gewirtz, and Ross (1959). These investigators were interested in showing that the vocalizations of young infants have operant properties. Because of their belief that vocalizations seem to provide an index of the whole social response, they used social reinforcement which "an attentive adult might naturally make when a child vocalizes" (p. 68). Clearly, the response had to be judged as such by $E$ doing the reinforcing. On those occasions when the response was ambiguous or otherwise difficult to judge, a reinforcement was probably delayed (and at times incorrectly administered). This disadvantage is probably unavoidable, considering the definition of the response employed:

> Every *discrete*, voiced sound produced by $S$ was counted as a *vocalization*. A number of other sounds characteristically made by very young infants, e.g., straining sounds and coughs, and the whistles, squeaks, and snorts of noisy breathing, were not counted as vocalizations. Sounds falling under the categories of protests, fusses, and cries . . . were recorded separately. No attempt was made to record any of the phonetic characteristics of any of the sounds or their duration (p. 69).

Their definition of the response clearly precludes any effective use of an electronic voice key, apart from other disadvantages implicit in that device. A voice key, of course, allows for objective recording and instantaneous programming. However, it also records, programs, and reinforces any stray sounds of sufficient intensity to be picked up, like chair squeaks, passing autos, dropped reinforcers, footsteps, or apparatus pounding. Some of the extraneous pickup can be reduced by using a throat microphone in those $S$s that will both tolerate and ignore it. A less useful method is to have older $S$s wear space helmets, in a spirit of "This is all part of the game (i.e., experiment)." The limitations of these methods are clear.

A second observer checked the reliability of $E$'s judgments, and $E$ and the observer traded roles for half the $S$s as a further check on their mutual reliability. Their percentage of agreement ranged from 67 to 100, with a median of 96, over some 27 three-minute periods involving 13 $S$s. The infants were observed lying on their backs in their cribs. The unit of observation was a three-minute period, usually grouped in blocks of three, separated by two-minute rest periods during which the $E$s moved away from the crib. An attempt was made to have three such blocks of observation every day: early morning, late morning, and post-lunch. The first two days of study constituted an operant level or baseline period, during which $E$ stood by the baby's crib looking down at him for three-minute periods with "an expressionless face," while the observer (out of the baby's sight) tallied vocalizations. During the second two days of study, vocalizations were reinforced by a smile, the sounds "tsk, tsk, tsk," and a light touch to the baby's abdomen. If the rate of vocalization increased sufficiently, reinforcement was then given successively on FR 2 and FR 3 schedules (but this was rare). The third two days of the study were an extinction period, identical in procedure to the first two days of baseline.

The two days of reinforcement significantly increased the rate to nearly double the baseline rate; two days of extinction returned the rate to very nearly the baseline level. This pattern is shown in Figure 9. The experiment was duplicated with minor changes and the results were similar in both sets of observations.

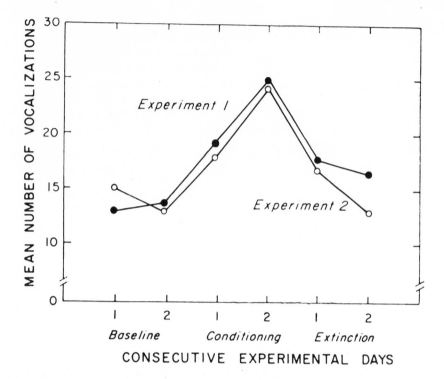

Figure 9. Vocalizations of three-month-old children as a function of reinforcement and extinction procedures. (From Rheingold, Gewirtz & Ross, 1959.)

The authors suggest, consequently, that infants' vocal behavior can be brought under experimental control and that a social event composed of ordinary acts performed by a relatively strange adult can function rather quickly as a reinforcer. They carefully point out, however, that identification of vocalization as an operant response requires observation of a condition in which the reinforcer is delivered as frequently but not contingent upon the response. Results obtained under this condition, when compared with the results reported, would indicate whether the social stimuli presented to the infant served to reinforce the preceding response or elicit the following one.

Weisberg (1963) extended the work of Rheingold, Gewirtz, and Ross along these lines by seeking the answer to two questions: Does the presence of a human adult elicit vocalizations? Can the infant's vocal behavior be controlled by social as well as nonsocial consequences? Thirty-three three-month-old institutionalized infants, divided into six groups, were studied over a period of eight consecutive days.

Group I. No *E* present. During days 1-8 the *E* was hidden from *S*'s view, keeping social stimulation to a minimum.

Group II. *E* was present. On days 1-2, no *E* present; on days 3-8, *E* was seated before *S* but his behavior did not depend upon *S*'s vocal behavior; he did not smile, frown, or make rapid jerky movements of his head.

As in the preceding group, the remaining four groups had no *E* present on days 1 and 2 and had *E* present on days 3 and 4.

Group III. Noncontingent social stimulation. On days 5-8, *S* received stimulation on a prearranged random schedule from *E* who was seated before *S*. This consisted of tactual contact with *S*'s chin, an open-mouthed smile and an aspirated "yeah" sound that we presented independently of *S*'s vocal behavior.

Group IV. Noncontingent nonsocial stimulation. On days 5-8, a door chime sounded on the same schedule as that of Group III while *E* was seated before *S*.

Group V. Contingent social stimulation. Conditioning was attempted on days 5 and 6 by presenting the social stimulus only after each vocalization; on days 7 and 8, social reinforcement was omitted.

Group VI. Contingent nonsocial stimulation. On days 5 and 6, the chime, in *E*'s presence was given as a possible reinforcer and was omitted on days 7 and 8.

Weisberg's findings indicated that the infant's rate of vocalizing: (1) increased when reinforced by the social consequences used in the study; (2) decreased under extinction after social reinforcement, but not to the level of baseline performance; and (3) did not increase when an unresponding adult was incorporated into the environment, when the social stimulus was noncontingent upon vocalization, or when the auditory stimulus was presented either independently of, or contingent upon, vocalization.

Lovaas (1961c) used a combination of differential reinforcement and instructions to achieve control of preschool children's speech. The children were shown two dolls seated on the top of a "talk-box" which contained a microphone. The box was placed beside a tray for receiving trinkets. One doll was clean and new; the other was badly soiled and old; otherwise they were identical. The child was instructed as follows:

This is a talk-box; when you talk to this box, it will give you toys right here (points to reinforcement tray). Now see here are two dolls. This (pointing) is the good doll; this (pointing) is the bad doll. Say "good doll" (if necessary coaches *S* to say, "good doll"; this response is reinforced). See what you got; this is your toy; you can keep it. Now say, "bad doll" (coaching if necessary; this response is also reinforced). See what the box gave you; this is your toy to keep. Now you sit here and tell the box all about the dolls; tell the box what is going to happen to the dolls (1961c, p. 331).

*E* then withdrew to a screened corner of the room, but coached *S* again in a similar way if necessary. All *S*s were reinforced for selected verbal responses (words, phrases, or sentences) until a rate of at least 12 verbal responses within a two-minute period was achieved. Half of the *S*s were then reinforced for aggressive verbal behavior, and half for non-aggressive verbal behavior. The only aggressive verbal behavior this sample emitted consisted of the phrases "bad doll," "dirty doll," and "doll should be spanked." Non-aggressive verbal responses included all other statements or words; however, if an *S* restricted his behavior to "friendly" behavior (e.g., "good doll" exclusively), then this was extinguished by non-reinforcement until other verbal responses, neither friendly nor aggressive, were produced (and reinforced). This was to ensure that the contrast between the groups could be fairly labeled *aggressive* and *non-aggressive* rather than *aggressive* and *friendly*. Conditioning was largely successful, as seen in Figure 10. Subsequent to the conditioning (and prior to it, as well) *S*s were confronted with a two-bar situation. One bar operated an innocuous ball-toy. The other bar activated a pair of mechanized puppets, one of which

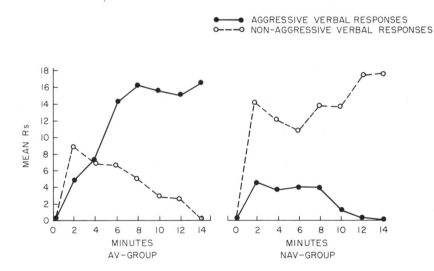

Figure 10. Mean number of aggressive and non-aggressive verbal responses during a verbal conditioning period, for *S*s being reinforced for aggressive verbalizations (AV) and non-aggresive verbalizations (NAV) separately. (From Lovaas, 1961c.)

struck the other with a stick when the bar was pressed, exemplifying an aggressive stimulus consequence of the response. Ss conditioned to give aggressive verbal responses showed a shift in behavior to this latter toy from pre- to post-sessions; the other Ss did not.

A use of social reinforcement has been developed by Baer (1962b) to study both verbal and non-verbal behavior. An animated cowboy puppet speaks to the child (E's voice is piped through the puppet while the jaw is worked in correlation with the words), attends to or ignores the child, and can press a puppet-sized bar much like the regular-sized one beside the child. In addition to giving social reinforcers, he can deliver trinkets from a built-in dispenser. A preliminary application of this technique to verbal behavior indicates that the inherent flexibility of the puppet has real advantages in studies of this sort. The puppet can tailor the stimulus consequences of the child's verbal behavior (or non-verbal behavior) to the particular child. That is, consequences can be "drawn out" by the puppet's taking the brunt of the conversation, answering his own questions, dispensing a good deal of approval, awarding an occasional trinket, and the like.

Bijou and Zylstra (unpublished data) have employed trinkets and visual feedback to strengthen verbal behavior in young children. In their situation the child sits facing a small box in which is mounted a microphone and either an oscilloscope or an "electric eye" tube. (The "electric eye" tube is of the sort commonly used in radio receivers to indicate the precision of tuning. It is more technically referred to as an electron-ray tube. Useful examples are identified by manufacturers as types 6E5, 6G5, and 6AD6G.) As the child speaks, he is reinforced both by the correlated changes in the pattern on the oscilloscope or eye tube and by scheduled trinkets. The use of a decibel meter as a measure of response strength offers an easy way of programming reinforcement for increasingly louder speech; E relies upon his ear for selective reinforcement of content.

A record of both the verbal behavior and various stimulus events correlated with it is easily obtained by a tape recorder. Stimulus events not audible to S can be recorded by E if the shield on the microphone lead is broken and the leads from it brought out to a hand switch (normally closed). E, by flicking the switch, records a correspondingly short 60-cycle buzz on the tape. A code is readily devised for a small number of stimulus events (e.g., one buzz for a reinforcement, two for an $S^D$ change, etc.). The tape can be played back later and E can transcribe the responses (and stimulus events) to a cumulative record by listening and pulsing the cumulative recorder appropriately. This procedure is more reliable than attempting to record the experimental behavior directly onto a cumulative recorder as it occurs.

Erickson (1963) used a technique which is suitable for children who can read, but departed somewhat from the flexibility of the free operant. She had fifth-grade Ss pronounce one of two nouns appearing on a display. One was an animate, the other an inanimate noun. Reinforcement was given for animate nouns after a baseline period to establish the operant level, and was either social ("good") or material (a marble). Immediately after reinforcement, the next pair of words was shown, allowing for a fairly good approximation to a free operant situation, much as in matching to sample. Some Ss experienced prior social deprivation (isolation for 15 minutes); and some, satiation for E's approval (30 instances of approval during 15 minutes of playing with a puzzle). Those Ss who had undergone social deprivation and were socially reinforced formed the verbal differentiation most clearly, saying the animate rather than inanimate noun increasingly often. Since none of the nouns was used twice during reinforcement, this amounted to a verbal concept of "animate" formed under selective reinforcement.

### Hesitant Speech

Two studies by Flanagan, Goldiamond, and Azrin (1958; 1959) have demonstrated experimental control of stuttering or hesitant speech through reinforcement procedures. Using a 6000-cycle tone at 105 db delivered to S through earphones in contingency with the stuttering response, they showed that presentation of the tone as a consequence of stuttering weakened stuttering (relative to speech rate), and that cessation of the tone as a consequence of stuttering strengthened the behavior. Their youngest S was 15.

Felty (1959) extended their procedure to children as young as 12 with known speech difficulties. He used both escape and aversive schedules, as in the Flanagan et al. studies. In the escape condition, the tone was continuously present and a five-second termination of it was contingent upon stuttering; in the aversive condition, a one-second blast of tone was presented following the response. The S read from material considered easy and interesting for his age level to supply an ongoing operant level of speech and stuttering.

A typical session involved three 25-minute periods: operant level, escape or aversive schedule of reinforcement, and recovery. Each S had two sessions on consecutive days, one with an aversive and one with an escape schedule. As in the Flanagan et al. study, the schedules produced the expected strengthening or weakening of the behavior, independently of overall reading rate. Figure 11 shows the response curves for one of Felty's Ss.

The definition of the response was accomplished by E listening to the speech from a control room. A stuttering response was considered to be "any hesitation, stoppage, repetition, or prolongation in the rhythmic flow of vocal behavior" (Flanagan et al., 1958, adopted by Felty). Obviously, this criterion requires a judgment by E who is recording the behavior as hesitant or stuttering and is programming reinforcement. Such judgments may be late or inaccurate, of course—a source of error which apparently must be ac-

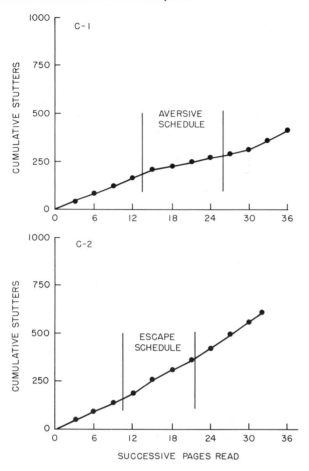

Figure 11. The course of stuttering behavior through aversive and escape schedules involving loud noise. (From Felty, 1959.)

cepted as a limitation on good technique when studying this kind of behavior.

After-the-fact assessments of the reliability of *E* in judging and reinforcing the response can be made in a variety of ways: by having two listeners independently rate a session of speech and/or a tape recording of the session, comparing ratings to produce a percentage of agreement (Felty's procedure); or by having two *E*s run cumulative recorders simultaneously as they listen to the speech, subsequently comparing the records visually for agreement, not in number of responses, but in changes of slope from moment to moment (Goldiamond, 1962); or by having *S* run a cumulative recorder, pulsing it every time *he* thinks he has stuttered and so producing a record which is compared to *E*'s (Flanagan *et al.,* 1959). These techniques are adequate to show only the reliability of *E* in the past session. Probably they best function as reinforcements to $E$ to improve and/or maintain his future performance.

### Thumb-sucking

In the course of studies dealing with the withdrawal of positive reinforcement, Baer noted an $S$ who watched movie cartoons and sucked his thumb almost continuously. The decision to apply withdrawal of reinforcement techniques to this response started a tangential study of thumb-sucking as a potential operant (Baer, 1962a). The technique which was developed involved giving $S$ a long (42-minute) session of cartoons which was broken into alternating periods of operant level and punishment of the thumb-sucking response. Punishment was accomplished by turning off the sight and sound of the cartoons as soon as $S$ put his thumb in his mouth, and re-presenting the films as the thumb was removed. This double-barrelled procedure (which punishes thumb-sucking and positively reinforces thumb removal) yielded increasingly greater depression of thumb-sucking during three consecutive sessions spaced a few days apart. During the interspersed operant level periods, however, the response quickly returned to its usual high rate, suggesting that the response was quickly discriminated to its own consequences rather than generally weakened. This is shown in Figure 12.

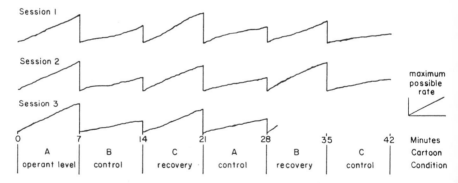

Figure 12. Cumulative thumbsucking rates of a young boy under alternating conditions of reinforcement-withdrawal ("control" in the figure) and recovery. The letters A, B, and C refer to three different cartoons shown in the sequence indicated (see text). (From Baer, 1962a.)

Two other $S$s with similarly high operant levels of thumb-sucking were run in a yoked situation: one experienced contingent withdrawal and re-presentation of the cartoons as a function of thumb-sucking as described above, while the other, watching the same movie screen, experienced the same withdrawals and re-presentations, but not contingent upon thumb-sucking. During the next session, their roles were reversed. Contingent withdrawal and re-presentation procedures yielded control of the response, but random, yoked withdrawal and re-presentation did not, indicating the importance of the contingency between the response and these withdrawal and presentation techniques.

The response was recorded as a cumulative response by using a programmer which pulsed the recorder for every three seconds of thumb-sucking. $E$ watched $S$ through a one-way mirror and activated a switch on the programmer as long as $S$ had his thumb in his mouth. The thumb-sucking response is a simple one to judge and shows nearly perfect reliability, as shown by having two judges simultaneously make cumulative records of the same performance. (It is necessary to isolate the recorders from the judges, since the clicking of one judge's recorder may serve as an $S^D$ to the other judge, if it is audible. A visual comparison of the records usually shows thorough agreement.)

## REINFORCERS AND CONTINGENCIES

Operant research with children has a distinctive aspect to its procedures, which sometimes seem divorced from the simplicities of the animal compartment. Probably this is due to the nature of the reinforcing stimuli in child studies. Typically, they are weak. This may be because they are in themselves low-order reinforcers with only a slight biological or learning basis, because they are subject to quick satiation, or because it is impractical to institute proper deprivation conditions for them. Any combinations of these reasons may hold. In any event, operant research with children has had to develop highly specialized techniques to make available powerful and lasting reinforcing stimuli, or has had to be restricted to short segments of behavior over only a few occasions.

Of course, these comments pertain only to the average child. Almost every $E$ working with children has come upon $S$s who give large quantities of behavior for a dozen plastic trinkets, or who will continue to behave under tight stimulus control for tokens despite the fact that they have acquired a large pile. An example in the University of Washington laboratory was a five-year-old boy who performed repeatedly and consistently for trinkets, finally on an FR 600, and showed great resistance to extinction. Such a performance is unusual in $S$s who have been to the laboratory long and often and have acquired a large number of trinkets. Investigation showed that at the end of each session, this child would gather up his trinkets and rush back to his play group, where he would show them to the other children and boast at length about the number he was building up, comparing this to the much smaller number of trinkets the other children had acquired in the laboratory. It is likely that the reinforcer dispensed was an acquired reinforcer, ultimately supported by social reinforcers on the playground on a sort of percentage schedule.

For the researcher interested in determining what stimuli have reinforcing strength for individual children, such $S$s are a delight and a challenge. But for the investigator (e.g., Witryol & Fischer, 1960) who wants a typically effective, durable reinforcer, to support the behavior of most children over long or repeated sessions while studying other variables (like discrimination or scheduling), there is no simple, satisfactory answer. Obviously, the deprivation procedures of animal experimentation cannot be applied, and strong aversive stimulation such as electric shock is inappropriate. Hence, two aspects of child operant research deserve discussion: the development of distinctive procedures yielding reinforcing stimuli adequate for protracted study, and specific reinforcers used in typical studies to date.

## The Development of Durable Reinforcers

In $S$s old enough to have an adequate reinforcement history for it, money in adequate denominations is probably the most durable reinforcer for experimental use. However, young children are inclined to respond to money essentially as to tokens. For dealing with children of all ages, however, it would seem that candy is probably the most available, universal, and durable reinforcer. Modern business technology has even supplied brightly colored M & Ms which will not melt in $S$'s hand but in his mouth. Hersheyettes and other common candies are also useful. However, there are two serious drawbacks. One is the growing concern of parents and school administrators over the effects of candy on tooth decay, which in some children results in the development of a history of conditioning to refuse candy. A second drawback is that although it is generally known that children will eat candy when they will not eat other food, candy is not insensitive to satiation. This occurs more quickly in children than in adults, due in part to the frequent feeding of children. It is difficult to find a child who is more than two hours away from his last feeding; it is virtually impossible to find a nursery school child who is.

One solution to the problem of satiation for candy (and for other reinforcers suitable for children) is the use of what Ferster and Skinner call "percentage" reinforcement (1957, p. 67). In this procedure some kind of conditioned reinforcer is introduced between primary reinforcers on an increasing VR schedule. Practically all experimental setups contain a certain number of cues on reinforcement occasions in addition to the reinforcer itself, such as the dispenser noise or deliberately added lights, buzzers, or tone (momentary room darkening is a favorite).

Percentage reinforcement involves the continued use of these cues *without the reinforcer* on an increasing percentage of response occasions ordinarily scheduled for reinforcement. Clearly, this involves a use of secondary reinforcers built up within the the experimental situation and kept from extinguishing by a certain percentage of reinforcement by the ultimate reinforcing stimulus.

In addition, the technique makes increasingly sparing use of the ultimate reinforcer, thus decreasing the rate of satiation. A procedure of this kind was mentioned by Keller and Schoenfeld (1950, p. 246), who described the general procedures as a "tempting" possibility but could find no data to support it at the time of their writing. Bijou (1958a) has since applied this technique to children, using trinkets as the ultimate reinforcer, but eventually presenting the trinket on about one third of the scheduled reinforcement occasions. On the other occasions (as well as on trinket occasions) the child receives only the motor noise of the reinforcement dispenser (which, in itself, has slight if any reinforcement value for most children). If the reduction in percentage of reinforcement occasions which produces a trinket is gradual, the method produces more behavior for the reinforcer than does dispensing it on every reinforcement occasion and more than a similar schedule of trinkets without the additional motor noises.

A variation of this technique, used by Bijou (unpublished data) and by Lovaas (1961a), allows the child to choose one toy from an array of attractive items. The selected toy is locked in a transparent box which can be seen throughout the experiment. The child is told that the toy will be his when he opens the box. He is shown that the box may be opened by dropping tokens in a tube projecting from the box. The number of tokens required to open the plastic box may be varied. Preliminary shaping of the routine is helpful in ensuring that the child can respond to the contingency and in establishing a VR schedule of token insertion for box opening. With this arrangement the tokens can support a considerable amount of nonverbal behavior such as bar pressing, or verbal behavior of a given class.

Ferster and DeMyer (1961) report another variation of percentage reinforcement which also requires shaping. In their experimental situation the child obtains coins or tokens by operating a switch or performing on a matching-to-sample task. The coins may have little intrinsic reinforcement value for some children but are used to obtain candy and other reinforcers from coin-operated dispensers. The machines work, however, only when signal lights are on; hence, coins inserted when the lights are off are wasted. This discrimination must be established first; then by keeping the signal lights off for an increasing percentage of the time, the child, in effect, is put on a percentage schedule. Thus, the reinforcer dispensed by the machine is used more sparingly, and increasingly long segments of behavior uninterrupted by reinforcer-consumption result.

Ferster and DeMyer also describe a "generalized reinforcer" which sustains substantial amounts of behavior over long periods. This was achieved by having a large number of reinforcement-dispensing devices in the room, all of which were operated by the coin given as reinforcement. Included were a vending machine with eight kinds of food, candy, toys, or trinkets to be chosen by coin insertion; a pigeon in a transparent box who performed for 30 seconds; a pinball machine simulating a baseball game and giving two balls to play; a phonograph playing children's music for 30 seconds; a color-wheel giving a kaleidoscopic display for 30 seconds; a portable electric organ which the child could play for 30 seconds; and a vending machine dispensing a one-ounce container of milk or juice.

> Such a conditioned generalized reinforcer has the advantage that it derives its reinforcing effect from other reinforcers which are effective under various kinds of deprivation. Should the level of deprivation in respect to several of the specific reinforcements used in the experiments be low, the generalized reinforcer would continue to maintain behavior through the remaining devices which might be relevant to current deprivations. If the number of reinforcing devices were large enough so that at least some of these would be reinforcing for each subject, the same experimental room could be used for a number of subjects. There is also the possibility that the generalized reinforcer may have its effect by the sum of the specific reinforcers (pp. 315-316).

Some of the studies with normal and retarded children at the University of Washington Developmental Psychology Laboratory have combined percentage and generalized reinforcement in experiments requiring long sessions. The technique involves dispensing two kinds of tokens, white and red. At first the red tokens are dispensed exclusively. Later they are dispensed less frequently with white tokens filling the time gaps. The child can "cash in" the red tokens at the end of the session for any of a variety of reinforcers offered to him then: toys, candies, trinkets, mechanical and electrical games, etc. Hence, the red token is a generalized reinforcer given on a percentage basis, and the white token is a tangible conditioned reinforcer. The white token cannot be traded for other reinforcers, but serves to inform the child that his behavior is of the reinforcible kind; and as such the white token acts as a stabilizing stimulus. One advantage of this procedure is that the session is not interrupted with reinforcer-consumption; the red tokens serve as reinforcement until the end of the session.

Other approaches to the development of a durable reinforcing stimulus have concentrated upon enhancing the "game" or "toy" aspects of the stimulus situation. In addition to decorated operanda, complex toys have been modified for experimental control and offered as reinforcers: animated dolls, electric trains, mechanical animals, movies, tape recordings of music or stories, etc. Some of these will be discussed later in this section.

### Specific Examples of Reinforcers Developed for Children

The following examples will illustrate a number of the stimuli which have been developed for experimental use as reinforcers for children and some of their possible contingencies. The discussion will follow this order:

1. Positive reinforcers produced by a response
2. Positive reinforcers lost or withdrawn by a response
3. Negative reinforcers produced by a response
4. Negative reinforcers escaped or avoided by a response

### Positive Reinforcers Produced by a Response

The most common experimental situation with children involves the presentation of positive reinforcers. Consequently, there exists a relative wealth of such studies in the literature. Such popularity probably stems from the fact that sensitivity to stimulus consequences is one basic criterion for establishing a response as an operant and that presentation of positive reinforcers is the most acceptable reinforcement operation to apply to children.

Bijou and Sturges (1959) classify these stimuli as consumable and/or manipulable. Consumables include candy (M & M's, gumdrops, "Little Gems," mints, small Hershey bars, jelly beans, corn candy, sour balls, Tootsie Rolls); other foods (raisins, currants, peanuts, cookies, and honey); and liquids (milk and fruit juices), which are, naturally, dispensed in sanitary, water-tight containers. (One way to accomplish percentage reinforcement is to schedule a certain number of empty containers on reinforcement occasions.)

Manipulable objects, which are typically less powerful as reinforcers, include dime-store toys; plastic trinkets or "charms" (of the sort dispensed by gumball machines); stuffed animals (teddy bears, etc.); pictures or "stickers" of animals, birds, and toys. Also included are mechanized toys with interesting routines, made available for watching rather than given as gifts. The use of action toys allows an increasing wealth of choice, as toy shops currently stock a great variety of mechanized toys, many of which are electrical and can be run on the rectified voltage from filament transformers with minimal filtering. Remote experimental control is readily accomplished.

Bijou and Sturges offer the following practical recommendations: (1) Before dispensing reinforcers to children, it is expedient to check with parents and/or custodians on their acceptability. *E* should not be surprised to enocunter vehement opposition, on occasion, to candy, electrical devices, toys that seem "aggressive," trinkets, religious symbols, and devices of somewhat ribald humor. Occasionally a parent will respond to the sanitary properties of experimentally dispensed consumable reinforcers. (2) It is often efficient to investigate the suitability of the intended experimental reinforcers for the age and economic class of the *S*s prior to conducting the main study. (3) Precise control over the delivering of reinforcers should be attempted. (4) A complete description of the method of delivery and the nature of the reinforcers should be given. Commercially available reinforcers are preferred over homemade ones, as they facilitate replication.

Now we turn to studies involving social reinforcement. This requires more exploration than was given to toys and edibles, since these procedures and stimuli require more engineering. An excellent analysis of the problems involved in social reinforcement is given by Gewirtz (1961).

A technique of social reinforcement applicable to three-month-old *S*s will be recalled from studies by Rheingold, Gewirtz, and Ross (1959) and Weisberg (1963). Brackbill's (1958) reinforcement of smiling in four-month-old infants is relevant here, and has been described previously (p. 742 ff). As soon as the infant smiled, *E* smiled in return, and began to speak softly to the infant, and picked it up. The baby was then held, jostled, patted, and "talked to" for 30 seconds before being replaced in the crib. The reinforcement procedure was recorded on 12 feet of color film and filed with the American Documentation Institute (Washington, D.C.).

Gewirtz and Baer have published two studies in which social stimuli served as reinforcers (1958a; 1958b). The child sat before a toy containing two holes in which marbles could be dropped. One of these responses was chosen for reinforcement.

> The reinforcer, designed to appeal primarily to the concept of approval, consisted most frequently of the word "Good!" and less frequently of such phrases as "Hm-hmm," "Good one!" "That's a good one!" and "Fine!" These reinforcers were delivered by *E* in a casual manner, according to a schedule incorporating four successive fixed ratios. . . (1958a, p. 50).

The schedule began with continuous reinforcement and progressed through FR 2 and FR 3 to FR 5, unless *S* made as many as five consecutive incorrect responses, in which case a retreat was made briefly to a lower ratio. Since the reinforcing stimulus was produced by an adult cognizant of the meaning of possible results, the adult was observed throughout the experiment and judged as properly standardized in his or her behavior by observers behind a one-way mirror. Similar use of social reinforcement has been made by Walters and Ray (1960), and Zigler, Hodgden, and Stevenson (1958).

Baer (1962b) studied social reinforcement in children by using a mechanized talking puppet. The puppet had an articulated jaw which could move in correlation with his "talking." It could also attend to (look at) the child or ignore the child, press a miniature bar, and deliver trinket or candy reinforcers (see Figure 13). *E* watched from behind a one-way mirror, spoke through the puppet, and programmed various contingencies. Preliminary work indicated that some of the stimuli produced by the puppet, such as his attention and verbal approval, functioned as social reinforcers for the children in that situation. The findings correlated well with judgments about the effectiveness of similar stimuli in other situations, such as nursery school.

There are at least two advantages of a talking puppet over a talking adult. One is the ease of standardizing the stimulus output of the puppet. Considering the variety and subtlety of stimuli which may function as social

Figure 13. An animated, talking puppet for studies of social reinforcement with young children. (From Baer, 1962b.)

reinforcers (nods, smiles, raised eyebrows, winces, and other facial expressions), it is important to ensure that only controlled delivery of such stimuli takes place. An adult may require considerable practice before achieving satisfactory uniformity in the output of social stimuli. The other advantage lies in the less forbidding aspect of an interaction with a puppet, as opposed to one with a relatively strange adult. Response to the puppet's social reinforcement develops more rapidly. However, it remains to be seen how fully these two advantages can be realized.

We close our discussion of this topic, positive reinforcers produced by a response, with a description of a series of studies in which social reinforcement was made contingent upon certain desirable responses of normal preschool children. All of these investigations were conducted in the natural setting of a university nursery school. Basically the procedures consisted of: (1) obtaining a baseline over several days; (2) observing changes in behavior under conditions of administering social reinforcement contingent upon the desired behavior, and withholding social reinforcement following the undesired behavior; and (3) reversing the contingencies once or perhaps twice. The data were gathered by a trained observer, with a second observer added from time to time to check on reliability. The reinforcers (social nearness, praise, support, encouragement, and the like) were administered by a trained teacher assigned to the task. In one study, a three-year-old girl, who persisted in crawling despite the fact that she had developed walking behavior in the usual manner, was reinforced for standing, walking, and running (Harris, Johnston, Kelley, & Wolf, 1964). After she had engaged in behaviors in upright positions for one week, the baseline conditions were reinstituted. Crawling behavior reappeared in high strength. "On-feet" behavior was again systematically reinforced while "off-feet" behavior was not. Again activities involving upright behavior occurred in high frequency. These contingencies were reversed again with the same results. The last phase of the study involved reinforcing on-feet behavior on a continuous and then an intermittent schedule. The same procedures were employed to weaken isolate play and strengthen group play in a four-year-old girl (Allen, Hart, Buell, Harris, & Wolf, 1964). They were also used to decrease the frequency of operant crying and to increase the occurrences of more acceptable verbal behavior in two four-year-old boys (Hart, Allen, Buell, Harris, & Wolf, 1964). These studies, together with three others involving another case of strengthening group play behavior in a three-year-old boy, heightening vigorous play behavior in a three-year-old boy, and increasing the verbal output of a four-year-old girl, were reported and analyzed by Baer, Harris, and Wolf (1963).

### Positive Reinforcers Lost or Withdrawn by a Response

The removal of a positive reinforcer from the possession of a child, contingent upon his response, has received little attention, probably because of the reluctance of many investigators to take candy from a near-baby. Nevertheless, the process deserves study.

Baer (1961) used movie cartoons as an ongoing state of positive reinforcement which could be terminated or withdrawn, contingent upon a response. Previous work had shown that these cartoons were excellent reinforcers for the great majority of young children (Baer, 1960), in that Ss would consistently press a bar to return them when withdrawn. The cartoons were of the Woody Woodpecker sort, and were shown on a Busch Cinesalesman, a 16 mm movie projector with built-in screen and sound system. This apparatus is particularly suitable as it never requires rewinding and can use "endless" reels of film which can be run over and over again indefinitely without pause. Withdrawal of the cartoons was accomplished by automatically flipping a shield over the lens and opening loudspeaker circuit. (It proved impractical to stop the film cleanly and repeatedly.) Ss were first taught a bar-pressing response for peanut reinforcement. After such training one group was extinguished and punished by the withdrawal of the cartoons for two seconds, contingent upon every bar-pressing response. Subsequent sessions with and without cartoons (but without peanuts or punishment) showed maintenance of the response-weakening effect in the punished group and the usual spontaneous recoveries in the other group. This is shown in Figure 14.

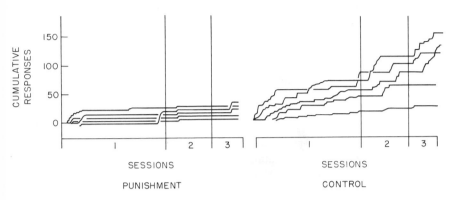

Figure 14. Individual response curves of Ss undergoing punishment in Session 1 (withdrawal of positive reinforcement) during extinction of a bar-pressing response, compared to Ss not being punishing. (From Baer, 1961.)

A similar application of cartoon withdrawal was made to the thumb-sucking response of three preschool boys (Baer, 1962a). It was shown that thumb-sucking was weakened by withdrawing the cartoons as long as S had his thumb in his mouth, but the response recovered quickly during periods of no withdrawal or withdrawal not contingent upon thumb-sucking (see p. 751 f).

Cartoons are not convenient for reinforcing behavior for a few seconds at a time, contingent upon responding. Unless a continuous schedule of reinforcement is used, only scattered and disjointed bits of the cartoons are seen, since the projector continues to run film even if the picture is not projected. Such discontinuity detracts somewhat from its reinforcing value. (Some of this difficulty might be avoided by the use of taped music developed by Jeffrey [1955]. Children listen to the music through earphones, which probably enhances its reinforcing value. There is the problem, however, of rapid satiation.) An alternative to continuous reinforcement would be percentage reinforcement, where the reinforcer may be tokens which, at the end of the session, would be used by the child to run the projector continuously through one or more cartoons.

### Negative Reinforcers Produced by a Response

As would be expected, there is a scarcity of research dealing with punishment in children through the presentation of a negative reinforcer. The major emphasis has been an auditory stimuli. As mentioned previously, Flanagan, Goldiamond, and Azrin (1958; 1959) used a 6000-cycle tone at 105 db, delivered through earphones, contingent upon stuttering in Ss 15 years of age and older. It is probably the hesitancy of Es to use intense stimuli, rather than the suitability of the technique, which will determine the lower age limits to which this method will be extended.

Tyler (1960) utilized a pair of heavy-duty relays in a flip-flop circuit which produced a loud and rapid clatter. Ss were taught a discrimination, some with the relay clatter used as a consequence of $S^\Delta$ responding, some with a mild tone used in the same role, and some with no added stimulus consequences of $S^\Delta$ responding. For some Ss, the relay clatter served as a punishing stimulus in the acquisition of the discrimination, and in the maintenance of the discrimination under extinction procedures with both relay and positive reinforcement absent. Other Ss responded to the clatter as a positive reinforcer.

Young (unpublished data) has done some preliminary work on the presentation of negative social reinforcement contingent upon preferences for colors. The Ss were preschoolers; the response was filling in outlined patterns with chips of colored wood. The task was much like putting together a picture puzzle, except that there were many identical pieces in piles of four different colors. Young obtained baselines of color preference over several blocks of responses, and then negatively reinforced a preferred color by saying, "No," "No no," "Uh-uhh," whenever the child picked up a piece of that color. Without exception, the first delivery of negative reinforcement stopped ongoing behavior. Subsequently, the further use of the disapproved color markedly decreased in most Ss. There were a few children who were less sensitive to disapproval as trials progressed. No doubt, children could be found who would respond to this stimulus as positive reinforcement.

### Negative Reinforcers Escaped or Avoided by a Response

Most avoidance situations present S with a negative reinforcer which he must endure until the "correct" response is made. For this reason it is, again, a difficult technique to engineer with children. Two compromises are possible: (1) the use of sufficiently mild stimuli or limited durations of more intense stimuli, and (2) the use of withdrawal of positive reinforcement as the punishing event which can be avoided.

The Robinsons (1961) exemplify the first procedure in their use of a 50 db, 2300-cycle tone lasting up to ten seconds and programmed as an interruption of an ongoing tape recording of music and stories. Light cues were given 1.5 seconds prior to the onset of the noise, and a plunger-pulling response would avoid the noise (or, if late, would turn it off). However, the Robinsons point out that the noise alone would not support avoidance behavior in nursery school children. Complex instructions were required. It is quite possible that they added negative social reinforcement value to the noise.

Baer (1960) has used the withdrawal of movie cartoons as a negatively reinforcing event which could be escaped and/or avoided by a bar-pressing response. The movies were withdrawn after a three-second (or five- or ten-second) interval, and could be re-presented only by a bar press. In one schedule, any bar press served to delay the next withdrawal for three (or five or ten) seconds. $S$ could never be more than three (or five or ten) seconds away from the next withdrawal. In another schedule any response served to add three seconds to the interval between that response and the next scheduled withdrawal, so that time could be "saved up" by responding and $S$ could be several minutes away from the next withdrawal. (This is a minor variation on Sidman's "escalator" schedule. See Chapter 10 in this book.)

Under the first schedule practically all children showed highly consistent, precise, and durable "escape" responding, escaping from the withdrawal condition by reacting immediately as the cartoons went off. A few showed some tendency to develop additional responses which would avoid the next withdrawal for some time, but these patterns were not consistent and tended to disappear in the course of a dozen sessions. Using the escalator schedule, however, many children of preschool age showed response patterns which maintained the cartoons uninterruptedly for increasingly long periods; a few children developed quite efficient rates of response which prevented all but a few of the scheduled interruptions during a half-hour session.

In an extension of this technique to social reinforcement, Baer (1962b) made the attention of a mechanized talking puppet contingent upon bar pressing which avoided its withdrawal (see Figure 13). Again, the escalator schedule was used, with a three-second interval. (That is, any response added three seconds to the interval between the response and the next scheduled withdrawal of attention.) The quickness with which preschool $S$s learned to avoid the withdrawal of the puppet's attention, and their efficiency in maintaining the attention, correlated well with ratings of attention-seeking tendencies in the nursery school setting.

## DISCRIMINATION PROCEDURES, DISCRIMINATIVE STIMULI, AND SECONDARY REINFORCEMENT

Operant discrimination serves as an organizing section in this chapter because it is conceived of as a basic process in children's behavior, and because of its role in general behavior theory. The study of discriminative processes in children has generated a number of distinctive procedures. Occasionally it is simply the choice of the discriminative stimulus itself, rather than the discrimination process in which it functions, which deserves attention. And since an equation is usually made between discriminative stimuli and secondary reinforcers, the few studies of secondary reinforcement in children involve discrimination procedures as an essential ingredient. Hence the tripartite nature of this section.

## Discrimination Procedures

Most studies of the discriminative process in children use ordinary discriminative stimuli and focus attention on reinforcement and extinction contingencies. Many of these arrangements are an almost literal translation of animal discrimination procedures. Indeed, a great number of studies employ techniques which reflect common Y- and T-maze situations, which are in effect variations on restricted operant procedures. (See Spiker, 1960, for a review of literature involving such techniques.) The restricted operant multiple-choice situations have many advantages such as simplicity, ease of instrumentation, economy of operation, and little or no preliminary training. Furthermore, these devices are often thought to resemble common learning situations in school and other aspects of everyday life.

The restricted operant multiple-choice techniques have a number of disadvantages, when compared to a free operant situation. One is the lack of sensitivity to slight changes in the controlling variables (probably due to the spaced and inflexible response rate involved). Another is the difficulty of examining the strength of one of the responses except as relative to the others. That is, the child can respond to either of, say, two stimuli, $S^D$ or $S^\Delta$. He makes either an $S^D$ or $S^\Delta$ response on discrete occasions, and his score is the relative proportion of $S^D$ responses to $S^\Delta$ responses over a block of responses. As soon as $S^D$ responding has increased in strength sufficiently, $S^\Delta$ responses disappear; but it is possible that $S^\Delta$ responses have not extinguished completely. There may still be responses to $S^\Delta$, but stronger responses to $S^D$ are prepotent. Furthermore, since the child now does not respond further to $S^\Delta$, thorough extinction may be prevented by the adequate power of $S^D$ to control responding.

It is, of course, possible to examine the strength of $S^D$ and $S^\Delta$ responding separately in a two-choice situation, for example, by presenting only $S^\Delta$ on some trials, with the $S^D$ position empty or blank. However, this is a new stimulus situation in the child's training history, and results obtained by such a procedure are confounded by the novelty and/or ambiguity of the procedure.

Still another limitation of restricted operant multiple-choice discrimination techniques is the impression they produce (often unintentionally) that discrimination is a response in itself, which is strengthened or weakened as a unitary organization of behavior. Since responses to the two stimuli in a two-choice situation are typically not independently examined, the simpler processes underlying a discrimination cannot be brought out.

Some of these difficulties may be overcome by eliminating the restricted character of this operant situation, so as to allow a rapid and flexible response rate to both $S^D$ and $S^\Delta$. This was done by Gewirtz and Baer (1958a; 1958b) and Stevenson and Fahel (1961), in a situation in which the child dropped marbles down either of two holes (one $S^D$, the other $S^\Delta$) at a high rate. However, such methods merely allow for greater sensitivity in showing the rate at which $S^D$ responses increase in strength until they successfully compete with $S^\Delta$ responses. They do not reveal the strength of $S^D$ responding independently of $S^\Delta$ responding.

The combination of a free-operant and a multiple schedule has its virtues. In a multiple schedule there are two or more component schedules of reinforcement, each with its distinctive $S^D$. For the study of discrimination processes, it may be advantageous to use extinction as one of the schedule components (its $S^D$ thereby being properly labeled as $S^\Delta$), and any convenient reinforcement schedule (e.g., VI or VR) as another. $S^D$ and $S^\Delta$ periods are programmed in either regular or irregular alternations, and the response rate of a free operant can then serve as a measure of the ability of both $S^D$ and $S^\Delta$ to control the response. These measures are independent of each other, if taken as absolute rates; alternatively, rate under $S^\Delta$ can be expressed as a proportion of rate under $S^D$ if a relative measure is desired.

Bijou (1961) made a direct application of multiple scheduling to discrimination problems in young children. The multiple schedule consisted of two components, one a VR 50 schedule of reinforcement, with the illumination of an amber light on the left side of the response device as $S^D$; the other, extinction, with the illumination of a blue pilot light on the right side of the response device as $S^\Delta$. Stable discrimination developed in six or seven 20-minute sessions, spaced about a week apart. This is shown in Figure 15, curve A.

Also apparent in Figure 15 (curves B, C, and D) is the effect on the discrimination of a change in the experimental situation in which two switches were added that could be used by the child to turn off the $S^D$ and $S^\Delta$ lights. Turning off a light did not alter the contingencies associated with it; they remained in force for the time called for by the program. Responding during $S^D$ periods was greatly disrupted at first (curve B), but response during $S^\Delta$ remained virtually zero, testifying to the effectiveness of the extinction procedures inherent in this type of discrimination training. In the second session following the change (curve C), response during $S^D$ periods recovered its smoothness; in the third session (curve D), $S^D$ rate was even higher than at the beginning of stable discrimination (curve A). Bijou argued that such discrimination performance, with its distinctive pattern of response to $S^D$ and $S^\Delta$, is highly appropriate to the individual analysis of children, "since a clear functional relationship has been shown between a stable baseline performance and the introduction of a special stimulus condition" (p. 170).

The establishing of the discrimination, in this study as in others, was accomplished by an initial shaping and strengthening of the response in the continuous presence of the $S^D$. Subsequently $S^D$ was removed and $S^\Delta$ was presented, with extinction programmed. After a fixed time of extinction

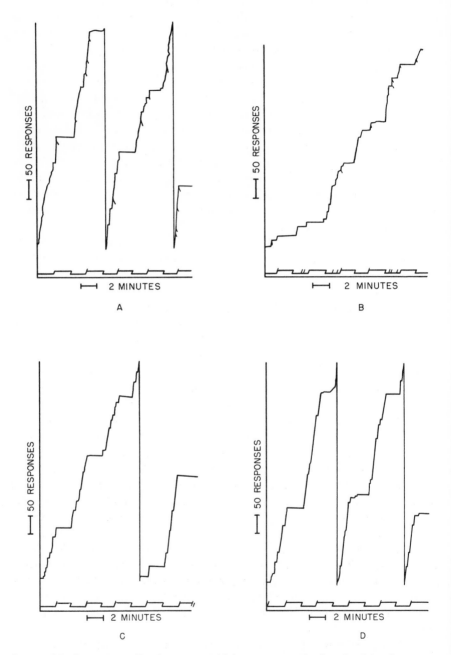

Figure 15. Response of a four-year-old boy to a multiple-schedule discrimination training procedure. Periods of VR 50 alternate regularly with extinction periods. In B, C, and D the effects of a new variable are shown. (From Bijou, 1961.)

under S$^\Delta$, the S$^D$ was re-presented and the response was again reinforced according to schedule. Thus, S$^D$ and S$^\Delta$ periods of standard lengths were alternated, the response being strengthened under S$^D$ and extinguished under S$^\Delta$. The discrimination was considered to have been acquired when response rate under S$^D$ exceeded a certain value, and/or response rate under S$^\Delta$ fell below a certain value, and/or S$^D$ rates exceeded S$^\Delta$ rates by a certain proportion.

With this technique many Ss achieved the discrimination criterion only after considerable training, probably because the initial shaping and strengthening of the response gave it considerable resistance to extinction, which the relatively short periods of S$^\Delta$ extinction did not diminish sufficiently to produce discriminated behavior. Through generalization, the frequently interspersed S$^D$ periods of reinforcement probably contribute too often and too much to response rates under S$^\Delta$, sometimes directly reinforcing these rates.

Bijou and Orlando, in a series of papers (Orlando & Bijou, 1960a; unpublished manuscript; Bijou & Orlando, 1961), have described a procedure which produced a rapid acquisition of multiple-schedule discrimination performance in retarded children. The technique involved manipulation of the relative lengths and distribution of S$^D$ and S$^\Delta$ periods, and considerable care to the specific steps in the initial shaping and strengthening of the response. Basically it consisted of a drl contingency between response during S$^\Delta$ and the presentation of the next S$^D$ period. That is, during S$^\Delta$, not only were all responses extinguished, but in addition any response served to delay the next presentation of S$^D$ for a certain number of seconds. Hence, the S$^\Delta$ extinction schedule remained in effect until the response was extinguished sufficiently to produce an interresponse interval, or pause, exceeding a certain time limit. Then S$^D$ was re-presented, and responding during the S$^D$ period was reinforced. With the next presentation of S$^\Delta$, the pattern was repeated. As S's behavior began to shape to the reinforcement contingencies, the length of pauses during S$^\Delta$ required for presentation of the S$^D$ was increased according to objective criteria, and the length of S$^D$ periods was also increased. (Initial S$^D$ periods terminated with the first response, which was always reinforced. Subsequently, S$^D$ periods were lengthened to half-minute, minute, and two-minute intervals, with FR, VR, FI, or VI schedules of reinforcement, which also were increased as the discrimination stabilized.)

An additional technique in the training program was an initial *rate evaluation* phase with a one-minute period of FI 15-second reinforcement in the presence of the stimulus to be established as the S$^D$. If S made fewer than 20 responses during this first minute, an additional minute was programmed. If no acceleration in rate was observed, use was made of ratio scheduling to increase rate, prior to any discrimination training. However, if S made 20 responses or more, S$^D$ was replaced by S$^\Delta$, the drl ("pause-building") contingency was put into effect, and discrimination training began. The authors state that

. . . if training on low rates of responding [to Sᐃ] is undertaken when the initial rate is low . . . extinction may develop. Hence, this stage includes operations designed to strengthen rate when required. On the other hand, if pause training is attempted when the initial rate is very high, pausing may require an excessive amount of time to develop and stabilize. The second function of the evaluation procedure, therefore, is to detect high rates as early as possible to avoid dispensing any more reinforcers than necessary (Bijou & Orlando, 1961, p. 10).

Figure 16 shows the results of this procedure on the performance of three retarded children. Sᴰ presentations are shown as offset portions of the lower timeline. Reasonably stable discriminations are shown by the second session.

From these curves it is possible to inspect in detail the simultaneous

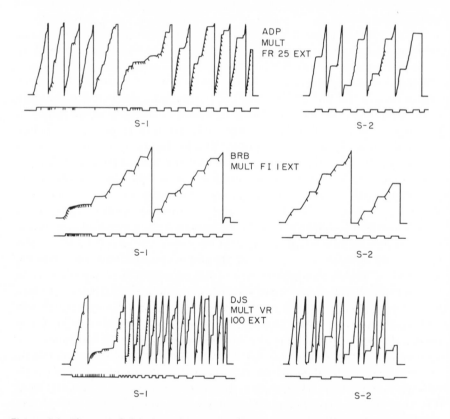

Figure 16. The rapid development of a multiple-schedule discrimination through the use of drl contingencies during extinction responding, as seen in three subjects. Sᴰ times correspond to offset portions of the lower timeline. Blips in the cumulative curves mark reinforcement occasions. Sessions are labeled S-1 or S-2 to indicate their sequence. (From Bijou & Orlando, 1961.)

strengthening of response to $S^D$ and weakening of response to $S^\Delta$; the strength of $S^D$ and $S^\Delta$ responses is seen independently *and* relatively; and an emphasis is achieved which defines discrimination as the result of several simpler concurrent response processes, rather than as a unitary process or unique response. Furthermore, this procedure focuses on the formation of the discriminated behavior, rather than concentrating on previously formed discriminations in the way that much of formal education does.

Orlando (1961a) analyzes the classical response pattern to fixed interval scheduling as a complex discrimination. The usual pattern of response after extensive fixed interval schedules of reinforcement is a low rate of responding, restricted mainly to moments just prior to the regularly spaced times when a response will be reinforced. Orlando suggests that there are, in fact, two component discriminations involved. "The first is the use of temporal interval as a discriminative stimulus and the second is withholding from responding in the presence of stimuli associated with non-reinforcement" (p. 615). A test of this hypothesis involved three discriminations, each considered simpler than, but relevant to, optimal fixed interval response: (1) The simplest discrimination was a two-choice situation in which $S$ had to discriminate the position of a stimulus light alternating between two locales. The alternations occurred randomly but on the average every 30 seconds. At each locale was a Lindsley operandum. Response to the plunger located by the light was reinforced (VI 10 seconds), and response to the other plunger was extinguished. This procedure was used as a screening device to eliminate $S$s lacking the behaviors which the discrimination involved. Two of 12 $S$s were eliminated. (2) The second problem was a simplification of fixed interval scheduling, involving a "crutch" which consisted of a buzzer-produced tone to mark the time when the response would be reinforced. Technically, this was a single-response, multiple crf extinction schedule, the extinction component having a 40-second duration. That is, every 40 seconds a buzzer would sound, whereupon the next response would be reinforced, and the buzzer would terminate. No responses would be reinforced until 40 seconds later, when the buzzer would sound again. Stable discrimination of this pattern of reinforcement indicated that $S$ could withhold responding when appropriate, apart from any discrimination of temporal stimuli. Eight of the ten $S$s screened made this discrimination. (3) The third problem was a standard FI 40-second schedule, identical to the second "crutch" problem except that there was no stimulus except for the passage of time to mark occasions when a response would be reinforced. This task involved not only the withholding of response, but the discrimination of temporal stimuli as well. The four $S$s who showed appropriate behavior under this fixed interval schedule were drawn at random from the eight who had solved the "crutch" problem.

Orlando analyzed discrimination behavior into simpler components in another study (1961b) involving a two-response situation. In this experimental situation, there were two Lindsley response devices, each on its own panel, and each with its own pair of red and blue $S^D$ lights. The program consisted of alternating two-minute periods, during which one panel would have a red light illuminated and the other, a blue. $S$ was reinforced for responding to the panel with the red light and extinguished for responding to the panel with the blue. The reinforcement schedule was developed to VR 100, and the discrimination was made so stable that a two-minute period of correct responding without reinforcement did not disturb the pattern of response. Then, after demonstration of the stability of the discrimination to periods of non-reinforcement, either the $S^D$ cue from the correct panel, or the $S^\Delta$ cue from the incorrect panel was eliminated for a two-minute period of non-reinforcement. $E$ was interested in seeing whether $S$ was responding to the panel *with* a red light, or to the panel *without* a blue light. Results indicated that one $S$ stably showed one pattern and two the other; none of the three $Ss$ tested showed both. "The method avoids the confounding effects of novelty in a restricted-operant ambiguous-cue technique and permits repeated measures on the same $Ss$" (pp. 160-161). Furthermore, it re-emphasizes one of the more basic corollaries of operant-respondent conditioning: the multiplicity of learning histories which can produce behaviors similar in appearance, and the consequent need for the experimental analysis of complex behaviors into the varieties of simpler components.

Long (1959b; 1962) has shown techniques for establishing multiple-schedule control in young children through the use of different kinds of reinforcers under two schedules. The experimental situation involved is described on p. 727. The behavior of his $Ss$ became discriminated to the schedule components, not only to the $S^D$s programmed with these schedule components, but also to the different reinforcements associated with each schedule.

The two-component schedules were FI and FR ranging between FI 1.5 FR 10, and FI 3 FR 10. Some children were reinforced with a penny plus a "highly valued trinket" under FR schedules, but with a "less valued trinket" alone under FI schedules. For other children, the reverse was true. Within two to four sessions the two procedures, which, incidentally, proved to be equally serviceable, produced consistent multiple control in ten $Ss$. Eight previous sessions using the same reinforcers (pennies and trinkets) uniformly under both schedules failed to produce stable multiple-schedule effects. In other words, the nature of the reinforcer seems to have been a cue to the next phase of the multiple schedule.

Long followed up this work with an extensive exploratory study of chained and tandem schedules on school children between four and seven years of age (1963). Trinkets and pennies served as reinforcers on chain drl FR, chain dro FR, chain FI FR, tand FI FR, and tand dro FR. (The dro schedule is one in which reinforcers are delivered for any behaviors *other* than the one reinforced during the other components of the schedule.

The initials stand for *differential reinforcement of other responses*. This schedule allows reinforcers to be delivered at the usual rate to the subject, but not contingent on previously reinforced behavior; thus it constitutes an extinction condition minimally different from the reinforcement conditions of the schedule.)

> Chain drl FR and chain dro FR schedules almost always produced strong schedule and stimulus control, but chain FI FR schedules rarely did if additional techniques were not used. Strong control was produced with chain FI FR schedules, however, if: (a) the FR component was increased in size; (b) schedule and stimulus control was first established with chain drl FR or chain dro FR schedules before shifting to the chain FI FR; or (c) an external clock was attached to the FI. Tand FI FR schedules never produced regular or repeatable patterns of responding when additional procedures were not used. Rate patterns resembling those of chain FI FR schedules were produced by tand FI FR schedules, however, if: (a) an external clock was attached to the FI component or (b) control was established by means of tand dro FR schedules before the tand FI FR was used. Stimulus control was found to be exercised by specific signal stimuli, change in stimuli, and schedule order (Long, 1963, p. 459).

Stoddard (1962) studied timing behavior per se in children two to ten years of age by means of drl schedules. The *S*s were required to wait at least 10 (or 20) seconds between responses; otherwise responses went unreinforced. *S*s who attended a median of 20 sessions were also observed under conditions of VI and multiple schedules. All *S*s learned to make appropriately spaced responses under the drl contingency. Stoddard concluded: "The processes by which children discriminate time intervals, such as the mediating function of collateral behavior patterns, can be studied systematically" (p. 143).

### Discriminative Stimuli

In most studies of discrimination, the stimuli serving as $S^D$ or $S^\Delta$ are of the types convenient for laboratory work: pilot lights, illuminated panels, room lights, buzzers, relay clicks, tones from audio-oscillators, pictures, or projected slides, etc. (see, for example, Lane & Curran, 1963; Risley, 1964). Ordinarily the choice of the stimuli follows from considerations of simplicity and economy, coupled with the importance of presenting a stimulus display as obvious as possible. (Exceptions to this are the situations in which *S*'s current ability to respond to minimal stimulation is of interest, as in threshold determinations.) Although important from a systematic point of view, there is little in the work of this sort which requires discussion here. There are, however, a few problems which merit discussion because they pose technical or procedural difficulties or because they deal with particularly interesting or unusual $S^D$s.

### Technical Procedures

A common problem in the programming of discriminative stimuli is the discovery that unwanted stimuli are systematically presented on $S^D$ or $S^\Delta$ occasions. This may be especially common in child research, where the physical limitations of the usual laboratory make it difficult to insulate the child completely from the controlling apparatus. A frequent discovery is that the child is responding not to a visual $S^D$ but rather to an audible relay click from the programmer which also marks stimulus changes. Techniques to counter this possibility range from better sound insulation of the child and/or the relay to the introduction of masking noises in the child's room. A simple method for accomplishing the latter is to set aside an interval programmer with a short interval VI tape running a relay. This device programs a random series of clicks for the child, which are indiscriminable from the other relay clicks emanating from the control apparatus, and thus may rob all such noises of their discriminative possibilities.

Occasionally an $E$ who wishes to use visual stimuli will find it necessary to ensure that $S$ attends to the stimuli, especially when weak reinforcing stimuli are used. Two simple options are available. One is to make the visual display extremely obvious—for example, by using changes in the room illumination as the $S^D$ or by using so large an illuminated panel that changes can be seen from most angles of visual regard. Another method is to use an auditory stimulus to mark visual stimulus changes. If the child is not looking at the visual display at the moment of change, a click or buzz serves as an additional $S^D$ marking stimulus changes and often will cause the child to look back immediately at the stimulus display. This procedure, however, can establish the auditory stimulus as functional in place of the visual stimulus. To avoid this the auditory "warning" stimulus can be programmed occasionally during $S^D$ periods as well as whenever $S^D$s change.

Several devices are available commercially which simplify the devising and presentation of complex discriminative stimuli. One of these, distributed by Grason-Stadler and Foringer, and used by Ferster, Levitt, Zimmerman, and Brady (1961), is the Miniature Display unit which contains 12 different stimuli, any one of which can be selected for display on the screen of the unit. Selection and change are immediately accomplished through proper switching. There are a great variety of stimulus patterns (letters, numbers, geometric figures, etc.) available for it, and any special stimuli can be made to order by the manufacturer. Another device, and one more flexible, is the projector-programmer, a 35 mm slide projector which accomplishes both $S^D$ presentation and programming through holes punched on the slides which control photo-electric sensing units (Hively, 1962; Holland, 1963).

### Interesting Discriminative Stimuli

A stimulus may be "interesting," in this context, for one of several reasons. It may represent a stimulus of systematic significance in behavior theory (e.g., frustration); it may be a stimulus that, at first glance, would seem difficult to translate in the laboratory (e.g., social stimuli); it may be a stimulus frequently encountered in real-life situations (e.g., aggression); or it may be a stimulus, varied over a wide dimension, that has potential significance for a technology of education (e.g., conceptual stimuli, such as "mirror images"). The studies which follow exemplify responses with one or more of these possibilities.

Lovaas (1961b) found that certain movie cartoons could serve as a device for presenting aggressive stimulus events of a wide variety and at a high rate to children. He used the Official Films' cartoon "Rassling Match," which "was cut to give an almost continual display of aggression (hitting, biting, etc.) inflicted by one human-like cartoon figure upon another" (p. 38). (The slight amount of cutting required is a comment on what is considered a suitable cartoon for children by film makers.) As a control condition, a non-aggressive film (Castle Films: "Bear Facts") was found and also edited to depict "three bear cubs and a mommy bear engaging in pleasant human-like play" (p. 38). These five-minute stimulus presentations were used between pre- and post-measures of aggressive responding, i.e., responding to make one animated doll strike another. Lovaas found an increase in responding in those $S$s exposed to symbolic aggressive stimuli.

In a similar study, Larder (1962) used the animated puppet developed by Baer (1962b; see also p. 757 f above) to tell either an aggressive or non-aggressive story to the child, again using the hitting dolls as a pre- and post-measure. The story was taped and played "through" the puppet, whose jaw was worked in coordination with the words so that he appeared to be telling the story. Her findings were that the group given the aggressive story tended to increase in aggressive responding to the dolls, while those children given the non-aggressive story tended to decrease or increase only slightly.

Baer (1962b) has made some preliminary use of the same puppet to provide social discriminative stimuli to preschool children. In one case, $S$ had been shown to be insensitive to the puppet's attention, which was designed to serve as a positive reinforcer. However, $S$ was brought to stable performance after the puppet, through conversation and demonstration, had made his attention discriminative for trinket-reinforcements which were effective for the child. In another case, the puppet pressed a miniature bar-pressing apparatus while giving social reinforcement to the child talking with him. On some occasions, especially when receiving positive social reinforcers from the puppet, the child developed a similar bar-pressing response, even though no reinforcement was programmed for it. Here the puppet's bar-pressing behavior provided a discriminative stimulus to the child.

Baer and Sherman (1964) made a study of such imitative responding by reinforcing children who imitated other responses by the puppet, such as head nodding, mouthing, and verbal nonsense-syllable chains. Children reinforced by approval from the puppet for such imitation also typically began imitating his bar-pressing behavior, although this response was never reinforced by the puppet. This generalized imitative bar pressing was sensitive to time-out or extinction procedures applied to the child's other behavior emitted in imitation of the puppet's responses.

Other studies of social discriminative stimulation are found in the work of Azrin and Lindsley (1956; see above, p. 738) and Cohen (1962). The latter provides a more elaborate use of social stimuli as discriminative for reinforcement contingencies. This study used two Ss working in adjoining rooms connected by a clear plexiglass window through which each could view the other under certain conditions (See Figure 17).

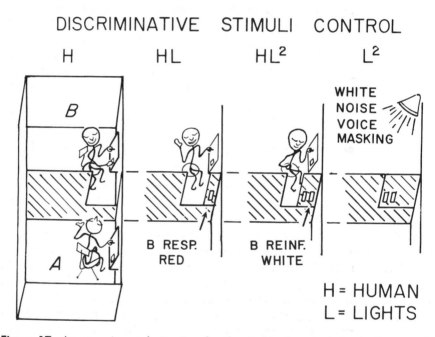

Figure 17. An experimental situation for the study of cooperative and competitive responding, using the behavior of another subject as discriminative stimuli. In the H condition, the discriminative stimuli are "human" only, produced by subject B; in the HL condition, a red light marks B's responses as well; in the HL$^2$ condition, a white light is added to mark B's reinforcement occasions; and in the L$^2$ condition, only the lights remain as discriminative stimuli. (From Cohen, 1962.)

An opaque sliding panel could be closed in several stages to block the plexiglass window. Mounted on each side of the panel were two lights which acted as mechanical stimuli. One light (red) flashed on when the person in the other room pulled his plunger; the other light (white) flashed on when he was reinforced. By successively sliding the panel it was possible to have only human stimuli (H), human stimuli and the response light (HL), human stimuli and both lights (HL$^2$), or the response and reinforcement lights alone (L$^2$) (pp. 699-700).

Cohen devised reinforcement contingencies which required discrimination by each $S$ of the other's responding, and he collected data in terms of individual and team responses. The latter required the participation of both $S$s. As individual A pulled his plunger, the movement was converted into a brief electric impulse. Similarly, B's response was converted into an electric impulse. Responses were divided into four groups: A followed by B (AB); B followed by A (BA); A followed by A (AA); B followed by B (BB). AB and BA were team responses; AA and BB were individual responses.

In order to facilitate the study of socially defined or team behavior the individual responses were mildly punished. The punishment for an AA consisted of A's room being darkened for two and one-half seconds during which a pure tone (500 cycles) was sounded through his speaker (see Ferster & Skinner, 1957, p. 35). When either A or B was being blacked out, no responses entered the sequence analyzer.

Cooperation was operationally defined as behavior in which both $S$s were involved and in which both were reinforced on a given trial. Competition was defined as behavior in which both $S$s were involved and only one was reinforced. That is, cooperation and competition were team responses differentiated on the basis of the reinforcement, or "pay-off" contingency.

One of the two $S$s was always Justin, a 13-year-old boy. The other was, from occasion to occasion, his mother, his brother (age 16), his sister (age 14), a close friend (age 13), or a stranger (age 14). Cohen's findings led him to conclude that "the close similarity between the experimentally measured patterns and the extra-experimental relationships as determined by questionnaires and interviews demonstrates that these experimental measures have high validity" (p. 717). The experimentally measured patterns referred to are findings that for a given pair of subjects, cooperation was more likely than competition, or that cooperation was frequent only when A led and B followed his lead, while for another pair (Justin and someone else), different relationships held.

Recently a series of studies have been concerned with programming complex auditory and visual stimuli for normal and deviant children. They might be viewed as interesting in that they deal with perceptual, conceptual, and "cognitive" processes and have implications for training, remediation, and psychotherapy. For example, Audrey L. Holland and Mathews (1963) evaluated the effectiveness of three programs for teaching discrimination of the "s" phoneme to children with defective "s" articulation in order to develop a machine suitable for presenting the programs. Their $S$s, normal children ranging in age from 8 to 11, were required to listen to tape recordings. Every time they heard an "s" they pushed a blue button, and every time they heard any other sound, they pressed a red button. In Program I they were required to discriminate isolated sounds spaced five seconds apart, then to discriminate the sound in words, then to identify the position of the sound within a word, and finally to discriminate correctly articulated from misarticulated sounds within a word. In Program II they were required to differentiate only between the "s" sound and other speech sounds when they were not embedded in phonetic context; and in Program III they were given training similar to that in Program I, except that the last phase—identifying the position of "s" within a word—was extended. They found Program I to be adequate in improving scores on the "s" discrimination test and concluded that techniques for the improving of "s" discrimination in children who misarticulate "s" are amenable to teaching-machine programming.

Another example is the work of Hively (1962). He studied concept formation in five- and six-year-old children by means of a two-choice, matching-to-sample technique (decribed on p. 770), employing visual material that differed systematically in shape, size, and color. On the basis of an analysis of errors he concluded that: (1) the difference between consecutive discriminations, and (2) the amount of training at each level of discrimination play a part in facilitating or retarding progress through the sequence. Still another illustration is the investigation by J. G. Holland (1963). Working with Long, he explored "inductive reasoning" by presenting a picture of a series of objects, uniform in size and shape, that differed in color and/or horizontal or vertical position. S's task was to select from five alternatives the pictures of the object which continued the series; in other words, the task was a variation of a non-verbal analogies test. The material was presented to children between the ages of six and nine and to institutionalized retarded Ss, by means of an automated matching-to-sample apparatus (see p. 770). The last example is the study by Bijou (Bijou & Baer, 1964), who used the apparatus and procedures of Holland and Long to program nonsense forms (all with right angles, straight lines, and identical areas). The forms were systematically modified and arranged to train young normals (three to six years of age) and institutionalized retarded children to discriminate patterns despite rotations in the vertical and horizontal planes.

Instructions to Ss, as a class of operations, might be considered discriminative stimuli. Ordinarily, it could be argued, instructions provide a complex set of stimuli which are discriminative for a correspondingly complex series of responses by the child. The details of these discriminated operants lie presumably in his history of conditioning to verbal stimuli and to the various social reinforcers implicit in most instructions. However, primarily because there are so few experiments which manipulate instructions as such (as is done with most discriminative stimuli) instructions will not be considered in this section but in the section on setting events.

## Secondary Reinforcement

Findings from the meager literature on secondary reinforcement processes in children largely mirror those from the more extensive literature on the same problem in animal behavior: the results are inconsistent in general, and the procedures show varying degrees of commitment to making the potential secondary reinforcer truly discriminative for reinforcement. The most frequent practice is to present the reinforcer-to-be on reinforcement occasions, with the hope that $S$ will discriminate it. If $E$ places any confidence in the equation of secondary reinforcers to stimuli having prior discriminative value, then it would seem reasonable that he present data showing that a stimulus did indeed have a discriminative function before testing it to determine its secondary reinforcing value.

Such guarantees are readily possible in the laboratory. In the usual paradigm, there is a dispenser for reinforcers (candy, money, etc.), and a hopefully neutral stimulus, the reinforcer-to-be, which can be presented on reinforcement occasions. (Elementary precautions will ascertain that the reinforcers, rather than $E$'s instructions, are effective for each $S$, and that the "neutral" stimulus is initially neutral for each $S$ and not either positively or negatively reinforcing.) A series of trials is instituted in which the stimulus is presented on some schedule in conjunction with, or briefly preceding, the reinforcer. This allows $E$ to observe $S$'s dispenser-approaching responses, and to note when they have become discriminated to stimulus occasions and extinguished to all other occasions. Given such observations, it may be concluded that the stimulus has a discriminative function, and that it is meaningful to test its reinforcing properties.

Since in this procedure it is essential to note some response coming under the discriminative control, the response should be one which is easily observable by $E$ and which does not occur all the time. Approach to the reinforcer-dispenser tray is usually convenient. The aspect of the approach response selected as the dependent variable should be other than mere looking at the chute, or standing by it, since such responses may occur continuously and may thus not become discriminated. It may be necessary to arrange the situation so that countable responses are highly probable. For example, one solution is to place a panel, which must be opened by $S$, over the tray; this has the advantage of being suitable for mechanical recording. Rate of door opening in the presence of the reinforcer-to-be, compared to rate of door opening in its absence, permits quantitative judgment of the discriminative function of the stimulus in question. Furthermore, it should be clearly demonstrated that it is the reinforcer-to-be which fills this discriminative function, and not some other stimulus like the hum of the dispenser or the rattle of the reinforcer falling down the chute.

Finally, much confusion can be avoided if the prospective secondary reinforcer is tested by making it a consequence of some new response, one having minimal resemblance to the dispenser-approaching response for which it is discriminative. If the new response is strengthened, it is more likely that the effect is due to the reinforcing function of the stimulus than to its discriminative function. That is, it is more likely that the stimulus strengthened the response that produced it than that it set the occasion for the response that followed it.

A study by Lambert, Lambert, and Watson (1953) on nursery school children is an example of an elaborate experimental situation within which both the discriminative and the reinforcing properties of the same stimulus may have operated on the dependent variable. The experiment employed the Solomon token-reward vendor (see Figure 7), a box with a crank which can be turned repeatedly, a chute from which tokens fall, a slot for the insertion of the tokens, and a second chute which deposits candy in a trough. One of the more complex procedures was as follows: The child turned the crank nine times, which produced a click followed by a red token; the red token was inserted in the slot, whereupon the handle was turned nine times again, producing a second click followed by a white token; the white token, when inserted in the slot, produced a different sound, and a piece of candy was dropped into the trough. During extinction of this sequence, the chain was broken in the following four places for four groups: (1) after the first nine turns (no red token was produced); (2) after the insertion of the red token (repeated turning produced another red token); (3) after the second nine turns (no white token was produced); and (4) after the insertion of the white token (no candy). It was found that the first and second groups resisted extinction longer than the third and fourth groups. The results might be attributed to the various secondarily reinforcing values of the stimuli in this chain, or to their varying resemblance to the training situation, since the response is the same in both cases (crank turning), or to the work involved in crank turning.

This experimental situation contains many possibilities for further investigation of discrimination and secondary reinforcement processes. However, it might be enhanced by adding two other features: (1) A door might be fitted over the reinforcer trough, which would have to be opened to obtain the reinforcers. This operandum would bring the final approach response under the discriminative control of preceding stimuli. (2) *Two* slots might be provided for token insertion, one for red and one for white. This situation would establish response differentiation to the tokens on the basis of color.

Myers (1960) performed a study with apparatus functionally similar to that of Lambert *et al.* It consisted of a clown face with red jewel-light eyes, a push-button nose and a slot-tray mouth.

When the nose of the clown was pressed, a token was delivered from the clown's mouth. The token was inserted in the ear of the clown, and the nose pressed again. This time a candy fell from the mouth. . . . Each child received either 10 or 20 conditioning trials, with either 50% or 100% token reinforcement, and 50% or 100% candy reinforcement, followed by 40 5-sec. extinction trials. . . . Groups receiving the token during extinction showed considerably greater resistance to extinction than did groups receiving no token. Furthermore, these token-in-extinction groups differed significantly in the number of responses in extinction from a control group which received tokens for nose-presses, but which had never received candy conditioning (pp. 178-179).

Thus Myers, like Lambert *et al.,* has shown that the token was discriminative (for an ear-insertion response which produced reinforcement), and in addition has controlled for the reinforcing value of the tokens per se. However, as in the work of Lambert *et al.,* the same response was used in training and extinction; hence, results may be attributed to the reinforcing and/or discriminative value of the tokens.

A more recent study by Myers, Craig, and Myers (1961) employed the same situation, with the addition of another push-button to the clown's face. Pushing one button produced a token; after token insertion, pushing the other button produced candy. During extinction more candy-button responses were made by groups receiving tokens; more token-button responses were made by the groups receiving nothing (extinction). Again, the discriminative function of the stimulus is confounded with its possible reinforcing function.

## SETTING FACTORS OR EVENTS

"Setting factors or events" is a term from Kantor's writings which serves to describe a large class of stimulus operations pertinent to both operant and respondent behavior.

Such setting factors as the hungry or satiated condition of the organism, its age, hygienic or toxic condition, as well as the presence or absence of certain environing objects, clearly influence the occurrence or non-occurrence of interbehavior or facilitate the occurrence of the activities in question in varying degrees (Kantor, 1959, p. 95).

These are the operations to which the term *motivation* has been so widely, loosely, and variously applied as to rob it of any consistent meaning. The concept of setting events helps to avoid most of this ambiguous connotation. Another advantage is that it encourages an initial description of operant behavior in terms of the reinforcement contingencies that control it. Setting events subsequently can account for variance in the effectiveness of reinforcing stimuli resulting from other stimulus operations, such as deprivation. Hence, most of the studies reviewed have been cited under concepts such as response, reinforcer, contingency, and discrimination. There remain only a few researches which need mentioning in this section: the major concern will be with the concept of deprivation; the rest of the section will deal briefly with instructions. This plan of treatment does not imply that the effect of instructions is slight. Very likely the opposite is true. Unfortunately, however, there exists little literature dealing with demonstrated effects of instruction.

## Deprivation, Satiation, and Sex-Membership

In an attempt to apply the concept of deprivation to the behavior of children for social reinforcers, Gewirtz and Baer (1958a) argued that

> . . . relevant stimuli (e.g., food, water) acquire maximal reinforcing value for an organism only subsequent to its recent deprivation of them. Other reinforcers of no apparent biological importance, like that provided by the opportunity to make a brief observation response, appear also to be raised in effectiveness following preceding periods of deprivation. In this context, it is a provocative question whether *social* reinforcers (those dispensed by people), postulated to possess reinforcing value through a history of conditioning, respond in a similar manner to deprivation (p. 49).

The method used to study this question involved a two-response marble game (previously described) and adult approval, contingent upon dropping marbles down one of two holes to accomplish response (hole) differentiation. The degree to which such differentiation took place (relative to operant level) was taken as a measure of the reinforcing strength of the adult's approval for the S on that occasion. For each S, there were two critical conditions. One, labeled a *non-deprivation* session, consisted of reinforcing the correct response for ten minutes, after establishment of the operant levels of the two responses, with no previous deprivation of S (at least, not by E). The other, designated a *social deprivation* condition, involved isolation accomplished as follows:

> On this occasion, when S (escorted by E) arrived at the experimental room, a familiar adult would appear to announce that the toy was "broken" and was "being fixed." S was given plausible assurance that the toy would be repaired "in a few minutes," and that since E wanted him not to miss his turn with the game, he might as well wait in the experimental room, since the adjoining "repair" room was clearly crowded. S was then left to wait alone without playthings in the experimental room with the door closed (or slightly ajar if he was more comfortable that way), while both adults retired to "repair" the toy. (During this process, occasional appropriate noises were emitted to indicate that repairs were progressing.) This procedure was carefully structured so as not to imply sanctions and appeared adequate to guard against the possibility that S might feel rejected. If S

poked his head out and asked to leave during the 20-minute isolation period, he was warmly reassured that the toy was "almost fixed," and he returned to the room. (This rarely occurred.) After 20 minutes, *E* returned with the "repaired" toy, and the game was played in the usual fashion (Gewirtz & Baer, 1958a, p. 50).

Under the non-deprivational condition, *S* began the game immediately upon his arrival at the experimental room from his nursery group.

This study has given rise to a rather large number of replications and elaborations. Some of these clearly were intended to reproduce the phenomena sensitive to this operation and analyze it further. Others were apparently aimed at demonstrating that the isolation procedures of Gewirtz and Baer were not essentially deprivation procedures but instead presented the child with discriminative stimuli, for punishment perhaps, or for especially powerful reinforcement of subsequent obedience or affiliation. (Thus, any increase in later behaviors by the child for social approval might be attributed to causes other than deprivation *per se,* according to such arguments.) At any rate, some of the replications did reproduce the same effects as Gewirtz and Baer had demonstrated; other failed to do so. It would seem likely that the operations for accomplishing the deprivation or satiation of social reinforcers for a child could hardly be so straightforward as those accomplishing the same operations for a lower organism with reinforcers like food or water. Consequently, we have reproduced the authors' description of these procedures in detail (and will do the same later in the case of their satiation procedures); it is likely in such research that differences in results will parallel rather detailed differences in procedures.

The effect of *this* deprivation operation was to accomplish a significantly greater strengthening of the approved marble-dropping response than was possible when *S* was not deprived. However, the effect was qualified by a significant relationship which also may be characterized as a setting event: an interaction between the condition of deprivation and cross-sex relationship of the child and *E*. Deprivation had consequences only with boys reinforced by a female *E,* and with girls reinforced by a male *E*. (Indeed, a male *E* appeared to lose effectiveness with boys after deprivation.)

A similar cross-sex pattern was found in a study by Gewirtz (1954) in which children's attention-seeking behavior to *E* was related to the sex of the child, the sex of *E,* and the availability of *E*. "High availability" meant that an adult was sitting near the child (who was engaged in easel painting) and attending to him continually. By contrast, "low availability" meant that an adult was maintaining some distance between himself and the child, i.e., busily engaged in paperwork and attending to the child only when addressed. As in the deprivation study, low availability of the adult showed its greatest effect in the increased attention-seeking behavior of the child when the unavailable adult was of the opposite sex. The similarity of the results in the two studies is seen in Figure 18.

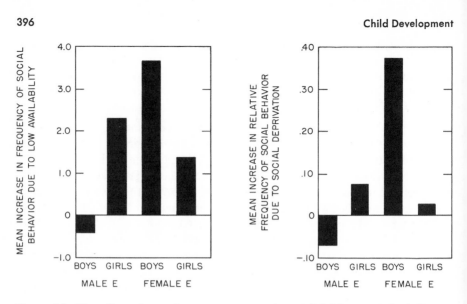

Figure 18. The effect of sex of experimenter and sex of child on social-reinforcer effectiveness in two studies by Gewirtz (1954) and Gewirtz and Baer (1958a). (From Gewirtz, Baer, & Roth, 1958.)

Reviewing the similarity of findings on cross-sex interaction, Gewirtz, Baer, and Roth (1958) argued that both social deprivation and low availability are experimental procedures which involve a simple dimension of the relative supply of social reinforcers. Hence availability of reinforcers might as well be labeled as a satiation-deprivation concept.

A second study by Gewirtz and Baer (1958b) replicated the deprivation and non-deprivation conditions, adding a satiation operation.

> . . . each of these $S$s was introduced to $E$ in the classroom by the teacher, but during the walk to the experimental room, $E$ maintained a very pleasant and interested attitude toward $S$, responding to all details of his comments and questions, asking questions to draw out more of $S$'s conversation, and generally approving of anything about $S$ which might reasonably be praised or admired. Upon reaching the experimental room, $E$ showed $S$ around the room, seated him, told him that the game was in use elsewhere and that she would go fetch it in a little while when it would be free. She suggested that meanwhile $S$ might like to draw pictures or cut out designs, and proferred the essential materials. Then for 20 minutes $S$ drew or cut out designs, while $E$ maintained a stream of friendly conversation with him, inducing him to talk about himself if he did not do so naturally. The $E$ alternated her praise and admiration of whatever $S$ did with whatever he said about himself, all in an appropriate fashion, and attempted to dispense 30 such reinforcers during the 20-minute satiation period at an approximate rate of three every two minutes (p. 166).

The game was played in the usual manner. $E$'s ability to accomplish response differentiation within the game, with her approval as a reinforcer, was minimal following satiation, intermediate following nondeprivation, and maximal following deprivation. Only a female *E* was used. Half the *S*s were boys; half were girls. No pattern involving the sex-membership of *E* or the *S*s emerged as statistically significant; however, satiation seemed to have appreciably more effect on girls than on boys.

A different approach to the concept of deprivation as a setting event is exemplified in the work of Stevenson and Fahel (1961) and Zigler, Hodgden, and Stevenson (1958). In these studies deprivation is considered as a long-term operation, or as a complex series of operations over a long period. Procedures are more or less similar to those of Gewirtz and Baer in testing the effectiveness of social stimuli as reinforcers, and the patterns of results generally agree (not always, see Stevenson & Fahel, 1963) in showing that institutionalized children are more sensitive to social reinforcement than non-institutionalized children. Subsequently, Zigler (1961) has argued that histories of institutionalization may be considered not simply as long-term deprivational conditions, but rather as histories establishing behaviors discriminated to the presence or absence of adults.

Still another study relevant to a deprivation-satiation dimension is by Stevenson and Odom (1961). They show that children with a pre-session of playing with tops differ from controls, on a bar-pressing response reinforced by pictures of animals. Here the similarity between the stimuli of the pre-session and of the test are rather different. The generalization of the effects of satiation has not been explored.

### Instructions

Only one study will be cited in which instructions were manipulated in a free-operant situation. This is the one by Walters and Ray (1960), in which two sets of preliminary instructions were administered, prior to a marble-game test of the effectiveness of adult approval as a reinforcer (similar to the Gewirtz and Baer method). In one procedure,

> The assistant knocked on the classroom door and unless the teacher answered, asked for the teacher by name. By prior arrangement the teacher called *S* to the door and said, "I want you to go with this man." The assistant then said to *S*: "Come with me into the next building." He did not introduce himself or explain why *S* was being taken out of the class. He initiated no conversation, answered *S*'s questions in a brief, aloof manner, and deliberately avoided giving any information about the nature of the experiment. . . . *S* was brought to the outer of two adjoining rooms and told:
> "We have something for you to do, but we are not ready yet. You wait in this room until we fix the machine. You sit here (indicating an adult-size chair), and I shall be back for you in a little while when the machine

is ready. Do not touch anything in the room and do not leave the room until I come for you" (p. 360).

In the other procedure, the school secretary brought $S$ to the experimental room, in a friendly and relaxed manner, and introduced him to the $E$, saying:

This is a friend of mine, Mr. Ray. I want you to play a game with him, but I'm afraid the game is broken right now. I do not want you to miss your turn, so why don't you wait in this room (indicating the adjoining room) while we fix it. It won't take long. You can sit here (indicating a child-size chair), and Mr. Ray will call you as soon as the game is ready. Be a good boy and don't come out until you are called (p. 360).

After these instructions were given, some children experienced a 20-minute period of isolation. Others were handled in the same two ways, but with the instructions tailored to avoid any reference to a delay while the machine was being "fixed," and played the game immediately.

The first set of instructions produced a greater sensitivity to $E$'s approval than the second, whether followed by deprivation (isolation) or not. (However, deprivation is probably not critical in this study, because one of the setting events is the similarity of sex-membership of $E$ and $S$s. This is the sex-by-sex condition which Gewirtz and Baer found to be insensitive to the effects of deprivation.)

It seems clear that if differences in instructions such as these can produce significant statistical differences, then many of the instructions in child studies are probably at least equally effective in contributing to differences in performances. One program of research awaiting intensive investigation concerns the role of instructions in providing social reinforcement to individual $S$s in a manner which differs from that intended by $E$.

Some examples of instructions which seem likely to contain surplus social reinforcement for the behavior observed are listed here:

1. Each $S$ was told to push the button-nose, insert the token, and push again to see what happens. When another token appeared, $E$ exclaimed, *"Another penny!* What do you do now?" When $S$ replied that he put it in the ear, $E$ answered, "That's right, now do you understand how to play this game? Go ahead."

2. "Something funny happens when you press his nose. Let's see what happens."

3. "See? Here's candy for you. Now you do it. You get candy."

4. "Go ahead and get some candy. I'll be back when it is time for you to go."

5. "We're going to play a game today. I think it will be fun."

6. "I'll tell you when to stop."

In these instructions, as well as in many others, it is a question of whether a particular $S$ is performing under the control of the experimental reinforcer (candy, penny, token, etc.) or under the control of $E$'s remarks. Is the reinforcer the penny or $E$'s delight over the penny? Is it the candy or $E$'s command to get more of it? When $E$ says, "Let's see what happens," is it the experimental reinforcer or the child's history of reinforcement for what constitutes an adequate demonstration of "what happens" that determines "resistance to extinction?" If $E$ says, "The game is fun," does the child perform under the control of the reinforcer contained in the game or under the control of his history of reinforcement for doing what strange adults in authority say? When $E$ says, "I'll tell you when to stop," how does he separate the child's sensitivity to the experimental reinforcer from his history of training in obedience to adults? Also, when the words, "I'll tell you when to stop" are followed by experimental social reinforcement, it is possible that approval of the experimental response may serve to terminate responding. The response of approval may be responded to as: "I am now telling you to stop."

Three recommendations evolve from this discussion on instructions. The first is to study systematic variations of instructions and other statements by $E$ to determine the nature and range of their effects on individual children. The second is to eliminate them when their effects in a given experimental situation are not separately evaluated. Perhaps it is undesirable for $E$ to emulate a deaf-mute when dealing with child $S$s; however, a close approximation to such a practice would seem to be the safest and most economical alternative to an extensive study of the effect of $E$'s statements. The third is to exploit the advantages of individual experimental analysis. Since the effect of instructions will never be uniform for all children, or even nearly so, verbal instructions and demonstrations may be evaluated and separated from the effects of other experimental stimuli more readily for individuals than for groups of children.

A future chapter of operant methods in child research would be expected to have a large section on setting events. Variables such as social-class membership, histories of institutional deprivation, education, socialization, injury, medication, etc. will probably have been studied in relation to operant techniques. This section may be closed, then, with the characterization of such variables as one of the promising and interesting areas for future investigation.

## REFERENCES

Allen, K. Eileen, Hart, Betty, Buell, Joan S., Harris, Florence R., & Wolf, M. M. Effects of social reinforcement on isolate behavior of a nursery school child. *Child Develpm.*, 1964, *35*, 511–519.

Azrin, N. H., & Lindsley, O. R. The reinforcement of cooperation between children. *J. abnorm. soc. Psychol.*, 1956, *52*, 100–102.

Baer, D. M. Escape and avoidance response of pre-school children to two schedules of reinforcement withdrawal. *J. exp. Anal. Behav.*, 1960, *3*, 155–159.

Baer, D. M. Effect of withdrawal of positive reinforcement on an extinguishing response in young children. *Child Develpm.*, 1961, *32*, 67–74.

Baer, D. M. Laboratory control of thumbsucking through the withdrawal and re-presentation of positive reinforcement. *J. exp. Anal. Behav.*, 1962, *5*, 525–528. (a)

Baer, D. M. A technique for the study of social reinforcement in young children: behavior avoiding reinforcement withdrawal. *Child Develpm.*, 1962, *33*, 847–858. (b)

Baer, D. M., Harris, Florence R., & Wolf, M. M. Control of nursery school children's behavior by programming social reinforcement from their teachers. Paper read at Amer. Psychol. Ass., Philadelphia, Pa., September, 1963.

Baer, D. M., & Sherman, J. A. Reinforcement control of generalized imitation, *J. exp. child Psychol.*, 1964, *1*, 37–49.

Bijou, S. W. A systematic approach to an experimental analysis of young children. *Child Develpm.*, 1955, *26*, 161–168.

Bijou, S. W. Methodology for an experimental analysis of child behavior. *Psychol. Rep.*, 1957, *3*, 243–250. (a)

Bijou, S. W. Patterns of reinforcement and extinction in young children. *Child Develpm.*, 1957, *28*, 47–54. (b)

Bijou, S. W. Operant extinction after fixed-interval schedules with young children. *J. exp. Anal. Behav.*, 1958, *1*, 25–29. (a)

Bijou, S. W. A child-study laboratory on wheels. *Child Develpm.*, 1958, *29*, 425–427. (b)

Bijou, S. W. Discrimination performance as a baseline for individual analysis of young children. *Child Develpm.*, 1961, *32*, 163–170.

Bijou, S. W., & Baer, D. M. *Child development*. Vol. 1. *A systematic and empirical theory*. New York: Appleton-Century-Crofts, 1961.

Bijou, S. W., & Baer, D. M. Some methodological contributions from a functional analysis of child development. In L. P. Lipsitt and C. C. Spiker (Eds.), *Advances in child behavior and development*. New York: Academic, 1964.

Bijou, S. W., & Oblinger, Barbara. Responses of normal and retarded children as a function of the experimental situation. *Psychol. Rep.*, 1960, *6*, 447–454.

Bijou, S. W. & Orlando, R. Rapid development of multiple schedule performances with retarded children. *J. exp. Anal. Behav.*, 1961, *4*, 7–16.

Bijou, S. W., & Sturges, Persis T. Positive reinforcers for experimental studies with children—consumables and manipulatables. *Child Develpm.*, 1959, *30*, 151–170.

Brackbill, Yvonne. Extinction of the smiling response in infants as a function of reinforcement schedule. *Child Develpm.*, 1958, *29*, 115–124.

Cohen, D. J. Justin and his peers: an experimental analysis of a child's social world. *Child Develpm.*, 1962, *33*, 697–717.

Crowell, D. H., Peterson, J., & Safely, Mary Anne. An apparatus for infant conditioning research. *Child Develpm.*, 1960, *31*, 47–51.

Dockery, F. C., & Valentine, W. L. A new isolation cabinet for infant research. *J. exp. Psychol.,* 1939, *24,* 211–214.

Ellis, N. R., Barnett, D. C., & Pryer, Margaret W. Operant behavior in mental defectives: exploratory studies. *J. exp. Anal. Behav.,* 1960, *3,* 63–69.

Erickson, Marilyn T. Effects of social deprivation and satiation on verbal conditioning in children. *J. comp. physiol. Psychol.,* 1962, *56,* 953–957.

Felty, J. The operant nature of stuttering behavior of adolescent boys. Unpublished Master's thesis, University of Washington, 1959.

Ferster, C. B. The use of the free operant in the analysis of behavior. *Psychol. Bull.,* 1953, *50,* 263–274.

Ferster, C. B., & DeMyer, Marian K. The development of performances in autistic children in an automatically controlled environment. *J. chron. Dis.,* 1961, *13,* 312–345.

Ferster, C. B., & DeMyer, Marian K. A method for the experimental analysis of the behavior of autistic children. *Amer. J. Orthopsychiat.,* 1962, *32,* 89–98.

Ferster, C. B., Levitt, E. E. Zimmerman, J., & Brady, J. P. The measurement of hypnotic effects by operant-reinforcement techniques. *Psychol. Rec.,* 1961, *11,* 427–430.

Ferster, C. B., & Skinner, B. F. *Schedules of reinforcement.* New York: Appleton-Century-Crofts, 1957.

Flanagan, B., Goldiamond, I., & Azrin, N. Operant stuttering: the control of stuttering behavior through response-contingent consequences. *J. exp. Anal. Behav.,* 1958, *2,* 173–177.

Flanagan, B., Goldiamond, I., & Azrin, N. Instatement of stuttering in normally fluent individuals through operant procedures. *Science,* 1959, *130,* 979–981.

Gewirtz, J. L. Three determinants of attention-seeking in young children. *Monogr. Soc. Res. child Develpm.,* 1954, *19,* (2).

Gewirtz, J. L. A learning analysis of the effects of normal stimulation, privation and deprivation on the acquisition of social motivation and attachment. In B. M. Moss (Ed.), *Determinants of infant behavior.* New York: Wiley, 1961.

Gewirtz, J. L., & Baer, D. M. The effect of brief social deprivation on behaviors for a social reinforcer. *J. abnorm. soc. Psychol.,* 1958, *56,* 49–56. (a)

Gewirtz, J. L., & Baer, D. M. Deprivation and satiation of social reinforcers as drive conditioners. *J. abnorm. soc. Psychol.,* 1958, *57,* 165–172. (b)

Gewirtz, J. L., Baer, D. M., & Roth, Choya L. A note on the similar effects of low social availability of an adult and brief social deprivation on young children's behavior. *Child Develpm.,* 1958, *29,* 149–152.

Goldiamond, I. The maintenance of ongoing fluent behavior and stuttering. *J. Mathetics,* 1962, *1,* 57–95.

Harris, Florence R., Johnston, Margaret K., Kelley, C. Susan, & Wolf, M. M. Effects of positive social reinforcement on regressed crawling of a nursery school child. *J. educ. Psychol.,* 1964, *55,* 35–41.

Hart, Betty M., Allen, K. Eileen, Buell, Joan S., Harris, Florence R., & Wolf, M. M. Effects of social reinforcement on operant crying. *J. exp. child Psychol.,* 1964, *1,* 145–153.

Hively, W. Programming stimuli in matching to sample. *J. exp. Anal. Behav.*, 1962, *5*, 279–298.

Holland, Audrey, & Matthews, J. Application of teaching machine concepts to speech pathology and audiology. *Asha*, 1963, *5*, 474–482.

Holland, J. G. New directions in teaching-machine research. In J. Coulson (Ed.), *Proceedings of the conference on applications of digital computers to automated instruction.* New York: Wiley, 1963.

Jeffrey, W. E. New technique for motivating and reinforcing children. *Science*, 1955, *121*, 371.

Jensen, K. Differential reactions to taste and temperature stimuli in newborn infants. *Genet. Psychol. Monogr.*, 1932, *12*, 361–479.

Kantor, J. R. *Interbehavioral psychology.* (Rev. ed.) Bloomington, Ind.: Principia Press, 1959.

Keller, F. S. Animals and children. *Child Develpm.*, 1950, *21*, 7–12.

Keller, F. S., & Schoenfeld, W. N. *Principles of psychology.* New York: Appleton-Century-Crofts, 1950.

Lambert, W. W., Lambert, Elizabeth C., & Watson, P. D. Acquisition and extinction of an instrumental response sequence in the token-reward situation. *J. exp. Psychol.*, 1953, *45*, 321–326.

Lane, H., & Curran, C. Auditory generalization gradients of blind retarded children. *J. exp. Anal. Behav.*, 1963, *6*, 585–588.

Larder, Diane L. Effect of aggressive story content on non-verbal play behavior. *Psychol. Rep.*, 1963, *11*, 14.

Lindsley, O. R. Operant conditioning methods applied to research in chronic schizophrenia. *Psychiat. res. Rep.*, 1956, *5*, 118–139.

Lipsitt, L. P. Conditioning in the human infant. Paper read at Amer. Psychol. Ass. meeting, Chicago, September, 1960.

Lipsitt, L. P., & De Lucia, C. A. An apparatus for the measurement of specific response and general activity of the human neonate. *Amer. J. Psychol.*, 1960, *73*, 630–632.

Long, E. R. The use of operant conditioning techniques in children. In S. Fisher (Ed.), *Child research in psychopharmacology.* Springfield, Ill.: Charles C Thomas, 1959. (a)

Long, E. R. Multiple scheduling in children. *J. exp. Anal. Behav.*, 1959, *2*, 268. (b)

Long, E. R. Additional techniques for producing multiple schedule control in children. *J. exp. Anal. Behav.*, 1962, *5*, 443–462.

Long, E. R. Chained and tandem scheduling with children. *J. exp. Anal. Behav.*, 1963, *6*, 459–472.

Long, E. R., Hammack, J. T., May, F., & Campbell, B. J. Intermittent reinforcement of operant behavior in children. *J. exp. Anal. Behav.*, 1958, *4*, 315–339.

Lovaas, O. I. The control of operant responding by rate and content of verbal operants. Paper read at Western Psychol. Ass. meeting, Seattle, June, 1961. (a)

Lovaas, O. I. Effect of exposure to symbolic aggression on aggressive behavior. *Child Develpm.*, 1961, *32*, 37–44. (b)

Lovaas, O. I. Interaction between verbal and nonverbal behavior. *Child Develpm.*, 1961, *32*, 329–336. (c)

Moustakas, C. E., & Berson, Minnie P. *The nursery school and childcare center.* New York: Morrow, 1955.

Myers, Nancy A. Extinction following partial and continuous primary and secondary reinforcement. *J. exp. Psychol.*, 1960, *60*, 172–179.

Myers, Nancy A., Craig, Grace J., & Myers, J. L. Secondary reinforcement as a function of the number of reinforced trials. *Child Develpm.*, 1961, *32*, 765–772.

Orlando, R. Component behaviors in free temporal discrimination. *Amer. J. ment. Defic.*, 1961, *65*, 615–619. (a)

Orlando, R. The functional role of discriminative stimuli in free operant performance of developmentally retarded children. *Psychol. Rec.*, 1961, *11*, 153–161. (b)

Orlando, R., & Bijou, S. W. Single and multiple schedules of reinforcement in developmentally retarded children. *J. exp. Anal. Behav.*, 1960, *3*, 339–348.

Orlando, R., Bijou, S. W., Tyler, R. M., & Marshall, D. A. A laboratory for the experimental analysis of developmentally retarded children. *Psychol. Rep.*, 1961, *7*, 261–267.

Rheingold, Harriet L., Gewirtz, J. L., & Ross, Helen W. Social conditioning of vocalizations in the infant. *J. comp. physiol. Psychol.*, 1959, *52*, 68–73.

Rheingold, Harriet L., Stanley, W. C., & Cooley, J. A. A crib for the study of exploratory behavior in infants. *Science,* 1962, *136*, 1054–1055.

Risley, T. Generalization gradients following two-response discrimination training. *J. exp. Anal. Behav.*, 1964, *7*, 199–204.

Robinson, Nancy M., & Robinson, H. R. A method for the study of instrumental avoidance conditioning with young children. *J. comp. physiol. Psychol.*, 1961, *54*, 20–23.

Screven, C. G. The effects of interference on response strength. *J. comp. physiol. Psychol.*, 1954, *47*, 140–144.

Shakow, D. Research in child development: a case illustration of the psychologist's dilemma. *Amer. J. Orthopsychiat.*, 1959, *29*, 45–59.

Simmons, Mae W., & Lipsitt, L. P. An operant discrimination apparatus for infants. *J. exp. Anal. Behav.*, 1961, *4*, 233–235.

Skinner, B. F. *The behavior of organisms.* New York: Appleton-Century-Crofts, 1938.

Skinner, B. F. *Science and human behavior.* New York: Macmillan, 1953.

Spiker, C. C. Research methods in children's learning. In P. H. Mussen (Ed.), *Handbook of research methods in child development.* New York: Wiley, 1960.

Stevens, S. S. Psychology and the science of science. *Psychol. Bull.*, 1939, *36*, 221–263.

Stevenson, H. W. Social reinforcement with children as a function of CA, sex of *E,* and sex of *S. J. abnorm. soc. Psychol.*, 1961, *63*, 147–154.

Stevenson, H. W., & Cruse, D. B. The effectiveness of social reinforcement with normal and feeble-minded children. *J. Pers.*, 1961, *29*, 124–135.

Stevenson, H. W., & Fahel, Leila S. The effect of social reinforcement on the performance of institutionalized and noninstitutionalized normal and feebleminded children. *J. Pers.*, 1961, *29,* 136–147.

Stevenson, H. W., & Odom, R. D. Effects of pretraining on the reinforcing value of visual stimuli. *Child Develpm.*, 1961, *32,* 739–744.

Stoddard, L. T. Operant conditioning of timing behavior in children. Unpublished doctoral dissertation, Columbia University, 1962.

Tyler, R. M. Discriminative behavior of developmental retardates under conditions of discriminative and negatively reinforcing stimulation. Unpublished Master's thesis, University of Washington, 1960.

Walters, R. H., & Ray, E. Anxiety, social isolation, and reinforcer effectiveness. *J. Pers.*, 1960, *28,* 358–367.

Weisberg P. Social and nonsocial conditioning of infant vocalization. *Child Develpm.*, 1963, *34,* 377–388.

Witryol, S. L., & Fischer, W. F. Scaling children's incentives by the method of paired comparisons. *Psychol. Rep.*, 1960, *7,* 471–474.

Zigler, E. F. Recent findings on social reinforcement. Paper used at meeting of Soc. for Res. in Child Develpm., Pennsylvania State University, 1961.

Zigler, E. F., Hodgden, L., & Stevenson, H. W. The effect of support on the performance of normal and feeble-minded children. *J. Pers.*, 1958, *26,* 106–122.

Zylstra, J. The interaction of extinction of simultaneously occurring verbal and manual operants. Unpublished Master's thesis, University of Washington, 1961.

# index